Dwelling House Construction

Dwelling House Construction

fifth edition

Albert G. H. Dietz

The MIT Press
Cambridge, Massachusetts
London, England

Original edition published by D. Van Nostrand Company, Inc., Princeton, New Jersey, and © 1946 and 1954 by Walter C. Voss and Albert G. H. Dietz.

New material © 1991 Massachusetts Institute of Technology.

This book was set in Melior by Achorn Graphics and printed and bound by Maple-Vail, Inc. in the United States of America.

Fifth edition (third MIT Press edition), 1991.

Library of Congress Cataloging-in-Publication Data

Dietz, Albert G. H. (Albert George Henry), 1908–
  Dwelling house construction / Albert G. H. Dietz.—5th ed.

    p. cm.
  ISBN 0-262-04108-1
  1. House construction. I. Title.
TH4811.D5   1990
690′.837—dc20   90-5651
                                                              CIP

This book is dedicated to Ross Francis Tucker, whose interest in young people and construction left an indelible mark on the personnel of the industry.

Contents

Preface

Developments in materials and construction techniques since the last (1974) revision of this book make another edition desirable. Some sections have been retained essentially unchanged; others have been moderately revised; still others have undergone major changes; and some entirely new material has been added.

One general change has been the elimination of specification clauses. Standard specifications are widely employed, or specific specifications, not generally applicable, must be written for specific cases.

New sections on materials as such, covering wood, concrete, steel, and masonry, have been introduced to provide some understanding of the properties and limitations of these materials. With the growing importance of synthetics in coatings, the formerly separate chapters on plastics and coatings have been combined into one. The discussion of the growing number of building boards, composite panels, and structural members has been expanded. A section on wood foundations, made possible by improved wood-treating processes, has been added. In light of the trend toward multiple housing, a section on light steel framing has been introduced, and the discussions of masonry construction have been expanded. The chapter on roofing has been revised considerably to take new developments into account. There have been similar revisions in the treatment of insulation.

Some sections have been reduced. Among them are the sections on braced and balloon framing, now seldom used. Standardized regulations respecting septic tanks have led to a shortened presentation. Traditional lath-and-plaster wall covering is now seldom used in dwellings, and the treatment of this is curtailed (although the increasingly popular veneer plaster is discussed).

Though the treatment of traditional but now seldom-used practices has been reduced, the existence of millions of older houses makes it desirable to retain enough information to impart some familiarity with these practices. This has been done in both the text and the illustrations. Thus, braced and balloon frames are still discussed and illustrated in some detail, as are wood double-hung and casement windows, the principles of which are similar for both traditional and contemporary forms. Traditional and contemporary building boards are both shown in details of construction.

As in all previous editions, the objective of this book is to present those fundamental principles of dwelling-house construction that change little, not being subject to fashion or whim. It is hoped that the book will be useful to the student and the practitioner.

This book is intended to be primarily an introduction, not a set of detailed instructions. In preparing it, recourse has been had to many carefully chosen resources considered to be reliable, including government publications, manufacturers' literature, trade associations, reference works, and individuals. Within these limitations, reasonable care has been taken to ensure accuracy, but the author and the publisher do not assume responsibility for accuracy and completeness, or for applicability to particular cases.

The user of the book is expected to judge the applicability and the limitations of its contents, and should consult original sources and seek additional information and advice as is desirable or necessary.

Acknowledgments

This edition of *Dwelling House Construction* was made possible by the contributions of many individuals and organizations. It is impossible to thank them all, but the following deserve special mention.

My former colleague Edward Allen carefully reviewed the entire book and made many highly valuable suggestions whose incorporation has greatly enhanced the text. Werner Gumpertz, another former colleague, undertook the revision of the chapter on roofing, in which he is a specialist, thereby considerably extending its coverage and increasing its value. Professor Walter Jones of the Wentworth Institute of Technology reviewed the book and made many suggestions that have expanded and clarified the text. Professor Eric Dluhosch reviewed the coverage of manufactured homes, thereby keeping it abreast of continuing developments.

Neal Mongold carefully drafted new illustrations and revised existing ones, skillfully blending the old and the new. Paula Maute and Charlotte Peede struggled to convert often indecipherable manuscript into typed text.

Many organizations and sources such as Sweet's and other literature have been drawn upon for assistance, revision, and clarification. The American Plywood Association has provided illustrations and brought many tables up to date. The McGraw-Hill Publishing Company gave permission to use illustrative material from J. H. Callender's *Time Saver Standards*. Others drawn upon include the American Architectural Manufacturers Association, the National Forest Products Association, the National Association of Home Builders Research Foundation, the Asphalt Roofing Manufacturing Association, the U.S. Forest Products Laboratory, the American Society for Testing and Materials, Acorn Structures, the Marino Industries Corporation, the Wood Foundation, the American Wood Preservers Association, and the Construction Lending Guide of the United States Savings and Loan League.

Finally, my wife Ruth, who was of immeasurable help and displayed monumental patience in the writing of the previous volumes, was again crucial in encouraging the preparation of this edition.

Dwelling House Construction

1 Inspection of the Site

1.1 General

a. Before construction proceeds, it is customary, in the case of contract or custom building, for the owner and the architect to invite a selected number of builders to prepare estimates of cost and to submit bids, i.e., their proposals for building the structure for a specified sum of money in accordance with plans and specifications. The builder must be acquainted with the site of the proposed structure, and must investigate the various factors which will influence costs of construction before he can make an intelligent estimate. The builder who builds for sale must be equally familiar with the site and other factors affecting costs.

b. The builder must closely investigate the location and the physical features (e.g., soil and water table) of the site, the availability of utilities, the legal restrictions (zoning ordinances, building codes), and labor and materials.

c. Although a custom builder need not consider orientation with respect to sunlight (because plans are given him), an owner planning his house or a builder planning for sale should be aware of north, east, south, and west exposures. West-facing windows, in particular, can lead to uncomfortable solar overheating, whereas south-facing windows can be shaded by overhangs against the summer sun while permitting the low winter sun to penetrate.

d. Many more considerations affect the owner's selection of a site. These do not concern the custom builder directly, but they do affect the builder who builds to sell. They include community facilities such as schools and shopping facilities, transportation, the immediate neighborhood, and the orientation of the site.

THE BUILDING SITE

1.2 Location

The following general questions immediately arise: What is the location of the site in the community? On what street or streets does it face? Which direction will the house face with respect to the points of the compass and with respect to the site? Are the boundaries well marked by surveyors' stakes, bounds, or some other means? If not, have provisions been made to have the boundaries clearly delineated?

1.3 Roads

a. What is the elevation of the site with reference to the road, and is the road private or public? Private roads are often narrow, little improved, and likely to follow existing surface contours. If taken over by public authority, such roads are likely to be straightened, widened, and leveled, thereby probably altering the position of a house with respect to the road. It is wise to ascertain whether plans have been made to alter the roadway which a house is to face, and to locate the house in such a manner as to avoid its being adversely affected. This may or may not be up to the custom builder, depending upon whether or not a plot plan is provided. It is of considerable importance to the developer.

b. Of immediate concern to the builder is the condition of the roads. If roads are good, he can count on easy access to the site at all times; if poor, he may have to bring in and store considerable amounts of material when the roads are passable.

1.4 Abutting Properties

a. What is the general elevation or "lie of the land" of abutting properties? This is important because of drainage. If abutting properties are higher, they may drain onto the plot in question, and the builder may be called upon to correct this condition by filling, grading, and sloping the finished ground level so as to divert drainage elsewhere. A matter of law may be involved that varies in different localities. Although a property owner may not be liable for the drainage from his land onto his neighbor's if it is natural drainage, he is not permitted to deliberately alter existing topography so as to cause a bad flow from his property to his neighbor's if that flow did not exist before.

b. If the custom builder follows instructions regarding grading which may result in lawsuits from adjoining owners because of altered drainage, he can be held liable unless he protects himself by securing a written acceptance of responsibility by the owner. Therefore, to avoid later complications, the prudent builder determines from his inspection of the site and the finished grades indicated on the drawings whether such a contingency can arise. The developer of land and the builder for sale must keep such contingencies in mind when developing and building on a site.

c. This is only one example of the care which must be taken to protect adjacent properties. In general, it is required by law that no permanent injury to abutting properties may result from building operations, and that any temporary injury must be made good.

PHYSICAL FEATURES

1.5 General Topography

Is the site on a hill, in a valley, or on flat land? If it slopes, how much is the slope and in what direction? Are the new grades to be the same as the old, or will there be a considerable amount of cutting, filling, and regrading? If there is to be much change, is an accurate plot plan available showing both existing and final grades? Will the final grades be such as to pose the problem respecting drainage toward and away from the house? (An excellent time to inspect a site is immediately after a heavy rain. Low spots and drainage features are then plainly visible, whereas they might escape notice when the site is dry.) Will walks and curbs have to be protected, or replaced because of breakage when heavy loads pass over them?

1.6 Soil

a. What is the depth and composition of the topsoil, the surface layer of earth? The owner is interested because of its gardening possibilities. The builder is interested primarily because he should strip the topsoil and stack it to one side for future finish grading. Usually the stripped area is about 20′ greater each way than the size of the house.
b. The best way to examine the character of the soil is to dig a pit on the site of the house. Sometimes cuts or excavations in the neighborhood give sufficient information, and frequently builders or excavators know subsoil conditions by experience. However, it is necessary to be careful, because the character of the subsoil may change over a short distance.
c. With the exception of rock, clay is the most troublesome material with which to deal. Since clay is both relatively compressible and impermeable, it may allow settlement and make quick drainage difficult. As a consequence, water may be held against foundation walls and eventually find its way through, thereby causing leaks that call for waterproofing. Heaving brought about by freezing in winter may cause considerable damage unless all foundations are carried below the frost line. In some parts of the country, expansive soils cause uneven swell-

ing and settlement. Special measures may be needed to deal with them.

1.7 Rock and Ledge

a. Are there any outcroppings of rock? The answer is often obvious, but sometimes the rock barely penetrates the surface or is slightly below it. If there is reason to suspect the presence of rock, it is wise to drive a sharpened iron bar into the ground at a sufficient number of points to determine its depth and location. These investigations should go at least as deep as the proposed excavation.

b. As a rule, a rocky site is undesirable, not only because it is expensive to excavate but also because a ledge often carries subsurface water, which may cause wet basements unless it is brought under control.

c. Architects who have reason to suspect that hidden rock may exist often insert a clause in their specifications calling for rock above a certain size, such as one-half cubic yard or more, to be removed at a specified cost per cubic yard. This approach allows the excavation cost estimates to be based on ordinary soil; otherwise they may be generously increased to take care of an unknown quantity of rock excavation at an increase in price which may not be justified by subsequent actual excavation.

1.8 Water

a. Are there any low or damp spots, which may indicate the presence of springs? It is wise to dig into such spots to see if springs actually exist. Sometimes springs do not appear until excavation has commenced, and then they present difficulties of a serious character, such as the necessity for continuous pumping or for complete waterproofing of the foundation at additional cost. The contract builder may or may not be able to secure extra remuneration for this.

b. Water cannot be ignored or neglected; it always asserts itself and it often causes trouble. It frequently occurs in rock or clay formations, and it usually presents a problem that is expensive to solve. The presence of water is one of the most important items to look for during the inspection of the site. If a water condition exists, the most prudent course is not to build on the site. If construction must proceed, adequate steps to remove the water by drainage must be undertaken. In extreme cases, this may require a permanent pumping installation.

1.9 Trees

Trees are a valuable feature of any home site. As few as possible should be felled, and those remaining should be carefully protected. Every effort should be made to avoid needless destruction by judiciously relating the house to the trees. In any event, the position, size, species, and condition of the trees on the site should be noted on the plot plan. Trees may be killed by altering the grade of the soil surrounding them, especially by heaping soil around the trunks or by cutting important roots.

1.10 Utilities

a. Are sewer, water, gas, telephone, and electricity services available?

b. Sewer. Is there a sewer in the street? If so, what is its size? What is its depth below the surface? What is the direction of its flow? It is important to know the depth, if only to determine whether plumbing fixtures in the lowest part of the house can drain by gravity flow into the sewer. If not, pumps are required. It is important to know the direction of the flow of the street sewer so that the connection of the house sewer to it may be made in the direction of the flow and not against it. In communities which have sewage-disposal systems, rain water cannot ordinarily be discharged into the sewer, as this may interfere with the sewage-disposal process or increase its cost. Other means, usually dry wells, must be found for the disposal of rain water.

c. If there is no sewer, and a household disposal system such as a septic tank is required, the proper soil conditions are essential. The soil must be permeable to allow suitable leaching of the effluent from the system. The size and the arrangement of the system are strongly influenced by the soil (chapter 3).

d. Water. Where is the water main? What is its size? What is the pressure? Where is the water connection for the site? If no water main exists, a well has to be dug. A careful survey should be made by a well-drilling expert to determine at what depth an adequate supply of water may be found, and what the cost will be. The quality of the water must be determined.

e. Gas. If gas is to be used, ascertain the location, depth, size, and pressure of the main and the location of the house connection. If there is no main, determine the means and the cost of supplying gas.

f. Electricity. Ascertain whether electric power and telephone lines are in or whether they will have to be brought in and at what cost. Are the lines overhead or underground? Will the house lines be overhead or underground?

1.11 Plot Plan

a. Figure 1.1 illustrates a plot plan for a house to be built on rather heavily wooded, sloping terrain. A topographical survey can be a decided help in locating and planning a house, as well as to the contract builder in making his estimate. As the contours show, the long dimensions of the house follow the topography rather than the lot lines. Cutting and filling are necessary to meet the requirements for a level drive and a terrace on the downhill side of the house. The house corners are situated to conform to zoning requirements. Trees which may have to be removed or protected during construction are marked, as are outside individual trees. Lot lines have been surveyed and located by stone bounds or pipe stakes. Notes respecting the subsoil have been made. Any changes in the topography are not of such a nature as to affect the neighboring properties. Water, gas, and electrical lines are available. If there is a sewer, it will have to be extended to the property; otherwise, a septic tank will be required. The subsoil and the natural drainage are ideal for the latter, but the installation will have to be located carefully to avoid spoiling the wooded lower slope, and must be far enough from the lake shore to conform to sanitary regulations. The owner must decide which to use, if he has a choice. With this plan and a checklist of the other major items mentioned in this discussion, the builder should be in a position to make a good estimate of costs and to determine his final building procedure. **b.** If more than one house is to be built, as in the operations of a tract builder, a plot plan is drawn for the entire tract. It shows the streets and utilities, the individual lots, the location of each house on its lot, and all other pertinent information.

LEGAL RESTRICTIONS

1.12. Zoning and Deed Restrictions

a. Most communities have zoning laws which restrict specified areas to certain uses, such as industrial, business, general residential, and single residential. In addition, they usually require that the buildings, especially residences, be kept back a certain distance from the front

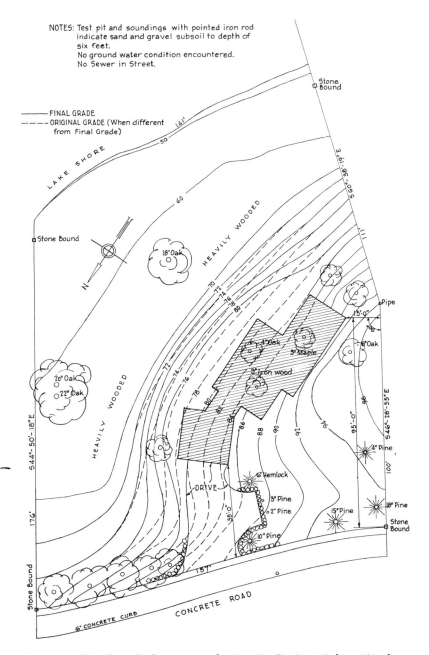

Figure 1.1 Plot plan of a house on a sloping site. Pertinent information for construction of the building is given.

lot line. They almost always require setbacks from the side and back lines as well. Sometimes the percentage of total area of the lot which may be covered by buildings is restricted.

b. Deed restrictions may affect the position of a house on a site, in addition to limiting cost, type, and other features.

c. The builder should check into these matters carefully, because any infringements of ordinances which are his fault may require costly alterations at his expense. It is most disconcerting to find that a whole house must be moved several feet after it is well along toward completion.

1.13. Building Code

a. Most municipalities have building codes which specify minimum requirements for construction. The builder must be thoroughly familiar with the building code, because it profoundly influences his practice and procedure as well as the costs of construction. A builder going into a new locality should first of all familiarize himself with the building code. This is logically a part of his general inspection of the site.

b. It by no means follows that because two communities are adjacent, they have identical building codes. The opposite is often true, and what is considered excellent practice in one municipality may be expressly prohibited in its neighbor. Furthermore, state codes of practice must be considered, and if the provisions of the state code are more stringent than those of the municipality, the state code must be observed.

c. Fees for the issuance of building permits and for inspection by the building commissioner's office are usually required. The builder should ascertain these costs as a part of his general inspection.

2 Building Layout

2.1 General

a. The first step in actual construction is to locate the house or houses upon the land. This is known as the "stake-out." Generally this takes place once, but occasionally the building is laid out twice, once for the excavation and again for the foundations.

b. All buildings of whatever kind must be built with "lines." The outside faces of the foundation walls are the building lines, and the chief outside walls of the structure are known as the main building lines. These lines are used as reference or base lines from which any subsidiary portions of the buildings are laid out. The dimensions between building lines are shown on the plans, especially the foundation plans, and these figures must be transferred and located on the ground so that the construction of the building may follow them with precision.

c. It cannot be emphasized too soon, too strongly, or too often that all good building is "precision" building, which means that floors must be level, walls must be plumb, lines must be straight, corners must be square, and dimensions must be correct, precisely as called for by the plans.

d. In order to lay out the building precisely, a system of stakes, lines, and batter boards or offset stakes is customarily used. These are placed after the topsoil has been stripped. Surveyors' instruments, especially the transit, are convenient for making the layout, but they are not essential, and accurate work can be done without them. Only methods which do not require instruments will be considered here.

2.2 Establishing Building Lines

a. The front building line is in many ways the most important because it is the starting point for all others. Furthermore, in most municipalities zoning ordinances establish minimum distances from the front lines of buildings to front lot lines, and if through error the building is not back sufficiently far, it may entail costly tearing down and rebuilding to correct the error. It is permissible to go back farther than the minimum, but often the owner wants to stay directly on the line. Almost always the "front line" refers to the outside face of the foundation wall under the front wall of the house proper, exclusive of porches, stoops, areas, and so forth, but local zoning peculiarities must be checked to make sure.

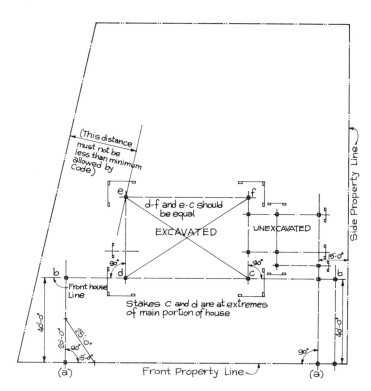

Figure 2.1 The procedure for layout of a house on its site. The building lines are established first. Batter boards for excavated and unexcavated portions are located to determine the building lines during excavation.

b. The builder must have clearly defined lot boundaries from which to work. Generally these are defined by surveyors' stakes or bounds of some kind situated at the corners of the lot. If such stakes or other clear markers are not present, the builder should require that they be given him; otherwise he cannot be responsible for errors in establishing house lines.

c. Suppose a plot plan shows a house to be 40' from the front line and 15' from one side line, and that this conforms to zoning regulations (figure 2.1). To locate and lay out this house the builder would proceed about as follows. Two stakes (a) are driven on the front property line and a mason's line is stretched between them. These stakes are farther apart than the width of the house. At each stake another line is erected perpendicular to the base line, measured back 40' with the tape, and two more stakes (b) are driven. The right angle between the perpendicular and the front property line can be laid off by using the familiar 3-4-5 right triangle. This is accomplished by measuring off from each front stake, along the front line, some convenient multiple of 3′ (say 15′), then measuring off on the perpendicular the same multiple times 4′ (20′ in this instance), and finally making the hypotenuse of the right triangle 25′. If the front lot line is on a curved street, it is necessary to work from a tangent to the curve, or to work from a setback such as a chord of the curve. Here regular surveyors' instruments such as a transit are most useful.

d. A line is now stretched between the two house-line stakes, and the extreme edge of the house is located by measuring in 15′ from the side lot line, as shown on the plot plan. The side wall of the main portion of the house is next located, and a stake (c) is driven at that point. The length of the front wall of the main portion of the house is measured off along the mason's line, and another stake (d) is driven.

e. With the front wall established, side walls are next laid off perpendicular to it by stretching lines from these stakes (that is, from nails driven in the tops), at right angles to the front line, measuring back the correct distance, and driving stakes (e, f), as before. Here great care must be exercised when laying out the 3-4-5 triangle to make sure it contains a true right angle. These four corner stakes, if correctly located, define the four sides of the main body of the house. They are checked by measuring the distance between the rear stakes and finally by measuring the diagonals d–f and e–c (the most important check of all). If the opposite sides are equal and the diagonals are equal, the figure is a true rectangle.

f. Any ells, wings, areas, etc. which may be attached to the main body of the house are laid off in the same way, using one of the sides of the main body as a base line. In each instance the diagonals of the rectangle are measured as a final check.

g. The stakes establish the corners of the house itself, but the excavation must be somewhat larger in order to allow room for the masons to lay up the foundation walls, or for the carpenters to build their forms. Also, when the footings are built, they extend beyond the foundation wall. Only in very rare instances will an earth bank stand vertically; usually it must be sloped back varying amounts, depending upon the soil. The excavation lines, therefore, must be set out from the house lines 1′ or more, depending upon the depth of the excavation.

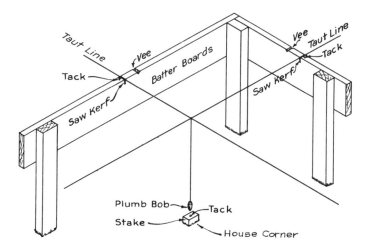

Figure 2.2 Batter boards. Lines drawn taut at vee, saw kerf, and nail establish several building lines. Top of the batter board establishes grades.

2.3 Batter Boards and Offset Stakes

a. Batter boards or offset stakes are employed to fix the building lines during excavation, since the corner stakes themselves are lost. Batter boards, as illustrated in figure 2.2, consist either of a pair of boards nailed to three uprights so as to form a right angle at exterior corners of buildings or of a single board nailed to two uprights at intermediate points. When batter boards are in place, the building lines are transferred to them from the corner stakes, as shown in figure 2.2, by holding plumb bobs over the tacks or nails in the tops of the stakes and moving a taut mason's line into contact with the plumb line. The crossing of the mason's line and the batter board is marked by a saw kerf or some other means. As shown in figure 2.2, several lines may be so marked but the marks must be distinct enough to avoid any possible confusion. In the illustration the three sets consist of "vees," saw kerfs, and nails, each distinctive enough to avoid any mistakes.

b. Positions of batter boards for the house plan in figure 2.1 are shown. For the main portion of the house, which is to be excavated, batter boards are placed far enough back to avoid being disturbed. For the unexcavated portion they are placed much closer to the building lines.

c. Offset stakes (figure 2.3) are simply stakes driven far enough away from the corner stakes to avoid being disturbed by the excavation but

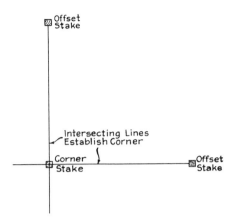

Figure 2.3 Offset stakes used to establish building lines.

so situated that when mason's lines are drawn between pairs of stakes the crossings of the lines locate the house corners.

2.4 Establishing Grades

a. The excavator now is enabled to place the cellar hole properly, but he must also know how deep to go. This means establishing the grade of the house and from it the finish grade of the lot, particularly if (as is often true) the finish grade is not to be the same as the natural grade.
b. Any point in the house could be used as a reference point for the establishment of all other grades. For many reasons, the top of the foundation wall is the most convenient, although the finished first-floor line is also much used. In any event, either the owner or the architect must tell the builder what the height of the finished first floor or some other point in the house is to be, or information must be given which will enable the builder to determine it. For instance, in level country, the owner may wish to have his first-floor line at the same elevation as those of his neighbors. In that event, the builder can level across from the neighboring house to the site of the new house and establish the first-floor line on a stake driven there. This point can also be located on the batter boards by placing the tops of the boards at the desired level. When a line is stretched across the boards, it establishes the building line and the reference elevation.
c. The plan may show a uniform pitch of grade from front lot line to house. If this were ½″ per foot, for example, and the house were 40′

back, the grade would be 20″ higher at the house than at the front lot line. If then the drawings indicated that the top of the foundation wall was, for example, 8″ above finished grade, the foundation line would be established at 28″ above the front lot line. By setting a stake at the front lot line with its top 28″ above finished grade, the top of the foundation wall could be established by leveling back from front lot line to the batter boards or the grade stake.

d. Once the house has been located on the lot and the grade established, the excavator is ready to proceed, because he can easily check the depth of his excavation from the grade marker and from the depths indicated on the drawings. Similarly, if the house is to be built on a slab at grade level, such excavation, grading, leveling, and other preparation as may be necessary can proceed.

2.5 Tract Layout

If more than one house is to be laid out, as in a housing tract, standard surveying instruments — especially transit, level, and tape — are much faster and more efficient in laying out the individual houses than the method described above. An experienced surveying team should be employed for such a project.

3 Excavation and Sanitary Systems

EXCAVATION

3.1 General

a. Most excavations, even small ones, are now made with power tools, but if a power shovel or other excavator is not available or the conditions are not favorable for its use, excavation by hand tools and light power equipment becomes necessary. Besides, whether power tools are used or not, on every building operation there is always a certain amount of hand excavation, such as trimming banks and so on.
b. Knowledge and understanding of the kinds of soil to be excavated and of the working conditions are essential in order to determine how many men to employ and what equipment to use.
c. Excavation is the most variable of all operations associated with building. Once a building is "out of the ground," job conditions are fairly well under control and can be predicted with some degree of certainty. With excavation, however, the story is different. Soil conditions vary with almost every site. Working conditions vary with every operation. Even the best knowledge gained from test pits and other sources gives only a general idea of what is to be expected, and many factors may enter to affect the final result. Good management and good judgment will accomplish much and are indispensable, but the best of these may be upset by unforeseen circumstances. Bad weather and a variety of other unanticipated possibilities may call for unexpected measures.

3.2 Classification of Soils

Much of the procedure on any excavation job depends on the nature of the soil. Although excavators frequently lump soils into convenient classifications, such as light, medium, and heavy, these classifications are often oversimplified and may lead to faulty decisions. A classification of soils developed by the Corps of Engineers and the Bureau of Reclamation is summarized in table 3.1, which also shows the relative suitability of the various soils for foundations of dwelling houses and for domestic sewerage systems. The relative numerical ratings are applicable within the individual columns only, and not from column to column. The numeral 1 indicates the best condition, and larger numerals indicate progressively poorer conditions. NS indicates that the soil is not suitable.

Table 3.1 Classification of Soils

	Relative Desirability for Various Purposes				
	Foundations			Sewage Disposal	
	Undisturbed		Disturbed (Fill)	Undisturbed	Disturbed (Fill)
	Dense	Loose			
1. Coarse-grained soils					
Gravels					
Clean (little or no fines)					
Well-graded gravel, gravel-sand mixture	1[a]	1	1	1	1
Poorly-graded gravels or gravel-sand mixtures	1	2	2	1	1
With fines in appreciable amounts					
Silty gravels, gravel-sand-silt mixtures	2	2	3	2	2
Clayey gravels, gravel-sand-clay mixtures	3	1	4	2	2
Sands					
Clean (little or no fines)					
Well-graded sands, gravelly sands	1	1	2	1	1
Poorly-graded sands or gravelly sands	1	2	4	1	1
With fines in appreciable amounts					
Silty sands, sand-silt mixtures	2	2	4	2	2
Clayey sands, sand-clay mixtures	3	2	5	2	NS[b]
2. Fine-grained soils					
Silts and clays, liquid limit less than 50[c]					
Inorganic silts and very fine sands, rock flour, silty or clayey fine sands or clayey fine sands or clayey silts with slight plasticity,	3	3	7	2	NS
Inorganic clays of low to medium plasticity, gravelly clays, sandy clays, silty clays, lean clays,	3 Expansion dangerous if dry	3–5	6	2	NS
Organic silts and organic silty clays of low plasticity	4 Expansion dangerous	4	8	2	NS
Silts and clays, liquid limit greater than 50[c]					
Inorganic silts, micaceous or diatomaceous fine sandy or silty soils, elastic silts	5	4	9	2	NS
Inorganic clays of high plasticity, fat clays	5 Expansion dangerous if dry	4 Expansion may be dangerous	8	NS	NS
Organic clays of medium to high plasticity, organic silts	6 Expansion dangerous	5	10		
3. Highly organic soils					
Peat and other highly organic soils	7	NS	NS	NS	NS

[a] The numeral 1 indicates best conditions; progressively larger numerals indicate progressively poorer conditions in any one vertical column.

[b] NS = not suitable.

[c] An arbitrary limit between the liquid and plastic states of consistency of a soil. Measured in a standard liquid limit apparatus.

Source: *Engineering Soil Classification for Residential Developments*, Federal Housing Administration, Washington, D.C., 1959.

3.3 Excavation Equipment

a. Equipment for hand excavation is quite simple: shovel (short- or long-handle, depending upon the locality), pick, and means of dirt removal (usually motor truck).

b. The difference in type of shovel used is just one of many instances which show that building has not yet fully emerged from its intensely local character. Although good work can be and is done with both types of shovels, certain regions prefer a short handle; others, a long handle.

c. The pick, used to loosen soils too heavy to dig directly, is often aided by the mattock, or grub hoe, which is similar to the pick except that the points are replaced by shorter, flat blades at a right angle.

d. Hand tools are used primarily for digging trenches and trimming excavations otherwise made principally with power equipment.

e. The power equipment usually used for house excavation is a tractor-driven bulldozer, a dipper-type shovel, or a clamshell mounted on a power crane. The dipper and the clamshell are usually used if the excavations are too deep for convenient maneuvering by bull-dozer; otherwise the bulldozer is used for simultaneous loosening and removal of the soil to one side. Large or long trenches are commonly dug by trenching machines.

3.4 Procedure

a. Once the building lines are located, the excavation can begin. No two excavations are alike, but the general procedure is more or less the same for all. Any job is divided into two classes of work: first, the main excavation, including trimming of banks; second, trenches of all kinds, including footings, piers, foundation trenches for basementless portions of the building, and trenches for services such as sewer, water, and gas. Portions of these two classes of work, such as the general excavation and trenches for services, can proceed simulta-neously; others of necessity have to follow one another.

b. Removal of topsoil. As mentioned in chapter 1, it is generally nec-essary to remove the topsoil and store it at a point where it will not be disturbed during construction, and subsequently to replace it as the last step in the finish grading. Topsoil ordinarily is 8″ to 12″ deep. It is moved to the designated point, the area cleared usually being consid-erably larger than the ground area of the house. Because the topsoil is removed over a fairly large area, batter boards or offset stakes should not be placed before this operation is completed. It is necessary, in this event, to make a preliminary rough layout so that the topsoil will be stripped over the correct area. For a basementless house, the area of topsoil removal is smaller, and this may complete the general excavation, leaving only trenches to be excavated.

c. General excavation. When excavation is performed by bulldozer, the machine simply moves back and forth over the site to be excavated, loosening and pushing the earth to the ends of the excavation, digging deeper on successive passes. The direction of motion is generally the long direction of the excavation. This procedure results in a more or less dish-shaped excavation whose edges may have to be trimmed to proper dimensions.

d. Trenches and miscellaneous holes. As has been noted, a fairly large amount of hand work is necessary on any excavation job. In the case of a dwelling house, this takes the form of trimming as well as the digging of small trenches, pier holes, and, frequently, fairly deep holes for dry wells and septic tanks. This work is seldom very complicated, and only occasionally is much bracing required to keep banks from caving in.

e. Most trenches are fairly shallow, and excavated earth from the bottom can easily be thrown directly up onto the bank. The chief exception to this rule is the sewer trench, which frequently is quite deep and may require excavated earth to be rehandled from an intermediate level before it is thrown onto the bank. This can be accomplished by digging the trench in steps; the material from the lower level is thrown onto the higher step and then thrown from there onto the bank. Staging may also be built into the trench as it goes down, so that earth from the lower level may be thrown onto the staging, to be rehandled. Detailed discussion of the various methods of bracing and sheet-piling deep trenches and other deep excavations will be omitted here, except to mention that trenches may be continuously sheeted if the soil is very loose (figure 3.1a), or braced with horizontal lagging at intervals if the soil is fairly firm (figure 3.1b).

f. Usually, separate trenches are required for the various services, because they come in at different depths and because the street connections for the house are at different points. Occasionally, several services can be placed in the same trench. Pipes should not be placed directly over one another, because subsequent repairs to the lower

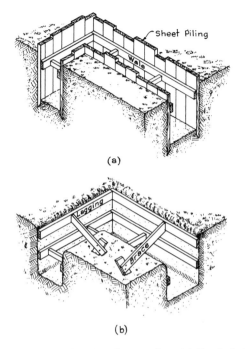

(a)

(b)

Figure 3.1 Bracing for trenches. (a) Vertical sheet piling. (b) Horizontal lagging.

ones are made difficult if others are in the way. Water and sewer lines should be separated as far as possible if in the same trench, because simultaneous leaks in the two lines might pollute the water supply. Water lines should be placed above sewer lines, preferably not directly above but offset to one side.

g. Certain precautions must be observed when digging trenches or deep holes for dry wells, septic tanks, and so forth. Earth is treacherous, and a bank that looks perfectly safe may slide. Sometimes warning is given by cracks appearing in the surface of the earth along the top of the trench. Earth trickling down the side of the bank also indicates that it may give way soon. In any event, all excavated material should be thrown well back and not piled close to the trench. If bracing is not to be used, the banks should be sloped sufficiently to avoid a cave-in; the looser the soil, the gentler the slope. Finally, once the excavation is made, it should receive whatever it is to contain — pipes, tanks, crushed stone, etc. — as rapidly as possible. Steep banks stand for a short time, but with time, rain, and vibration they may slide.

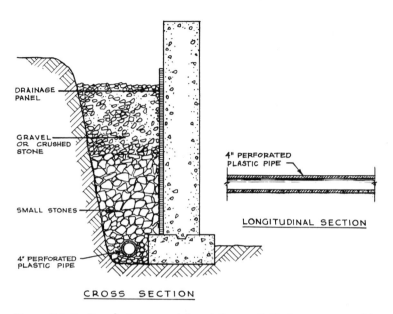

DRAINAGE PANEL

GRAVEL OR CRUSHED STONE

SMALL STONES

4" PERFORATED PLASTIC PIPE

4" PERFORATED PLASTIC PIPE

LONGITUDINAL SECTION

CROSS SECTION

Figure 3.2 Footing drains around foundation wall. Drainage promoted by gravel or drainage panel.

DRAINS AND DRY WELLS

3.5 Wall Drains

a. When foundations are built in impermeable soils, such as clay or mixtures of clay and sand, underground water is apt to be held in contact with the walls and to cause leakage, particularly after heavy rains or in wet seasons.

b. One of the simplest methods of draining the soil adjacent to walls is to lay a line of perforated pipe all around the base of the foundation, and to lead the line into a large dry well, preferably at a low point and at least several feet from the house. Drainage pipe is generally perforated plastic. It should be carefully bedded in a layer of small stones. Strips of tarred felt may be laid loosely over the pipe to prevent clay or silt from entering. The space adjacent to the walls is filled with crushed stone or gravel to within a foot or two of the finished grade. Finish grading with topsoil subsequently covers the gravel fill. Backfill should be compacted to avoid future settlement (figure 3.2).

c. A drainage panel or blanket, consisting of a porous outer membrane covering a series of pores or channels and an impervious inner membrane, may be applied to the outer surface of a foundation wall to accomplish the same purpose as the gravel or crushed stone (figure 3.2).

3.6 Roof Drains

a. Roof drains, called conductors, leaders, or downspouts (chapter 9), must be led into underground drainage basins, or dry wells, unless roof water can be led into the house sewer and into the municipal sewerage system, or unless the water can be discharged upon the ground. The underground drain, leading from downspout to dry well, must be watertight, unlike the wall drains discussed in the previous section. Plastic or various composition pipes are customarily employed for the horizontal underground portion. This is connected by an elbow to a vertical soil pipe into which the downspout is led at or just above the grade line.

b. If rain water is permitted to run into the house sewer, an encircling drain, connecting all conductors, may be built as shown in figure 3.3.

c. A rule for establishing proper grading for a drain is usually stated as follows: To 1' of fall in a drain, allow a length of 10' for each inch of diameter of the pipe.

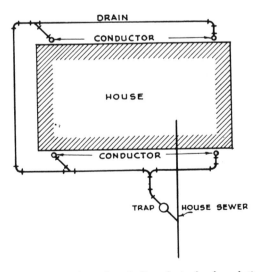

Figure 3.3 Plan of encircling drain for foundations.

d. To make a formula of this rule, we would have, if f = fall in feet, l = length of drain in feet, and d = diameter of pipe in inches,

$$f = \frac{l}{10d}.$$

Thus, for a 6″ drain 60′ long, the fall required would be 60/(10 × 6) = 1′.

3.7 Dry Wells

a. Dry wells are devices for disposing of excess water conducted from roofs or carried away from foundation walls by drain pipe. They are most effective in sandy or gravely soils because their function is to distribute the waste water into the subsoil, and in impermeable soils such as clay this cannot be accomplished satisfactorily.

b. Dry wells are simply fairly deep, fairly large excavations filled with crushed stone, gravel, broken brickbats, or other broken masonry, into which waste water is led for distribution to the surrounding soil. For roof water, dry wells must be away from the house a sufficient distance to prevent the water seeping into the soil from building up to a hydrostatic head against the foundation walls. Usually there are several dry wells for roof water, one for each principal downspout. They may be anywhere from 4′ to 6′ or 7′ in diameter and as deep; the size depends on the amount of roof water to be disposed of and on the permeability of the surrounding soil.

c. The dry well for the collection of water around the foundation walls, served by the wall drains, is usually considerably larger than the others, and its top is at the elevation of the footing drains. Its size, which may be from 6′ to 8′ each way, depends on the size of the house and the permeability of the soil, as well as on the condition in the site. A section through a typical dry well is shown in figure 3.4.

SANITARY SYSTEMS*

3.8 Sanitary Waste Disposal

Household and human wastes must be disposed of in such a way as not to contaminate drinking water, not to be accessible to insects, rodents, or other disease carriers, not to be accessible to children,

---

*Source: *Manual of Septic-Tank Practice*, Publication 526, Public Health Service, U.S. Department of Health, Education, and Welfare.

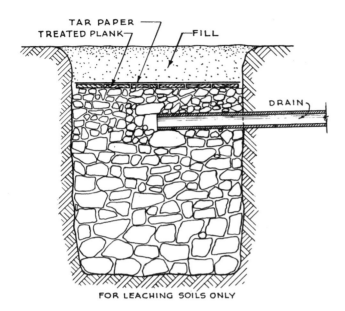

Figure 3.4 Section through dry well.

not to violate laws governing pollution, not to pollute beaches and streams, and not to create a nuisance due to odor or appearance. By far the best way is to discharge such wastes into an adequate community sewerage system. If this is impossible, a carefully designed and constructed and properly maintained septic-tank system can be satisfactory.

3.9 Septic-Tank System

a. A septic-tank system consists essentially of two parts: the tank, into which wastes are discharged to be digested and in which solids are separated from liquids and the liquids are prepared for disposal; and the disposal field, in which the liquids are allowed to percolate into the soil. Anaerobic bacteria (bacteria not dependent on free oxygen) accomplish much of the digestive action in the tank; aerobic bacteria (bacteria requiring free oxygen) in the soil attack the liquid effluent, pathogens are removed by percolation, and disease bacteria eventually die in the unfavorable environment of the soil. Although detergents in the quantity usually used do not affect the system as such, they are often highly resistant to digestion and may not be removed. If they penetrate into water supplies, they may cause foaming and other undesirable effects. Special care should therefore be taken to avoid penetration of potable-water supplies by detergent effluent. The soil *must* allow the effluent to percolate away readily. Impervious soils, therefore, are not suitable for septic-tank systems.

b. Most localities require septic tanks to be designed by registered sanitary engineers in accordance with local law and the results of percolation tests.

c. The most important function of the septic tank is to separate out solids that would otherwise quickly clog the soil in the disposal field. The rate of flow of sewage discharging from the house is reduced upon entering the tank, thereby allowing solids to sink into the sludge at the bottom or rise to the scum at the top. The clarified effluent is discharged to the disposal field.

d. Solids and liquids in the tank are attacked and decomposed essentially by anaerobic bacteria. The treated effluent sewage may be more highly septic and malodorous than the raw sewage (hence the name septic tank), but it causes less clogging than untreated wastes.

e. No matter how efficient the septic tank may be at decomposing and digesting wastes, residual solids remain compacted at the bottom and scum containing solids and grease floats partially submerged at the top. The septic tank, therefore, must provide storage space for sludge and scum between periodic cleanings.

f. Septic tanks should be at least 10′ away from any building, should not be in swampy ground, and should be situated far enough away both vertically and horizontally from wells or other sources of potable water to avoid contamination. The depth and direction of flow of underground water sources should be considered when selecting the site for a septic-tank system.

g. The general arrangement of a typical septic-tank system is shown in figure 3.5. Household wastes discharge through a liquid-tight sewer line into the liquid-tight septic tank. The effluent discharges from the tank into a distribution box and is there directed into the disposal field consisting of drain lines such as perforated pipe or drain tile with open joints, laid in gravel or crushed stone.

h. Tanks must be large enough to handle the expected wastes. Local or state codes specify sizes and details. The construction materials should not be corroded or otherwise attacked by the contents or the surrounding soil. Concrete, properly coated metal, vitrified clay, con-

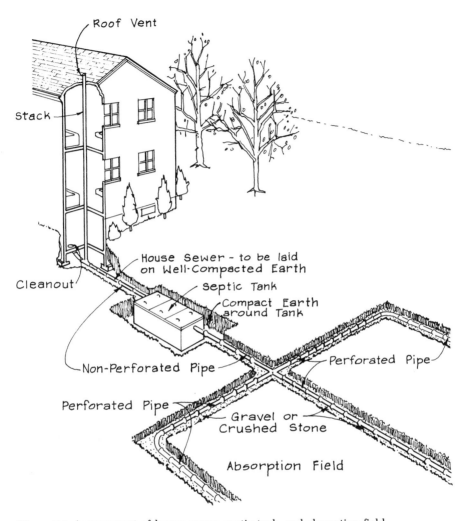

Figure 3.5 Arrangement of house sewer, septic tank, and absorption field.

crete blocks, and hard-burned bricks have been found suitable. Job-built masonry tanks should have all joints well filled.

i. Adequate access for cleaning and inspection must be provided at both the inlet and outlet ends, and in each compartment if there are several.

j. The first step in the design of a septic-tank system is to determine whether the soil is suitable for percolation of the effluent. If it is not, the system is not feasible. The soil must have an acceptable percolation ratio without interference by ground water, rock formations, or other impervious strata. Procedures for percolation tests are set up by local or state codes.

k. Two types of soil-absorption systems or disposal fields are generally used: standard trenches and seepage pits. Either should be kept a safe distance from water supply and dwellings. Local conditions and codes dictate the details. Seepage pits should be avoided where wells are shallow, or where underground channels may connect with water sources.

4 Foundations

4.1 General

a. In many respects, foundations are the most important part of any structure. Once built, little can be done to alter them. If they are adequate, the building remains stable, level, and plumb; if not, differential settlement causes cracks and leaks in the foundation, sloping floors, binding windows and doors, cracked plaster, and general racking of the superstructure.

b. Foundations normally consist of two principal parts: footings and walls. The materials generally employed are cast concrete and concrete block, although brick and rubble masonry are found. When no basement is desired, the substructure may consist merely of piers resting on footings.

c. Many basementless houses are built on slabs resting on soil at grade level. A peripheral footing integral with the slab is employed, and similar integral footings support bearing partitions, chimneys, and other local loads.

d. An important aspect of all foundation design and construction in cold areas is to make sure that expansion ("heaving") of soil because of frost action will not cause distortion of the structure. This means the provision of good drainage to carry away soil water which might cause trouble, or extending the bottoms of foundations or footings below the frost line (the greatest depth to which frost penetrates).

FOOTINGS

4.2 General

Footings may be required under foundation walls, piers, and posts, to spread the load to such an extent that settlement either is negligible or is uniform under all portions of the structure. In firm soils, such as compact sand and gravel, footings can often be omitted if the foundation wall is cast concrete, especially if it is reinforced. Walls of concrete blocks, brick, and stone should have footings no matter what the soil.

4.3 Footing Design

a. Footings for dwelling-house foundation walls are seldom designed; they are usually built by rule of thumb. Generally speaking, the depth of the footing should be the same as the thickness of the wall above it. Its width is 3″ to 4″ greater on each side than the wall above. As a

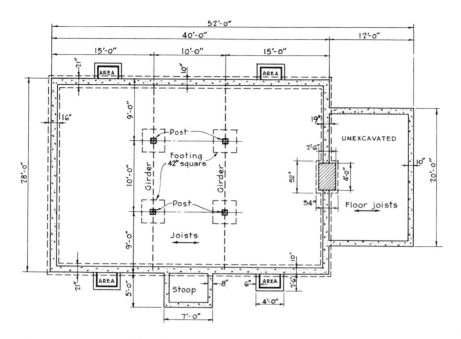

Figure 4.1 Footing and foundation plan, with footings proportioned for approximately equal load distribution.

matter of design, the footings ought to be proportioned to the loads transmitted to them from the building, in order to spread the loads uniformly on the soil and, thereby, prevent differential settlement. Dwelling-house loads are generally so light, however, that wider footings than those indicated are seldom necessary. Nevertheless, where unusually soft soils are encountered, the footings should be carefully proportioned to spread loads evenly and over a sufficient area to avoid overloading the soil beneath.

b. Figure 4.1 shows a typical house foundation plan. Part is excavated, part is not; a chimney is placed at one point, and there are several areaways, as well as a stoop. Two girders running the width of the house are supported at their ends by the foundations and at two intermediate points by posts. The foundation walls support the exterior walls, the floors, and the roof. The floor and ceiling of the ell are supported by the long outer wall and by the right-hand wall of the main foundation. The roof of the ell is supported by its two short foundation walls.

c. If this house were to be built on yielding soil, it would be well to investigate the probable loads on the various portions of the footing and to proportion them accordingly. The following computations are based on customary design assumptions respecting the weights of cast concrete and masonry, the live load plus the dead load on floors and roofs, and the weights of walls and partitions. The computations are based on a 1' length of wall, the total weight of the chimney, and the total tributary load on a post.

d. Examination of the computations in table 4.1 shows that minimum loads per foot of length are found under the ell walls. At 1,200 to 1,360 lb per ft under 10"-thick walls, the bearing on the soil is approximately 1,400 to 1,600 lb per sq ft. This is not excessive for moderately dense clay, and footings could be omitted under the ell walls. With loads of 1,600 lb per sq ft, the sizes of footings shown in the computations are found to be necessary for the other walls, the chimney, and the posts if approximately uniform load intensities are to be maintained on the soil. With other allowable bearing loads on soil, other footing sizes are needed.

e. With only two posts per girder, the load per post becomes large and the footings become correspondingly large. Unless they are reinforced, the footings must be approximately 20" deep, requiring a considerable amount of concrete and adding over 200 lb per sq ft to the load on the soil. It would be preferable to use three posts, thereby cutting down the load per post as well as reducing the size of the girder.

f. The floor and roof loads are "live" (i.e., intermittent), whereas the chimney load is permanent. Where such a condition exists and the soil is soft, it is a good plan to tie the footings together by embedding short lengths of reinforcing steel in the concrete at the juncture of the footings. In soft soils, this is also advisable at corners and other spots where breaks in the direction or width of the footing occur. Such spots are otherwise likely to develop cracks because of load concentrations and changes.

4.4 Forms

a. Footing forms (figure 4.2) are often omitted when the soil is firm enough to stand as a vertical wall for a short time. A shallow trench the size of the footings is dug and concrete is immediately deposited in it. While this is the easiest way to form the footings, it often leaves them uneven on top and may consequently cause some trouble with

Table 4.1 Footing Sizes for Approximately Equal Load Distribution (See Figure 4.1)

		Footing (Width)
Main portion, load per running foot		
Long walls		
Foundation, 8′ x $\frac{10}{12}$ x 140 lb/cu ft	940 lb/ft	
Walls, 2 stories high, 18′ x 20 lb/sq ft	360	
Ends of girders (see posts) spread over 10′ of footing, 4½′ x 1985 lb/ft = 8,900 lb ÷ 10 =	890	
Roof, 14′ x 30 lb/sq ft	420	
	2,610 lb/ft	19″
Short walls		
Left		
Foundation, 8′ x $\frac{10}{12}$ x 140 lb/cu ft	940 lb/ft	
Floors, first and second, 2 x 7½′ x 50 lb/sq ft	750	
Wall, 2 stories plus gable, 23′ x 20 lb/sq ft	460	
	2,150 lb/ft	16″
Right		
Foundation (omitting chimney)	940 lb/ft	
Floors, main house	750	
Ell, 6′ x 50 lb/sq ft	300	
Ceiling, ell, 6′ x 10 lb/sq ft	60	
Wall	460	
	2,510 lb/ft	19″
Ell, load per running foot		
Short walls		
Foundation, 6′ x $\frac{10}{12}$ x 140 lb/cu ft	700 lb/ft	
Wall, 1 story, 10′ x 20 lb/sq ft	200	
Roof, 10′ x 30 lb/sq ft	300	
	1,200 lb/ft	none
Right wall		
Foundation, 6′ x $\frac{10}{12}$ x 140 lb/cu ft	700 lb/ft	
Wall (part gable), 12′ x 20 lb/sq ft	240	
Floor, 6′ x 50 lb/sq ft	300	
Ceiling, 6′ x 20 lb/sq ft	120	
	1,360 lb/ft	none
Posts		
Load per foot of girder		
First and second floors, 2 x 12½′ x 50 lb/sq ft	1,250 lb/ft	
Bearing partitions above, first and second floors. 18′ x 20 lb/sq ft	360	
Attic floor, 12½′ x 30 lb/sq ft	375	
	1,985 lb/ft	
Loads per post, 9½′ x 1985 lb/ft =	18,900 lb	42″ x 42″
Chimney block, approximate total weight		
Average solid masonry 38′ x 3′ x 1.33′ x 120 lb/cu ft	18,300 lb	34″ x 52″

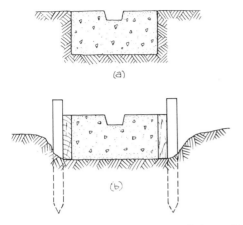

Figure 4.2 Footing forms. (a) Trench form. (b) Plank form.

the subsequent erection of wall forms. Tops of such footings should, therefore, be made as level as possible by lining up with level and cord.

b. When the top of the footing projects above the level of the basement excavation, or when the soil will not stand as a vertical cut, it is necessary to build some kind of footing form. This is most conveniently done by placing on edge in the trenches 2″ planks of the proper width, and holding them in position by stout stakes driven into the ground at intervals of 5′ to 6′. The planks are lightly nailed to the stakes after their top edges are leveled at the proper height. Concrete deposited in such forms can easily be brought to a level and straight line.

4.5 Sizes

a. Unreinforced solid concrete foundation walls for full-depth basements are usually 10″ to 12″ thick, although 8″ often meets requirements. Very thin walls and piers must be used with considerable caution, for while they may meet load-bearing requirements, they have a tendency to fail in shear or to buckle because of earth and water pressure. It is a good rule, therefore, whenever walls or piers less than 10″ thick are used, to reinforce them. Another useful rule of thumb is to limit the height of unreinforced walls to approximately ten times their thickness; if the ratio is greater, reinforcement should be used.

b. The thickness of a wall is often determined by the superstructure, rather than by the loads it is to carry. The thickness of a frame wall is usually 5″ to 6″. An 8″ wall will do in this case. A brick-veneer wall is at least 9″ thick, and at least 9″ or 10″ of foundation wall must be provided. For stone face and backing, 16″ to 18″ may be necessary (chapters 5 and 10).

c. The nature of the soil has its influence. Heavy impervious clay generally creates a water condition outside the walls; if the basement is to be kept dry, the walls may have to be heavier, waterproofed, and/or provided with special drainage (chapter 3).

4.6 Forms

a. The lumber used in the foundation forms of a dwelling house may subsequently be used in the superstructure. This consists of studding and rough flooring, sheathing, or plywood, the studs usually 2 × 4 and the boards 1 × 6 to 1 × 10 square-edged or matched material (chapter 5). As this lumber is to be used again, it should be cut as little as possible. For instance, some stud heights of the house may be 7′8″ and others 8′3″, but studs are not usually to be had in these lengths. Therefore, 16′ material is purchased and cut into two pieces. Such irregular lengths may be used for form studs, as these need not be uniform in height. Further, since lengths of boards are multiples of 2′ and plywood is usually 4′ wide, it is ordinarily best to space the form studs 2′ on centers so that as little waste as possible results from cutting.

b. Sheathing, if of boards, must be sound and free of large knots or knotholes; otherwise it does not withstand the pressure of wet concrete and does not provide a smooth wall. Studding must be examined, and any defective pieces laid aside to avoid any danger of failure in the forms. The same holds true in even larger degree for the rangers.

4.7 Types of Forms

a. Simple stud. The simple form shown in figure 4.3 consists of vertical studs faced with boards or plywood. This is simple but not very robust, and it should be used, if at all, only for minor walls. Fresh concrete weighs approximately 150 lb per cu ft, and when soft exerts a hydrostatic pressure equal to 150 lb times the depth in feet. Consequently, if such a form is filled too rapidly, it either bulges or collapses.

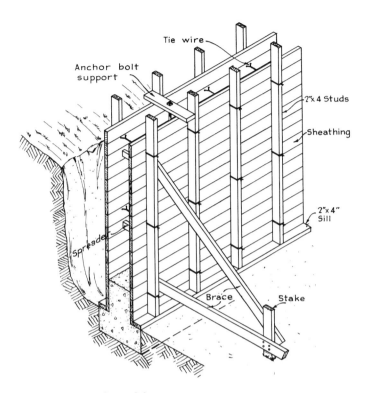

Figure 4.3 Simple stud form.

b. The studs are set opposite one another and are tied together at several points in their height. Since these ties take all the stress, there must be enough of them to withstand the pressure of fresh concrete.
c. Braces are required at frequent intervals with this type of form because there is no lateral stiffness except that provided by the sheathing. Furthermore, there is nothing to keep the form in alignment except the braces.
d. Stud and ranger. Because of their lack of rigidity, simple stud forms are reinforced, when greater strength is needed, by rangers running horizontally, as shown in figure 4.4. Rangers are placed on both sides of the form and are tied together. With this construction, only enough braces are needed to keep the form from overturning. With studs, rangers, and braces properly spaced, it is possible to deposit concrete to the full height of the wall without danger of distortion.
e. Rangers should always be used if it is important to have a perfectly straight wall, free of undulations and true to line. Moreover, if the

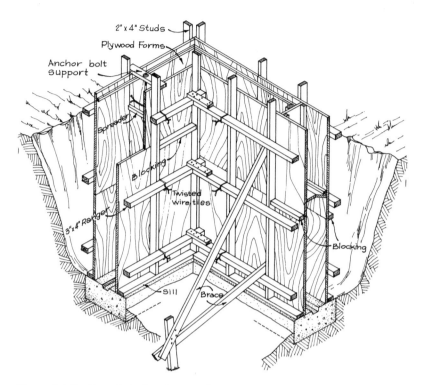

Figure 4.4 Section of stud-and-ranger form.

rangers instead of the studs are tied together, studs on opposite sides of the wall need not be in pairs. The rangers stiffen the entire form so that fewer braces are necessary. Any breaks or weaknesses in the form are held in check by the rangers.

f. Rangers are commonly 3 × 4 or two 2 × 4s.

g. Standard practice is to space studs 2' on centers. The strength of a 1″ board (chapter 5) or of plywood in bending controls this distance, and the load on the board, in turn, is governed by the hydrostatic head or height of the soft concrete above it. For heights up to 5', deflection is not noticeable in such a board if studs are 2' on centers. For heights more than 5', studs must be closer together, unless the concrete is deposited slowly enough to allow the initial set to take place at the bottom, thus reducing the hydrostatic pressure. Forms are generally built completely around the wall, and the concrete is deposited in layers.

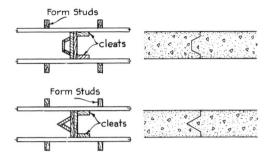

Figure 4.5 Method of framing vertical joints in concrete walls.

h. Rangers are spaced varying distances apart vertically, but are closer together at the bottom to resist the increased pressure. The lowest ranger is ordinarily 1' from the bottom, the second is 2' to 3' above that, and the third is about 1' down from the top. In dwelling-house work, three rangers are usually enough, but they should not be more than $3\frac{1}{2}'$ to 4' apart vertically if casting is continuous.

i. Rangers must be especially straight and should be at least 16' long. Their ends should be butted and the joints spliced with pieces of board at least 3' long. If rangers are doubled 2 × 4s, splices are made by staggering the joints.

4.8 Prefabricated Reusable Forms

Prefabricated reusable sectional forms may be employed. These are commonly boxes made of studs with waterproof plywood on each side. The sections are set adjacent to one another and braced (figure 4.6). Such sectional forms are especially useful in tract housing, where many identical foundations are built. Prefabricated forms may also be metal.

4.9 Spreaders and Wiring

a. In order to ensure uniform thickness in the completed wall, the forms must be kept a uniform distance apart and be held there while the concrete is setting. This is accomplished by spreaders and wire ties or other devices, the spreaders giving the proper thickness and the ties preventing the forms from yielding (figure 4.7). The principle is illustrated here with spreaders and ties, but a number of proprietary devices are commonly used to achieve the same effect.

b. Spreaders are short metal bars or wood sticks (figure 4.7a), usually

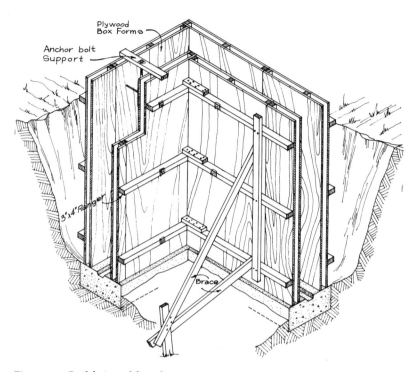

Figure 4.6 Prefabricated box forms.

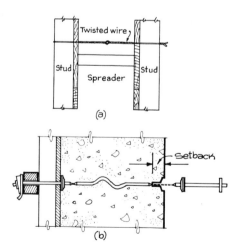

Figure 4.7 (a) Spreader and wires. (b) Metal bar spreader-tie with snap-off ends.

about 1″ × 2″ in cross-section and of length equal to the thickness of the wall. They are inserted between the sides of the form and are held in place by the pressure exerted against their ends by the ties, which should be of fairly heavy, soft, black, annealed iron wire because they must withstand both tension and severe twisting stresses without breaking. Number 8 wire is best; not only is it strong enough, but it twists rapidly and does not cut into the wood as badly as does smaller wire. However, no. 10 or 12 is suitable for simple stud forms, which are usually small.

c. Wires are inserted as the forms go up. In the simple stud form, the wires may be placed in the joints between boards. Plywood sheathing and the ranger type of form requires $\frac{3}{8}$″ to $\frac{1}{2}$″ holes to be bored in the sheathing to allow wires to pass around studs or rangers on both sides. Fresh concrete readily chokes these holes.

d. Many proprietary devices are available to perform the combined functions of spreader and tie wire. These are usually easily and quickly put in place in the forms, and they stay in place in the concrete when the forms are removed. Some provide a device which can be snapped off or otherwise removed at the surface of the concrete, leaving a depression which can be filled with mortar or caulking material. One type is illustrated in figure 4.7b. This device holds forms the proper distance apart, but the ends of the tie are snapped off when forms are dismantled, leaving part of the bar in place and leaving a small depression at the surface that can be left exposed or mortared over.

4.10 Erection

a. Forms may be erected one side at a time or both sides may be thrown up simultaneously. In the former procedure, the outer side is built first and ties may be inserted loosely in the sheathing as it goes up. If the form is a large one, the studs are erected in place, are nailed to a lower horizontal 2 × 4 member called a *shoe*, and are temporarily braced. The sheathing is then nailed to the studs. (Small forms can advantageously be built on the flat and lifted into place when finished.) The inner side is then erected. As it goes up, the ties and spreaders are placed between the two sides and tightened.

b. When both sides are built simultaneously, both sets of studs are erected at once and the sheathing goes up on each set at the same time.

c. In either procedure, rangers may or may not be placed as the sheathing goes on, but usually it is best to place them at once so that the form is straight from the very start.

d. Braces are set more or less simultaneously with the studs and sheathing. Enough must be placed at the beginning to hold the form in alignment, and when the sheathing is in place enough must be added to hold the form rigid. The simple stud type may require braces at every other stud, the ranger type seldom any oftener than every fourth or fifth stud.

4.11 Runways

a. When concrete is to be deposited by wheelbarrow or buggy, runways may be built which are partially supported by the forms. For easy dumping, the top of the runway should be at the level of the top form board and should be wide enough to permit two vehicles to pass.

b. With the ready-mix concrete commonly employed, it is usually possible to bring the ready-mix truck into position and to deposit the concrete directly by chute into the forms, thus eliminating the runways.

4.12 Top of Form

The importance of leveling the top of the concrete wall cannot be overemphasized. In order to stop the concrete at the proper height, a guide must be provided which indicates the top of the wall. This may consist of nails driven 2' to 3' apart in the top form board along a straight level line established at the proper elevation. A more accurate method is to nail a wood strip along this line and cast the concrete to the underside of the strip. Some form builders cut the top of the sheathing along this line so that the wall cannot be carried too high and a good level surface can readily be achieved.

4.13 Openings and Sleeves

a. Provision must be made in the form for openings such as doors and windows. Finished wood frames should not be concreted in place, because they are likely to swell and become distorted. Openings should be boxed and the frames set later. In the boxing, provision should be made for later anchoring the wood frames to the concrete. Bolts, clip angles, or other similar devices may be used. When steel window frames are used, the frames are built into the boxes with the edges of the frames protruding. Concrete is cast around the frame, thereby firmly anchoring it in place.

b. Pipes for water, gas, oil, and electricity are brought through the foundation, and openings for these must be left in the wall. Openings are most conveniently provided by placing in the forms pieces of pipe or metal sleeves whose length equals the thickness of the wall and whose inner diameter is slightly larger than the pipes that are to pass through them.

4.14 Anchor Bolts and Reinforcement

a. If the superstructure is to be frame, it should have a sill, generally bolted to the foundation walls. These bolts — commonly $\frac{1}{2}''$ in diameter, provided with $2''$ washers or hooked at the lower end, and usually spaced $4'$ to $8'$ apart — are suspended in the forms at the proper height and concreted in. Later the sill can be slipped over them and fastened down by nut and washer (chapter 5). Other anchoring devices include metal straps and a variety of proprietary devices. Powder-actuated studs driven (by explosive cartridges) through the sill into the concrete are also used.

b. A common way to reinforce walls is to put No. 6 bars ($\frac{6}{8}''$, i.e. $\frac{3}{4}''$) at the top and the bottom of the form, resting on form ties.

CONCRETE

4.15 Material

a. Composition and mixes. Concrete is a mixture of large mineral particles called *aggregate*, small mineral particles or sand, cement (almost always portland cement), and water. When first mixed it is plastic, but it hardens when the cement hydrates and "sets."

b. Of the five types of cement classified by the American Society for Testing and Materials (ASTM C150), general-purpose or Type I is by far the most common. Others are employed for more special purposes — e.g., Type II for somewhat slower set and less heat evolution, Type III for high early strength if fast setting is a critical requirement, Type IV for minimum heat evolution in mass concrete, and Type V for high-sulfate resistance. All may be modified with air-entraining ingredients and called Type IA, etc. Plastic cements contain up to 12 percent plasticizing agents.

c. The most common aggregate for standard concrete is gravel or

crushed stone. Other aggregates include air-cooled blast-furnace slag, furnace clinkers or cinders, expanded slag, expanded clay and shale, raw and sintered pulverized-fuel ash, diatomite, expanded mica (vermiculite), expanded volcanic ash (perlite), pumice, and scoria. Concrete may be foamed mechanically or by chemical reaction of aluminum and portland cement; in the latter case, the hydrogen gas released serves as a blowing agent. The various aggregates and foaming methods are often used for special purposes, such as thermal insulation and reduced weight. Standard concrete weighs 140–150 lb per cu ft; most lightweight concretes range from 90 to 115 lb per cu ft.
d. Concrete cast in the field is generally standard concrete employing gravel or crushed stone aggregate (or slag when it is readily available). Other aggregates are more common in blocks (sections 4.18ff.) and other precast units.
e. The ready-mixed concrete commonly employed in the field is specified by 28-day strength, and the actual mix is left to the provider of the concrete. If concrete is mixed on the job, it may be done by hand or machine. Hand mixing is used only for small batches. Simple easy-to-measure ratios, such as 1-2-4, 1-2.5-5, and 1-3-6 are common, meaning 1 cubic foot (one sack) of cement to 2 cubic feet of sand to 4 cubic feet of aggregate and so forth. The higher the cement content the higher the strength, *provided the water-to-cement ratio is constant.* Strength is seldom a great factor in house foundations, so more economical mixes are commonly employed, but they must be sound and dense enough to prevent leakage.
f. The purchasing of premixed concrete is becoming more and more common, especially in larger urban centers, and has many advantages.
g. Machine mixing. The usual concrete mixer consists of a rotating drum containing oblique blades. The dry ingredients — sand, aggregate, and cement — are placed in the drum and mixed, after which water is added and the mass is turned over long enough to achieve thorough mixing. The drum is then tilted downward and the soft mix is deposited in whatever vehicles are employed to transport the concrete to the forms.
h. Workability. Hard to define, "workability" is one of the most important attributes of good concrete. "Plasticity" is another term. It means the property of flowing easily (not running like water) into and filling all the parts of a form completely without segregation of the ingredients of which the concrete is composed. Good workable con-

crete does not show free water at the surface; when poured out of a bucket it forms a pancake curling under at the edges, and it quakes when shaken or prodded. Workability is a matter of good proportions, size of aggregate and sand particles, and, above all, the proper amount of water. *Small variations in water content make large differences in workability, strength, and density.*

i. Depositing. Concrete must not be dropped from a height of more than 3′ or 4′. For greater height, a trough or chute should be used. Dropping causes sand, water-cement paste, and aggregate to separate. Individual loads should be spread, not merely dumped. Spreading remixes the ingredients, which may have started to separate, and mixes the entire mass in the forms more uniformly.

j. Working. Once in the forms, the concrete must be worked into all corners, and any entrapped air must be removed. This is done by spading and rodding or by means of mechanical vibrators. Rodding and spading are done most vigorously in the center and less so at the form faces. Concrete must be carefully worked. If it is neglected, "honeycombs" or pockets form in which there is no concrete. Too much working tends to separate the ingredients, the lighter material rising to the top as a milky scum called "laitence." It consists of a very fine, overwatered or "drowned" cement, which is worthless, soon disintegrates, and causes much of the trouble encountered with concrete. Too much working brings this to the top or to the face of the wall, where it subsequently forms a film that continually dusts off, or leaches when water strikes it.

k. Filling. Forms may be filled in horizontal layers all around the structure or in full-height sections adjacent to one another. In small structures, the horizontal-layer method is commonly employed, because it is easier and it permits lighter forms. It does require that forms be built completely around the wall. Sometimes the forms cannot be filled in one day's operation by this method; consequently, horizontal joints occur between successive days' work.

l. The vertical-section method, more commonly employed on large structures, calls for heavier forms and for bulkheads to be built inside the forms between successive sections (figure 4.5). However, forms need not be built entirely around the structure, since sectional forms can be reused. Their chief advantages are the elimination of horizontal joints and the regular spacing of vertical joints in the wall. Vertical joints must be provided in long walls; otherwise, shrinkage causes irregular vertical cracks. In small foundation walls, such as in dwelling houses, this is not a particularly serious matter and is seldom taken into account.

m. Where watertight construction is required (as in cisterns or other liquid-containing structures), concrete must be cast continuously to completion because joints of any kind are almost sure to leak under hydrostatic pressure.

n. Bonding. Bonding new to old concrete is one of the most important and difficult aspects of concrete work. In continuous pouring, the bond is automatic because successive wet masses are merged into one another. The merging process can be carried on anytime within 2 hours or so, but after that the concrete enters its first hardening stage, called the "initial set," and should not be disturbed. New concrete will not merge satisfactorily with old after this time. After about 8 hours, the concrete enters its second hardening stage, called the "final set," and new concrete will not merge with the old at all.

o. Fresh concrete can be bonded to hardened material only by adhesion. For a good bond:

1. Laitence must be removed. Laitence forms a plane of cleavage, does not adhere to either old or new concrete, and gradually crumbles or leaches away. It should be thoroughly chipped, scraped, or brushed off.

2. Any dirt, dust, or other foreign matter must be cleaned off thoroughly by wire brushing and by flushing the surface with a hose. Water must be allowed to drain away before new concrete is deposited.

3. The surface should be roughened to increase the area for adhesion. This can be done by chipping when laitence is removed. Sometimes, to form projecting keys for the new concrete, fairly large pieces of aggregate are embedded in the surface of the old concrete while it is still fluid.

4. The new concrete must be carefully deposited, spread, and thoroughly rammed and rodded so that no air remains at the surface of the old. A grout with a low water-cement ratio may be placed first and thoroughly worked into the new concrete.

5. Mixes of sand, cement, and a variety of latex materials based on plastics and other polymers are available to provide strong bonds to old concrete.

p. Curing. Concrete should not be permitted to become too hot, too cold, or too dry. The best concrete is obtained by curing at 50–70°F. Above that range, the speed of set is accelerated, but strength and hardness are impaired, largely because of the too-rapid evaporation of water. High temperatures are, therefore, best offset by constant sprinkling.

q. Set is retarded at low temperatures, and it stops below freezing because the water congeals and no longer reacts with the cement. Frozen concrete is dormant; after it has thawed, it continues to set, probably with some loss of strength. Alternate freezing and thawing has a disrupting influence and may ruin concrete. Therefore, concrete is best kept from freezing, and if it has once frozen it should be kept heated until it has passed well beyond the final set. Hard concrete rings when struck with a hammer; frozen concrete gives a dull thud and shows a wet spot where the hammer strikes.

r. Concrete permitted to dry before it has completely set soon disintegrates because hydration of the cement is incomplete, and the unhydrated portion acts as if it were dust mixed into the mass. During cure, therefore, concrete should be kept as wet as possible. Several days to a week of wetting down with a hose and covering with wet burlap or with an impervious plastic film is good treatment.

4.16 Stripping Forms

a. After the concrete has attained its final set, it can stand unsupported and forms may be removed. If just enough nails have been used to hold the forms together, they come apart easily and with little broken material. Inasmuch as studs and boards are to be reused, the stripping should be done carefully so as to waste as little material as possible. Boards and studs should be cleaned of nails, and any adhering concrete should be scraped off. They should then be piled neatly and straight with spacers so that they may dry quickly without warping or twisting.

b. Protruding wires should be cut off flush with the face of the wall and patched over with mortar, or proprietary spreader-ties should be removed as directed. Any open spots (which should not occur in a well-rodded and spaded wall) should be filled with a 1-3 cement-sand mortar to which has been added about 15 percent lime.

4.17 Finishing

a. Exterior faces of concrete walls exposed above grade may be treated in some manner to remove the marks of form boards and to improve their appearance, but the rough wall is often left as it comes from the forms.

b. Several finishing methods are employed, of which the following are the most common:

1. *Coating.* Cement plaster, consisting of sand, cement, and water, is troweled or spatter-dashed onto the wall. This is the easiest and by far most common method, but frost action may eventually dislodge the coating.

2. *Rubbing.* As soon as possible, the form boards are removed and the surface rubbed down at once, e.g., with a carborundum brick and plain water or a paste (grout) of water and cement.

3. *Brushing.* Forms are removed as soon as the concrete will stand, and the still-soft surface is wire-brushed.

4. *Hammering.* The hardened surface is gone over with a bush hammer (a hammer with a serrated face).

CONCRETE BLOCK

4.18 Units

a. Instead of solid concrete, cast in place, walls are frequently built of concrete blocks small enough to be handled by one man, and laid up in much the same way as brick (figure 4.8). Foundation blocks are generally standard concrete, but blocks for other purposes (such as insulation and backup) are often made with other aggregates or by foaming (sections 4.15b, 4.15c).

b. Although at one time there was a great multiplicity of sizes and shapes, concrete blocks have now been more or less standardized. The sizes most frequently used are $7\frac{5}{8}''$ × $15\frac{5}{8}''$ on the vertical face, with thicknesses varying from $3\frac{5}{8}''$ to $11\frac{5}{8}''$ in $2''$ multiples. The $7\frac{5}{8}''$ thickness is most common. With $\frac{3}{8}''$ mortar joints, all these blocks are $8''$ × $16''$ on the face. To decrease weight and to save material, vertical open spaces are left in the interiors of the blocks. For corners, special blocks with smooth end faces supplement the ordinary blocks with hollowed ends. Many special blocks, including concrete brick, are made; these call for various special interlocking and cross-tying systems. Special sculptured or otherwise treated surfaces are available. Glazes, and coatings based on various polymeric materials (chapter 16), may be applied. Surfaces may be ground smooth.

c. Blocks should be well cured by autoclaving or aging, to reduce subsequent shrinkage and cracking in the wall.

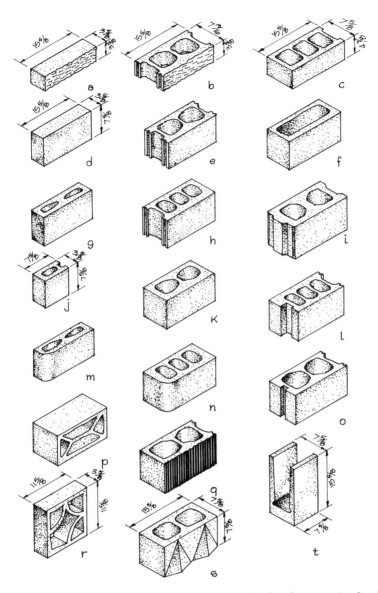

Figure 4.8 Types of concrete block. (a) 4″ × 4″ split. (b) 4″ × 8″ split. (c) 4⅞″ starter. (d) 4″ × 8″ solid. (e) 8″ stretcher. (f) 8″ conduit. (g) 4″ stretcher. (h) 8″ stretcher-corner. (i) 8″ control joint. (j) 4″ half-stretcher. (k) 8″ double corner. (l) 8″ wood sash. (m) 4″ single bull nose. (n) 8″ single bull nose. (o) 8″ steel sash. (p) 8″ screen. (q) 8″ striated. (r) 4″ × 12″ × 12″ screen. (s) 8″ sculptured. (t) 8″ × 16″ lintel.

4.19 Use

Concrete blocks are widely used for foundations. They are also frequently built into upper walls, often faced with stucco, brick, or with integral surfaces (see above). Blocks with a finished surface, or split blocks, are employed with no further facing. In such instances, they are in the same category as cut stone. Blocks may be made especially to conform to particular wall openings, or the openings may be arranged to meet the stock sizes of blocks (sections 4.20c, 5.46ff.).

4.20 Laying Up

a. Coursing. Blocks are laid end to end, "stretcher" fashion, completely around the wall; the first course is brought to a true and level line on top of the footing so that subsequent courses will also be true. The next course is laid on top of the first but with the vertical joints offset or "broken" half the length of a block. Therefore, joints in every other course are directly above one another. Blocks lap over each other at the corners and provide a good bond (figure 4.9). If the walls are to be concealed below ground, standard blocks may be employed at the corners in place of the special smooth-ended corner blocks.

b. Wall height. Since blocks are normally 8″ high, including a $\frac{3}{8}$″ mortar joint, any wall height which is not a multiple of 8″ has to be attained by (1) courses of brick, (2) half blocks laid on the flat, (3) thickening all horizontal "bed" joints, or (4) a combination of these methods.

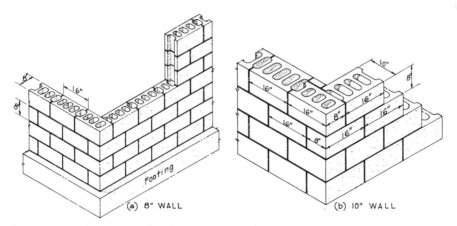

Figure 4.9 Laying concrete-block walls.

c. By far the simplest procedure is to lay out wall heights, and the heights of openings such as doors and windows, in multiples of standard block heights. Similarly, horizontal dimensions, including lengths of walls and widths of openings, are best laid out in half block lengths. With the commonly employed nominal 8″ × 16″ block, for example, this means that vertical and horizontal dimensions are in multiples of 8″. With other than 8″-wide blocks, special details at corners may be required (figure 4.9).

d. **Openings in walls.** Wherever doors, windows, or other openings occur, frames are often erected before the wall is started so that the wall may be built tightly against the frames. Anchorage blocks are built into the wall directly adjacent to the frames, and the frames are subsequently fastened to these blocks. Preferred construction calls for openings to be built into the wall and frames to be inserted later. Offset jamb blocks are employed to provide a recess into which the frames are fitted. Nailing blocks, strap anchors, or other fastening devices are built into the wall to hold the frames in place.

e. Concrete blocks can be carried across openings on lintels. Several types of lintels are shown in figure 4.10, including steel and one-piece cast-in-place or precast reinforced-concrete lintels. Another type is formed by laying special U-shaped lintel blocks side by side, placing reinforcing steel is the channel thus formed, and filling the channel with concrete; this is usually done in place.

f. A commonly used deflection limitation for hard, brittle materials is $\frac{1}{360}$ of the span. For example, the maximum deflection permitted on a 10′ span (120″) is $\frac{1}{3}$″. For concrete blocks, with their greater tendency to crack, especially at the joints, it is safer to limit the deflection still more; $\frac{1}{480}$ of the span is recommended by engineers.

g. **Mortar.** Although high-cement mortars have long been commonly used for concrete block, there is a decided tendency toward higher-lime mortars because of their greater workability and the more intimate contact they give between block and mortar. Therefore, a mortar composed of 1 part cement, 1 part lime putty, and 5 to 6 parts sand is generally recommended. Sufficient water is added to obtain good workability. Special mortars formulated for blocks are available.

h. **Returns, pilasters, and piers.** Where changes in direction or "returns" in walls occur, care must be exercised to build the corner straight and plumb, and to make sure that no long vertical joints occur. Such vertical joints are avoided by carrying the succeeding

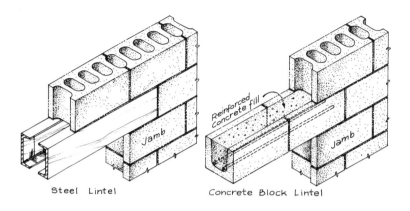

Steel Lintel   Concrete Block Lintel

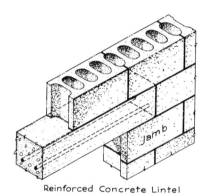

Reinforced Concrete Lintel

Figure 4.10 Lintels.

courses of block into the corner alternately from one side and the other, much as logs in a log cabin are laid on top of one another at the corner.

i. Pilasters are short sections of the wall which are increased in thickness throughout its height, usually to carry concentrated loads such as girders. Since there is a return at each side of a pilaster, the same precautions respecting long vertical joints hold as for corners. The pilaster must be built as an integral part of the wall by bonding wall and pilaster block together. To obtain odd dimensions, brick and half-block must often be employed.

j. Piers are free-standing posts, usually square in cross-section, which support concentrated loads. Again, by lapping block in succeeding courses, long vertical joints are avoided. Often, voids in concrete-

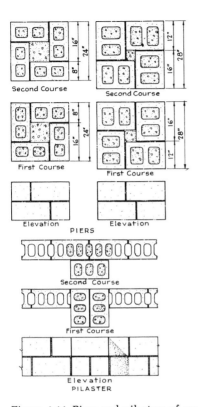

Figure 4.11 Piers and pilasters of concrete block.

block piers and pilasters are filled with concrete to produce completely solid structures.

4.21 Anchor Bolts

Anchor bolts may be needed to prevent displacement of the superstructure by wind, earthquake, or other forces. In the case of concrete block and other masonry units this is not accomplished as easily as in the case of cast concrete, but it can be done by carrying the bolts down some depth into the wall. In concrete block, this should be equal to at least two courses of block. For firm anchorage, the lower ends of the bolts are provided with steel plate washers, which are embedded in the horizontal mortar joint. The bolts extend upward through the openings in the block and are fixed in place by filling the openings with mortar. Steel strap anchors are commonly bent at the bottom and embedded in a mortar joint.

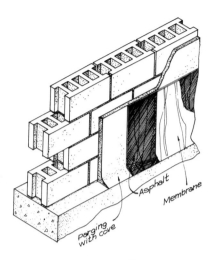

Figure 4.12 Parging and waterproofing of concrete-block foundation wall.

4.22 Waterproofing

a. In wet locations concrete block walls are apt to leak, so extra precautions must be taken to ensure dry walls. Drain tile is placed around the outsides of footings to prevent a head of water from being built up in some soils. The drains lead into dry wells or into the municipal sewerage system (chapter 3). Even in relatively dry locations it is desirable to "parge" or plaster the outside of the wall with two layers of mortar, each ¼″ thick, troweled and pressed on firmly. This helps seal the fairly porous surface (figure 4.12). A foaming-agent admixture in the mortar is helpful in promoting workability, adhesion, and watertightness.

b. Asphalt coating and membrane waterproofing. Both of these are essentially the same as the waterproofing and built-up roofing found in larger structures. Asphalt coatings are asphaltic mixtures applied either hot or cold to the wall. Their effectiveness depends upon the care and thoroughness with which they are applied and upon the wall not cracking. Membrane waterproofing consists of alternate layers of hot asphalt and builders' felt. This is a much more dependable method of waterproofing.

4.23 Advantages and Disadvantages

a. Advantages of block construction are the elimination of forms and the speeding of construction. Block walls are ready for the superstructure almost as soon as they are finished, and need be allowed to stand only long enough for the mortar to set. Solid concrete walls must be allowed to harden; then the forms must be removed.

b. Disadvantages of block walls are possible poor anchorage, greater likelihood of leakage, and greater likelihood of cracking. A concrete block wall does not have the strength of a solid wall, and any settlement is more apt to cause cracks than in solid concrete.

4.24 Reinforced Block Masonry

If lateral forces, such as may be caused by earth pressure or earthquakes, are expected, block walls may be reinforced in a variety of ways, as shown in figure 4.13. The footing is reinforced against cracking, and vertical rods, embedded in the footing, are carried upward at corners, openings, and intersections through the holes in the cores of the blocks. These holes are then filled with mortar or concrete. Wire reinforcing is laid in the horizontal joints. At the top of the wall a continuous beam is formed by lintel blocks, reinforcing steel, and concrete.

4.25 Types of Rubble Masonry

a. The foundation walls for a dwelling are sometimes built of stone. Since a house may be built entirely of stone, this discussion will not be confined to the foundation walls in particular, but will consider the subject as a whole, with particular emphasis on random rubble.

b. In general, stone masonry is divided rather roughly into two classes: rubble and ashlar. Ashlar is a facing of stone (usually cut stone with regular squared joints) backed with other material (usually brick). Rubble masonry is usually homogeneous; that is, the entire wall is built of the same stone, takes all of the load, and is an integral structure. Many large and famous buildings, such as ancient churches and castles, are so built.

c. Rubble masonry is composed of stones or stone fragments irregular in any or all of the elements of size, shape, and jointing. The irregularity may be somewhat ordered in any of these particulars, and the degree of such ordering has given rise to the broad classifications of random rubble and coursed rubble.

d. *Random rubble* (figure 4.14) is the roughest and most casual of all stonework. Little attention is given to coursing, but each layer should contain stones bonding through the wall in sufficient number to produce a closely knit structure. The remaining interstices are filled with

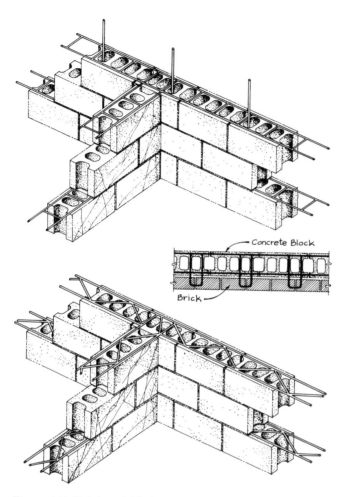

Figure 4.13 Reinforced block: (top) vertical; (bottom) horizontal; (center) brick-to-block tie.

Figure 4.14 Random rubble.

Figure 4.15 Coursed rubble.

smaller stones of convenient size and shape. Such walls may be used for both foundations and superstructure. The most attractive random rubble is composed of good-sized stones, with a minimum of small chips as fillers. It should never be pointed with full mortar pointing to hide the natural shapes of the stones. The pointing should be kept well back of the outer surface. "Builds" or "vertical" joints need not be truly vertical, but "beds" should be approximately horizontal for stability and appearance.

e. *Coursed rubble* (figure 4.15), as its name implies, is assembled of roughly squared stones in such a manner as to produce, at intervals, approximately continuous horizontal bed joints separated by variable vertical distances from similar neighboring joints. It is necessary to have only fairly level beds and approximately vertical builds and faces. Such masonry may either be irregularly coursed or squared, as the specifications may direct.

4.26 Wood Foundations

This short treatment is general. Original sources should be consulted—for example, *All-Weather Wood Foundation Systems* (National Forest Products Association).

a. Wood foundations may be employed for light structures, but they require careful attention to details and to failure (e.g., decay and insect attack). The frame and the foundation must be able to support the superstructure. At this point the techniques must be considered innovative, and caution is advised.

b. The framing (figure 4.16) is standard platform framing (section 5.6), usually made up in panels, and assembled on the footings. The studs (generally 2 × 4 or 2 × 6) must be deep enough and spaced closely enough to be able to carry wall and floor loads from above in addition to lateral soil pressure. Lintels above openings such as windows must be strong enough to carry superimposed loads. Plywood is generally $\frac{1}{2}''$

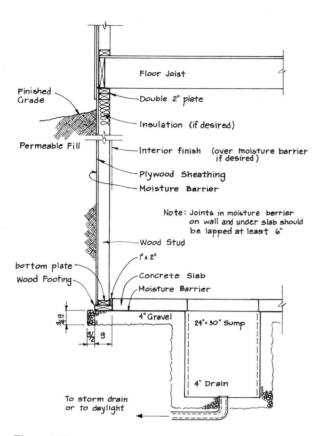

Figure 4.16

with standard stud spacing, but $\frac{5}{8}''$ or more may be required with wider stud spacing and with heavy soil pressures.

c. All materials must be pressure-treated according to rigid industry standards. Only nonleaching preservatives are approved. Metal parts must resist corrosion by soil or preservative.

d. Plywood (section 5.3) must be bonded with exterior glue, and must conform to U.S. Department of Commerce Product Standard for Construction and Industrial Plywood. Species employed in plywood (and all lumber) should accept the required retention. Heartwood of some common species is difficult to treat. Specifications may limit such heartwood.

e. Members should be fabricated to shape and size before treatment. Cutting of surfaces after treatment should be avoided. If it occurs, the surfaces should be soaked or thoroughly brushed with a strong solution (at least triple strength) of the preservative employed.

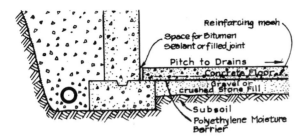

Figure 4.17 Concrete floor.

f. Although specifications require caulking in joints between panels, the best precaution against penetration by water is to make certain that the soil is thoroughly drained to avoid water pressure against the wall, by means of drain pipe in porous fill such as gravel or crushed stone. Tile should lead to daylight or storm drains. A sump in the basement is recommended (figure 4.16). It may be an open sump, as shown, or it may be filled with gravel or crushed stone, with a perforated pipe extended upward into the fill.

g. The footing at the base of the wall may be concrete, similar to the footings under concrete block walls, but is commonly a plank, 2 × 6 or 2 × 8 for 2 × 4 or 2 × 6 studs, resting on well-consolidated gravel or crushed stone. A concrete-slab floor is ordinarily employed, but the floor may be treated wood on treated sleepers resting on a bed of consolidated gravel or crushed stone. The footing must be able to sustain safely and spread the superimposed load to avoid undue settlement.

4.27 Floors

a. The basement floor is not placed at the same time that the foundation walls are built. It must wait until the house is framed and all the necessary underground service lines have been placed under the basement, but it should be cast as soon as possible in order to allow it to dry thoroughly before the finish lumber arrives. Otherwise, dampness originating in the basement may cause swelling and warping in the kiln-dried millwork used for the interior finish.

b. Unless the subsoil is itself dry, sandy, and gravely, it is wise to put down a layer of gravel or crushed stone, from 4″ to 6″ thick, before the concrete is cast (figure 4.17). To avoid future settlement or cracks, the fill must be well tamped. Preferably, it should be dampened at the same time to make it compact better. Too much water merely soaks it and tends to float the finer particles to the top.

c. Concrete for basement floors should be quite stiff, to reduce the amount of water that must be evaporated, to increase the density, and to provide a harder, more wear-resistant surface than would be found if the concrete were soft.

d. If floor drains are provided, the floor should be gradually but uniformly sloped toward the drains from all directions. To make sure that the slope is correct, stakes are set and the tops of the stakes are brought to the proper pitch with a level and straight edge. Concrete is cast and leveled to the tops of the stakes, which are removed as the concreting progresses. After the concrete is deposited and brought to the proper elevation, it is surfaced by working the face with a wooden float (a wood block with a handle) or a steel trowel. Floated finishes are slightly rough and pebbly; troweled surfaces are smooth.

e. Although concrete basement slabs are commonly cast directly against foundation walls, it is wise to leave a space to be filled subsequently with bitumen or other sealant (figure 4.17). Otherwise, shrinkage of the slab is likely to open a peripheral crack, which may let in water.

f. Wire-mesh reinforcement not only helps to strengthen the concrete; especially over possible hollow spots below, it helps to prevent large cracks from developing. A polyethylene-film moisture barrier under the slab, over the fill, helps to prevent moisture from migrating up through the slab.

5 Framing

5.1 General

a. The frame is the structural skeleton of the building. In light construction such as dwelling houses it consists mainly of relatively small pieces of timber ranging from 2″ to 6″ or 8″ in thickness and from 2″ to 12″ in width. The frame is assembled on the foundations, and to it are fastened windows, doors, roof covering, exterior covering, interior covering, and floor. Light steel framing is increasingly common (section 5.13).

b. The species of wood used in framing vary with the locality; in any one place, those species that are most available and economical are used. By and large, spruce, hemlock, yellow pine, and Douglas fir are most commonly used. Since appearance is no factor (because the frame is subsequently covered), those grades are employed which are most economical but still possess the requisite strength and rigidity.

5.2 Wood

a. The commercially important species of wood employed in dwelling houses are divided into two broad groups: "softwoods" (derived from conifers or needle-bearing trees) and "hardwoods" (from broad-leafed trees). These terms are used commercially, even though many "softwoods" are considerably harder than many "hardwoods."

b. Trees used for construction lumber grow by adding layers of new wood under the bark. Trees in temperate or cold zones grow during the warm seasons, rapidly in the spring and more slowly in the summer, and are dormant in the cold. One year's combined lightweight "springwood" and dense "summerwood" provides an annual ring, usually easily seen on a cross-section of the trunk; counting the rings establishes the tree's age. Trees in tropical regions with distinct wet and dry seasons show similar rings, but trees whose growth is more or less continuous may not.

c. The relatively narrow outer rim of the stem consists of living wood called *sapwood*. The no-longer-living inner part is the *heartwood*. Sapwood is characteristically light-colored; heartwood may be darker and distinctively colored (e.g., redwood, black walnut).

d. Wood and bark consist of hollow cells, loosely called *fibers*, consisting mainly of cellulose bonded together by lignin. The great majority are long and narrow (0.6–3 mm long in hardwood and 2–7 mm long in softwood, and about a hundredth of the length in diameter).

They grow parallel to the axes of the stems or trunk of the tree. Others, short and chunky, grow radially in wood rays. In living sapwood and inner bark, sap moves upward; food manufactured in the leaves or needles moves downward, passing from cell to cell through openings called *pits*.

e. Some softwoods, such as pines, contain resin in resin ducts or canals; others, such as redwood, do not. Presence or absence of resin can affect use. All hardwoods, but no softwoods, contain specialized cells called *pores* to facilitate passage of sap and food. In some, such as maple, they are small and inconspicuous, and the wood is called *close-grained*; in others, such as oak, the springwood pores are large and prominent, and the wood is called *open-grained*.

f. "Grain" has various meanings. "Along the grain" means longitudinal or parallel to the axis; "across the grain" is at a right angle, or at least a substantial angle, to the longitudinal or axial direction. "Fine-grained" wood has a fine appearance, often associated with a radial ("quarter") cut or with narrow growth rings; "coarse-grained" wood is coarse in appearance, often associated with a tangential ("flat") cut or with wide growth rings.

g. Some woods, such as cedar, have distinctive odors. Figure and texture, closely allied to "grain," result from growth features such as crotch, stump, burl, and direction of cut.

h. Many of the properties of wood, such as strength and tendency to shrink and swell, are related to the density or "apparent" specific gravity. This is the ratio of the weight of a given volume of wood to the weight of an equal volume of water. "Solid" wood (that is, solid cellulose and lignin) has a specific gravity of about 1.5. Actual wood has much open space, so that the apparent specific gravity is less — sometimes as low as 0.10 and occasionally above 1.00 (will not float).

i. A living tree is normally saturated with moisture: "imbibed" water in cell walls and "free" water in the hollow cell interiors. When a tree is cut into lumber, the moisture evaporates, the free water leaving first. The point at which all the free water has left but imbibed water is still present is called the *fiber-saturation point*. The wood is still "green." As imbibed water subsequently leaves the cell walls, the latter shrink and thus the wood shrinks (almost entirely across the grain, practically not at all along the grain). Tangential shrinkage is about 50 percent greater than radial. The range from green to completely dry (oven-dry) is greater for higher-density species, as is shown in table 5.1a. Values for selected commonly used species are given in table 5.1b.

j. Moisture content eventually comes to equilibrium with the relative humidity of the surrounding air. At the fiber-saturation point, most species contain about 28–30 percent moisture (weight of water divided by oven-dry weight of wood). "Air-dried" wood (wood dried naturally, not in a kiln) generally has a moisture content of about 12 percent; the moisture content of kiln-dried wood is likely to be about 6–7 percent. Commercial "dry" lumber, such as that used in house framing (sections 5.5ff.) has a moisture content of 19 percent or less. Kiln-dried wood is employed for furniture and for finish such as flooring and trim (chapter 13) to avoid shrinkage and splits or open joints. Average moisture contents of woods used in various parts of a house are given in table 5.1c.

k. Apparent specific gravity (see above) is usually measured oven-dry, air-dry (12 percent), and at fiber-saturation point, or "green." Boards cut with wide faces tangent to annual rings (slash or flat cut) shrink and cup so that the flat surface is curved (figure 5.1). Circular-cut posts become oval, and square-cut ones become rectangular or diamond-shaped.

l. Boards cut along the radius, with wide faces perpendicular to the annual rings (quarter-sawn or edge-grain), do not cup but remain flat and merely become smaller. This is an advantage of this cut, which is favored for flooring and trim as well as for furniture. A board cut from diagonal-grained material tends to twist while drying. Other changes of shape caused by drying are bow and crook (figure 5.1). Shrinkage values for several commercially important species are given in table 5.1.

m. The principal destroyers of wood are fire, decay, and animal organisms.

Wood chars and begins to burn at approximately 400°F as volatile gases are evolved and tissue ignites. Thick timbers tend to build up charcoal surface layers that inhibit penetration of fire, but wood members usually employed in dwelling-house construction are relatively thin.

Decay is caused by fungi, which are plants that need air, moisture, and food (in this case, wood). Decay is prompted by damp warm conditions. Air-dried wood does not ordinarily decay, nor does wood kept immersed in water.

Table 5.1

a. Shrinkage Ranges of Different Species, Green to Oven-Dry

Tangential	4 to 14
Radial	2 to 8
Longitudinal	0.1 to 0.8
Volumetric	7 to 21

b. Shrinkage Values for Selected Woods Grown in the United States (Percentages)

	Shrinkage (percent of dimension when green) from green to—								
	Air-dried to 12% to 15% moisture (estimated values)			Kiln-dried to 6% to 7% moisture (estimated values)			Oven-dried to 0% moisture (test values)		
Species	Radial	Tan-gential	Volu-metric	Radial	Tan-gential	Volu-metric	Radial	Tan-gential	Volu-metric
Birch	3.4	4.4	8.2	5.2	6.7	12.2	6.9	8.9	16.3
Cedar									
Eastern red	1.6	2.4	3.9	2.3	3.5	5.8	3.1	4.7	7.8
Western red	1.2	2.5	3.8	1.8	3.8	5.8	2.4	5.0	7.7
Douglas fir									
Coast region	2.5	3.9	5.9	3.8	5.8	8.8	5.0	7.8	11.8
Rocky Mountain region	1.8	3.1	5.3	2.7	4.6	8.0	3.6	6.2	10.6
Fir									
Commercial white	1.6	3.6	4.9	2.4	5.3	7.4	3.2	7.1	9.8
Gum Black	2.2	3.8	7.0	3.3	5.8	10.4	4.4	7.7	13.9
Hemlock									
Eastern	1.5	3.4	4.8	2.2	5.1	7.3	3.0	6.8	9.7
Western	2.2	4.0	6.0	3.2	5.9	8.9	4.3	7.9	11.9
Larch, western	2.1	4.0	6.6	3.2	6.1	9.9	4.2	8.1	13.2
Maple									
Red	2.0	4.1	6.6	3.0	6.2	9.8	4.0	8.2	13.1
Sugar	2.4	4.8	7.4	3.7	7.1	11.2	4.9	9.5	14.9
Oak									
Red	2.2	4.5	7.4	3.2	6.8	11.1	4.3	9.0	14.8
White	2.7	4.6	8.0	4.0	7.0	12.0	5.4	9.3	16.0
Pine Loblolly	2.4	3.7	6.2	3.6	5.6	9.2	4.8	7.4	12.3
Longleaf	2.6	3.8	6.1	3.8	5.6	9.2	5.1	7.5	12.2
Northern white	1.2	3.0	4.1	1.7	4.5	6.2	2.3	6.0	8.2
Ponderosa	2.0	3.2	4.8	2.9	4.7	7.2	3.9	6.3	9.6
Shortleaf	2.2	3.8	6.2	3.3	5.8	9.2	4.4	7.7	12.3
Sugar	1.4	2.8	4.0	2.2	4.2	5.9	2.9	5.6	7.9
Western white	2.0	3.7	5.9	3.1	5.6	8.8	4.1	7.4	11.8
Redwood	1.3	2.2	3.4	2.0	3.3	5.1	2.6	4.4	6.8
Spruce									
Eastern	2.2	3.8	6.3	3.2	5.8	9.4	4.3	7.7	12.6
Engelmann	1.7	3.3	5.2	2.6	5.0	7.8	3.4	6.6	10.4

c. Moisture Content (Percentage of Weight of Oven-Dry Wood) for—

	Dry South-western States		Damp South-ern Coastal States		Remainder of United States	
Use of Lumber	Average	Individual pieces	Average	Individual pieces	Average	Individual pieces
Interior finish woodwork and softwood flooring	6	4–9	11	8–13	8	5–10
Hardwood flooring	6	5–8	10	9–12	7	6–9
Siding, exterior trim, sheath-ing, framing	9	7–12	12	9–14	12	9–14

Source: U.S. Forest Products Laboratory.

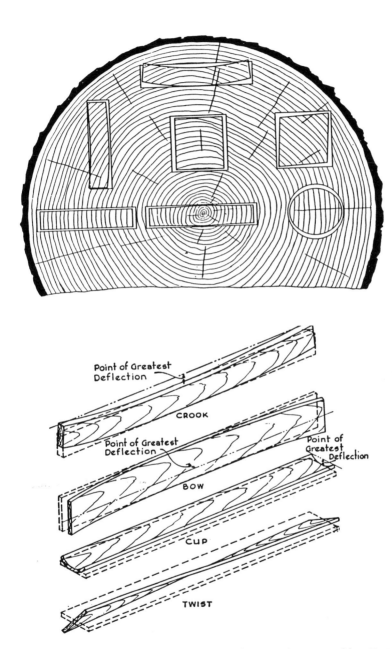

Figure 5.1 Top: shrinkage of members cut from various parts of log. Bottom: types of warp. Courtesy of U.S. Forest Products Laboratory.

The animal organisms that attack wood include, primarily, insects and salt-water organisms such as the teredo and the limnoria. Sea-borne attack is limited to marine structures. The insects that destroy wood are primarily termites, carpenter ants, and the grubs of a variety of beetles, such as the powderpost. Termites may be subterranean (nesting in the ground and fanning out to find wood, often by means of earth tubes) or of the damp-wood or the dry-wood variety (nesting directly in wood). Subterranean termites are found throughout the United States except in Alaska; the others are restricted mostly to southern coastal areas. Carpenter ants excavate wood for their nests but do not eat it. Beetle larvae burrow in wood until maturity, leaving the wood as adult beetles after depositing their eggs.

n. Wood can be protected from destroyers by various treatments. The most effective is impregnation by vacuum-pressure processes that force preservatives into the wood. Dipping and brushing are largely ineffective, although some end-grain penetration may be achieved.

For fire resistance, the salts monoammonium phosphate, diammonium phosphate, ammonium sulfate, zinc chloride, sodium tetraborate, and boric acid are often used. Pressure-treated wood does not support its own combustion but can be destroyed by hot fires. A second fire treatment for wood is intumescent paint, a surface coating that bubbles upon heating, forming an insulating layer of hardened froth containing inert gas.

Decay and attack by animal organisms are combatted by oily, solvent-soluble, and waterborne preservatives. Creosote, the most effective oily preservative, is excellent for exterior structures but is dark, oily, and smelly. Pentachlorphenol, carried by solvents, is less dark and less odoriferous. The most commonly used waterborne salts are chromated copper arsenate (CCA) and ammoniated copper arsenate (ACA), both of which are resistant to leaching, and chromated zinc chloride and fluor-chrome-arsenate-phenol, which do leach in wet conditions. Unlike oily and solvent-borne preservatives, salts are clean, have no residual odor, and can be painted.

o. Wood members should be cut to size and shape, and bored (if necessary), before being treated, to ensure adequate penetration at all surfaces. If cutting must be done after treatment, exposed surfaces should be thoroughly soaked with preservative.

p. Strength and stiffness are important in framing lumber, which must sustain loads. Hardness may be more important in such items as trim and flooring.

Wood is extremely strong in tension along the grain, but extremely weak in tension across the grain. It is not often used in direct tension along the grain, and it should not be depended upon across the grain. Bending strength is important in beams and joists (sections 5.16ff.). Here, again, strength parallel to the grain is quite high (about 60 percent of tension) but strength across the grain is not to be depended upon. Direct compressive strength parallel to the grain is good (about 40 percent of tension), useful in studs and posts. Compressive strength across the grain is sufficient for such purposes as the bearing of joists and studs on sills or plates but may fail in crushing under concentrated loads. Shear strength parallel to the grain (where there is a tendency to split, with the pieces sliding past one another) is generally high enough in beams and joists unless they are short, deep, and heavily loaded.

Stiffness, as measured by the modulus of elasticity, varies with species, and must be sufficient — especially in long bending members (joists, rafters, beams) — to avoid undue deflection under load, and to avoid buckling in long compression members (posts, studs). Increasing moisture content decreases most mechanical properties; it decreases tensile strength least and compressive strength most, with bending intermediate.

q. Most mechanical properties are related to density or apparent specific gravity (see item h above). The higher the apparent specific gravity, the more woody tissue and, in general, the greater the strength, stiffness, hardness, and shrinkage and swelling with moisture changes.

r. The principal characteristics that affect strength, in addition to apparent specific gravity, are the following:

Diagonal grain. Because of the low cross-grain tensile strength of wood, even small deviations of grain direction from parallel cause marked decreases in parallel tensile and bending strength. Deviations (slope of grain) greater than about one part in twenty cause noticeable loss, and deviations greater than one in ten may rule out load-bearing uses.

Knots. Branches begin at the pith of the tree trunk and grow larger as the tree grows. Knots are cuts through branches. They may vary from round to oval or "spike" (cut along the branch) and can be intergrown, encased, sound, loose, or absent (knot hole). Because they cause severe local grain distortion, they weaken the nearby wood.

Splits. When wood dries it may split or "check" longitudinally. Splits (called *shakes*) may also occur in living trees. Splits reduce the shear strength of wood parallel to the grain.

s. Diagonal grain, knots, and splits are taken into account when wood is graded for structural strength. Working stresses in bending, compression, and shear are assigned on the basis of size, frequency, and distribution.

t. For general-purpose lumber, additional grading features may include color, resin pockets, stain, and manufacturing blemishes (for example, raised and torn grain, skips, and distortion such as crook and bow).

u. In dwelling-house construction, wood is employed chiefly in the forms of lumber, plywood, laminated wood, and derived boards (chiefly fiberboard, particle board, wafer board, and strand board).

5.3 Lumber, Plain and Reconstituted

a. "Softwood" lumber is used almost exclusively for framing. Softwood is classified as *seasoned* or *dry* if its moisture content is 19 percent or less, and as *unseasoned* or *green* if its moisture content is greater than 19 percent.

b. Softwood is classified according to use as follows:

Yard lumber (figure 5.2a). Grades, sizes, and patterns generally in-

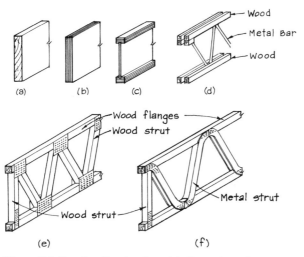

Figure 5.2 Construction lumber: (a) dimension; (b) veneer; (c) I-section; (d–f) open web joists.

tended for ordinary construction and general building; mostly used for house construction.

Structural. Lumber more than 2″ in nominal thickness, used where large stress-graded engineered lumber is required.

Factory and shop. Used primarily for remanufacturing, e.g., into sashes and doors.

c. Softwood is classified according to extent of manufacture as follows:

Rough. Sawed, edged, and trimmed but not dressed (surfaced).

Dressed (surfaced). Planed to obtain smoothness and uniformity of size, on one side (S1S), two sides (S2S), one edge (S1E), two edges (S2E), or a combination (S1S1E, S1S2E, S2S1E, S4S). S4S is the most common in dwelling-house construction.

Worked. Not only dressed, but matched, shiplapped, or patterned (see figure 5.14).

Matched. Worked with a tongue on one edge and a groove on the other.

Shiplapped. Rabbetted on both edges.

Patterned. Shaped to a patterned or molded form.

d. Softwood is classified as to nominal size, i.e., the size originally cut from the tree. Actual sizes (table 5.2) are less because of drying shrinkage and dressing. Actual sizes are different for seasoned, or dry, lumber (19 percent or less) and unseasoned, or green, lumber (more than 19 percent).

Boards. Less than 2″ nominal thickness, 2″ or more nominal width. (Boards less than 6″ wide may be called *strips*.)

Dimension. Nominal thickness 2″ to less than 5″, nominal width 2″ or more. Classified as framing, joists, rafters, studs, small timbers, etc.

Timbers. Least nominal dimension 5″ or more. Classified as beams, stringers, posts, caps, sills, girders, purlins, etc.

e. Yard lumber is graded on the basis of quality as follows:

Select. Good appearance and finishing qualities.

Natural (transparent) finishes:

Practically clear (A Select)

Generally clear, high quality (B Select)

Often these grades are combined into "B and Better."

Paint finishes:

High-quality paint finish (C Select)

Table 5.2 Nominal and Actual Sizes of Board and Dimension Lumber

Nominal (in.)	Actual (in.) Unseasoned	Seasoned
Board		
1 × 2	$\frac{25}{32}$ × $1\frac{9}{16}$	$\frac{3}{4}$ × $1\frac{1}{2}$
1 × 3	$\frac{25}{32}$ × $2\frac{9}{16}$	$\frac{3}{4}$ × $2\frac{1}{2}$
1 × 4	$\frac{25}{32}$ × $3\frac{9}{16}$	$\frac{3}{4}$ × $3\frac{1}{2}$
1 × 6	$\frac{25}{32}$ × $5\frac{5}{8}$	$\frac{3}{4}$ × $5\frac{1}{2}$
1 × 8	$\frac{25}{32}$ × $7\frac{1}{2}$	$\frac{3}{4}$ × $7\frac{1}{4}$
1 × 10	$\frac{25}{32}$ × $9\frac{1}{2}$	$\frac{3}{4}$ × $9\frac{1}{4}$
1 × 12	$\frac{25}{32}$ × $11\frac{1}{2}$	$\frac{3}{4}$ × $11\frac{1}{4}$
Dimension[a]		
2 × 2	$1\frac{9}{16}$ × $1\frac{9}{16}$	$1\frac{1}{2}$ × $1\frac{1}{2}$
2 × 3	$1\frac{9}{16}$ × $2\frac{9}{16}$	$1\frac{1}{2}$ × $2\frac{1}{2}$
2 × 4	$1\frac{9}{16}$ × $3\frac{9}{16}$	$1\frac{1}{2}$ × $3\frac{1}{2}$
2 × 6	$1\frac{9}{16}$ × $5\frac{5}{8}$	$1\frac{1}{2}$ × $5\frac{1}{2}$
2 × 8	$1\frac{9}{16}$ × $7\frac{1}{2}$	$1\frac{1}{2}$ × $7\frac{1}{4}$
2 × 10	$1\frac{9}{16}$ × $9\frac{1}{2}$	$1\frac{1}{2}$ × $9\frac{1}{4}$
2 × 12	$1\frac{9}{16}$ × $11\frac{1}{2}$	$1\frac{1}{2}$ × $11\frac{1}{4}$

[a]Thicknesses of seasoned nominal 3″ and 4″ lumber are $2\frac{1}{2}$″ and $3\frac{1}{2}$″, of unseasoned lumber $2\frac{9}{16}$″ and $3\frac{9}{16}$″. Widths are the same as given above.

Intermediate between high-finishing and common grade (D Select)

Common. Suitable for general construction and utility where appearance is of secondary importance.

For standard construction:

No. 1 Common. Better construction.

No. 2 Common. Good standard construction.

No. 3 Common. Low-cost temporary construction.

For less exacting purposes:

No. 4 Common. Low quality.

No. 5 Common. Lowest recognized usable grade.

Other terms are often used in the trade. The select boards may be called, for example, Supreme (B and Better), Choice (C), and Quality (D). The Nos. 1 to 5 Common boards may be called, e.g., Colonial, Sterling, Standard, Utility, and Industrial. Light Framing Common dimension lumber may be called Construction, Standard, Utility, and Economy, whereas Structural Light Framing Common dimension may be called Select Structural, No. 1, No. 2, No. 3, and Economy. The latter terms are also used for structural joists and planks.

f. Structural lumber, not often used for dwelling-house construction but used for engineered structures, has assigned values for modulus of elasticity and working stresses in bending, compression parallel and perpendicular to the grain, and horizontal shear.

g. Factory and shop lumber is graded according to the sizes and percentages of pieces clear on one or both sides that can be cut from it for such things as sash and door parts and other general cutup uses.

h. Thin sheets of wood, called *veneers,* are glued together into thick panels with the grain in the layers parallel. Panels are cut into members (figure 5.2b) called laminated veneer lumber (LVL) or parallel-laminated veneer (PLV). By selecting veneers and species and judiciously placing features and blemishes such as knots and splits, quality can be controlled, and long lengths can be achieved by offsetting (staggering) joints in veneer layers. Thicknesses and widths of this veneer lumber are the same as for corresponding dimension lumber sizes (section 5.3d). Properties are similar to those of equivalent lumber, and may be higher because blemishes are judiciously placed and wood is dry at manufacture.

i. Open-web joists (figure 5.2d,e,f) consist of plain wood or parallel-laminated veneer flanges with webs of wood or formed metal bars, typically fastened together with multiple-nail plates (section 5.33o) or with steel pins.

j. Wood veneers are assembled in layers into panels called *plywood,* each layer consisting of one or more veneers. Layers, whether single or multiple veneers, are called plies. They are glued together with grain direction of adjacent plies at right angles. An odd number of plies (from a minimum of three) is used. Plywood thicknesses ordinarily used in dwelling-house construction range from $\frac{5}{16}''$ to $1\frac{1}{8}''$. Outer plies are called *faces* or *face* and *back;* the center ply is the *core;* intermediate plies, if any, are *crossbands. Exterior* panels have fully waterproof bonds and must withstand permanent exposure to weather and moisture. *Exposure 1* panels also have waterproof bonds but are not expected to be exposed to as severe conditions as Exterior panels. *Exposure 2* panels have intermediate moisture-resistant glues and are designed for protected conditions. *Interior* panels are for indoor use only. The cross-plied construction gives the resulting board practically the same properties in all directions, allows the manufacture of large thin boards, and reduces the shrinkage in all directions to a small amount because the longitudinal grain in both directions resists the tendency to shrink or swell in the transverse direction. Splitting is markedly reduced, so that nails or screws can be driven close to the edge with little danger.

k. Some 70 species of wood are employed in plywood. They are divided according to strength and stiffness into five groups (table 5.3), Group 1 the highest. A group number is assigned to a plywood panel depending upon the face and back veneers. If the face and the back are different groups, the higher number is generally used except for sanded and decorative, where the face number is used.

l. Veneer grades are the following:

N: smooth surface, natural finish, select heartwood or sapwood, minor wood repairs

A: smooth and paintable; limited natural finish, neat repairs permitted

B: solid surface veneer; circular repair plugs and tight knots

C: knot holes to $1''$, some to $1\frac{1}{2}''$ within specified limits; some splits; synthetic and wood repairs

Table 5.3 Species Groups and Span Ratings of Plywoods

Species group				
1	2	3	4	5
Apitong	Cedar, Port Orford	Alder, Red	Aspen	Basswood
Beech, American	Cypress	Birch, Paper	Bigtooth Quaking	Poplar, Balsam
Birch Sweet Yellow	Douglas fir 2[a]	Cedar, Alaska	Cativo	
	Fir	Fir, Subalpine	Cedar	
Douglas Fir 1[a]	Balsam California Red	Hemlock, Eastern	Incense Western Red	
Kapur	Grand	Maple, Bigleaf	Cottonwood Eastern	
Keruing	Noble	Pine	Black (Western Poplar)	
Larch, Western	Pacific Silver White	Jack Lodgepole Ponderosa	Pine	
Maple, Sugar	Hemlock, Western	Spruce	Eastern White	
Pine Caribbean	Lauan	Redwood	Sugar	
Ocote	Almon	Spruce		
Pine, South. Loblolly Longleaf Shortleaf Slash	Bagtikan Mayapis Red Tangile White	Engelmann White		

Table 5.3 (continued)

Species group 1	2	3	4	5
Tanoak	Maple, Black			
	Mengkulang			
	Meranti, Red[b]			
	Mersawa			
	Pine			
	Pond			
	Red			
	Virginia			
	Western			
	White			
	Spruce			
	Black			
	Red			
	Sitka			
	Sweetgum			
	Tamarack			
	Yellow Poplar			

[a] Douglas fir from trees grown in the states of Washington, Oregon, California, Idaho, Montana, Wyoming, and the Canadian Provinces of Alberta and British Columbia shall be classed as Douglas fir no. 1. Douglas fir from trees grown in the states of Nevada, Utah, Colorado, Arizona, and New Mexico shall be classed as Douglas fir no. 2.

[b] Red Meranti shall be limited to species having a specific gravity of 0.41 or more based on green volume and oven-dry weight.

Span rating

Thickness (inches)	C-C and C-D							Underlayment and C-C Plugged			
	12/0	16/0	20/0	24/0	32/16	40/20	48/24	16 oc	20 oc	24 oc	48 oc
$\frac{5}{16}$	4	3	1								
$\frac{3}{8}$			4[b]	1							
$\frac{15}{32}$[a], $\frac{1}{2}$				4[b]	1			1			
$\frac{19}{32}$, $\frac{5}{8}$					4[b]	1		4[b]	1		
$\frac{23}{32}$, $\frac{3}{4}$						4[b]	1		4[b]	1	
$\frac{7}{8}$							3[c]			3[c]	
$1\frac{1}{8}$											1

[a] Thickness not applicable to Underlayment and C-C Plugged.
[b] Use Group 3 stresses for Structural II.
[c] Use Group 4 stresses for Underlayment and C-C Plugged 24 o.c.
Source: American Plywood Association.

C plugged: improved C veneer; splits limited to $\frac{1}{8}''$, knot and borer holes limited to $\frac{1}{4}'' \times \frac{1}{2}''$; some synthetic repairs

D: knots and knot holes to $2\frac{1}{2}''$, some larger; limited splits

m. In *reconstituted* panels (figure 5.3), wood is broken down into fibers or fragments and recombined into panels.

n. In *fiberboard*, wood fibers are separated and then interfelted, using the natural lignin as binder with or without additives. *Insulating* board is a soft board consolidated enough to retain its integrity yet soft and light enough (well under 0.50 specific gravity) to give good thermal insulation. *Hardboard* is similarly composed of interfelted fibers, pressed in a hot-plate press to a specific gravity of 0.50 or higher. Additives may include resins for hardboard siding.

o. *Particleboard* is a panel consisting of wood chips or particles combined with synthetic resin binder and pressed in a hot-plate press to form a flat sheet. Particleboard may be made of random small particles derived from scrap or waste lumber. Structural particleboard is made from graded small particles, usually arranged in layers according to particle size. It is intended to carry loads (e.g., sheathing, floors).

p. *Flakeboard* is similar to particleboard except that the pieces of wood are large and waferlike. The configuration of the wafers and their planar orientation impart considerable strength.

q. In *strandboard* the particles are long and narrow. They may be incorporated in the panel in a random configuration or oriented, as in oriented strandboard (OSB). The configuration and orientation of the strands impart directional strength.

r. Particles, flakes, and strands may be combined, as in panels with particleboard cores and flakeboard facings.

s. Reconstituted panels may be faced with single or double veneers to provide stock for such items as table and counter tops, doors, and paneling in general.

t. In members subjected to bending (e.g., joists, rafters, and beams), maximum bending stresses occur at the top and bottom edges and maximum shear at the center of depth. Consequently, an efficient I-shaped member can be made with flanges of plain wood or parallel-laminated veneer lumber glued along the top and bottom edges of a plywood or oriented-strandboard web (figure 5.2c; see also section 5.18). Studs and other sizes of dimension lumber (section 5.3d) are made of strandboard cores edged with strips of veneer.

u. Adhesives for plywood and panel products are predominantly

Figure 5.3 Reconstituted wood panels. From top down: plywood, composite, wafer-board, oriented strandboard, structural particleboard. Courtesy of American Plywood Association.

thermosetting resins (section 15.3), urea-formaldehyde, phenol-formaldehyde, phenol-resorcinol-formaldehyde, and melamine-formaldehyde. Urea is used for moderate water resistance and minimum cost, the others for maximum water resistance. Melamine also provides colorless bonds.

v. Panels for carrying loads, especially roof and floor sheathing, are given span ratings in inches (e.g., distance in inches from center to center of joists and rafters). For example, 32/16 means the allowable span is 32″ on roofs and 16″ on floors. Some, such as combined floor and underlayment (section 5.22), are given only one span rating (table 5.3).

Among the principal classes of panels are sheathing, subflooring, subflooring plus underlayment, siding (various textures), sanded and touch-sanded (one or both sides to be exposed, exterior or interior), and various specialties such as concrete-form panels (with or without overlay), marine, decorative, and hardboard-faced. Panels may be treated with preservatives.

w. Although wood is the traditional dwelling-house framing material, the use of steel is increasing. Two types of framing members are most common: hot-rolled steel structural shapes and cold-formed light steel framing members. Hot-rolled shapes are mainly American Standard I, wide-flange, channel, angle (equal and unequal leg), and square, plus bar, rod, and plate (figure 5.4). Cold-formed members, made by shaping sheet steel of various gauges, are mainly channels (or tracks), C shapes, and I sections. Angles are combined with rods into open-web "bar" joists. I-shaped studs with spaced double webs, and joists with spaced double flanges, allow nails to be driven into the crimped double space (figure 5.4).

x. The mild carbon steel used for structural shapes, as specified by the American Society for Testing and Materials (ASTM A36), has the following principal properties: yield strength 36,000 psi,* allowable stress in bending 22,000 psi, modulus of elasticity 29,000,000 psi. When cold-formed, steel undergoes considerable strengthening and hardening but its modulus of elasticity (measure of stiffness) is unchanged. Alloy steels with higher yield strengths and allowable stresses are seldom found in light structures such as dwelling houses.

---

*psi: pounds per square inch

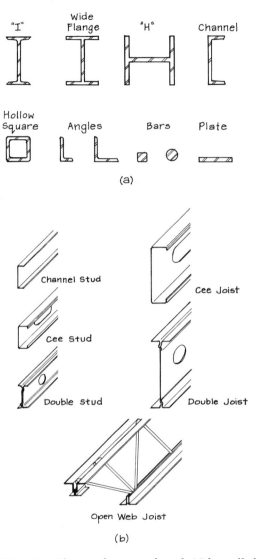

Figure 5.4 Shapes of structural steel: (a) hot-rolled, (b) cold-formed.

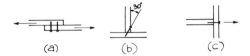

Figure 5.5 Nailing: (a) perpendicular to load; (b) diagonal or toe nailing; (c) end nailing, parallel to load.

5.4 Nails

a. Nails are discussed in detail in chapter 14. For framing, common nails are employed. In general, a nail should be about 3 times as long as the material through which it is driven. For example, to nail $\frac{3}{4}''$ sheathing to studs, the nail should be $2\frac{1}{4}''$ long. An 8d nail is $2\frac{1}{2}''$ long and, therefore, meets the requirements. For fastening dimension lumber, 10d and 16d nails are generally employed for nominal 2'' stock. Studs are commonly toe-nailed with 8d or 10d nails.

b. Nails may be driven (figure 5.5) perpendicular to the direction of load, parallel or in withdrawal (end nailing), or at an angle to the face of the piece being nailed (toe nailing). The best is perpendicular loading and the poorest is withdrawal, especially if the nail is driven parallel to the grain of the wood. Toe nailing is employed to fasten studs to sills.

c. A recommended nailing schedule for framing is given in table 5.4. Recommended nailing is also discussed in connection with specific construction details in this and other chapters. See also chapter 14.

5.5 Outside Wall Frames

In the United States today the type of frame known as the *platform frame* is practically universal. Historically, the *eastern braced frame* was widely used in the eastern part of the country. The lighter "balloon" *frame* came later in the midwest. The platform frame, once known as the western frame, has become general because of its simplicity and its ease of erection.

THE PLATFORM FRAME

5.6 General

a. The platform frame has the following parts (figure 5.6):
sill
posts

Table 5.4 Recommended Nailing Schedule

Framing, using common nails	
Joist to sill or girder, toe nail	3–8d
Bridging to joist, toe nail each end	2–8d
Ledger strip	3–16d at each joist
1″ × 6″ subfloor or less to each joist, face nail	2–8d
Over 1″ × 6″ subfloor to each joist, face nail	3–8d
2″ subfloor to joist or girder, blind and face nail	2–16d
Sole plate to joist or blocking, face nail	16d @ 16″ o.c.
Top plate to stud, end nail	2–16d
Stud to sole plate	
toe nail	4–8d
end nail	2–16d
Doubled studs, face nail	10d @ 12″ o.c.
Doubled top plates, face nail	10d @ 16″ o.c.
Top plates, laps and intersections, face nail	2–10d
Continuous header, two pieces	16d @ 16″ o.c. along each edge
Ceiling joists to plate, toe nail	3–16d
Continuous header to stud, toe nail	4–8d
Ceiling joists, laps over partitions, face nail	3–10d
Ceiling joists to parallel rafters, face nail	3–10d
Rafter to plate, toe nail	3–8d
1-inch brace to each stud and plate, face nail	2–8d
1″ × 8″ sheathing or less to each bearing, face nail	2–8d
Over 1″ × 8″ sheathing to each bearing, face nail	3–8d
Built-up corner studs	16d @ 24″ o.c.
Built-up girders and beams	20d @ 32″ o.c. along each edge

Source: *Manual for House Framing*, American Forest Products Association. For additional nailing schedules, see tables 5.5 and 5.7–5.9 and chapters 8, 10, and 12.

headers or bands
soles or sole plates
studs
plates
sheathing

b. The distinctive feature of this frame is that each floor forms a platform upon which are erected the studs for that story. Each story is, therefore, an entirely separate entity, and theoretically the construction could be repeated as often as desired to form a building of any height.

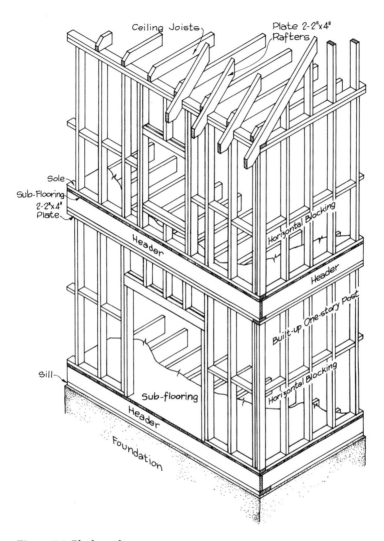

Figure 5.6 Platform frame.

5.7 Sill

a. The sill's function is to transfer the loads and wind stresses from the frame to the foundation wall, and to form a base upon which to erect the balance of the frame. In order for a sill to perform these functions properly, certain features must be incorporated into its construction.

b. Sills are customarily of 2″-thick materials, 4″, 6″, or 8″. If good continuous bearing on level cast-in-place concrete or concrete blocks with filled holes is available, the sill can be of 1″-thick material, or it can be eliminated altogether, provided that there is some means of holding floor joists in position. The top of the foundation must be level to avoid unevenness in the floor.

c. Anchors are generally set in the foundation wall (chapter 4). They serve to hold the sill down firmly to the foundation, to prevent any sidewise slipping and to counter the tendency to overturn. They also ensure a tight fit between the sill and the foundation wall.

d. Anchors are commonly $\frac{1}{2}$″ bolts (figure 5.7) set in the wall, as described in chapter 4. Other types of anchors include various steel straps fastened to the foundation by embedment or mechanical fastening and to the sill by nails, screws, bolts, and other means. Sometimes powder-actuated steel studs are driven through the sill into the foundation.

e. If bolts are employed, holes are bored in the sill at the proper intervals, the sill is slipped over the bolts, and nuts and washers are turned down tight.

f. The sill must be level and straight if the rest of the frame is to be plumb and the floor joists level. One method of ensuring a level bed is to place special compressible bedding or sealing strips on the founda-

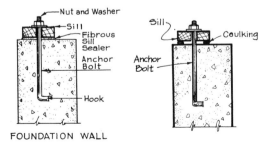

Figure 5.7 Anchor bolt. Left: fibrous sealer. Right: caulking beads.

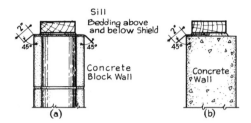

Figure 5.8 Termite shields. (a) Full. (b) Half.

tion and to press the sill tightly against them by means of anchor bolts. Nuts and washers are tightened as necessary to level the sill. A caulking bead along each edge of the sill similarly provides a watertight bed (figure 5.7). The classical method of bedding sills has been to string a bed of fresh mortar along the top of the foundation wall, with the sill immediately placed on it, leveled, and held in place by the anchors. Moisture in the mortar can cause the sill to cup.

g. Where termites are known to be present, one way of protecting the wood parts of the house is the use of metal (noncorroding) shields (figure 5.8). These extend across the top of the foundation wall continuously around its periphery, and are bent down 2″ at an angle of 45° both inside and out. Where the shield fits around anchor bolts the joint is sealed. In solid concrete walls, a half-shield may be employed provided it is solidly bedded and there is no chance that termites may work up the unprotected side. Termites are also combated by poisoning the soil around the foundation as it is backfilled.

h. Where sills are in danger of decay because of damp surroundings, it is advisable to use a naturally resistant species (such as redwood) or treated lumber (section 5.2n). If the latter, it is extremely desirable to have the individual pieces cut and bored before being treated. Whenever it is necessary to cut the pieces after treatment, the exposed surfaces must be thoroughly soaked with the preservative.

5.8 Posts

Posts are built up, as shown in figure 5.9. This arrangement provides a return for nailing interior wall surfaces such as wallboard and lath.

5.9 Headers or Bands

a. *Headers* (also called *bands*) are on-edge members, of the same size as the joists, which rest directly on the sill and run around the periph-

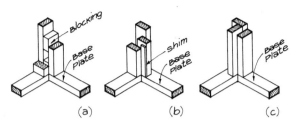

Figure 5.9 Built-up corner posts. (a) Studs plus blocking. (b) Offset plus shim. (c) L plus stud.

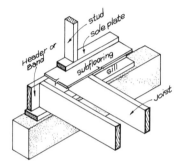

Figure 5.10 Sill detail (platform frame).

ery of the building. The joists are framed against the headers in the manner shown in figures 5.6 and 5.10. This type of sill-and-header combination, known as a *box sill,* is a distinctive feature of the platform frame.

b. Before any of the superstructure is erected, the first-floor subflooring is put down to form a platform upon which the carpenters can work, frame the material for walls and partitions, and assemble the members. Walls and partitions can be quickly assembled and nailed together flat on the floor and then tilted up into position. This feature makes the platform frame extremely convenient and gives it a distinct advantage over other types, although the Tee sill (figure 5.20) also provides a working platform.

5.10 Studs

a. Wall studs are commonly 2 × 4, but with the trend toward increased thermal insulation (chapter 11) 2 × 6 or larger studs are being utilized. Studs 2 × 6 or larger, or 2 × 4s widened with 2 × 2 or wider strips, are often required to provide a "wet wall" thick enough to accommodate plumbing lines. For one-story construction, 2 × 3 studs are often sufficient. Codes limit the number of floors plus roof that can be carried by various sizes of studs.

b. Spacing. Because wood lath was originally cut 4' long or some other multiple of 16", it has become common practice to set studs and joists 16" on centers, although joists are often set at different spacings. There is no structural reason for the 16" spacing; it is merely another instance of traditional usage (but see section 5.39). Because of this standard stud spacing, wallboards and plaster bases are customarily made in stock sizes which are multiples of 16" — commonly 48". It is common practice to space 2 × 6 studs 24" on center.

c. Openings. Wherever an opening such as a window or a door occurs, it must be framed in the studs to receive whatever member is to be placed in it. Framing consists of horizontal members called *headers*, vertical members called *trimmers*, and short studs called *cripples*.

Windows. Window openings must be framed large enough horizontally to admit the window frame and provide adjustment space between the frame and the trimmer. The opening must be large enough to admit the frame with adjustment. Since window sizes are specified by the size of the glass panes (called *lights* in builders' language), the horizontal opening dimension is made large enough to allow for two sash stiles, two frame thicknesses, and adjustment and blocking. The vertical dimension is similarly increased for three sash rails, the window sill, and the head of the frame. Manufacturers specify rough opening dimensions.

Doors. Door sizes are specified by the overall dimensions of the door; consequently, the opening must be framed large enough to admit the frame plus sufficient additional room to allow for adjustment, blocking, and leveling.

Framing (figures 5.6, 5.11). Framing around openings must perform two functions: (1) it must be sturdy enough to carry the superimposed wall loads around the opening without sagging or distortion; and (2) it must provide ample support for the frames of windows and doors and provide nailing for interior wall covering, sheathing, grounds, and exterior finish where they adjoin the opening. For both these reasons, the headers and trimmers should at least be double 2 × 4 members. When openings are large horizontally (more than 4', for instance), the upper header must be made considerably stronger than usual because it has to support a greater load over a longer span. This is accom-

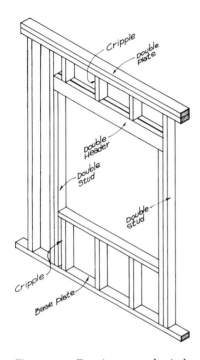

Figure 5.11 Framing around window opening.

plished most simply by making the header a pair of 2 × 6, 2 × 8, or larger members. This method, while simple, has the disadvantage that it introduces a large amount of wood which may shrink and swell across the grain and cause cracks. Composite wood members, such as I sections, largely eliminate such shrinkage and swelling.

5.11 Sole Plate and Plates

a. Directly on top of the subfloor is a horizontal member called the *sole*, the *base*, or the *sole plate*, which forms a base for the studs. It is the same cross-sectional size as the studs, and is nailed through to the headers and joists below. When studs are placed directly above joists, the sole plate can be 1″ thick.

b. Plates occur at every floor level above the first, and at the eaves. Usually they are doubled 2 × 4s, 2 × 6s, etc. The lower member is end-nailed to the upper ends of the studs, and the upper is nailed to the lower. Joints in the plates should be "broken" or staggered at least 1′.

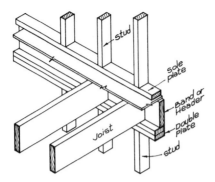

Figure 5.12 Floor framing at wall of second floor.

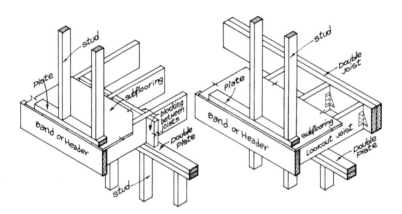

Figure 5.13 Framing overhang. Left: cantilevered joists. Right: projecting lookouts.

c. On top of the plate is the second-floor header or band, with the joists framing into it in the same manner as at the sill (figure 5.12). Therefore, the box construction occurs again at this point and at every subsequent floor level. Also, the second-floor subflooring is carried out to the edge. The second-story sole rests on the subflooring and the studs on the sole plate, as before.

d. The second floor sometimes extends beyond the first to form an overhang. Figure 5.13 shows alternative methods of framing. If the second-floor joists run at right angles to the wall, they are simply extended as cantilevers. If the joists are parallel to the wall, the second or third joist back is doubled, and short joists or "lookouts" are framed as shown.

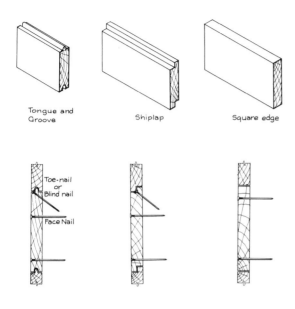

Application and Nailing

Figure 5.14 Sheathing boards, and their application and nailing.

5.12 Sheathing

a. *Sheathing boards* (figure 5.14) have traditionally been employed to cover the outside of the frame, but these have been largely replaced by various wallboards — particularly wood-based panels and other boards (sections 5.3h, 5.3q) — because these wallboards come in large sheets that are quickly applied. (See also chapter 12.)

b. Sheathing-grade plywood and reconstituted panels are applied with their long dimensions either vertical or horizontal. When properly nailed (table 5.5) and employed for the recommended spans (e.g., studs 16″ or 24″ on center), they withstand both bending loads and racking loads (such as wind) without bracing.

c. Siding-grade panels can be applied directly to wall framing and eliminate the need for sheathing. They can also be used over sheathing (chapter 10).

d. Fibrous wallboards, made of processed wood, cane, newsprint, and other materials, have become increasingly common sheathing materials, as has gypsum (see also chapters 10 and 12). They are sufficiently rigid to withstand handling and to provide moderate nail-holding

Table 5.5 Nailing Schedule for Wood-Based Panel Wall Sheathing[a] (continuous over two or more spans), Fiber Board Sheathing, and Gypsum Sheathing

Wood-based panel Span rating	Stud spacing[b]	Nail size[c]	Nail spacing Supported panel edges	Intermediate supports
12/0, 16/0, 20/0 or Wall-160c	16″	6d for panels $\frac{1}{2}$″ thick or less,	6″	12″
24/0, 24/16, 32/16 or Wall-240c	24″	8d for thicker panels		
Fiber board				
$\frac{1}{2}$″		1$\frac{1}{2}$″ galv. roofing or 6d common, or 16-ga. staple 1$\frac{1}{8}$″ long, minimum crown of $\frac{7}{16}$″	3″	6″
$\frac{25}{32}$″		1$\frac{3}{4}$″ galv. roofing or 8d common, or 16-ga. staple 1$\frac{1}{2}$″ long, minimum crown of $\frac{7}{16}$″	3″	6″
Gypsum		12-ga. 1$\frac{1}{4}$″, large head, corrosion resistant	4″	8″

[a]When wood-based sheathing panels are used, building paper and diagonal wall bracing can be omitted.
[b]When sidings such as shingles are nailed only to the sheathing, apply panels with long dimension or strong axis across studs.
[c]Common, smooth, annular, spiral-thread, or galvanized box; or T-nails of the same diameter as common nails (0.113-inch diameter for 6d, 0.131-inch for 8d) may be used. 16 ga. galvanized wire staples with a minimum crown width of ⅜ inch also permitted spaced 4 in. oc around entire perimeter of panel and 8 in. oc at intermediate supports. Minimum penetration of staples 1 inch into studs.
Sources: Panel schedule from American Plywood Association; fiber board and gypsum schedules from BOCA *Basic Building Code, 1970* (Building Officials and Code Administrators).

power. Half-inch-thick boards of this type are frequently employed, and provide approximately the same insulating value as wood sheathing. Because the boards are used in large sheets (commonly 4′ × 8′ to 4′ × 12′), they impart a high degree of stiffness to the wall when well nailed, in spite of the low bearing value per nail. Static tests indicate that when these wallboards are nailed as recommended in table 5.5, let-in bracing may be omitted.

e. Panels of plastic foam (chapter 15) or glass fiber mat are increasingly employed because of their high thermal insulating values. For the same thicknesses, they impart insulation superior to wood or dense materials such as gypsum. When soft sheathing is employed, plywood or reconstituted wood panels installed with their long dimensions vertical at the corners of the frame impart enough stiffness to eliminate bracing.

f. The wood boards used for sheathing (figure 5.14) may also be employed for roof boards and for subflooring. Joints must be made on studs and should be "broken" (that is, joints in successive tiers of boards should not be made on the same stud).

g. Each board should be nailed with at least two nails at every stud, and with three if the boards are more than 8″ wide (table 5.4). Such tight nailing makes for stiffness and helps to prevent warping and twisting if the boards become wet.

h. Because there are no braces in the platform frame itself, the lateral rigidity of the house must be provided by the sheathing or other bracing; otherwise the racking stresses are thrown into the interior wall covering, and cracks are an almost certain consequence.

i. In horizontal-board sheathing, nailing alone is not sufficient to prevent racking. With diagonal sheathing, racking stresses are transferred directly down the sheathing boards to the sill and thence to the foundation. Diagonal sheathing is, therefore, a stiffer, more enduring type of construction.

j. Bracing must be employed with non-structural sheathing panels or horizontal-board sheathing. Let-in bracing is often employed in the platform frame. It consists of boards, usually 1 × 4, let into the studs at the corners of the house and run diagonally from post to sill (figure 5.15). Properly done, this kind of bracing adds a great deal of rigidity to the frame; its use is sufficient to obviate the need for diagonal sheathing. Figure 5.15 shows let-in bracing in a platform frame. The same procedure is used with balloon framing. Bracing is also provided by flat or tee-shaped steel straps let into studs similarly to wood bracing.

k. Full 2 × 4 or 2 × 6 braces cut entirely through the studs are sometimes employed. They destroy the strength and continuity of the studs and are likely to be at too steep an angle to provide much bracing.

l. Depending on the type of exterior finish (chapter 10) and sheathing, wind-driven air and moisture may penetrate. Such penetration should be blocked. The many joints in wood sheathing boards may allow penetration; large panels such as plywood do not. When penetration is possible, a building paper is used over the sheathing. It should be a

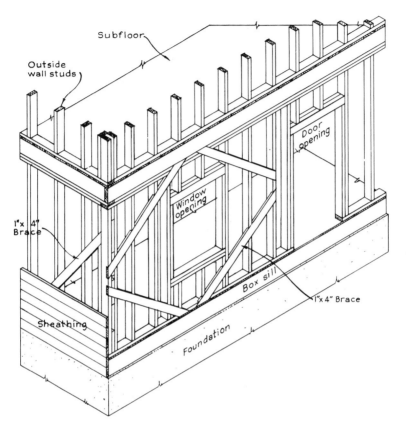

Figure 5.15 Let-in bracing.

wind barrier, but should allow water vapor to pass (chapter 11). Commonly used papers are matted synthetic fibers, vapor-permeable papers, and lightweight vapor-permeable asphalt felts.

5.13 Steel Framing

a. Although wood is the traditional framing material for dwelling-house construction, light steel framing has become increasingly common, especially for multiple housing. It is in general use for light commercial and industrial buildings. Steel framing members are described in section 5.3w and shown in figure 5.4. Their application in dwelling-house construction is largely adapted from standard platform framing. Some typical details are shown in figure 5.16. Members are customarily joined together by self-tapping screws and light welding.

b. Facing materials such as boards are commonly fastened with clips and self-tapping screws. I studs with spaced double webs, and joists with similar flanges, can have nails driven into the crimped space. Light-duty studs find use in non-bearing applications, but heavier-duty studs are load-bearing.

c. Auxiliaries such as small cold-rolled steel channels are used for stud stiffeners and for furring and runners in suspended ceilings. Formed sheet-steel screw-attached plain or resilient furring channels find similar use. Other formed sheet-steel channels and Z shapes are used to retain rigid foam insulation and to support boards such as gypsum (sections 12.3, 12.8).

THE BALLOON FRAME

5.14 General

a. The balloon frame, once popular, has been superseded by the platform frame. It is often found in older houses. It has the following parts (see figure 5.17):

sill
posts
ribbon (or ribband)
plate
studs
sheathing

b. A comparison with the parts of the platform frame shows two chief differences. Instead of a sill and header platform at the foundation, and a plate and header platform at upper floors, the balloon frame uses a one-member sill, and a ribband to support second floor joists. The rest of the members — sill, posts, plate, studs, and sheathing — perform essentially the same functions as in the platform frame, but certain important differences are to be noted.

c. Posts for the balloon frame are built up similarly to those for the platform frame, but they run full height from sill to roof plate, as shown in figure 5.17.

d. The ribband (figures 5.17, 5.18) is more commonly called the ribbon and forms the support for upper-floor joists. It is a square-edged board, 4" to 8" wide, which is let ("housed") into the studs so that the

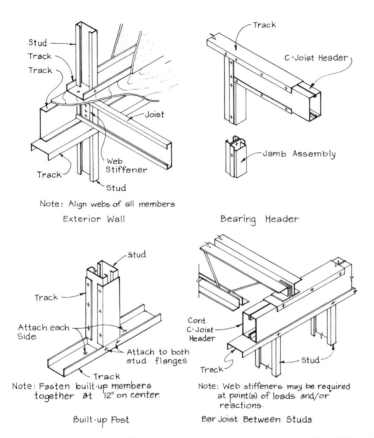

Figure 5.16 Light steel framing. (Left) Details at exterior wall and floor: bearing header; built-up post; bar joist support between studs. (Right) Wind bracing: X-bracing or single diagonal strap in tension. Courtesy of Marino Industries Corporation.

top of the ribband is at the elevation of the bottoms of the joists. The joists are set on the ribband and nailed to the studs. The ribband occurs only in those walls which run perpendicular to the direction of the joists.

e. The balloon frame is distinguished by studs that run full length from sill to plate.

f. The vertical spaces between studs are likely to act as flues to transmit flames if fire breaks out. These potential flues must be closed, particularly at the sill, where otherwise an unbroken sweep from basement upward would be afforded. Firestopping at this point may be incombustible filling. Wood blocking may be placed between joists.

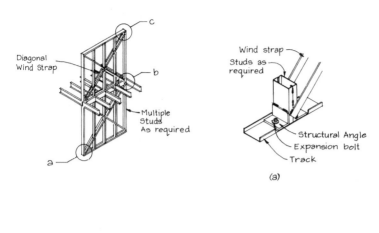

(a)

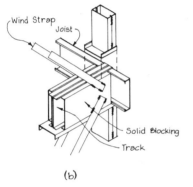

(b)

(c)

Types of firestops are shown in figures 5.17 and 5.18. One method of obtaining such firestopping is the tee sill (figure 5.20).

g. The observations made in regard to sheathing for platform framing are equally applicable to balloon framing.

THE BRACED FRAME

5.15 General

a. The braced or eastern frame, once mandatory under many codes in the northeastern United States, is a descendant of the heavy frames built during the Colonial period. It is still sometimes employed.

b. The braced frame has the following parts:

sill
girts

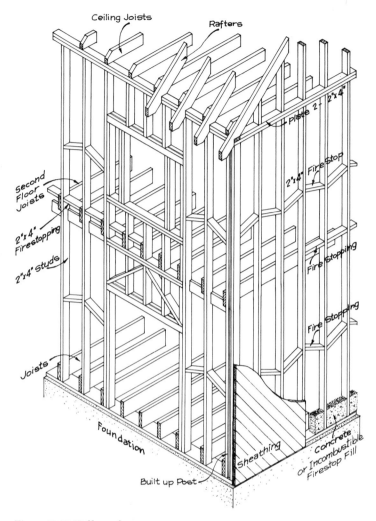

Figure 5.17 Balloon frame.

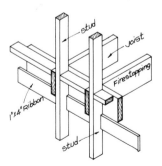

Figure 5.18 Ribbon and firestopping at second floor.

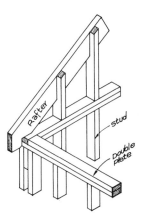

Figure 5.19 Roof plate and end rafter for gable roof.

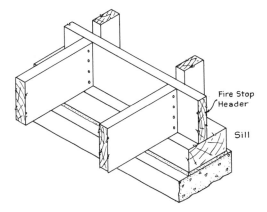

Figure 5.20 Tee sill construction.

plate
braces
studs
sheathing
c. In most braced frames, the sills, posts, and girts are of solid timber.
d. The sill for a braced frame is almost always 4″ thick; the usual size is 4″ × 6″.
e. Posts, usually 4″ × 6″ but occasionally 4″ × 8″, are placed at all corners of the exterior walls and at intermediate points where necessary. Posts run full length from sill to plate.

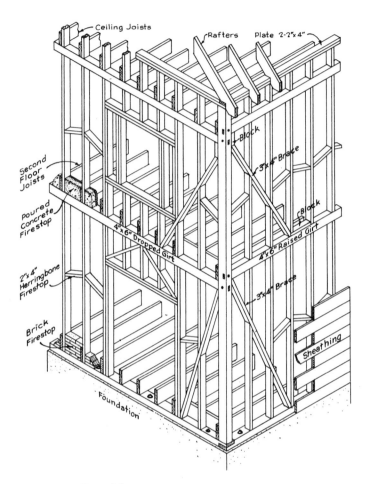

Figure 5.21 Braced frame.

f. *Girts* are horizontal members at the second floor. One supports the ends of second-floor joists and is called the dropped girt; the other, the raised girt, is parallel to the joists (figure 5.21).

g. The end corners of the outside walls and the important intermediate corners are braced to withstand the lateral racking caused by wind and nonuniform loads. The braces distinguish this type of frame and give it its name.

h. In older frames, knee braces, posts, and girts were mortised, tenoned, and pinned (figure 5.22).

i. The *single diagonal brace* (figure 5.21) is generally a 2 × 4 or 3 × 4

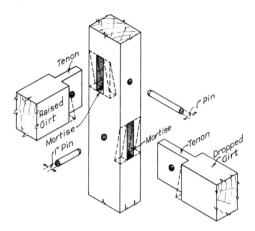

Figure 5.22 Pinned mortise-and-tenon connections of girts to posts in braced frame.

strut. In the first story, it runs diagonally from the intersection of the post and the girt to the sill. In the second story, it runs from the intersection of the post and the plate to the girt.

j. In the braced frame, the studs extend from the sill to the girt in the first story and from the girt to the plate in the second. They are toe-nailed to the sill and the girts. The framing around openings is similar to that for the platform frame, and includes headers for relatively small openings and trussed construction for wide openings.

k. The firestopping is similar to that described under balloon framing. Good practice calls for additional firestopping between the sill and the girt and between the girt and the plate. This takes the form of blocking — either horizontal or sloping ("herringbone") — between studs half way up the story height, as shown in figures 5.6, 5.17, and 5.21.

l. Sheathing boards have been customarily employed with the braced frame. This frame, however, has lateral bracing built into it and does not depend upon the sheathing to resist lateral racking. Consequently, wood sheathing boards can be applied horizontally instead of diagonally, without let-in bracing.

FLOOR FRAMING

5.16 General

a. Floor framing is simpler in its details than wall framing and is essentially the same no matter what kind of wall frame — platform, balloon, or braced — is used. The floor, regardless of the finish it is to bear, consists of rough subflooring resting on joists carried by girders, walls, or partitions. The girders are supported by posts or piers, which rest on footings. Joists are sometimes known as *floor beams,* but the term *joist* is much more commonly employed.

b. Although plain wood has been the traditional material for joists, the use of composite-wood members (sections 5.3h, 5.3i) is increasing, especially for long spans.

c. Cold-formed light steel joists and open-web "bar" joists (section 5.3w) are also employed, especially for long spans.

d. The simplest way to frame a floor would be to let joists run the full length from one outside wall to the other, but this would entail excessively long pieces, difficult to handle and expensive to purchase. Moreover, if these joists had no intermediate support they would have to be extremely deep to provide the requisite strength and stiffness. For these reasons shorter lengths, supported at their ends on girders, walls, or partitions, are employed.

e. Figure 5.23 shows a framing plan for a small dwelling. The left half of the house has joists running perpendicular to the front and back walls. The total distance is covered in two spans, the interior ends of the joists resting on a girder which runs parallel to the front and back walls. The right half of the house is framed with joists paralleling the front and rear walls; two sets of joists again make the total span, but

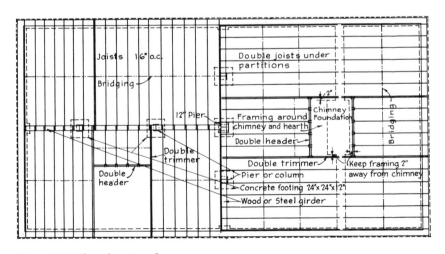

Figure 5.23 Floor framing plan.

their intermediate ends rest on a masonry or concrete wall. In general it is simplest to have all joists run in the same direction, but this is by no means necessary nor is it always feasible. Generally, joists should be so arranged as to give the shortest spans with the fewest intermediate supports. This makes for economy in labor and material: the shorter the span the shallower the joists can be, and the fewer the intermediate supports the less labor required in framing.

5.17 Posts

a. Some common supports for girders are hollow steel pipe, steel pipe filled with concrete, wood posts, masonry piers (brick or concrete block), and cast concrete piers.

b. No matter what the column or pier may be, it must have an adequate footing and a cap of some kind upon which the girder bears. The footing is usually concrete poured in place and is commonly 2' square and 1' thick. For large masonry piers these dimensions must be increased; for small wood or steel columns carrying light loads the dimensions can be reduced (chapter 4).

c. Brick piers must be at least 12" square unless the loads are very light and the piers are short. For large loads and tall piers the dimensions are increased to 16". Concrete block piers (figure 5.24a) have the same limitations, except that since most blocks are 16" long the piers are seldom smaller than that dimension in each direction.

d. Cast concrete piers should not be less than 10" round or square unless reinforced with laterally tied vertical rods.

e. Wood posts must not be permitted to stand in water or to become permanently damp. Therefore, their lower ends should be raised off the floor several inches so that any water standing on the floor will not cause them to rot. As shown in diagrams b and c of figure 5.24, a base of concrete or masonry, built on top of the footing, projects above the floor level and supports the column. When wood posts are used, the surrounding air must be dry enough to prevent rot unless the posts have been treated with preservative (section 5.2n).

f. Steel pipe columns, hollow or filled, are fitted with cap and base plates (figure 5.24c). Often the base plates are set directly on the footings and the entire foot of the column is concreted in. While this anchors the column firmly, it also permits water to reach and rust the steel parts. Rust-resisting coating should, therefore, be applied liberally to these parts before they are set and concreted. It is preferable to

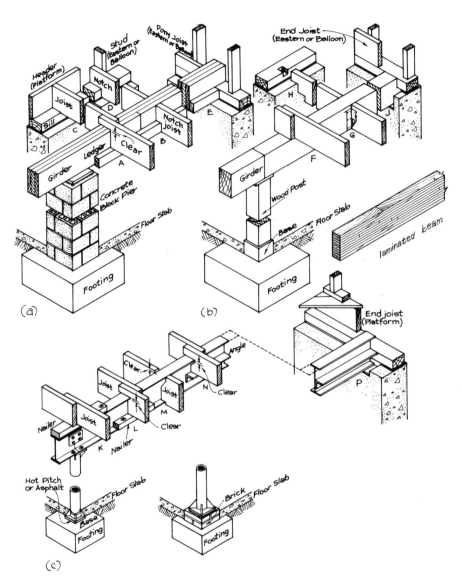

Figure 5.24 Details of post and girder construction for masonry, wood, and steel. (a) Block pier and built-up girder. (b) Wood post and solid girder. (c) Steel column and steel girder.

set these plates on concrete or masonry bases, as is done for wooden posts, or to set anchor bolts in the concrete and fasten the column and base plate to these bolts, on top of the floor slab.

g. Caps for columns of all kinds are commonly flat steel plates, $\frac{1}{4}''$ to $\frac{1}{2}''$ thick. Where wood posts are as wide as the girders above, the cap plate can be omitted.

5.18 Girders

a. Wood. In houses and other light construction, the girders are wood, or steel shapes such as I and wide-flange beams (section 5.3w), or reinforced concrete. Wood girders may be either solid or built up. The built-up timber consists of pieces of 2″ or 3″ stock set on edge and nailed or lag-screwed together to form a larger piece. Figure 5.24a shows a girder built up from three 2″ pieces. The solid timber (figure 5.24b) is simplest and gives the most actual timber for a given cross-section: a nominally 8″ wide solid timber is actually $7\frac{1}{4}''$ or $7\frac{1}{2}''$, whereas four 2″ pieces are actually $4 \times 1\frac{1}{2}''$ or $1\frac{9}{16}''$ (i.e., 6″ to $6\frac{1}{4}''$) wide. A built-up timber, therefore, would have to be made up of five 2″ pieces in order to contain as much wood as the solid stick. On the other hand, whereas solid pieces run only from support to support, built-up girders can be made continuous from one end of the building to the other, thereby tying the entire frame more closely together and adding to the stiffness of the girder. Thus, built-up girders can generally be the same nominal sizes as solid timbers. Solid timbers are also apt to shrink and check (split) more badly than built-up timbers, which are preferable. The larger sizes of timber call for an extra item in the lumber order, whereas the built-up timbers are made of the same stock that is used for floor joists. As a matter of practical engineering, joints in built-up girders should be well staggered or "broken" and ought to occur at approximately the quarter-points of the spans, not directly over the supports or at mid-span.

b. Wood girders may be laminated by gluing smaller pieces together to form larger timbers. Usually, nominal 2″ material is dressed smoothly and glued together to make up the desired depth. Casein is commonly used for indoor applications, but a waterproof glue is needed for exposure outdoors. After the glue has hardened, the timber is again dressed on all four sides to produce a clean, smooth surface (figure 5.24b). Scarf or fingered joints with slope $\frac{1}{10}$ or shallower are needed in the upper and the lower quarter-depth to resist bending stresses. Other joints can be butt joints (see also section 5.42).

c. Steel. Steel beams used as girders (figure 5.24c) introduce one or two new problems but are essentially the same in their action as wood girders. Usually, because of their weight, they run only from support to support instead of being continuous, and are held in place by bolts which engage the cap plates of steel pipe columns. They are held together, in addition, by steel splice plates bolted to the ends of two butted members.

d. Framing at exterior walls. Where the ends of wood or steel girders rest in exterior walls, recessed ledges are provided. The bottoms are best covered with steel bearing plates or carefully leveled (figure 5.24b,c). Such openings must be made large and deep enough to provide adequate ventilation around the ends of girders; otherwise dampness causes wood girders to rot and steel girders to rust.

e. Spacing. Since joists are cut in lengths which are multiples of 1' or 2', the best spacing of girders is such as to allow full use of these lengths without waste. If no other factors govern, girders should be so spaced. Frequently, however, girders are placed under important bearing partitions, and these in turn are regulated in their spacing by room sizes. Sometimes, moreover, it is desirable to place girders over basement partitions so that they will not project into the ceiling space in finished basement rooms.

f. Framing into sills and girders. The simplest and in many ways the best way to frame joists into their supports is merely to set them on top (see C, F, and K in figure 5.24). When so supported, joists are easily toe-nailed and end-nailed to the sill and the stud, making a good joint; similarly, they are easily lapped at the girders, nailed together and toe-nailed to the girder, again affording a strong joint. However, in-line and cantilever framing (section 5.39) make it desirable to keep joists in alignment.

g. Joists resting on girders pile up a good deal of wood in a direction perpendicular to the grain and make for excessive shrinkage if the wood is not seasoned. Measurements show that, with wide climatic and geographic variations, wood reaches an average final moisture content of roughly 12 percent in dwellings (section 5.2j). Consequently, even commercially "dry" wood (seasoned to 19 percent moisture content or less) is likely to show some shrinkage in place in a dwelling. This is especially serious at the girders, less so at the sill.

Moreover, dropped girders may require pipes and ducts to be carried very low, and may therefore call for extra depth in the basement.

h. Girders should, for the foregoing reasons, be kept as high as possible. This is best accomplished by the cleat or ledger, illustrated in figure 5.24 as ABE. The notched joists at A are to be carefully noted. Bearing must not in any case be permitted to occur at the notch; it must all occur at the bottom of the joist where it rests on the ledger. Hence the notch must be made high enough to clear the girder by at least $\frac{1}{2}''$, so that subsequent shrinkage in the joist will not cause bearing at the notch. Otherwise the joist is almost certain to split at that point. This is a general rule covering all deep notches: bearing must not occur at the notch; otherwise splits are almost certain to occur. This does not apply to shallow notches as illustrated at the sill at point C. These merely take up the slight inequalities in depth which often occur in joists, and allow the tops of all joists to be at the same level. When it is desired to have girders and joists flush at the bottom, joists may be notched as shown at B. Notches at this depth are not objectionable on deep joists of long span carrying fairly light loads. Heavy loads on short spans are apt to cause splits at the notch, as is also true of D unless the bottom of the joist is shimmed to bear on the foundation wall. The more complicated notch shown at H is open to the same general criticism. It was common in older construction, especially in the eastern braced frame, but is seldom used now.

i. Specially formed metal grip plates or framing anchors are available to fasten the ends of joists to the sides of girders by nailing (figure 5.25). Joists may also be hung from girders with hangers, as illustrated in figure 5.34b.

j. When steel girders are used (figure 5.24c), joists may rest directly on

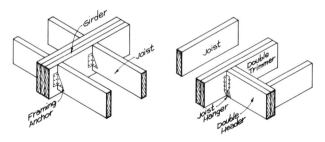

Figure 5.25 Joists and headers supported by framing anchors and joist hangers.

top. In that case a nailer (see K) may be bolted to the top flange to provide nailing for the joists. Joists may also rest directly on the bottom flange of the beam (see M); here too nailing may be provided by nailers bolted to the beam (see L). Support may also be afforded by angles bolted to the web of the beam (see N). To provide for shrinkage, notches at L and N and tops of joists at M should clear the top flanges of the girder by at least $\frac{1}{2}''$.

k. Any of the sill details C, D, H in figure 5.24 may be combined with any of the girder details A, B, F, G, K, L, M, N by altering the height of the girder and its wall supports EJ or P. As drawn, E corresponds to A and B; J corresponds to F; P corresponds to N.

l. Steel joists (section 5.3w) are handled somewhat similarly to wood joists, except that open-web joists commonly rest on the ends of their upper flanges (figure 5.16).

m. Framing around openings. Openings in floors are framed in essentially the same way as in walls, namely by a combination of trimmers and headers arranged around the opening. The joists (figures 5.22, 5.25, 5.26) that run parallel with two sides of the opening are doubled if necessary to carry the loads and are called *trimmers*. At right angles to the trimmers are set other joists called *headers* (doubled, if necessary), and into these headers are framed the shortened joists, known as *tail beams, tail joists,* or *header joists.*

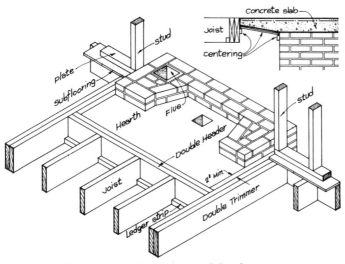

Figure 5.26 Framing around chimney and fireplace.

n. Where spans are short and loads are light, this whole assembly can be nailed together. Otherwise hangers or framing anchors ("grip plates") are used, particularly to support the headers on the trimmers. Sometimes the tail beams are supported on ledgers by notching, as illustrated in figure 5.26, but this is subject to the criticism already made regarding bearing on notches.

o. Framing around chimneys and fireplaces (figures 5.23, 5.26) is commonly held away 2″, and the space between is filled with incombustible insulating material. *Wood members must not be permitted, under any circumstances, to frame into a chimney,* although a pilaster or corbel may be built as part of a chimney to support wood framing members. (See also chapter 6.)

p. Framing under partitions. Nonbearing partitions resting on the floor and running perpendicular to the direction of the joists need no extra support. However, bearing partitions may impose enough load, if they are situated close to the centers of spans, to require additional strength in the supporting joists. These may be made deeper or may be doubled as shown in figure 5.27a. When a condition such as this exists, the loads imposed on the joists should be analyzed and the joists designed by elementary engineering procedures. Partitions run-

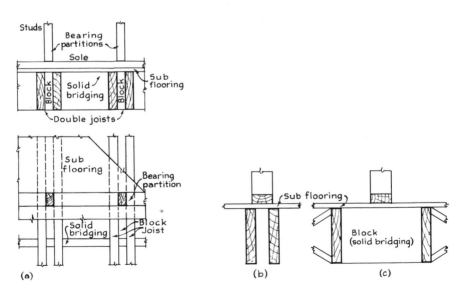

Figure 5.27 Framing under partitions. (a) Support for intermediate transverse bearing partition. (b, c) Support for nonbearing partitions.

ning parallel to the joists throw undue loads on single joists if additional support is not provided. Figure 5.27 shows two methods of obtaining this support. The simplest is merely to double the joist in question (b) if the partition happens to come directly over it. If the partition comes between two joists, short pieces of block (solid bridging) are nailed across between them, every 2' or so, in order to distribute the load to the joists (c).

q. Framing upper floors. Upper floors are framed the same as the first, except that the outer ends of joists rest on plates instead of on sills and the inner ends rest on partition caps instead of on interior basement walls or girders. Occasionally, however, girders are used to support second-floor joists over large rooms.

5.19 Interior Basement Walls

Joists supported by interior masonry walls are carried on sills. If there is a chance that lateral forces will be applied to the house (by heavy winds, or earthquakes), these sills should be anchored in the same way as the sills on exterior walls.

5.20 Joists

a. Joists must not only be large enough to carry the floor loads, but must also be stiff enough to prevent excessive deflection. The usual rule of thumb is to limit deflection at the center to $\frac{1}{360}$ of the span.

b. Table 5.6 lists spans for various sizes of joists at various spacings as limited by the rule above and by fiber stress in bending. The 50 lb per sq ft loading (including live load plus weight of floor structure) is a customary building code requirement for the living quarters of a house, with 40 to 20 lb per sq ft for sleeping quarters and attics. For a joist of a given grade and species, the modulus of elasticity E and the allowable bending stress F_b should be checked to see that the loading is safe.

c. Joists are commonly spaced 16" on centers, but this spacing can be varied. Joists are generally the same depth throughout the floor. That is, instead of making some spans of the first floor 2×8s and some 2×12s, all spans are 2×12s. The second floor might be all 2×10s or 2×8s. Quite often, second-floor joists are lighter than those on the first floor.

d. By varying the spacing it is often possible to save material. For instance, suppose all spans but one in a floor were 12' or less, but this one were 13'. Suppose that, except for this one span, all joists could

Table 5.6 Floor Joists[a]

	Joist spacing (in.)	Span and Fiber Stress Live Load 40 lb/sq ft[b] Modulus of Elasticity E, in 1,000,000 lb/sq. in.										
Joist size		1.0	1.1	1.2	1.3	1.4	1.5	1.6	1.7	1.8	1.9	2.0
2 × 6	12.0	9-2	9-6	9-9	10-0	10-3	10-6	10-9	10-11	11-2	11-4	11-7
		830	890	940	990	1040	1090	1140	1190	1230	1280	1320
	13.7	8-9	9-1	9-4	9-7	9-10	10-0	10-3	10-6	10-8	10-10	11-1
		870	930	980	1040	1090	1140	1190	1240	1290	1340	1380
	16.0	8-4	8-7	8-10	9-1	9-4	9-6	9-9	9-11	10-2	10-4	10-6
		920	980	1040	1090	1150	1200	1250	1310	1360	1410	1460
	19.2	7-10	8-1	8-4	8-7	8-9	9-0	9-2	9-4	9-6	9-8	9-10
		970	1040	1100	1160	1220	1280	1330	1390	1440	1500	1550
	24.0	7-3	7-6	7-9	7-11	8-2	8-4	8-6	8-8	8-10	9-0	9-2
		1050	1120	1190	1250	1310	1380	1440	1500	1550	1610	1670
	32.0	6-7	6-10	7-0	7-3	7-5	7-7	7-9	7-11	8-0	8-2	8-4
		1150	1230	1300	1390	1450	1520	1590	1660	1690	1760	1840
2 × 8	12.0	12-1	12-6	12-10	13-2	13-6	13-10	14-2	14-5	14-8	15-0	15-3
		830	890	940	990	1040	1090	1140	1190	1230	1280	1320
	13.7	11-7	11-11	12-3	12-7	12-11	13-3	13-6	13-10	14-1	14-4	14-7
		870	930	980	1040	1090	1140	1190	1240	1290	1340	1380
	16.0	11-0	11-4	11-8	12-0	12-3	12-7	12-10	13-1	13-4	13-7	13-10
		920	980	1040	1090	1150	1200	1250	1310	1360	1410	1460
	19.2	10-4	10-8	11-0	11-3	11-7	11-10	12-1	12-4	12-7	12-10	13-0
		970	1040	1100	1160	1220	1280	1330	1390	1440	1500	1550
	24.0	9-7	9-11	10-2	10-6	10-9	11-0	11-3	11-5	11-8	11-11	12-1
		1050	1120	1190	1250	1310	1380	1440	1500	1550	1610	1670
	32.0	8-9	9-0	9-3	9-6	9-9	10-0	10-2	10-5	10-7	10-10	11-0
		1170	1230	1300	1370	1450	1520	1570	1650	1700	1790	1840
2 × 10	12.0	15-5	15-11	16-5	16-10	17-3	17-8	18-0	18-5	18-9	19-1	19-5
		830	890	940	990	1040	1090	1140	1190	1230	1280	1320
	13.7	14-9	15-3	15-8	16-1	16-6	16-11	17-3	17-7	17-11	18-3	18-7
		870	930	980	1040	1090	1140	1190	1240	1290	1340	1380
	16.0	14-0	14-6	14-11	15-3	15-8	16-0	16-5	16-9	17-0	17-4	17-8
		920	980	1040	1090	1150	1200	1250	1310	1360	1410	1460
	19.2	13-2	13-7	14-0	14-5	14-9	15-1	15-5	15-9	16-0	16-4	16-7
		970	1040	1100	1160	1220	1280	1330	1390	1440	1500	1550
	24.0	12-3	12-8	13-0	13-4	13-8	14-0	14-4	14-7	14-11	15-2	15-5
		1050	1120	1190	1250	1310	1380	1440	1500	1550	1610	1670
	32.0	11-1	11-6	11-10	12-2	12-5	12-9	13-0	13-3	13-6	13-9	14-0
		1150	1240	1310	1380	1440	1520	1580	1640	1700	1770	1830
2 × 12	12.0	18-9	19-4	19-11	20-6	21-0	21-6	21-11	22-5	22-10	23-3	23-7
		830	890	940	990	1040	1090	1140	1190	1230	1280	1320
	13.7	17-11	18-6	19-1	19-7	20-1	20-6	21-0	21-5	21-10	22-3	22-7
		870	930	980	1040	1090	1140	1190	1240	1290	1340	1380
	16.0	17-0	17-7	18-1	18-7	19-1	19-6	19-11	20-4	20-9	21-1	21-6
		920	980	1040	1090	1150	1200	1250	1310	1360	1410	1460
	19.2	16-0	16-7	17-0	17-6	17-11	18-4	18-9	19-2	19-6	19-10	20-2
		970	1040	1100	1160	1220	1280	1330	1390	1440	1500	1550
	24.0	14-11	15-4	15-10	16-3	16-8	17-0	17-5	17-9	18-1	18-5	18-9
		1050	1120	1190	1250	1310	1380	1440	1500	1550	1610	1670
	32.0	13-6	13-11	14-4	14-9	15-2	15-6	15-10	16-2	16-5	16-9	17-0
		1150	1220	1300	1380	1450	1520	1580	1650	1700	1770	1830

[a]The first number under each modulus of elasticity value E is the span, in feet and inches, as limited by the allowable deflection (see note b), and the second number is the corresponding extreme fiber stress in bending for that span (note b).
[b]Design criteria for deflection under 40 lb/sq ft live load: Deflection is to be limited to span (in.) divided by 360. Strength: The resulting fiber stress value is determined by taking the live load (40 lb/sq ft) plus a dead load of 10 lb/sq ft.
Source: National Association of Home Builders Research Foundation, Inc.

Table 5.7 Typical Allowable Bending Stresses

Species	Floor joists[a] (lb/sq. in.)	Modulus of elasticity (lb/sq. in.)
Douglas fir, larch	1,450	1,700,000
Eastern hemlock	1,250	1,100,000
Eastern spruce	950	1,400,000
Hem-fir	1,150	1,400,000
Southern pine	1,400	1,600,000
Spruce-pine-fir	1,000	1,300,000

[a] Allowable stresses for rafters are increased 15 percent because of the short duration of loads such as snow and wind.

be 2 × 8s. Since deflection for uniform floor loading increases as the fourth power of length, the 2 × 8s to be used on a 13' span would have to be spaced more closely to reduce the load per joist. The ratio of spacing would be $(13)^4:(12)^4$. This is almost exactly 4:3. Therefore, the 2 × 8s spaced 12" on centers over this one span would be satisfactory and all joists could be 2 × 8s. Similarly, spacing could be increased above 16" in other instances (see table 5.6).

5.21 Bridging

a. Bridging has traditionally been considered necessary to keep long, deep floor joists from tending to buckle sidewise at the bottom. Tests indicate that bridging, except in unusual cases, is not really necessary; however, many codes require it.

b. As shown in figure 5.28, bridging consists of short pieces set in crosswise between the joists and nailed top and bottom. Bridging is commonly 1 × 2 or 1 × 3 for joists up to 2 × 10 , and 2 × 2 or 2 × 3 for deeper joists. Customarily, there is a line of bridging for each 6' to 8' of unsupported length of joist. Steel bridging is also employed. Solid bridging consists of blocks of joist material set between joists.

5.22 Subflooring

a. When ¾" square-edged or matched boards are used for rough flooring, they are best laid at 45° to the joists when the finish floor is wood strip flooring (chapter 13). Such flooring should not run in the same direction as the rough floor and, since the finish floor may change direction in various rooms, this can be avoided only by laying the subfloor diagonally. The best board subfloor is 6" or 8" tongue and groove or shiplap driven up tight and nailed with at least two nails at

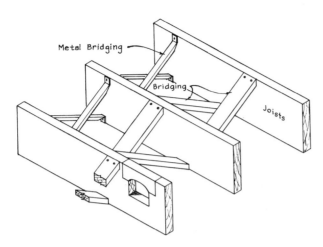

Metal Bridging

Bridging

Joists

Figure 5.28 Bridging floors and cutting holes for piping.

every joist. Unless the flooring is well nailed, it may warp and twist upon wetting and provide a poor nailing surface for the finish floor.

b. Wood-based panels are used extensively for subflooring as single thickness and as double thickness with subflooring and underlayment (figures 5.29, 5.30). As a general rule, panels should be laid with the long dimensions or strength axes perpendicular to the direction of the joists.

c. Some recommended grades, thicknesses, spans, and nailing schedules for sheathing-grade panels used as subflooring under tongue-and-groove wood strip and block flooring (chapter 13) or lightweight concrete are given in table 5.8. The panels are continuous over two or more joists, and the long dimensions or strong axes run across the joists.

d. As shown in figure 5.29, a ⅛" space should be left between panels at the end and edge joints. If the finish floor is wood block, the edges of the panels should be supported by blocking between joists unless the edges are tongue and groove. End joints in adjacent tiers of panels are staggered (broken).

e. For support of resilient flooring (chapter 13), underlayment provides a smooth surface over panel subflooring or over boards. Recommended grades, thicknesses, and fastener (nail or staple) spacings are given in table 5.8. Joints in underlayment are offset from joints in panel subflooring.

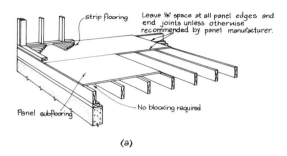

(a)

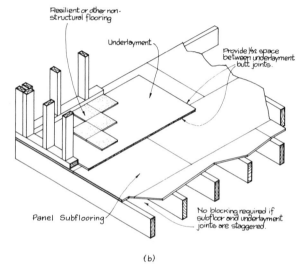

(b)

Figure 5.29 (a) Panel subflooring with wood-strip flooring. (b) Panel subfloor and underlayment for resilient flooring.

f. Panel subfloor and underlayment may be combined into one thickness to eliminate the double labor of installing two layers. Some recommended grades, thicknesses, spans, and nailing are given in table 5.9.

g. Panels $1\frac{1}{8}''$ thick are employed in systems of construction in which joists or floor beams are spaced $32''$ to $48''$ apart.

h. In one system, tongue-and-groove plywood, $1\frac{1}{8}''$ thick, is utilized to provide combination subfloor and underlayment of sufficient strength and stiffness to span the $32''$ and $48''$ distances. Because of the tongue-and-groove construction, no edge blocking is required.

i. When plywood is glued to the floor joists, with nails used only to apply the necessary pressure to the glue, a considerable increase in

Table 5.8 Nailing Schedule for Panel Subflooring[a] (C-C Exposure 1, Structural I C-D Exposure 1, C-C Ext., Structural I C-C Ext.)

Panel span rating (or group number)	Panel thickness (in.)	Maximum span (in.)	Nail size and type	Nail spacing (in.)	
				Supported panel edges	Intermediate supports[f]
24/16	$\frac{7}{16}$	16	6d common	6	12
32/16	$\frac{15}{32}, \frac{1}{2}, \frac{5}{8}$	16[b]	8d common[c]	6	12
40/20	$\frac{9}{16}, \frac{19}{32}, \frac{5}{8}, \frac{3}{4}, \frac{7}{8}$	20[d]	8d common	6	12
48/24	$\frac{23}{32}, \frac{3}{4}, \frac{7}{8}$	24	8d common	6	12
$1\frac{1}{8}''$ groups 1,2[e]	$1\frac{1}{8}$	48	10d common	6	6

[a]For subfloor recommendations under gypsum concrete, contact manufacturer of floor topping.
[b]Span may be 24″ if $\frac{3}{4}''$ wood-strip flooring is installed at right angles to joists.
[c]6d common nail permitted if panel is $\frac{1}{2}''$ or thinner.
[d]Span may be 24″ if $\frac{3}{4}''$ wood-strip flooring is installed at right angles to joists or if at least $1\frac{1}{2}''$ of lightweight concrete or 1″ of some gypsum concrete products is applied over panels.
[e]Check availability with dealer.
[f]Applicable building codes may require 10″ o.c. nail spacing at intermediate supports for floors.

Table 5.9 Plywood Underlayment

Plywood grades[a]	Application	Minimum plywood thickness (in.)	Fastener size and type	Fastener spacing (in.)[b]	
				Panel edges	Intermediate
APA UNDER-LAYMENT, APA C-C Plugged EXT, APA RATED STURD-I-FLOOR ($\frac{19}{32}''$ or thicker)	Over smooth subfloor	$\frac{1}{4}$	18 ga. staples or 3d ring-shank nails[c,d]	3	6 each way
	Over lumber subfloor or other uneven surfaces.	$\frac{11}{32}$	16 ga. staples[c]	3	6 each way
			3d ring-shank nails[d]	6	8 each way
Same grades as above, but species Group 1 only.	Over lumber floor up to 4″ wide. Face grain must be perpendicular to boards.	$\frac{1}{4}$	18 ga. staples or 3d ring-shank nails[c,d]	3	6 each way

[a]In areas to be finished with thin floor coverings such as tile or sheet vinyl, specify Underlayment, C-C Plugged or STURD-I-FLOOR with "sanded face." A-C Underlayment, B-C Underlayment, Marine EXT or sanded plywood grades marked "Plugged Crossbands Under Face," "Plugged Crossbands (or Core)," or "Plugged Inner Plies" may also be used under thin floor coverings.
[b]If green framing is used, space fasteners so they do not penetrate framing.
[c]Use 16 ga. staples for $\frac{19}{32}''$ and thicker plywood. Crown width $\frac{3}{8}''$ for 16 ga. $\frac{3}{16}''$ for 18 ga. staples, length sufficient to penetrate completely through, or at least $\frac{5}{8}''$ into, sub-flooring.
[d]Use 3d ring-shank nails for $\frac{1}{2}''$ panels and 4d ring-shank nails for $\frac{5}{8}''$ or $\frac{3}{4}''$ panels.
Source: American Plywood Association.

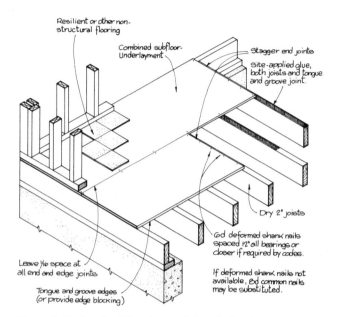

Figure 5.30 Panel subflooring nailed and glued to joists.

strength and stiffness results because the plywood now acts together with the joist as a Tee beam. A bead of elastomeric high-strength adhesive is applied with a caulking gun to the upper edge of the joist and in the groove of the tongue-and-groove edge of the plywood. As shown in figure 5.30, end joints are staggered and a $\frac{1}{8}''$ space is left between panels. Nailing is according to table 5.10. Table 5.11 gives recommended spans and spacings for selected glued panel-joist combinations.

j. Special preparation is needed for the bathroom floor if it is to be tile (figure 5.31). In the upper view, the tops of all joists are first chamfered; then 1 × 3 strips are nailed to the sides of the joists, 3″ down from the top. On these strips are placed short lengths of rough flooring fitted between joists. The concrete base for tile is then cast on these boards. Wire mesh, run continuously over the chamfered tops of joists, is embedded in the final mortar bed, upon which the tiles are placed. A more desirable method is shown in the lower portion of figure 5.31. Here the tendency to incipient cracking in the floor above the usual chamfered joists is avoided because the concrete is of uniform thickness. (See also chapter 13.)

Table 5.10 Rated Sturd-I-Floor[a]

Span rating (maximum joist spacing, in.)	Panel thickness[b] (in.)	Fastening: Glue-nailed[c]			Fastening: Nailed-only		
			Spacing (in.)			Spacing (in.)	
		Nail size and type	Supported panel edges	Inter-mediate supports	Nail size and type	Supported panel edges	Inter-mediate supports[g]
16	$\frac{19}{32}$, $\frac{5}{8}$, $\frac{21}{32}$	6d ring- or screw-shank[d]	12	12	6d ring- or screw-shank	6	12
20	$\frac{19}{32}$, $\frac{5}{8}$, $\frac{23}{32}$, $\frac{3}{4}$	6d ring- or screw-shank[d]	12	12	6d ring- or screw-shank	6	12
	$\frac{11}{16}$, $\frac{23}{32}$, $\frac{3}{4}$	6d ring- or screw-shank[d]	12	12	6d ring- or screw-shank	6	12
24	$\frac{7}{8}$, 1	8d ring- or screw-shank[d]	6	12	8d ring- or screw-shank	6	12
48 (2-4-1)	$1\frac{1}{8}$	8d ring- or screw-shank[e]	6	(f)	8d ring- or screw-shank[e]	6	(f)

[a]Special conditions may impose heavy traffic and concentrated loads that require construction in excess of the minimums shown.

[b]As indicated above, panels in a given thickness may be manufactured in more than one Span Rating. Panels with a Span Rating greater than the actual joist spacing may be substituted for panels of the same thickness with a Span Rating matching the actual joist spacing. For example, $\frac{19}{32}$"-thick Sturd-I-Floor 20 o.c. may be substituted for $\frac{19}{32}$"-thick Sturd-I-Floor 16" o.c. over joists 16" on center.

[c]Use only adhesives conforming to APA Specification AFG-01, applied in accordance with the manufacturer's recommendations. If non-veneered panels with sealed surfaces and edges are to be used, use only solvent-based glues, check with panel manufacturer.

[d]8d common nails may be substituted if ring- or screw-shank nails are not available.

[e]10d common nails may be substituted with $1\frac{1}{8}$" panels if supports are well seasoned.

[f]Space nails 6" for 48" spans and 12" for 32" spans.

[g]Applicable building codes may require 10" o.c. nail spacing at intermediate supports for floors.

Source: American Plywood Association.

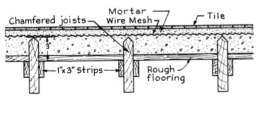

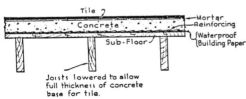

Figure 5.31 Preparation for tile floor.

Table 5.11 Maximum Joist Spans with Underlayment Panels[a,b] in Glued Floor System

Species and grade of joist	Joist size	Joists @ 16" oc		Joists @ 19.2" oc		Joists @ 24" oc
		Under-layment 16 or 20 oc	Under-layment 24 oc	Under-layment 20 oc	Under-layment 24 oc	Under-layment 24 oc
Douglas fir-Larch No. 1	2 × 6	11'0"	11'4"	10'6"	10'6"	9'5"
	2 × 8	14'3"	14'7"	13'7"	13'10"	12'5"
	2 × 10	17'11"	18'3"	17'0"	17'4"	15'10"
	2 × 12	21'7"	21'11"	20'6"	20'10"	19'3"
Douglas fir-Larch No. 2	2 × 6	10'6"	10'6"	9'7"	9'7"	8'7"
	2 × 8	13'10"	13'10"	12'7"	12'7"	11'3"
	2 × 10	17'7"	17'7"	16'1"	16'1"	14'5"
	2 × 12	21'3"	21'5"	19'7"	19'7"	17'6"
Douglas fir-South No. 1	2 × 6	10'4"	10'8"	9'11"	10'2"	9'1"
	2 × 8	13'4"	13'8"	12'8"	13'0"	12'0"
	2 × 10	16'8"	17'0"	15'11"	16'3"	15'4"
	2 × 12	20'1"	20'5"	19'1"	19'5"	18'4"
Douglas fir-South No. 2	2 × 6	10'1"	10'1"	9'3"	9'3"	8'3"
	2 × 8	13'1"	13'4"	12'2"	12'2"	10'11"
	2 × 10	16'4"	16'8"	15'6"	15'6"	13'11"
	2 × 12	19'8"	20'0"	18'8"	18'10"	16'11"
Hem-Fir No. 1	2 × 6	10'3"	10'3"	9'5"	9'5"	8'5"
	2 × 8	13'7"	13'7"	12'5"	12'5"	11'1"
	2 × 10	17'0"	17'4"	15'10"	15'10"	14'2"
	2 × 12	20'6"	20'10"	19'3"	19'3"	17'2"
Hem-Fir No. 2	2 × 6	9'4"	9'4"	8'6"	8'6"	7'7"
	2 × 8	12'4"	12'4"	11'3"	11'3"	10'0"
	2 × 10	15'8"	15'8"	14'4"	14'4"	12'10"
	2 × 12	19'1"	19'1"	17'5"	17'5"	15'7"
Mountain Hemlock No. 2	2 × 6	9'6"	9'6"	8'8"	8'8"	7'9"
	2 × 8	12'6"	12'7"	11'6"	11'6"	10'3"
	2 × 10	15'8"	16'0"	14'8"	14'8"	13'1"
	2 × 12	18'9"	19'2"	17'9"	17'9"	15'11"
Mountain Hemlock-Hem-Fir No. 2	2 × 6	9'4"	9'4"	8'6"	8'6"	7'7"
	2 × 8	12'4"	12'4"	11'3"	11'3"	10'0"
	2 × 10	15'8"	15'8"	14'4"	14'4"	12'10"
	2 × 12	18'9"	19'1"	17'5"	17'5"	15'7"
Western Hemlock No. 1	2 × 6	10'8"	10'10"	9'11"	9'11"	8'10"
	2 × 8	13'10"	14'1"	13'0"	13'0"	11'8"
	2 × 10	17'4"	17'8"	16'6"	16'7"	14'10"
	2 × 12	20'11"	21'2"	19'10"	20'2"	18'1"
Lodgepole Pine No. 2	2 × 6	8'11"	8'11"	8'2"	8'2"	7'3"
	2 × 8	11'9"	11'9"	10'9"	10'9"	9'7"

Table 5.11 (continued)

Species and grade of joist	Joist size	Joists @ 16" oc		Joists @ 19.2" oc		Joists @ 24" oc
		Underlayment 16 or 20 oc	Underlayment 24 oc	Underlayment 20 oc	Underlayment 24 oc	Underlayment 24 oc
	2 × 10	15'0"	15'0"	13'8"	13'8"	12'3"
	2 × 12	18'3"	18'3"	16'8"	16'8"	14'11"
Western Cedar	2 × 6	8'11"	8'11"	8'2"	8'2"	7'3"
No. 2	2 × 8	11'9"	11'9"	10'9"	10'9"	9'7"
	2 × 10	15'0"	15'0"	13'8"	13'8"	12'3"
	2 × 12	18'3"	18'3"	16'8"	16'8"	14'11"
Southern Pine	2 × 6	11'0"	11'4"	10'6"	10'10"	9'8"
KD15 No. 1	2 × 8	14'3"	14'7"	13'7"	13'11"	12'9"
	2 × 10	17'11"	18'3"	17'0"	17'4"	16'3"
	2 × 12	21'7"	21'11"	20'6"	20'10"	19'7"
Southern Pine	2 × 6	10'8"	10'8"	9'9"	9'9"	8'8"
KD15 No. 2	2 × 8	13'10"	14'0"	12'10"	12'10"	11'6"
	2 × 10	17'4"	17'8"	16'4"	16'4"	14'8"
	2 × 12	20'11"	21'2"	19'10"	19'11"	17'9"

[a]Based on live load of 40 lb/sq. ft, total load of 50 lb/sq. ft deflection limited to 1/360 at 40 lb/sq. ft.
[b]Glue tongue-and-groove joints. If square-edge panels are used, block panel edges and glue between panels and between panels and blocking.
Source: American Plywood Association.

k. Joists for bathroom floors must be set with care because they carry especially heavy loads and because plumbers are very apt to cut holes and notches in them indiscriminately to get their pipes in place. These joists should therefore be set in consultation with the plumbing foreman and should be cut only under the supervision of the carpenter foreman or the builder. Figure 5.28 shows a method of cutting holes for piping that weakens the joist only slightly. Holes may also be strengthened by reinforcing the adjoining areas with wood scabs or steel plates or shapes, securely nailed, screwed, or bolted.

PARTITION FRAMING

5.23 General

a. A partition is merely an interior wall. It is framed almost exactly the same as the exterior wall of the platform frame, i.e., it possesses a sole plate or sole, studs, and a top plate. Studs are usually 16" on center.

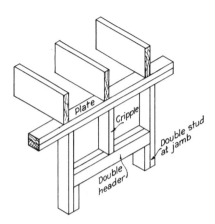

Figure 5.32 Framing above openings.

b. Partitions are either bearing or nonbearing — either they help support the joists above or they do not. In bearing partitions, the studs are 2 × 4s and the top plate is a doubled 2 × 4 (although a single 2 × 4 is sufficient if the joists bear on the plate directly above the studs). The studs of nonbearing partitions may be 2 × 3 or less, and closet partitions are often built with the studs set the 2″ way to save floor space. On the other hand, where waste pipes come down through partitions they may have to be framed with 2 × 6 studs or with 2 × 4 studs thickened with 2 × 2 strips.

c. Framing around door openings is the same as in the exterior walls; it consists of doubled studs at the sides and a header across the top (figure 5.32). For larger openings, the header is made deeper. Openings for doors are made 1″ to 2″ larger on each side to allow the door frames to be fitted in, squared, plumbed, blocked, and nailed. Manufacturers specify rough opening sizes.

d. The simplest way to build partitions is to put down the subfloor over the entire floor area, then assemble the partitions — sole, studs, plate, and all — on the floor and raise them into place. The sole may be put down first and the rest of the partition set on top of it, particularly in the case of nonbearing partitions erected after upper-floor joists are in place.

e. In platform framing, it is best to have all partitions built in the same manner as the outside walls — that is, starting with a sole on top of the subfloor and ending with a plate under the joists above. If, in addition, first-floor joists rest on ledgers at the girders, shrinkage is

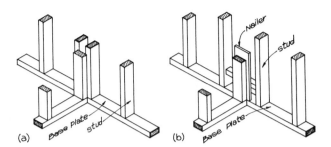

Figure 5.33 Intersection of partitions and walls to provide support for interior wall finish. (a) Paired studs. (b) Nailer and blocking between studs.

practically equalized throughout the structure. No matter what the framing, the moisture content of the lumber ought to be as close as possible to the final condition to avoid settlement caused by subsequent shrinkage.

f. Where partitions adjoin other partitions or exterior walls so as to form an internal corner, as shown in figure 5.33, it is necessary to provide nailing for wallboard or lath, just as it is at the corner posts. The two most commonly used methods are shown. Type a is preferred. Type b is an excellent method provided adequate blocking, securely nailed to the two adjacent wall studs, is provided behind the nailer; otherwise, the nailer is likely to work loose and allow cracks to open at the corner. Tops of partitions which run parallel to the joists above are often provided with a nailer much the same as that shown in figure 5.33b, except, of course, that the nailer is fastened to the plate and blocking is between adjacent joists above.

STAIR FRAMING

5.24 General

During framing, it is necessary to allow openings in the floors for the stair wells and to provide framing for any landings that may be desired. Rough stairs are commonly built at this time to allow ready access from floor to floor until the finished stairs can be installed.

Stair construction will be discussed in detail in chapter 13.

5.25 Openings

Ordinary rectangular openings in floors for stair wells are framed with the usual headers and trimmers (figures 5.25, 5.26). If the opening contains an angle (figures 5.34, 5.35), the corner may be supported in

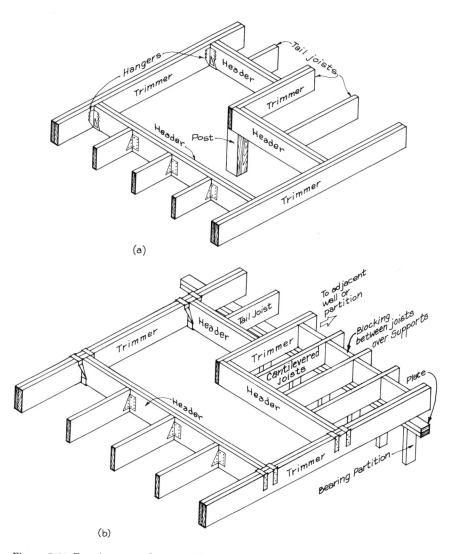

(a)

(b)

Figure 5.34 Framing around rectangular stair openings, with headers supported (a) by nailed hangers and (b) by older-style strap hangers. In diagram a the corner is supported by a post; in b the corner framing is supported by cantilever joists.

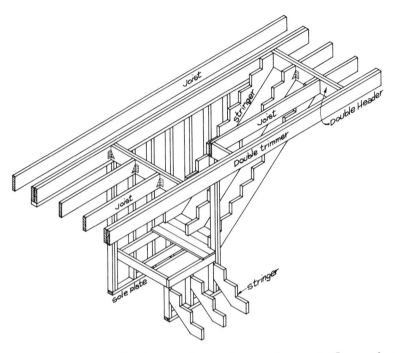

Figure 5.35 Stairway framing, showing landing, rough supports, floor, and partition.

a number of different ways:

a. Post. Where a header and a trimmer intersect, a post is inserted below to carry the load. The post may be free standing, or may form part of a partition (figure 5.34a). This is generally the easiest and most satisfactory method.

b. Cantilever. If the angle is close to a partition below, and joists from an adjacent span can be run out far enough to frame the angle, cantilevering (figure 5.34b) is possible. A projecting structure such as this tends to deflect more than if it is supported from below. Occasionally a corner is supported by a rod or wood tension member suspended from above.

5.26 Landings

Landings (small floors intermediate between main floors) serve to break the continuity of stairs, either in a straight run or in a turn. Landings are supported by adjacent partitions, usually by nailing but occasionally by resting the ends of landing joists on horizontal intermediate plates provided in the partition framing.

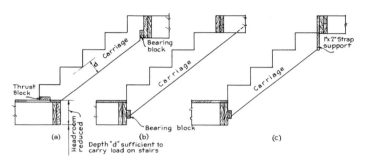

Figure 5.36 Rough stringers or carriages for stairs.

5.27 Stringers

a. The structural support for finished stairs is usually provided by rough carriages, also called *stringers* and *horses*, running from floor to floor, floor to landing, or landing to landing. Stringers are cut to the profile of the undersides of risers and treads (chapter 13), and enough are provided to carry the load. For the usual 3'-wide stair, when built in place rather than in a shop, this generally means three stringers: two near the edges of the stair and one at the center.

b. Stringers or carriages are framed into floors and landings in various ways, of which several are shown in figure 5.36. Of these, the type shown in diagram a is in many ways the simplest and best. The lower end of the carriage bears directly on the floor and is prevented from moving by the thrust block. The upper end bears directly against the framing of the floor or the landing. The objection to it is that the headroom may not be adequate at the bottom of the stair because the floor or landing framing projects downward. In a landing at a right-angle turn, it is difficult to use this type of framing at the interior corner. Consequently, the types shown in diagrams b and c are favored for built-in-place stairs. In shop-built stairs, the carriages are part of the finished stair structure, and the difficulties pointed out above largely disappear (chapter 13).

c. Figure 5.35 shows a typical framed stairwell with floor framing, landing partition, and stair stringers.

5.28 Partitions

Stairs may be enclosed between partitions, or they may be open (with one or both sides exposed). If open, they may be completely exposed, or partitions may be carried up from below to the undersides of the carriages on the open side. In the latter instance, both sides of the stairway are supported throughout its length — desirable in any stairway containing landings. If such support is not available, the outside carriages and stringers (outer edge of stairs into which risers and treads are fitted) must be strong enough to carry the stairs from floor to floor — a somewhat difficult task when breaks in the continuity of carriages and stringers occur at landings. In any event, the unbroken depth of the carriage (figure 5.36, distance d) must be great enough to carry the load on the stair.

ROOF FRAMING

5.29 General

Although the function of a roof is to protect the house from the elements, it also adds greatly to its appearance. Its shape is therefore dictated both by climatic and by architectural considerations. With the increasing efficiency of roofing materials, however, the climatic considerations are becoming less important. Traditionally, low flat roofs have been used in warm climates where only water has to be shed, and steep roofs have been used in cold climates in order to shed snow as well as water.

5.30 Types

Roofs may take many shapes, but the most commonly found are the following:
shed or lean-to
gable
hip
gambrel
mansard
deck

5.31 Parts of a Roof

a. Roof plate. Already discussed under wall framing, this is the double member that rests on top of the studs.
b. Ridge. The peak of the roof. It is found on all but shed and deck roofs. The *ridge board* or *ridge pole* is the member against which the rafters bear. It forms the lateral tie that holds them together at that point. In a hip roof over a square house the ridge dwindles to a point.

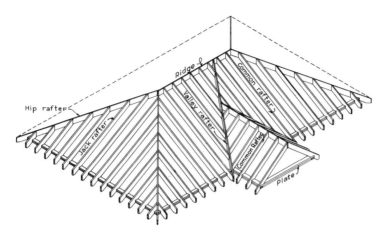

Figure 5.37 Framing members in hip roof.

c. Eaves. The lowest part of the roof. It is the section formed by the rafter ends, the plate, and the cornice.

d. Cornice. The ornamental detail found at the juncture of the roof and the wall. It is made up of a combination of moldings and boards, and usually includes the gutter as a part of its design (chapter 9).

e. Rafters. The structural members of the roof. They correspond to the joists in the floors, and carry all the loads, whether dead, snow, or wind. Like the joists, they must be designed to perform this function satisfactorily, but unlike the joists, deflection is usually not a prime consideration. For long rafters, in which deflection rather than strength may be the controlling consideration, L/180 is often taken as limiting. (Codes differ.) Common rafters run from the ridge to the plate at right angles to the wall. At the intersections (hips) of the roof planes of a hip roof are found hip rafters, running from the exterior corners of the plate to the ends of the ridge. Framing into the hips are shorter rafters, running from plate to hip rafter, called *jack rafters*. Jack rafters are short rafters of any kind which do not run the full length from plate to ridge. They may run from ridge to hip, plate to hip, ridge to valley, valley to plate, or hip to valley. Jack rafters are, therefore, found on any kind of roof that is broken up in some manner (figure 5.37).

f. Hip. The intersection of two roofs which meet at an exterior angle of the building. The roofs slope down and away from the hip in each direction.

g. Valley. The intersection of two roofs which meet at an interior angle of the building. The roofs slope down toward the valley from each direction.

h. Purlin. The intersection of the two slopes of a gambrel roof. The name is also applied to the horizontal member that forms the support for the rafters at that point. More generally, a purlin is a member spanning roof supports, such as a roof beam running from truss to truss and, in turn, supporting rafters or planking.

5.32 Pitch

The "pitch" of a roof is its slope. It may be expressed in a variety of ways. The most obvious is to express the slope in degrees, i.e., the size of the angle which the roof makes with the horizontal. This is seldom done, however, because in practice it is cumbersome. More commonly, pitch is expressed as a ratio. The units used to express the pitch are the rise and the run. The rise is the vertical projection of the slope (sine of the angle); the run is the horizontal projection (cosine of the angle). Evidently the pitch can be expressed easily and unmistakably as a ratio of rise to run, and this is most commonly done. For convenience, the rise is always expressed as a certain number of inches per foot of run. Thus, a rise of 6″ means that the roof rises 6″ for each 12″ that it runs horizontally; the pitch is 6 to 12.

5.33 Analysis and Framing

a. Loads are primarily vertical (caused by gravity) and lateral (primarily wind; in some areas, earthquake; in others, flood). Vertical loads are usually classified as dead (caused by the weight of the building) or live or movable (exemplified by people, furniture, and snow).

b. Figure 5.38 illustrates vertical loads (P) and lateral loads (W) acting on roofs of various configurations. Wind causes pressure on vertical surfaces, inward or positive on the windward side and outward or negative on the leeward side. Wind blowing across horizontal surfaces causes uplift, or negative pressure. On sloping surfaces, upward forces on windward surfaces diminish with increasing slope, becoming positive as the slope increases, but negative (uplift) on leeward surfaces.

c. Shed. The shed roof, as its name implies, is merely a single inclined plane. It may cover the main structure, or it may cover an ell which adjoins a higher structure (in which case the term *lean-to* is more appropriate). Many so-called flat roofs are actually shed roofs

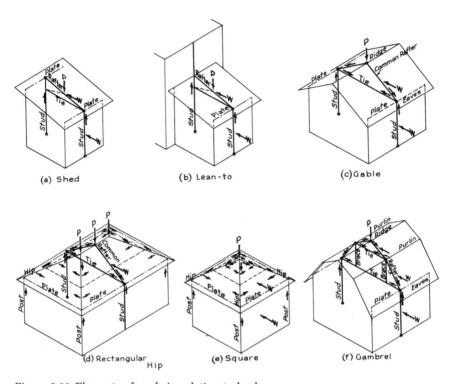

Figure 5.38 Elements of roofs in relation to loads.

with a very small slope to shed water and prevent "ponding." Ponding is to be avoided unless water is wanted on the roof for cooling purposes.

d. In figure 5.38a, a vertical load *P* is seen to induce vertical reactions in the studs. Under a lateral load *W*, such as wind, the frame (consisting of studs and rafter) would distort if there were no roof to act as a stiff diaphragm to transmit the load to stiff end walls or interior partitions. A ceiling joist acting as a tie would also impart stability, by inducing bending in the stud, which would have to be strong enough and continuous (e.g., by being supported on a ribbon, as in figure 5.39a). Essentially the same considerations hold true of the lean-to show in figure 5.39b, except that lateral loads (such as wind) may be transferred to the main structure. Figure 5.39 shows several ways of framing shed and lean-to roofs.

e. Gable. The gable roof consists of two inclined planes which meet in a peak over the center line of the house and slope down to two

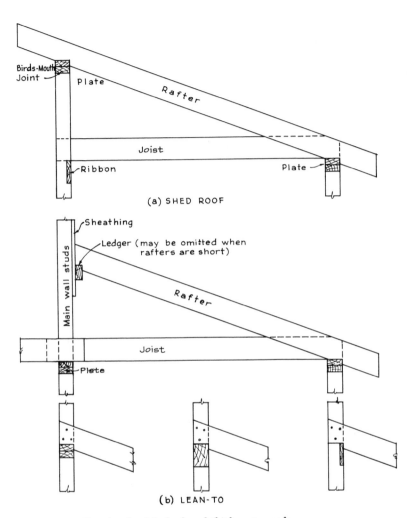

Figure 5.39 Framing for (a) shed and (b) lean-to roofs.

opposite roof plates. At the two ends are triangular sections of wall called *gables* or *gable-ends*. When a vertical load P acts on the roof, the rafters tend to push out at the eaves and to displace the studs unless some kind of tie is provided. Generally, the attic floor joists are oriented in this direction and provide the necessary tie, as shown in figure 5.40.

f. The outward thrust of the rafter may be large. It must be securely nailed to the side of the attic floor joist, or to the plate, which in turn must be well nailed to transmit the thrust to the attic floor joist. Similarly, where attic floor joists lap at the interior bearing partition, they must be securely nailed to each other, or to the partition cap, or be spliced together. When trussed rafters (o below) are employed, the upper chords act as rafters and the lower chords as horizontal ties.

g. The stud-rafter-joist combination is unstable against lateral loads, such as winds. These must be resisted by the end walls (braced, plywood, rigid wallboard, or diagonally sheathed) and by interior partitions. Floors act as stiffening diaphragms.

h. The triangular cut commonly made in the rafter to allow it to rest on the plate is known as a *bird's mouth joint* and is illustrated in figures 5.39–5.41. It provides bearing on the plate and allows for toe-nailing. The projection beyond the plate depends upon the cornice detail which is ultimately to be built around the rafter ends. The cut at the upper end depends upon the pitch of the roof. In order to allow the entire area of this cut to bear against the ridge board, the latter must be made deep enough to equal the length of the cut.

i. The ridge board may be omitted, but it helps to line up the peak, which otherwise may be crooked. Frequently the board is a 1″ piece, but 2″ stock is more likely to keep the ridge straight. Two-inch-thick ridge boards may or may not be chamfered at the top (figure 5.41).

j. Wind blowing across a roof usually exerts downward pressure on the windward side and an upward pull on the leeward side because of the reduced atmospheric pressure to leeward. Where winds are heavy, it is, therefore, not enough to attach the roof to the house in such a manner as to resist the downward pressure; it must also be anchored against uplift, which tends to raise the roof off the plates and to pull the two sides of the roof apart at the ridge. This is accomplished by collar ties below the ridge and various kinds of grip plates at the eaves (figure 5.40).

k. Collar ties (figure 5.40) are short pieces of 2 × 4 or 1 × 6 or 1 × 8

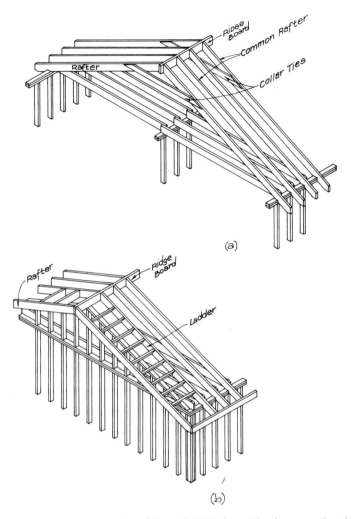

Figure 5.40 Framing for gable roof. (a) Rafter, ridge beam, and ceiling joist resting on wall plate. (b) Framing for overhanging end.

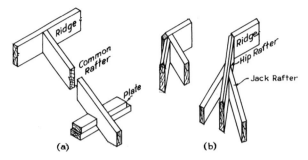

Figure 5.41 Details of roof framing. (a) Rafter to ridge and plate. (b) Rafter to hip and ridge.

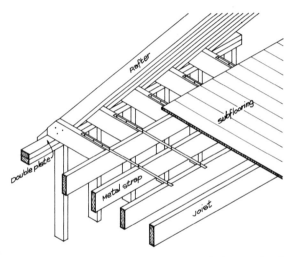

Figure 5.42 Framing to absorb outward thrust of rafters, with ceiling joists parallel to wall.

nailed to the sides of pairs of rafters some distance below the ridge. They tie the pairs of rafters together and prevent them from pulling apart in a high wind. They reduce the clear span of the rafters and thereby reduce the sizes which must be used. They also reduce the outward thrust of the rafters at the eaves.

l. If the attic is finished, collar ties are placed at ceiling height and form the ceiling joists. In gambrel roofs, they have the further important function of serving as horizontal ties to resist the outward thrust of the upper rafters at the purlins (figure 5.43).

m. If ceiling joists run parallel with the walls instead of at right an-

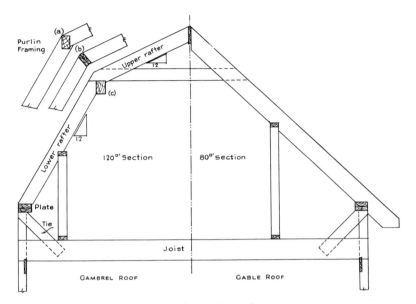

Figure 5.43 Sections of gambrel and gable roofs.

gles, some other means of absorbing the outward thrust of the rafters must be provided. One method is shown in figure 5.42. Short lengths of joists are brought against the sides of the rafters at the plate and butted against the side of a joist. Steel straps tie the two together. Subflooring assists in transmitting the thrust into the floor by acting as a diaphragm.

n. A projecting gable may be framed as shown in figure 5.40b. A "ladder" is built of short "lookout" rafters framing into the side of the end rafter and resting on the gable wall, in turn framed with short studs resting on the wall plate.

o. Gable rafters are often prefabricated into trussed rafters, as shown in figure 5.44. These are preassembled in the shop, sent to the site, and erected quickly, in contrast to the often awkward task of hoisting and assembling pairs of rafters to a plate and ridge. The sizes of rafters (top chords), ceiling joists (bottom chords), and diagonals depend upon the span, but are most commonly all 2 × 4 for the usually encountered spans, with 2 × 6 not unusual for top chords. Connections are most commonly made by means of steel plate connectors, a few of which are shown in figure 5.45. These have claws or prongs stamped integrally from the sheet. They are usually pressed into the

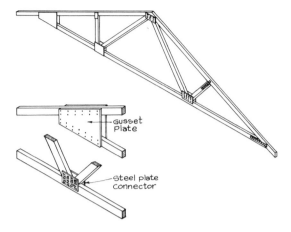

Figure 5.44 (top) A trussed rafter. (bottom) A glued and nailed plywood gusset and a steel plate connector.

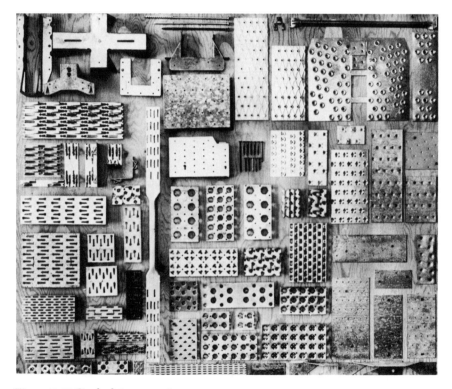

Figure 5.45 Steel plate connectors.

wood, on each side of the joint, in the assembly jig. Glued and nailed plywood gussets are also employed (figure 5.44a).

p. Hip. When a roof slopes down in four inclined planes to four plates, it is called a *hip roof*. The plan may be rectangular or square (figures 5.37, 5.38d,e).

q. A vertical load applied to the peak of a square hip roof is distributed among the four hips, and the vertical components are transmitted to the corner posts. Any spreading tendency caused by the horizontal components is taken up by the skin of the roof (roof boards). No lateral ties are theoretically required, because the roof is a self-contained unit. Actually, the attic joists do provide a lateral tie in one direction. In the opposite direction on large roofs it may be advisable to employ knee braces or ties on the longest jack rafters.

r. The end portions of a rectangular hip roof behave in the same way as the square hip just described. The central portion behaves and is framed in the same manner as a gable roof.

s. The framing of the intersection of the hip, the ridge, and the common rafter is shown in figure 5.41. Jack rafter cuts are also shown.

t. Hip rafters carry no appreciable bending load and need, therefore, not be especially heavy. Two-inch stock is preferable to keep the hip line straight and to provide nailing. Hip rafters may or may not be chamfered on top.

u. Gambrel. Unlike the gable, which is two inclined planes running from peak to plate, the gambrel roof consists of four inclined planes, two on each side of the peak, the upper plane on each side fairly flat and the lower one fairly steep (figures 5.38f, 5.43).

v. A vertical load P applied as shown in figure 5.38f induces a tendency to spread at the lower ends of both upper and lower rafters. Ties are therefore required at both points, and usually consist of collar ties (simultaneously acting as ceiling joists) and second-floor joists. So tied, the frame is in equilibrium under vertical loads, but tends to collapse under lateral loads, such as winds, unless vertical braces, such as those shown, are provided.

w. From a utilitarian standpoint, the chief advantage of the gambrel roof is the additional space it provides at no increase in the height of the ridge as compared with the gable. This is especially true of headroom, which occupies a much larger portion of the usable space under a gambrel than under a gable roof. The two sections shown in figure 5.43 have the same rise and span, but the gambrel has 50 percent more useful space than the gable.

x. Purlins may be framed so as to be completely enclosed by rafter ends (figure 5.43a,b) or may be exposed underneath (c). The latter is frequently supported by partition studs and may merely be the cap of a partition. The purlin shown at b is simpler than either a or c, may be either solid or built up as shown, and behaves much as if it were a secondary ridge board.

y. Mansard. If a gambrel roof is visualized as running up from all four plates, instead of from two, and if the lower plane on each side is made very steep while the upper is very flat, the result is a *mansard* roof. This type was commonly used on the mansions built in the late nineteenth century and was often varied by flaring out the lower slopes in a sharp curve.

z. Deck. The *deck roof* is merely a hip roof with the top sliced off and a flat platform substituted. It was often used on large houses with steep roofs where the roof would otherwise have been high. The dotted lines in figure 5.38e show the relationship of hip and deck roofs.

5.34 Ells

a. Roofs over ells are framed in the same manner as the main roof, with ridge board, common and jack rafters, and so forth. Usually, however, the ell is not as wide as the main house; its roof does not rise so high as does the main roof, and its ridge consequently ends against the side of the main roof instead of joining the main ridge.

b. Two ways of making the juncture between main and ell roofs are possible. If the ell is small and there is no reason why its attic space should be accessible or continuous with the main attic, the main roof rafters can all be carried down to the plate, the roof boards on the main roof carried beyond the point of intersection of the main and ell roofs, and the ell roof merely rested on top of the main roof by fastening valley members (2 × 4 pieces are usually sufficiently large) on top of the main roof and allowing the ell's valley jacks to frame into the valley members. If, on the other hand, the ell is quite large and its attic space is to be continuous with the main attic, a valley rafter is first framed full length from plate to ridge of the main roof as shown in figure 5.37 and a secondary valley rafter on the other side is brought from main roof plate to the first valley rafter. Jack rafters from both roofs then frame against these valley rafters, the ell roof framing is completed, and roof boards are carried into the valleys from both main and ell roofs.

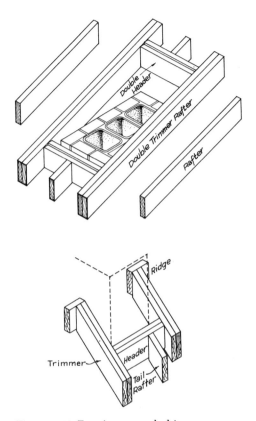

Figure 5.46 Framing around chimneys.

c. Valley rafters, unlike ridge and hip rafters, must withstand the downward thrust of the two portions of roof which frame into the valley, and must therefore be of heavy material. Usually they are made quite deep (2 × 10, or 2 × 12 on medium-size roofs), and they may be doubled on larger roofs. Where the spans are long, they may be given additional interior support by posts resting on bearing partitions below.

5.35 Framing around Openings

This is essentially the same as the framing around openings in walls and floors. The rafters at the two sides of the openings are doubled and are, therefore, trimmer rafters. Across the ends of the opening are placed doubled headers. The rafters that frame into the headers are called *header rafters* or *tail rafters*. If the opening is at the ridge, the two sets of trimmers react against each other at the ridge the same as do pairs of rafters.

5.36 Dormers

a. Whenever it is necessary to have a vertical wall rising out of a roof, the construction by which this is accomplished is known as a *dormer*. Usually dormers are employed to allow windows in the attic space, and such windows are called *dormer windows*.

b. Most dormers are quite small, and provision for them is most easily made by framing a rectangular opening in the main roof in the same manner as for chimneys, i.e., by the trimmer-header combination. Within this opening are erected three walls — two sides and one front — which are framed the same as any wall, with a sole resting on the attic floor, studs running from the sole to a plate, and a plate which supports the dormer roof. Sometimes, instead of starting at a sole set on the floor, side wall studs are rested directly on the double trimmer rafters, and front wall studs are rested on the double header at the bottom of the opening. Sometimes, also, some of the side wall studs start at the floor and others are cut off below the trimmer. This detail depends upon the architectural treatment of the attic space, which may or may not be finished. The opening for the window in the front wall is framed the same as any window opening, with double studs at the sides (trimmers) and headers top and bottom. Where space is restricted, the plate across the front may at the same time form the upper header for the window opening.

c. The dormer roof consists of the same parts as any other roof and may be either gable or hip. Figure 5.47 is a detail of a gable roof. The rafters rest on the plates, the ridge ends at the main roof, and ceiling joists span from one side wall plate to the other. This type of construction gives a flat dormer ceiling.

d. If a peaked ceiling is desired, the upper header in the original opening in the main roof is framed higher, beyond the dormer ridge board, and two short valley rafters are inserted below it, running from the center of the header to the two side trimmers. The dormer ceiling joists are omitted and the wall finish is carried up under the dormer rafters.

e. Large dormers are framed in essentially the same way as small except that instead of using two headers in the original opening in the main roof the upper header is left out and a pair of valley rafters

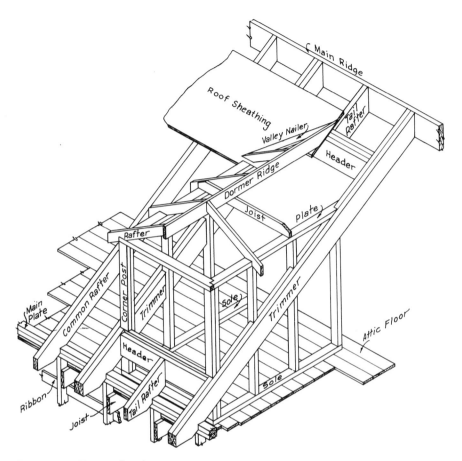

Figure 5.47 Dormer framing.

inserted, one running from trimmer to main ridge and the second from trimmer to the first valley rafter. This is the same framing as the second type described for ell roofs (figure 5.37).

5.37 Roof Boards

a. The manner in which roof boards are put on depends upon the kind of roofing which is to be applied. Usually the roof is tight-sheathed, that is, roof boards, when used, are driven up tightly against each other, or plywood or other board is employed. Unlike walls and floors, roof boards are not laid on a diagonal. They are laid with broken (staggered) joints, all joints are made at the rafters, and they are securely nailed with two 8d or 10d nails per board per rafter. The first board is started at the eaves, is nailed down tight and straight, and the others follow until the ridge is reached, where the top boards from both sides are cut off on a straight line along the ridge.

b. An exception to this procedure is a roof which is to be covered with wood shingles or shakes (chapter 8). Since wood rots when kept continually damp, and since rain water manages to work under shingles at least to a slight extent, sufficient ventilation should be provided under wood shingles to dry any dampness as quickly as possible. This is most easily done by spacing the roof boards apart several inches. In this case, square-edged strips, usually approximately 3″ wide, are nailed to the rafters and are spaced center to center a distance equal to the amount which the shingles are subsequently to be exposed to the weather.

c. Plywood and reconstituted wood panels are commonly employed for roof sheathing. They are similarly started at the eaves and carried on up to the ridge. Because they are made in 2′ multiples, rafters and trussed rafters are customarily spaced 2′ on centers, occasionally 12″ with thin (e.g., $\frac{3}{8}$″) panels. End joints are offset (staggered) so as not to have adjacent joints on the same support. Table 5.12 gives values, loads, and spans. Edge blocking, tongue and groove, or panel clips are employed to support panel edges if spans are greater than tabulated. Panels should be spaced $\frac{1}{8}$″ apart at edges and ends.

5.38 Roofing Paper

a. Roof boards are covered with roofing paper or felt to provide a surface tight against rains. This paper should be a good quality paper, applied so as to give a watertight roof. (A "square" in roofers' language is 100 sq ft.) This is accomplished by starting at the eaves and applying the paper in layers, each layer overlapping the preceding one by at least 2″, and all securely nailed with flat-headed roofers' nails or staples every 6″ along the edges. End laps should be at least 3″.

b. If there is any likelihood that the roof will not be covered with the final roofing for some time and the paper may be subjected to high winds, the nails can be driven through metal discs or caps which hold the paper much more firmly and with less likelihood of tearing than would be true of nails alone. Reinforced paper, similarly, is more resistant to tearing (chapter 8).

Table 5.12[e,f] Recommended Uniform Live Loads for PS-1 Plywood Roof Sheathing with Long Dimension Perpendicular to Supports[d] (Rated Sheathing and Structural I and II Rated Sheathing Marked PS-1)

Span rating	Plywood thickness (in.)	Maximum span (in.)	Unsupported edge-max. length (in.)	Recommended live loads (lb/sq. ft)[a] Spacing of supports center-to-center (in.)									
				12	16	20	24	30	32	36	40	48	60
12/0	$\frac{5}{16}$	12	12	125									
16/0	$\frac{5}{16}$, $\frac{3}{8}$	16	16	135	65								
20/0	$\frac{5}{16}$, $\frac{3}{8}$	20	20	165	90	55							
24/0	$\frac{3}{8}$, $\frac{1}{2}$	24	20, 24[b]	230	125	85	50						
32/16	$\frac{15}{32}$, $\frac{1}{2}$, $\frac{5}{8}$	32	28	325	180	120	75	40	35				
40/20	$\frac{19}{32}$, $\frac{5}{8}$, $\frac{3}{4}$, $\frac{7}{8}$	40	32		325	225	135	70	60	45	35		
48/24	$\frac{23}{32}$, $\frac{3}{4}$, $\frac{7}{8}$	48	36			280	175	110	95	55	45	35	
2-4-1[c]	$1\frac{1}{8}$	72	48				375	235	205	125	100	65	40
1-1/8" Grp. 1 and 2	$1\frac{1}{8}$	72	48				290	185	160	95	75	50	30

[a]Values based on 10 psf dead load.
[b]Maximum unsupported length 20 inches for 3/8-inch plywood, 24 inches for 1/2-inch plywood.
[c]2-4-1 is synonymous with APA Rated Sturd-I-Floor 48 o.c.
[d]When roofing is to be guaranteed by a performance bond, check with roofing manufacturer for minimum thickness, span and edge support requirements.
[e]Use 6d common, smooth, ring-shank, or spiral-thread nails for $\frac{1}{2}$" thick or less, and 8d common, smooth, ring-shank, or spiral-thread for plywood 1" thick or less. Use 8d ring-shank or spiral-thread or 10d common smooth-shank nails for 2·4·1, $1\frac{1}{8}$" panels. Space nails 6" at panel edges and 12" at intermediate supports, except that where spans are 48" or more, nails shall be 6" at all supports.
[f]Uniform load deflection limitation: $\frac{1}{180}$ of the span under live load plus dead load, $\frac{1}{240}$ under live load only.
Source: American Plywood Association.

Table 5.13 Recommended Uniform Loads (lb/sq. ft) for Nonveneer Rated Sheathing with Long Dimension Parallel to Supports[a]

Thickness (in.)	Span rating	Maximum span (in.)	Number and length of span					
			Four @ 12"		Three @ 16"		Two @ 24"	
			Live ld.	Total ld.	Live ld.	Total ld.	Live ld.	Total ld.
$\frac{7}{16}$	24/0, 24/16	16	155	240	50			
$\frac{15}{32}$, $\frac{1}{2}$, $\frac{9}{16}$	32/16	24[b]	185	245	60	85	25	30
$\frac{5}{8}$	40/20	24			135	175	50	65

[a]When roofing is to be guaranteed by a performance bond, check with roofing manufacturer for panel type, minimum panel thickness, span, and edge-support requirements.
[b]Solid blocking recommended at 24" span.
Source: American Plywood Association.

IN-LINE FRAMING AND POST, PLANK, AND
BEAM CONSTRUCTION

5.39 In-Line Framing

a. When large standard-size sheets such as plywood are employed for subflooring, sheathing, and roof boards, it is desirable to frame the house in such a way as to eliminate as much cutting of the wallboard as possible, to save on waste and labor. This makes it desirable to have all framing members — joists, studs, and rafters — in line and at such spacings that ends of wallboard sheets fall on framing members. With plywood or reconstituted wood board of the proper thickness for subflooring, sheathing, and roofboards, framing members are customarily placed 24″ on centers.

b. The basic platform frame plus trussed rafters or spliced rafter-ceiling joist connections makes such in-line framing possible if joists are also framed in-line instead of lapped, as is customary.

c. Figure 5.48 shows such in-line framing. Floor joists are set in line with their ends butted and resting on an intermediate girder as shown at a. Metal or wood splices tie the joists together.

d. However, an alternative method of framing shown at b provides better continuity by having the joists cantilevered over the girder alternately from one side and the other, and making the splice at an intermediate point. This is best done at approximately one-third to one-quarter span, because the bending moment approaches zero and only shear must be resisted by the splice. This construction makes the joist continuous over the intermediate girder, and considerably reduces deflection, which is often the controlling factor in selecting joist sizes (table 5.6). Splices may be metal or plywood, the latter best nail-glued.

e. Lightweight I-shaped joists (section 5.3t) are available in lengths long enough to span from foundation wall to foundation wall (figure 5.48b). Web stiffeners may be needed at bearings or at other loading points.

5.40 Post, Plank, and Beam Construction

a. Instead of the multiplicity of joists and rafters found in standard framing, in post, plank, and beam construction planks, usually of nominal 2″ and 3″ thickness, are supported on beams spaced usually 4′ to 8′ apart. These beams, in turn, are supported on posts or piers.

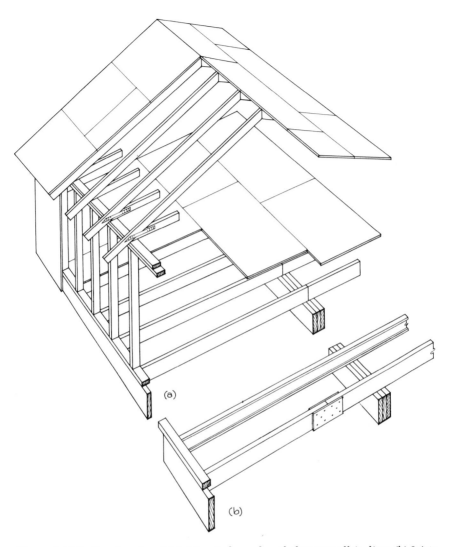

Figure 5.48 In-line framing. (a) Joists, studs, and roof elements all in line. (b) Joists made continuous by cantilevering and joining with splice plates, or utilizing long-span I joists.

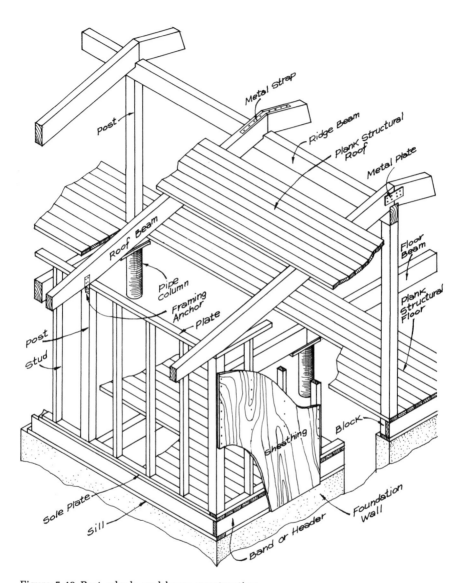

Figure 5.49 Post, plank, and beam construction.

Spaces between posts are filled in with studs or other framing as necessary to provide support for the enclosure. Stressed-skin or stressed-cover panels (section 5.45) find use in such walls. Partitions, likewise, are similar in construction to standard partitions with some exceptions. The supplementary framing in walls provides the lateral stability necessary against lateral loads such as winds. If partitions are tied into the main structure, they also provide such lateral stability in a manner similar to standard construction.

b. To take full advantage of the simplicity of plank and beam construction, it is desirable to carry out the design of the house with this type of construction in mind from the very beginning, rather than to try to adapt it after the design has been worked out. Windows and doors, for example, are best located between posts in exterior walls. Usually the wide spaces between posts are ample for this purpose. There must, however, be sufficient solid walls to provide the necessary lateral bracing. With a little forethought, it is possible to combine conventional and plank and beam framing.

c. The principal advantage of the system is its simplicity, leading to fewer members, which, in turn, can reduce the amount of labor required. A further advantage from the architectural standpoint frequently lies in the exposed plank and beam ceiling, which is often considered aesthetically pleasing and also provides higher ceilings than is true of joists and rafters covered with interior finish on their lower edges. The heavier flooring and framing members also lead to increased resistance to fire.

d. Limitations associated with plank and beam framing include the lack of concealed spaces for wiring and piping or duct work. Wiring and piping can sometimes be accommodated by making the beams of two pieces spaced apart to accommodate the wires and pipes (figure 5.50). A soffit board fastened to the bottoms of the two members can be used to conceal that space.

e. The planks employed in plank and beam framing are for moderate, distributed loads and not for heavy concentrated loads such as bathtubs, refrigerators, bearing partitions and similar loads. Where these occur, additional framing is needed under the planks to transmit these loads to the beams.

f. Where insulation is needed, it can be placed between the beams, but in that case, the lower surfaces of the planks are concealed and insulation is in view. The alternative is to place the insulation above

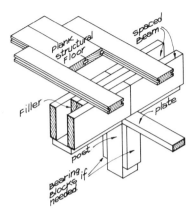

Figure 5.50 Spaced beam with post and plank.

the roof planks, in which case it should be rigid and capable of supporting the roofing material. Furthermore, a vapor barrier between the insulation and the planks is highly desirable (chapter 11).

5.41 Construction Details

a. Foundations for plank and beam construction may be continuous as shown in figure 5.49, or individual piers may be employed to support the posts and the ends of beams.

b. Posts must be adequate in size to carry the loads and should, in any event, be at least 4 × 4 in cross section or two 2 × 4s securely nailed together. Where the ends of beams abut and rest on a post, there should be at least 6″ of bearing parallel to the beams. This may be obtained by making at least one dimension of the post 6″, if solid, or by fastening at least three 2″ members together, or by using a plate at the top of the post to support the beams (figure 5.50).

c. The sizes of beams depend upon the spans and the loads being carried by them. Many building codes require, in addition to the dead load, a live load of 40 lb per sq ft on floors, and 20 to 40 lb per sq ft on roofs, depending upon the local climate. Beams may be laminated (section 5.18, figure 5.24) or one piece. They must be of sufficient structural quality to carry the loads.

d. Fastenings of beams to posts are usually accomplished by means of framing anchors or angle clips, nailed, bolted, or lag-screwed to the timbers (figures 5.49, 5.51).

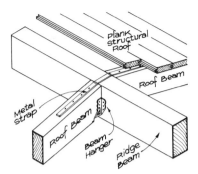

Figure 5.51 Roof beam framed to side of ridge, tied with metal strap.

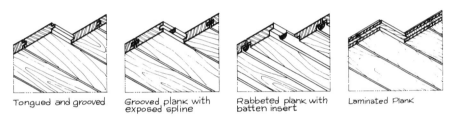

Tongued and grooved   Grooved plank with   Rabbeted plank with   Laminated Plank
                       exposed spline   batten insert

Figure 5.52 Types of planks.

e. The planks may be square-edged, but usually are matched in some way such as by means of tongue-and-groove, splines, or rabbetted battens, as shown in figure 5.52. Because planks are frequently exposed, it is highly desirable to have their moisture content at the time of installation as closely as possible matching the moisture content in actual use. This will avoid excessive shrinkage and opening of unsightly cracks at the joints between planks.

f. Planking may be laminated by gluing two or more nominal 1"-thick boards together. When three boards are employed to provide nominal 3"-thick planking, the center board or lamination can be shifted slightly sidewise to provide a tongue along one edge and a groove along the other. Furthermore, the center lamination can be shifted longitudinally to provide a tongue at one end and a groove at the other (figure 5.52). Among the advantages of glued-laminated planking are the fact that knots and other blemishes do not penetrate through the entire thickness, the thin boards before laminating are easily dried to a low moisture content (must be for successful gluing), and better-quality stock can be placed on the outside. The principal disadvantage is the cost of labor and materials as compared to "solid" unglued planking.

g. It is highly desirable to have planks continuous over more than one span to increase the stiffness of the floor. The plank that rests only on its ends will deflect approximately $2\frac{1}{2}$ times as much as a plank that is continuous over two spans. From the standpoint of appearance, it is probably best to have all joints between planks made over beams, but random lengths can be employed with joints coming between beams. In this case, it is essential that planks be matched by splines, tongue-and-groove, or similar means. End-matching, i.e., tongue-and-groove at the ends of planks as well as at the sides, is highly desirable.

h. Finish flooring should be laid at right angles to the directions of the planks, and if the planks are exposed below, care should be taken that the nailing for the finished floors does not penetrate through the planks.

i. Instead of plank, the floor may be heavy plywood or reconstituted board such as the $1\frac{1}{8}''$ thick plywood described under Subflooring (section 5.22, table 5.9). If the plywood is left exposed on the underside, a grade and group must be specified that has high-quality surface veneer at least on one side.

j. Most partitions in plank and beam construction are non-bearing because loads are supported on beams, in turn resting on posts. If bearing partitions occur, they are best placed directly over beams, which must be large enough to carry the additional load. If bearing partitions cannot be supported on the principal beams, supplementary beams are needed to support them.

k. If non-bearing partitions run at right angles to the direction of the planks, no additional support is necessary underneath them. Non-bearing partitions that run parallel to planks, however, should have additional support. This can easily be provided by a pair of 2 × 4s laid on edge. If this is not possible because of door openings, the 2 × 4 supporting members can be placed under the plank and, in turn, supported at their ends by framing anchors fastened to principal beams. This type of construction is shown in figure 5.53.

l. As figure 5.49 shows, a convenient method of handling roof framing is to utilize sloping beams resting on a ridge beam, in turn supported by posts. Roof beams may rest on top of ridge beams or may be framed into the sides and supported by beam hangers (figure 5.51). Metal

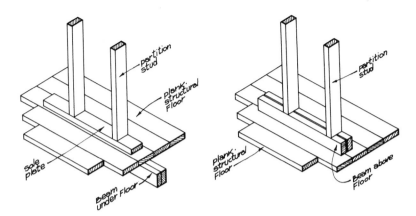

Figure 5.53 Supplemental support for partitions: double sole placed under or over floor plank.

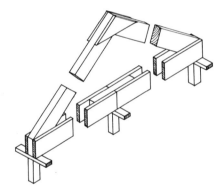

Figure 5.54 Roof beams and spaced ceiling beam.

straps across the top are desirable to provide a tie at this point; or metal plates fastened to the sides of the beams may also be employed.
m. If a ridge beam cannot be employed and roof beams consequently may provide outward thrusts at the walls, some kind of tie is required as in standard gable construction. One method of handling this is shown in figure 5.54, where a horizontal beam consisting of two members is framed into the ends of the roof beams and takes the horizontal thrusts at that point. The horizontal beam, in turn, may be spliced at its center or some other intermediate point and rest on a post.

n. The design of planking, beams, and posts is controlled by the necessity for adequate strength to carry the superimposed load and to provide sufficient stiffness to avoid excessive deflection under those loads. Building codes commonly specify floor and roof loading as well as wind loading. They may, in addition, specify deflection limitations such as some fraction of the span. These usually range from L/180 to L/360 to provide sufficient stiffness and a sense of security to the inhabitants. As pointed out above, stiffness in planking can be greatly enhanced by utilizing planking spanning at least two spans and preferably more. For example, a 12′-long plank will reach across two spans where beams are spaced 6′ on centers.

o. Framing anchors, angles, plates, and other means of fastening beams to beams and beams to posts must be adequate to transmit the loads involved.

p. As is true of any wood construction, it is desirable to detail the bottoms of posts so that they do not rest in moist conditions, and to allow plenty of ventilation around the ends of beams.

SPECIAL FRAMING

5.42 General

a. The foregoing sections of this chapter deal with types of framing employed in customary construction. Problems arise, however, involving exceptionally large spans for windows and interiors, openings in corners, wide overhangs, and the like. Usual procedures and rules of thumb often do not apply, and special techniques must be developed to meet special cases.

b. Frequently, the loads involved and the arrangement of members to handle the loads are such as to require engineering examination and design. No attempt at structural analysis will be made here, but some of the types of framing which have been found successful in meeting some typical design requirements will be described. Sizes of members cannot be given, since actual sizes depend upon the conditions of any particular problem.

5.43 Large Openings

a. Small and medium-size openings in walls and partitions are framed as previously described in this chapter. Large openings require heavier framing to carry the loads and to prevent excessive deflec-

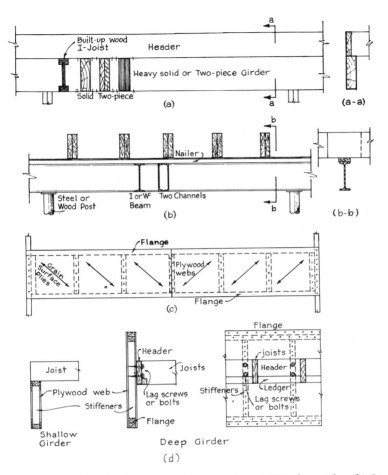

Figure 5.55 Methods of spanning large openings. (a) Timber girder. (b) Steel girder. (c) Box girder with plywood web. (d) Joists on shallow and deep girders.

tions. Figure 5.55 illustrates several possible methods. Simplest is the heavy single or two-piece girder shown at a. It is quickly erected, strong, and inexpensive. It has the serious drawback that any shrinkage in the girder is immediately made apparent by settling of the superstructure and by cracks in surface finishes. I-shaped beams of wood or veneer-wood flanges and reconstituted wood or plywood webs and trussed wood members avoid this problem (sections 5.3i, t). Laminated timbers (section 5.18) are usually dry when manufactured and can largely overcome this problem. A steel I beam or pair of channels may be employed, as shown at b. A nailer is necessary on

top, and should be provided on the bottom also if finished woodwork is to be applied later. End supports may be steel pipe columns or wood posts. Some kind of tie to the wood framing must be provided.
b. A built-up girder is illustrated at c, with $\frac{1}{2}''$ plywood webs and lumber top and bottom flanges and stiffeners. With nominal 2 × 3 stock, the total thickness is the same as a 2 × 4. For maximum efficiency, but with more waste, the grain in the surface plies runs in the diagonal direction shown. The large sheets of plywood impart stiffness and rigidity, particularly if they are glued as well as nailed to the frame.
c. Figure 5.55d illustrates two methods of supporting joists on built-up girders. Simplest is to rest the joist on top in the usual manner, but the total possible depth of girder is limited. On very long spans, where maximum depth is essential, floor joists may be framed into headers in turn bolted or lag-screwed to the stiffeners of the girder. Girders thus may be any convenient depth — from lower window head to upper window sill, for example.

5.44 Overhangs

a. Wide overhangs are frequently required, especially as sunshades over large deep windows. Simple overhangs are easily framed by projecting joists or rafters the required distance beyond the wall. Overhanging second stories are customarily built on the ends of projecting joists. If the overhang runs around the periphery of the building, framing is modified in the manner shown in figure 5.56. Lookout joists are framed into the side of a doubled regular joist or main header, and smaller lookouts frame into the side of a secondary header. If the overhang is large, the secondary header may be moved over one or two joist spaces and the lookouts become lookout joists resting on the plate in the same manner as the lookout joists shown. Lower edges of the overhanging portions of all members may be cut on a bevel (broken lines in figure 5.56), particularly if the superimposed load is small. Beveled cuts of this kind increase the angle at which the sun's rays may enter windows unobstructed.
b. Details are sometimes found in which large roof areas are supported on occasional posts instead of on continuous walls. One method of handling such details is shown in figure 5.57. The post, generally kept as slender as possible, supports a projecting girder strong enough to carry the load from its tributary area. Joists or rafters

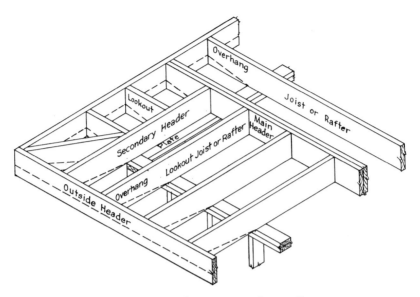

Figure 5.56 Framing for large overhang supported on wall.

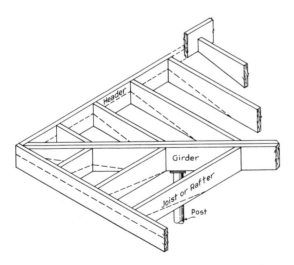

Figure 5.57 Framing for large overhang supported on post.

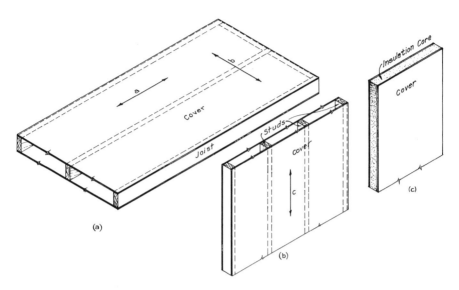

Figure 5.58 "Stressed cover." (a) Structural board glued to floor joists. (b) Structural board glued to wall studs. (c) Foamed plastic core.

span from girders to outside headers which are supported by the girders. Headers must be strong and stiff enough to support the outer ends of joists or rafters without sagging. This requirement often precludes any beveling of the lower edges of joists or rafters unless the upper edges of headers are raised as shown in the upper portion of figure 5.57. The joint at the ends of headers and girder is critical.

5.45 "Stressed Cover"

a. A technique which is employed in shop-fabricated panelized construction, but which also finds application in field construction, is the "stressed cover." In essence, it consists of a frame to which a continuous skin, e.g. plywood, is so firmly fastened that the entire structure acts as a unit and a considerable portion of the load is carried by the skin. Strength and rigidity are both markedly increased. Since it is essential that the frame and skin be tightly joined, nailing alone is not enough, and the skin is glued as well as nailed. Nails not only fasten the parts together but apply enough pressure to the glue line to effect a good bond. For floors a common combination is 2 × 6 joists, 2' on centers with $\frac{1}{2}''$ or $\frac{5}{8}''$ plywood top and $\frac{3}{8}''$ plywood bottom, glued with cold-setting casein or synthetic resin, nailed with 6d or 8d etched or coated common nails 6″ on centers. Walls may be $\frac{3}{8}$″ plywood outside and $\frac{1}{4}$″ inside with 1 × 2 studs 12″ on centers. Six-penny finish nails are favored. Although the greatest reinforcement for floor joists is obtained if face grain in the plywood runs in direction *a*, it is often placed in direction *b* to provide maximum stiffness between joists. Otherwise, excessive deflection would occur under concentrated loads placed halfway between joists. In wall panels, face plies run in direction *c*.

b. "Stressed-skin" or "stress-skin" sandwich panels consist of foamed plastic cores (chapter 15) with facings of plywood or one of the various reconstituted panels (section 5.3m), in which the facings perform the same function as the covers described above, and the core takes the place of the ribs. Such panels are particularly useful in walls spanning between members more widely spaced than usual, as in post and beam (sections 5.40, 5.41).

MASONRY

5.46 Burnt-Clay Units

a. Clay and shale, heated ("burned") at high temperatures, provide a wide variety of building units. The principal structural ones are brick (relatively small, essentially solid units) and structural tile (larger, hollow-cored, with relatively thin walls). Flat ceramic tiles are used principally as facings on walls and for floors (section 12.38).

b. Depending upon the raw materials and the time and temperature of burning, various degrees of color, hardness, durability, and fire resistance are attained. Some units, such as "salmon" brick, are underburned, highly porous, and of low strength. At the other extreme are vitreous brick, almost glass-hard and extremely strong. Units used in construction generally fall between these extremes.

5.47 Brick

a. The two broad classifications of building brick are *common* and *face*. Although essentially solid, wide faces of bricks may have depressions ("frogs") or holes passing through from face to face. Common brick may or may not be exposed to view, color can vary considerably, dimensions can vary, and moderate distortions of shape are permissible. Face brick is intended to be seen; its color may be rigidly controlled, its dimensions and shape must be within closer tolerances than for common, and its faces may be striated or mottled.

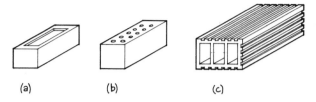

Figure 5.59 Burnt-clay units. (a,b) Brick. (c) Structural tile.

Table 5.14

Common	Face
SW (severe weathering)	SW (severe weathering)
MW (moderate weathering)	MW (all other)
NW (no exposure)	FBS (normal color range)
	FBX (minimum color range)
	FBA (maximum nonuniformity)

b. The American Society for Testing and Materials (ASTM) and the American National Standards Institute (ANSI) classify brick as detailed in table 5.14.

c. Common SW brick may be exposed to such extremes as frozen earth and may be used for all flooring purposes. Common MW brick is for all other exterior purposes. Both SW and MW may be used for interiors as well as exteriors. NW brick is for interior purposes except floors. Face SW brick is for the same purposes as common SW. Face MW is for all other purposes. The F grades are appearance grades, FBX the most stringent and FBA the least.

d. For SW, moisture absorption after 5 hours of boiling should average not more than 17 percent, with an individual maximum of 20 percent; for MW the percentages are 22 and 25, respectively. Soaking at room temperature for 24 hours should result in 80 to 90 percent of these figures. If absorption is too low, a good bond is not obtained between brick and mortar; if it is too high, water is drawn out of the mortar into the brick and a dry nonadherent layer is left between the mortar and the brick.

e. Sizes of brick vary. An ancient Greek brick was practically a 23″ cube. Some present-day bricks are as small as $1\frac{3}{4}'' \times 3\frac{3}{8}'' \times 4\frac{1}{2}''$. Brick may be modular or nonmodular. The dimensions of modular bricks are given as nominal size (that is, actual size plus mortar joint). For example, two common sizes of modular brick are $2\frac{2}{3}''$ or $4''$ high, $4''$ thick, and $8''$ or $12''$ long, the $2\frac{2}{3}''$ brick being the most common. If mortar joints are $\frac{3}{8}''$, for example, the actual brick dimensions are $\frac{3}{8}''$ less. Modular sizes are designed to conform to $4''$ multiples — e.g., three $2\frac{2}{3}''$-thick courses equal $8''$.

f. Nonmodular bricks do not necessarily conform to $4''$ multiples. The most commonly used size is $2\frac{1}{4}'' \times 3\frac{3}{4}'' \times 8''$ (actual dimensions). Course thicknesses depend upon the thickness of the mortar joint (figure 5.59).

5.48 Structural Clay Tile

a. Hollow burnt-clay units with parallel walls may be employed as load-bearing or non-load-bearing exposed units in walls and partitions, as a base for plaster or stucco, as fireproofing, and combined with brick in combination walls. In all of these applications they are in competition with concrete block (section 4.18).
b. Tiles may be laid up with cells horizontal or vertical. Sizes generally range from $2''$ to $12''$ in thickness, $8''$ to $16''$ in length, and $4''$ to $12''$ in height. Like bricks, they may be modular or nonmodular in size.
c. Finishes range from scored, combed, or roughened (for applied finishes such as stucco), to smooth, to opaque or transparent glazed.

5.49 Calcium Silicate (Sand-Lime) Brick

Sand and lime are combined and formed into solid bricks of the same size as standard clay bricks. Not as hard or durable as clay bricks, sand-lime bricks are employed largely as backup for clay bricks, or exposed for indoor applications where requirements are less severe than for clay units.

5.50 Mortar

Different types of mortar may be called for, depending on the requirements, such as strength, workability, bond, and weathering qualities. Not all qualities are necessarily found in the same mortar. High-strength mortar may not be as workable and may not bond as well as more moderate mortars. The principal ingredients are cementing material and mineral aggregate, typically sand or crushed stone. The most common cement is portland, usually type I or II (section 4.15), combined with various mixtures of masonry cement and hydrated lime ($Ca(OH)_2$) or lime putty. Although hydrated lime is most com-

Table 5.15 Mortar Proportion Specification Requirement (Parts by Volume)

Mortar type	Portland cement	Masonry cement	Hydrated lime or lime putty		Damp loose aggregate
			Min.	Max.	
M	1	—	—	$\frac{1}{4}$	Not less than $2\frac{1}{4}$ and not more than 3 times the sum of the volumes of the cements and lime used.
	1	1	—		
S	1	—	$\frac{1}{4}$	$\frac{1}{2}$	
	$\frac{1}{2}$	1	—		
N	1	—	$\frac{1}{2}$	$1\frac{1}{4}$	
	—	1	—	—	
O	—	1	—	—	
	1	—	$1\frac{1}{4}$	$2\frac{1}{2}$	

Source: Building Officials and Code Administrators Code

mon, some masons prefer to start with quick lime (calcium carbonate) burnt to calcium oxide (CaO) and "slake" it by adding water to form lime putty, also $Ca(OH)_2$. Slaking must be done carefully because much heat is involved; too little water causes overheating, too much "drowns" the lime; in either case the desired smooth "fat" lime putty is not achieved. Increasing lime increases workability, smoothness, and bond but decreases strength. For most building purposes maximum strength is not needed; a compromise involving the volumetric ratios of cement, lime or masonry cement and aggregate, is often chosen, higher in cement for rigorous purposes such as foundations, more lime for walls above ground. Generally the volume of aggregate lies between $2\frac{1}{4}$ and 3 times the combined volumes of the cement and lime used. Just enough water is added to make a workable mix. Table 5.15 gives recommended mixes. Type M may be used for all purposes except glass block, type S for all purposes, type N for most purposes above grade, and type O for walls of solid units and non-load-bearing partitions and fireproofing.

5.51 Joint Treatment (figure 5.60)

As masonry units are laid up, mortar projects beyond the joint and must be removed. The simplest is to "strike" off the excess with a trowel. The trowel may be held at an angle to provide a sloping surface as well as a shadow line. Alternatively, a separate tool may provide an ironed concave or V joint. The latter compress and densify the mortar and press it more firmly to the units than does striking.

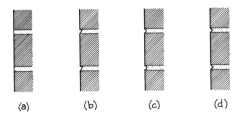

(a)   (b)   (c)   (d)

Figure 5.60 Joint treatments. (a) Flush. (b) Weathered. (c) Concave. (d) Vee.

5.52 Bond Patterns (figure 5.61)

a. Brick may be laid in a variety of patterns or "bonds," depending on the type of wall and on aesthetic and other considerations. The simplest is *running* bond, courses of stretchers (laid with the long dimension showing) with vertical joints in successive courses offset or "staggered" a half brick. This provides no tie between adjacent courses or wythes. Next is *English* bond, alternate courses of stretchers and headers (bricks laid with the ends showing). The headers tie together or bond adjacent courses. *Common* bond has several courses (usually about five) of stretchers and then one of headers. In *Flemish* bond, stretchers and headers alternate in the same course. Combinations of bonds (figure 5.61) can be employed to provide patterns.

b. Bricks laid on edge are called *rowlock*; on end, *soldier* courses. Successive courses, usually stretchers, with continuous vertical joints, are called *stacked bond*. Stacked bond is not as securely interlocked as bonds with staggered vertical joints (figure 5.62).

c. Walls may be solid or may have an opening or cavity between adjacent wythes (figure 5.63). Walls may be all brick or combinations of brick and block (section 4.18) or other units such as hollow tile (section 5.48). Solid walls (figure 5.64), either all brick or combination, may be bonded with header brick in any of the bonds described above except running bond. Cavity walls and solid running-bond walls have no cross-bonds, and the adjacent wythes are tied together with ties of various configurations laid in the mortar joints (figure 5.63). In outer walls, the cavity provides a space to drain water, such as from driving rains, that may penetrate an outer wythe. The cavity must be kept clear of mortar droppings, and small drainage openings or "weep holes" (usually small metal tubes) are provided, approxi-

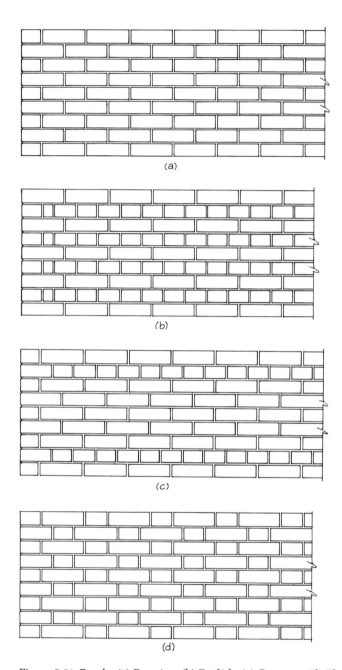

Figure 5.61 Bonds. (a) Running. (b) English. (c) Common. (d) Flemish.

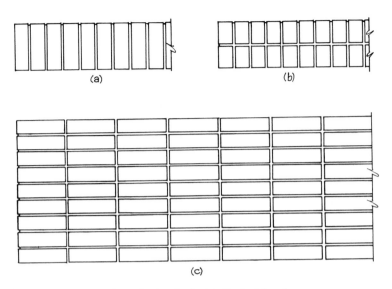

Figure 5.62 (a) Soldier. (b) Rowlock. (c) Stacked bond.

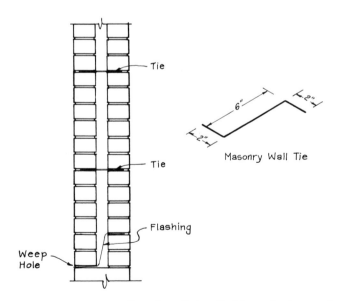

Figure 5.63 Cavity wall with wall ties, flashing at bottom, and weep holes.

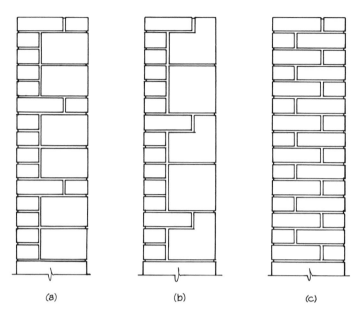

Figure 5.64 Types of solid walls. (a,b) Brick face, tile or block backup. (c) Solid brick.

mately 2' apart, at the bottom of the wall (figure 5.63). Flashing (chapter 8) diverts water to the weep holes. Figure 4.11 shows reinforced block and ties for combination brick and block walls.

5.53 Expansion Joints

a. All materials expand and contract with changes in temperature, moisture content, or both, and allowance must often be made. The faces of masonry walls are exposed to large temperature changes and to rain and sleet; allowance should be made for motion in long high walls by providing expansion joints. A common rule of thumb stipulates continuous vertical joints 50' to 200' apart with joints near external and at internal corners. Other vertical joints are conveniently made at changes in direction of the wall and at doors and windows. Horizontal joints are generally made at floor levels. In either case, the joint is free to move and is sealed with caulking capable of stretching and contracting as the joint opens and closes. Figure 5.65a shows an expansion joint in a brick wythe with a sealant at the exposed edge backed by a backing such as rubber or plastic foam, or a U-shaped

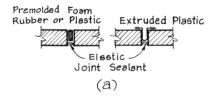

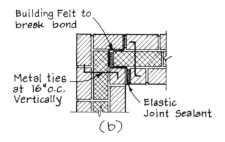

Figure 5.65 Expansion joints. (a) Joint in brick wythe. (b) Joint at corner.

insert, e.g., plastic or copper. Figure 5.65b shows a through-wall expansion joint at a corner.

b. In single-dwelling houses, the expansion joints are often omitted because wall areas are small. In multiple dwellings, the wall areas are likely to be large enough to call for such relieving joints.

5.54 Fire Cuts and Anchorages

a. Where ends of wood floor joints are built into masonry walls, a fire that causes a joist to collapse may cause the end of the joist to disrupt and overturn the wall as the joist falls. To avoid this, the ends of joists are cut diagonally so that the top of a joist clears the wall if the joist falls. This cut is called a *fire cut.*

b. To anchor wood joists into masonry walls, L-shaped or similar hooked metal straps are nailed to the bottom end of approximately every third joist, and built into the wall. The strap at the bottom does not tend to overturn a wall if the joist falls in a fire (figure 5.66).

PARTY WALLS

5.55 Function

a. Party walls separate horizontally adjoining dwelling units in multiple dwellings, variously known as *town houses, row houses,* and *clus-*

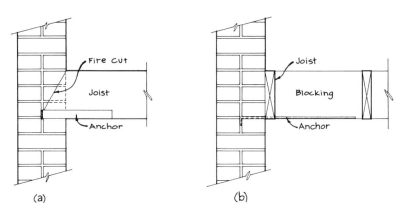

Figure 5.66 Anchorage and fire cut. (a) Joist resting in wall. (b) Joist parallel to wall.

ters. Such walls must meet code requirements, principally for fire resistance, sound attenuation, and thermal insulation.

b. Fire resistance is commonly specified in terms of hours of resistance to penetration by standard fire tests, such as those of the American Society for Testing and Materials (ASTM E119). Not only must a standard flame be kept from penetrating an enclosure in a specified length of time (such as 1, 2, or 3 hours), but the temperature on the side of the wall opposite to the fire must not rise high enough to set flammable materials on fire (250°F average, 325°F at any single point). For multiple residences, a common building-code requirement is 1 to 1½ hours.

c. Penetration of sound must be reduced by specified amounts in decibels, to keep to acceptable limits the sound levels on the side of the wall opposite the source. Codes may specify a "sound transmission class" (STC) or a reduction in sound level by a certain number of decibels (e.g., 45).

d. Resistance to heat flow is necessary to keep a cold unoccupied unit from causing excessive heat loss from an occupied adjoining unit.

e. Party walls may be constructed of all the common materials. Concrete-block walls (section 4.18) may be laid up additional stories high and carried up over the roof as parapets to heights specified by code. Surfaces may be left exposed or covered by wallboards, plaster, tile, or other facing materials (chapter 12).

f. Concrete party walls may be cast in place, utilizing formwork as

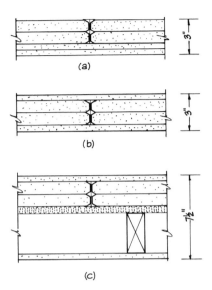

Figure 5.67 Gypsum or mineral board party walls. (a,b) Core plus facing boards. (c) Board plus thermal and acoustical insulation.

described in chapter 4. Precast concrete panels may be employed. Various facing materials may be applied.

g. Brick masonry, or brick and block, may be utilized. If the surface is exposed, face brick may be used; otherwise the brick may be common or sand-lime (sections 5.47–5.49).

h. Frame party walls of standard wood or metal (sections 5.5ff.) are common, especially if the rest of the construction is frame. Since the framing is not adequate for either fire or sound resistance, facing materials must be chosen to meet the requirements. Gypsum and other mineral boards, when applied in sufficient thicknesses, can provide the necessary fire and sound barriers, as can plaster on gypsum or metal lath (chapter 12).

i. Party walls may be solid board, consisting typically of laminated gypsum or other mineral board, built up to a thickness sufficient to provide the required fire and acoustical resistance (figure 5.67a,b).

j. Walls constructed as described above may provide the necessary thermal resistance. If not, thermal insulation (chapter 11) may be added. Figure 5.67c shows one type of construction that provides thermal insulation, two-hour fire resistance, and 56-dB STP sound insulation. Interstices in concrete block may be filled with poured-in insulation such as perlite or vermiculite. Faces of masonry and concrete walls may be covered with sheets of nonflammable board such as gypsum, glass fiber, or mineral fiber. Cavity walls may have sheets of insulating board (e.g., plastic foam or glass fiber board) inserted. Wood and metal frames may be insulated with the various types of insulation, preferably nonflammable, commonly used in frame construction (chapter 11).

k. Walls several stories high tend to be unstable and must be braced laterally. Such support is usually supplied by floors and roofs abutting the wall or framing into it. Ends of wood joists framed into party walls, for example, should be provided with fire cuts (section 5.54).

l. Party walls project beyond the roof as specified by codes. Walls are flashed and capped in a manner similar to details shown in chapter 8 for chimneys and walls projecting beyond a roof.

6 Chimneys and Fireplaces

6.1 General

a. Coincident with the framing of the house comes the construction of chimneys and fireplaces. If the chimney is an outside one (i.e., is on an outside wall), the lower part is built at the same time as the foundation walls and forms an integral part of the wall at that point. Otherwise, it may be begun at any time after the first-floor framing is finished. If it follows the framing, openings for it are left in the floor, wall, and roof framing.

b. To a large degree, the efficiency of any heating unit depends on the chimney. At the same time, the chimney constitutes a serious fire hazard. Consequently, its design demands careful planning and its construction meticulous attention to detail and good workmanship.

c. A chimney may be merely a simple flue or it may be a large piece of intricate masonry construction consisting of heater flues, ash pits, incinerators, ash chutes, fireplaces, and fireplace flues, all arranged to fit into the minimum space consistent with maximum efficiency.

d. In the following discussion, chimney construction is (for convenience) divided into two parts — the chimney proper and the fireplace — although the two are usually built as one operation. In ornamental fireplaces, however, rough openings may be left in the chimneys at the time of construction, and fireplaces later built into the rough openings.

CHIMNEY

6.2 Flues and Flue Linings

a. The *flue* is the open vertical shaft through which smoke and hot gases are carried from fire to open air. It must be designed to accommodate the unit to which it is connected. Its capacity is measured by the effective cross-sectional area, which in turn depends upon the path of the smoke and hot gases. When a current of warm air rises through a flue, it ascends in spirals and occupies the greater part of the center of the flue. If a circular flue is lined with smooth terra cotta flue lining, there is little or no drag, and the full area of the flue can be taken as its effective area. If the flue is square, the corners are occupied by cold air and soot, and the upward current of warm air must be considered as occupying only the central circular part of the flue. The effective area of a lined square flue is a circle whose diameter equals the width of the flue. A rectangular lined flue has an effective

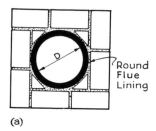

(a)

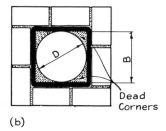

(b)

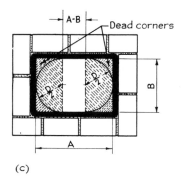

(c)

Figure 6.1 Total and effective areas of (a) circular, (b) square, and (c) rectangular flues.

area equal to the sum of the two semicircles inscribed in the ends of the rectangle, plus the intervening rectangular space. These principles are illustrated in figure 6.1.

b. The size of the flue required for a heating unit is dictated by its draft requirements and must be determined by the designer of the heating equipment. When it comes to fireplaces, the following rule of thumb has been found reliable: the effective area E of the flue should be from $\frac{1}{10}$ to $\frac{1}{12}$ the area of the fireplace opening. For example, a fireplace opening 42″ wide and 30″ high has an area of 1,260 sq in., and $\frac{1}{12}$ of that is 105 sq in. A 12″ circular flue lining has an actual and

Table 6.1 Flues, Areas, and Chimneys with Flue Linings

Nominal Sizes				
Round Flue Lining, Inside Diameter	Rectangular Flue Lining, Outside Dimensions	Actual Inside area (sq in.)	Effective Area E (sq in.)	Minimum Thickness of chimney Wall
. . .	4½″ x 8½″	23.6	21.3	3¾″
6 ″	. . .	28.3	28.3	3¾″
. . .	7½″ x 7½″	39.1	30.7	3¾″
. . .	4½″ x 13 ″	38.2	35.9	3¾
. . .	8½″ x 8½″	52.6	41.3	3¾″
8 ″	. . .	50.3	50.3	3¾″
. . .	8½″ x 13 ″	80.5	70	3¾″
10 ″	. . .	78.5	78.5	3¾″
. . .	8½″ x 18 ″	106	96.5	3¾″
. . .	13 ″ x 13 ″	127	100	3¾″
12 ″	. . .	113	113	3¾″
. . . .	13 ″ x 18 ″	177	150	3¾″
15 ″	. . .	177	177	3¾″
. . .	18 ″ x 18 ″	233	183	3¾″
. . .	20 ″ x 20 ″	298	234	8 ″
18 ″	. . .	254	254	8 ″
. . .	20 ″ x 24 ″	357	295	8 ″
20 ″	. . .	314	314	8 ″
. . .	24 ″ x 24 ″	461	346	8 ″
22 ″	. . .	380	380	8 ″
24 ″	. . .	452	452	8 ″

effective area of 113 sq in. and would be satisfactory. (See table 6.1.) A 13″ × 13″ flue lining (outside measurement) has a gross inside area of 127 sq in., and an effective area of 100 sq in., which would be a trifle small although it would do if the smoke chamber, the lip, and the length of the flue were adequate (see section 6.11c and table 6.2).

c. A single flue should not be used for more than one heating appliance if maximum draft is to be attained. Although this rule has certain common exceptions, such as the incinerator, it is true that for maximum efficiency there should be only the smoke inlet at the bottom and the outlet at the top.

d. It should be apparent from table 6.1 that square or rectangular flues have no inherent advantage over circular ones except that they are more easily built into the chimney.

e. When the direction of a flue must be changed (figure 6.2), the angle

Table 6.2 Flue Calculations (See Figures 6.7, 6.8)

$W = 2'6''$ to $5'0''$

$H = 2'6''$ to $4'0''$

but $H < W$ in all cases, and ranges from $2W/3$ to $3W/4$

$D = \dfrac{H}{2}$ to $\dfrac{2H}{3}$

but $\leq 26''$, $\geq 16''$ for coal and $\geq 18''$ for wood

$T \times W = 1.25A$ to $1.5A$

A^a
$\left\{\begin{array}{l}\\\\\\\\\\\\\\\\\end{array}\right.$

Rectangular Flue $\left\{\begin{array}{l} 20'0'' \text{ above hearth } = \dfrac{W \times H}{10} \\[2ex] 30'0'' \text{ above hearth } = \dfrac{W \times H}{12} \end{array}\right.$

Round Flue $\left\{\begin{array}{l} 20'0'' \text{ above hearth } = \dfrac{W \times H}{12} \\[2ex] 30'0'' \text{ above hearth } = \dfrac{W \times H}{15} \end{array}\right.$

Square Flue $\left\{\begin{array}{l} \text{Large enough to inscribe round} \\ \text{flue for similar conditions.} \end{array}\right.$

[a] Smoke chamber and lip of adequate size.

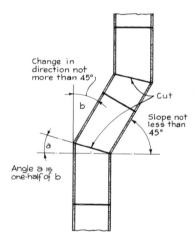

Change in
direction not
more than 45°

b

Cut

Slope not
less than
45°

a

Angle a is
one-half of b

Figure 6.2 Changes in direction and slopes of flues.

should in no case be more than 45°, and it is much better to make it 30° or less. The slope of a flue should not be less than 45°, and 60° or more is better. Sharp turns set up eddies which seriously impede the smooth motion of smoke and gases. Soot and dirt collect in sharp corners and on shallow slopes.

f. Care should be taken to set flue linings close and flush on top of one another, with the joints well filled and carefully struck on the inside to avoid rough spots and lodgement for soot. If the outside of the flue lining is packed tightly with mortar and brick, air leakage into the flue is prevented. On the other hand, many building codes advocate leaving an insulating air space between the flue lining and the brickwork to allow the flue to operate at higher temperatures and reduce the accumulation of caked soot (often called *creosote*). A section of flue lining is most readily cut with a power saw to make a smooth fit between cut surfaces. To change direction, the ends of both flue linings adjacent to the bend must be cut carefully to the proper angle — half the angle of the bend — and fitted tightly (figure 6.2). In this manner flues may be carried to almost any location.

g. Tops of chimneys must be carried high enough to avoid downdrafts caused by turbulence in the wind as it sweeps around nearby obstructions or over sloping roofs. In general, a chimney should project 2' to 3' above the ridge of the house, depending on its proximity to the ridge (figure 6.3). The steeper the pitch, the higher the chimney should be carried.

6.3 Chimney Wall Thicknesses; Withes

a. An 8" brick wall alone is not impervious to wind or weather. However, if we combine flue lining and 8" of brick, there should be no

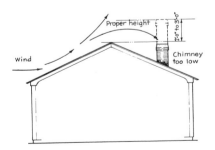

Figure 6.3 Height of chimney above roof.

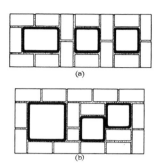

Figure 6.4 Thicknesses and withes of chimney walls.

trouble from this source, and this combination is recommended for the exposed portions of chimneys. Interior chimneys, or the interior portions of chimneys built into outside walls, may generally be only 4″ of brickwork if wood framing is held away from the masonry. For large flues, brickwork should be 8″ in any event (table 6.1).

b. The space between flues, when more than one flue occurs in a chimney, is called the *withe*. For best construction, this should be 4″, filled in solidly with brick (figure 6.4a). If space is at a premium the withe can be reduced to 1″, carefully and solidly filled with mortar. In this instance it is absolutely essential that joints in adjacent flue linings be staggered, that individual pieces of lining be sound and uncracked, and that joints between pieces be full, struck, troweled, smooth, and tight. It is highly desirable, in any event, to avoid having more than two flues adjacent to each other without full 4″ withes (figures 6.4b, 6.6).

6.4 Cleanouts

a. At the bottoms of all flues except those for fireplaces, there should be a cleanout door, so that soot or other accumulations can easily be removed from the chimney.

b. It is unnecessary to carry the bottom of the flue farther below the intake of the smoke pipe than is sufficient to install the cleanout door. All cleanout doors should fit tightly in their frames, which in turn should be carefully set in the brickwork and securely anchored to make them proof against air leakage.

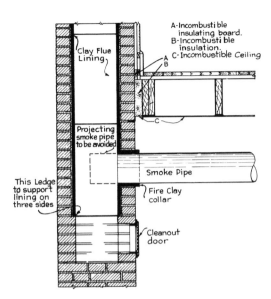

Figure 6.5 Cleanout, smoke pipe, and framing.

6.5 Smoke Pipe

a. An improperly located and protected smoke pipe from the furnace, stove, or other heating unit is a dangerous fire hazard in a dwelling house.

b. Care should be taken in setting the smoke pipe that it does not extend into the flue, as shown by the dotted line in figure 6.5. A metal or terra cotta collar should be built into the brickwork and the smoke pipe should be slipped into this collar, flush with the inside of the flue.

c. Many building codes require heater-room ceilings to be plastered or protected with incombustible wallboard as an essential part of the protection of the house from fire. In any event, the smoke pipe should be kept at least 10″ from the floor joists over it, even if the ceiling is protected.

6.6 Wood Framing

Framing members — floor and wall or partition — must be kept free of the chimney and should be insulated from it, especially if only 4″ of brick masonry surrounds the flue lining. The usual header and trim-

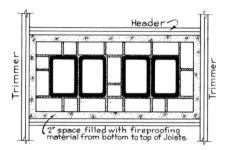

Figure 6.6 Framing around interior chimney.

mer construction is employed, with framing members held 2″ away from the masonry. See chapter 5 for a discussion of framing around chimneys and fireplaces. The space may be filled with incombustible insulating material, such as mineral wool, on an incombustible support.

6.7 Testing

Before apparatus is connected with any flue, but after the mortar has hardened, it is a good plan to apply a smoke test. One method is to build a smudge fire of paper, straw, wood, or tarpaper at the base of the flue and, when a dense column of smoke is ascending, tightly block the outlet. Leaks can be located at once by the appearance of smoke, and bad leaks due to carelessness in laying up masonry are often revealed. Such leaks may be into adjoining flues or directly through the walls or between the walls and the lining. A chimney that shows leakage should not be accepted until the defect has been remedied. Since stopping a leak after a chimney is complete is usually very difficult, it pays to watch the construction closely as it progresses.

6.8 Footings, Flashing, Cap

a. As was noted in chapter 4, a chimney is generally the heaviest portion of a structure and must have an ample footing. The footings should be designed to prevent differential settlement in the building by balancing the various loads on the footing.

b. Where a chimney penetrates the roof or comes in contact with the roof (as an outside chimney may), it must be flashed to the slope of the roof. Flashing is taken up in detail in chapter 8. Chimney flashing often consists of two parts: the *cap* and the *base*. The base is a bent sheet of metal fitted into the angle between the roof and the chimney. One part extends out on the roof under the shingles; the other lies flat against the side of the chimney. The cap is another bent sheet, built into the brickwork and turned down over the base flashing.

c. At the back of the chimney a flashed *cricket* (a small gable with a ridge at a right angle to the slope of the main roof) is built to divert the water and snow that come down the slope of the roof (chapter 8).

d. The top of any chimney must have a good and efficient wash. Often a cap of stone is provided, but in place of stone a thick bed of cement mortar, pitched to all sides to shed water quickly, may be spread over the whole top of the chimney. It is also desirable to let the flue project several inches above the chimney. Water must not be allowed to get into the brickwork at the top of the chimney, because it is likely to cause disintegration.

FIREPLACE

6.9 General

There are six principal items to be considered in the construction of a fireplace:

size and shape of fireplace opening
relation of size of fireplace opening to size of flue
size and shape of fireplace hearth or "underfire"
smoke shelf
smoke chamber
damper

6.10 Proportions

a. Most fireplace openings are rectangular, that is, wider than high, unless the fireplace is very narrow. Average widths for fireplaces are 36″ to 42″, and the average height is 30″, although the width and the height may be greatly extended. A room with 300 sq ft of floor space can well be served by a fireplace 36″ to 42″ wide. Fireplaces 48″, 54″, or 60″ wide are usually constructed in rooms of correspondingly greater dimensions.

b. The depth of the fireplace should not be too great; 18″ to 20″ suffices for the average fireplace up to 42″ wide, with slight increases in depth for wider openings. The shallower the fireplace, the more heat is reflected into the room.

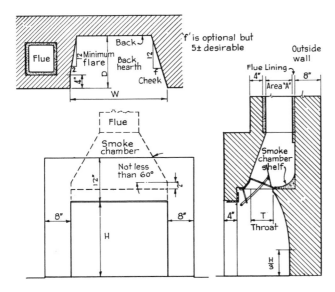

Figure 6.7 Fireplace relationships. (See table 6.2.)

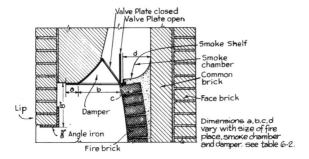

Figure 6.8 Detail of throat, showing damper, lip, and smoke shelf.

c. The back hearth (underfire) should not be square or contain square corners. The sides of the fireplace should slope inward from front to back approximately 5″ per foot of depth. Experiment has shown this to be the most effective angle, although it can be reduced to 2″ and still be satisfactory. Square corners cause eddies and smoke pockets which may interfere with combustion. Figures 6.7 and 6.8 and table 6.2 set forth relationships among the various parts of the fireplace which have been found workable in practice.

d. Figures 6.7 and 6.8 show sections which should be carefully noted. The back of the fireplace should be built vertical to ⅓ the height of the fireplace opening; then it should be sloped forward, so that at the top it comes to the back of the damper (or, if there is no damper, so as to allow a width of between 8″ and 10″ for the throat). At a point about 8″ above the top of the fireplace opening, the damper should be set and a shelf or ledge called the *smoke shelf* should be formed.

6.11 Damper

The damper is a large valve which can be adjusted to regulate the draft. Its position is important. Sometimes it is set directly at the top of the fireplace opening, but this is objectionable, because with a smoky fire in the fireplace, the draft is likely to carry the smoke against the top of the fireplace opening and so force some of it out into the room. A much better position is about 8″ above the top of the fireplace opening, as in figure 6.8. This arrangement allows the draft to carry the smoke up into the space back of the lip at the top of the fireplace opening and below the damper, so that it is more readily drawn through the damper into the space above.

6.12 Smoke Shelf

The smoke shelf is one of the most important features of a fireplace and must have close attention. With the central column of warm air rising in the flue, there is a downward current of cool air close to the walls of the flue. If there is no smoke shelf, this column or current of cool air reaches the throat of the fireplace, blocking the smoke and crowding it out into the room, as shown in figure 6.9. The function of the smoke shelf is to turn this current of cool air upward so that it will join with the upward current of warm air and not impede it. The width of the smoke shelf should be at least 4″.

6.13 Smoke Chamber

a. The next important feature is the smoke chamber. This is a large space over the damper and the smoke shelf (figures 6.7, 6.8). The back may go straight up, but the sides, starting at the ends of the damper, are sloped at the rate of 7″ in 12″ of height, and are carried up, converging, until the distance between the two sloping sides is equal to the inner dimensions of the flue lining, directly on the center line of the fireplace. The front of the smoke chamber may be sloped as needed to meet the flue at the same point. It is bad practice to have the

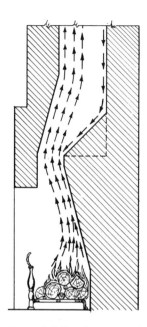

Figure 6.9 Poorly constructed fireplace, lacking damper and smoke shelf. Interference occurs at throat.

flue off the center line, because it causes the draft through the fireplace to be uneven. The first section of flue lining should be vertical, after which the flue may be turned or bent as desired.

b. Over the top of the fireplace opening, an angle iron (3″ × 3″ or 3″ × 4″) is generally set to carry the brickwork across the opening (figure 6.8). Some manufacturers make concrete or metal smoke chambers for each of their dampers. When the top of the fireplace opening is reached, the damper is set; then the metal or concrete smoke chamber of the proper shape and size is placed over it. Masonry is placed around the prefabricated smoke chamber.

6.14 Hearth

a. The hearth consists of two parts: the front or finished hearth and the back hearth or underfire. The front hearth is simply a precaution against flying sparks; although it must be noncombustible, it need not resist intense prolonged heat. It can, consequently, be finished with quarry tile, ordinary brick, stone (such as flagstone), concrete, or a similar material. The back hearth must withstand intense heat, as

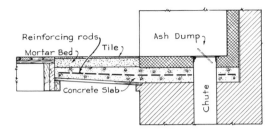

Figure 6.10 Trimmer-arch support for front hearth.

must the cheeks and back of the fireplace. These must be built of heat-resistant materials. Fire brick laid in fire clay is the best combination. As fire bricks are large, they can be laid on edge instead of on the flat. This saves brick and takes up less space. If the color of fire brick is objectionable, hard-burned clay brick can be employed; however, it may crack and spall after long exposure to hot fires.

b. As shown in figure 5.26, the floor framing around the space occupied by the front hearth is the familiar header-trimmer combination. The front hearth itself is supported on a concrete trimmer arch as illustrated in figure 6.10.

c. The framing for the concrete slab is much the same as for a tile floor. Nailing blocks are firmly nailed to the header framing the front hearth, and a brick corbel is built in the chimney at approximately the same height. Pieces of subflooring are laid on these supports. The concrete slab, at least 3″ thick, is cast on top of this platform and back into the rear of the chimney to form a base for the underfire or back hearth. Wire mesh is embedded in the concrete near the top of the slab and runs from the header to the back of the underfire. If an ash dump is to be provided, a box form is placed in the concrete at the proper place.

6.15 Ash Pit

The lower portion of a chimney containing one or more fireplaces is quite large and can conveniently be left hollow, both to save masonry materials and to form an ash pit into which ashes from the fireplaces can be chuted. The walls must be at least 8″ thick to support the chimney above, and if the latter is very large the ash pit's side and back walls should be 12″ thick. The front wall is usually 8″ thick, but may be 4″ in small chimneys since it does not carry much of the chimney load because this load is transferred to the side walls by the construction over the fireplace openings.

6.16 Construction Time

The fireplace may be built at the same time as the chimney or later when the house is nearly completed. If the fireplace is to be faced with ornamental material (such as tile or face brick) which may become soiled or damaged during the construction, it is much better to defer the building of the fireplace until just before the finish flooring is laid.

6.17 Examples

a. In figure 6.11, the foregoing principles are illustrated for a single large chimney, shown in elevation and in section. A main heater flue, on the left, is kept straight from bottom to top. A secondary flue, third from left, is shown as serving an incinerator. Although it is common practice to have incinerators utilize the main flue, it is better to provide a separate flue.

b. Two fireplaces, one offset above the other, have separate flues, each of which is centered over an ample smoke chamber and each of which rises straight for one length of flue lining before bending. No flue is inclined less than 60° to the horizontal. Joints in flue linings are staggered in adjacent flues, even though full 4″ withes are provided. The fireplaces have ash dumps and chutes, and are provided with proper dampers, lips, and smoke shelves. The lower trimmer arch is brick, now seldom used but once popular; the upper is concrete. Since the chimney is built into an outside wall, the outer three walls are 8″ thick, but the inner wall from above the lower fireplace to below the roof framing is 4″. At the roof it is corbeled (i.e., built out by projecting successive brick courses beyond the preceding ones — a common procedure) to 8″, so that above the roof all chimney walls are 8″ thick. Flue linings project beyond the generously pitched cap. Cap and base flashing is provided at the roof. The ash pit's top is arched, although it could well be corbeled. Its floor is raised above the basement floor to facilitate cleaning. Wood framing is held away from the brickwork at every point.

c. Figure 6.11 illustrates traditional fireplace and chimney construction. Figure 6.12 shows a more contemporary design with a raised

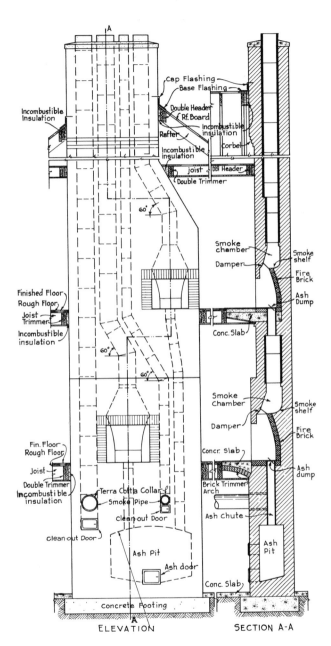

Figure 6.11 Chimney incorporating basement flues, two fireplaces, flues, and ash pit.

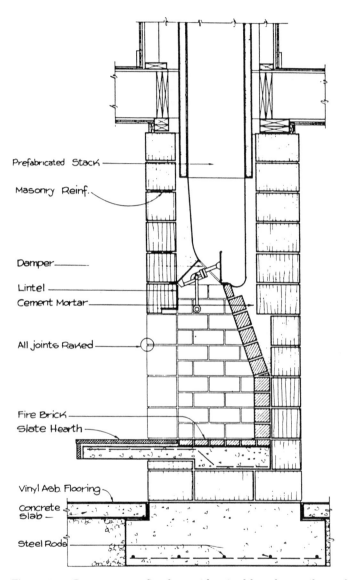

Prefabricated Stack

Masonry Reinf.

Damper

Lintel

Cement Mortar

All joints Raked

Fire Brick

Slate Hearth

Vinyl Asb. Flooring

Concrete Slab

Steel Rods

Figure 6.12 Contemporary fireplace with raised hearth, cantilevered front hearth, damper, lip, smoke shelf, and smoke chamber.

fireplace hearth and a cantilevered front hearth. Although the plan of the back hearth is rectangular rather than splayed, the general principles of the lip, the damper, the smoke shelf, and the smoke chamber are the same.

6.18 Prefabricated Chimneys and Fireplaces

Prefabricated flues typically consist of circular sections designed to fit snugly over one another with sealed joints similar to shiplap or tongue and groove. The inner lining is of a high-heat-resistance material such as fire clay. Surrounding it are several inches of heat-resistant insulation, in turn covered by a weather-resistant circular, square, or rectangular jacket of rust-resistant metal. Such flues must, of course, be adequate in size, as is true of any flue. Many varieties of prefabricated fireplaces or fireplace linings are to be found. Some are wall-hung; others rest on a base of some kind. Many have metal exteriors with heat-resistant insulating liners (e.g., fire brick). Their sizes, proportions, and flues should be checked to see that they will indeed draw properly without emitting smoke into the room.

6.19 Wood Stoves

Wood stoves, once almost universal then largely unused, have become popular. Most are based on the Franklin stove. Properly employed, they are markedly more efficient than fireplaces, but they can be hazardous when used improperly. Because of the amount of heat radiated, there should be at least 36″ between the stove and a wood-stud wall, even if the latter is covered with plaster or incombustible board (either of which can become so hot as to set studs or other wood in the wall ablaze). The flue must be carefully placed and safeguarded against overheating, especially if it penetrates walls or partitions. The juncture between the flue and the chimney should be treated like any smoke pipe as it enters a chimney (section 6.6).

7 Windows

7.1 General

A window performs either or both of two functions: to let in light and to provide ventilation. Light transmission is effected by glass or some other light-transmitting material, such as a plastic; ventilation should occur only when the window is open. If installed properly, a window is tight and allows only a small amount of air to leak past when it is closed; if a window is installed carelessly, not only does a great deal of air leak past but rain finds its way through and damages the adjacent wall. Tight windows are a matter of proper construction and proper detailing.

7.2 Window Types

a. Windows might be broadly classified as "fixed" (non-opening) or "ventilating." A ventilating window generally consists of one or more movable panels (*sashes*) within a fixed frame. Ventilating windows are generally classified by the manner in which the sashes open or operate.

b. Double-hung windows (two sliding sashes) and single-hung windows (one fixed sash, generally above; one sliding sash, generally below) open and close by sliding the movable sash vertically in grooves provided in the sides (*jambs* or *stiles*) of the frame, the sliding sash being held in the desired open or closed position by various spring balances concealed in the sash or frame (in jamb or head), by a manually operated or spring-actuated ratchet or peg arrangement between the sash and the frame, or by a friction-type control. Formerly, double-hung sashes were customarily counterweighted.

c. Horizontal "traverse" windows open and close by sliding or rolling the sash horizontally in grooves or tracks provided in the top (head) and bottom (sill) of the frame, the sliding sashes generally being limited to the smaller sizes or lighter glazing by their operating friction. When such windows are full length, to the floor, they are sliding doors, sometimes called patio doors.

d. Casement windows formerly included all those in which the sashes were hinged to the frame at one edge (rail or stile), opening inward or outward at the opposite edge, as well as the fixed or fully encased windows. In current usage, however, the term *casement* generally refers only to those windows in which the sashes are supported or "hung" at one side (jamb or stile) and open outward or inward at

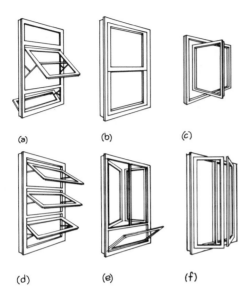

Figure 7.1 Types of windows. (a) Projected. (b) Double-hung. (c) Reversible, pivoted. (d) Awning. (e) Casement (top) and hopper (bottom). (f) Outswinging casement.

the opposite side, the outward-opening casements being the more common. Top-hung sashes opening outward at the bottom are now generally called *awnings*; bottom-hung sashes opening inward at the top are referred to as *hoppers* or *hopper-vents*. Top-hung in-swinging sashes are also available.

e. Though sashes of the above casement varieties are often supported from the frame, or swung on hinges or butts (chapter 14) of various types, they are often of the projected type, in the opening of which the retained rail or stile of the sash slides toward the center of the frame on shoes from which the sash pivots as it moves to the open position. In both methods, the sashes are held in the open position by extension arms. One end of these arms is attached to a shoe which slides in a track or groove at the edge of the sash, the other end being pivoted on the frame. Projected sashes are generally of the awning or the hopper-vent type.

f. Jalousie or louvered windows are a variety of awning windows in which numerous narrow horizontal lights of glass, each pivoted at its top edge (generally by a metal rail or muntin), operate in unison and overlap slightly in the closed position.

g. Various combinations of ventilating sashes and fixed glass in a single frame are often used in residential construction as picture windows, window walls, bow windows, etc. Folding windows are a less-frequent combination in which several sashes in a single frame are hinged together, turning on pivots supported by shoes which slide on tracks or in grooves in the frame and permitting the sash to fold away from the opening in accordion style.

h. Pivoted sashes, which open only by turning either horizontally or vertically about the centers of their rails or stiles, are less frequently employed in residential construction because of the problem presented by insect screening. A combination pivoted and double-hung (or horizontal traverse) sash in a reversible window is occasionally employed, however, to simplify the cleaning of both sides of the sash from the inside without removal.

i. Because of the great diversity of window types, materials, and details, only the major ones are described below, and only in sufficient detail to set forth principles. Wood windows are used to illustrate many of these principles because they were the most common original prototypes; many later windows of metal and other materials were derived from them.

7.3 Materials

a. Windows are generally constructed primarily of wood or metal, the metals most commonly employed for this purpose being aluminum and mild carbon steel. Windows constructed of stainless steel or bronze are available, but are rarely used in residential work because of the cost. Windows are also constructed entirely or partially of plastics.

b. Though the great majority of residential windows have traditionally been double-hung or outswinging casements, increased use is being made of awnings, ventilators, and jalousies, as well as of horizontal sliding (or rolling) windows. In residences, steel projected casements, hopper vents, and awning ventilators are employed principally in foundation walls, brick-veneered frame construction, and solid masonry construction.

7.4 Glass

a. Window glass is made by the *flat-drawn* and *float* processes. Flat-drawing consists of drawing a continuous sheet of glass from a molten mass and slowly cooling or annealing it through a long tunnel. Float glass is made by casting a sheet of glass continuously on a bed of

Table 7.1 Residential Glass

Type	Weight (oz/sq ft)	Max. Area 100 mph (sq ft)
Single strength $\frac{3}{32}''$	18–21	8
Double strength $\frac{1}{8}''$	24–26	13
$\frac{3}{16}''$	36–40	24
$\frac{7}{32}''$	44–45	30
$\frac{1}{4}''$	50–52	35

molten tin, where it spreads to a uniform thickness and flat surfaces by surface-tension forces. The sheet is drawn through and slowly cooled in a long tunnel. Flat-drawing is employed especially where minimum optical distortion is required.

b. In building, the thickness of glass is known as its *strength*. The two most commonly used strengths are "single strength" (ss) and "double strength" (ds). Clear-glass designations in current use for residential work are given in table 7.1. Figured glass (glass with a patterned surface, which transmits light but not clear images) is generally $\frac{1}{8}''$ or $\frac{7}{32}''$ thick.

c. Single-strength glass is used only in small lights. Where there is a likelihood of heavy wind pressures, or where the lights are larger, double-strength glass is needed. The heavier grades are used for still larger windows, such as store fronts and large "picture windows."

d. The maximum glass area depends upon the expected wind pressure. Wind velocities of 100 mph exert pressures of roughly 30 lb per sq ft. Manufacturers recommended that glass areas be no larger than the values give in table 7.1. Clear plastics, although more easily scratched, are often employed where the breakage hazard is high (section 15.2).

7.5 Sashes

a. The vertical side members of sashes are called *stiles*, the horizontal top and bottom members are called *rails*, and the smaller members which divide the glass into smaller panes — called *lights* in building language — are called *bars and muntins*, or just *muntins*. Muntins or grilles may be integral (as shown in figure 7.2), lower sash, or snap-in wood or plastic, as shown in the upper sash. The latter are obviously for appearance only, but can be removed to make washing of glass easier. Sash details are many and varied.

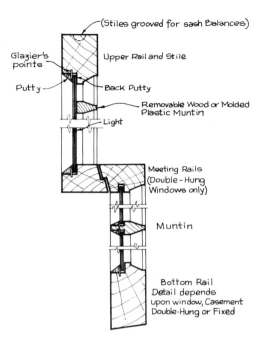

Figure 7.2 Parts of window sash.

b. Wood sashes and frames are generally constructed of kiln-dried, clear, straight-grained Western or Ponderosa pine, and are factory-treated with a toxic, water-repellent preservative. Stock wood sash thicknesses vary from $1\frac{3}{8}''$ to $2\frac{1}{4}''$, depending upon the size of the opening and the thickness of the glazing units. (Single glass or double "insulating" glass may be used.)

c. Sash members are rabbeted on the outside to receive the lights and the putty. They are finished with a molding on the inside. This molding is often an ogee (cyma), but it may be any detail the architect or manufacturer may desire. Figure 7.2 shows the essential parts. Details vary greatly.

7.6 Glazing

a. The process of inserting lights into sashes is called *glazing*. It must be done carefully, or else air and water may find their way around the edges of the glass.

b. Lights are cut approximately $\frac{1}{16}''$ to $\frac{1}{8}''$ smaller than the sash opening to provide enough clearance and to permit slight distortions of the sash without cracking the glass. Before a light is inserted, the sash rabbet is painted with a drying oil; then a thin layer of putty is spread over the back of the rabbet or struck on to the edges of the glass. The glass is next pressed firmly against the bed of putty. This *back-puttying* is essential to a tight joint, inasmuch as direct glass-to-wood contact would not be absolutely continuous. Flat triangular or diamond-shaped zinc "points" are next laid on the glass and forced into the wood so that $\frac{1}{8}''$ to $\frac{3}{16}''$ is left projecting to hold the glass in place. Various other clips and holding devices are employed, especially with metal and plastic sashes. Finally, the rabbet is filled with putty sloped to the outer edge of the sash.

c. A good putty is made of precipitated whiting (calcium carbonate) or marble dust ground in drying oil. This makes a hard, durable putty which adheres firmly to wood and glass. In order to make any putty adhere satisfactorily to wood, the latter must first be painted with drying oil; otherwise the raw dry wood absorbs too much of the oil from the putty.

d. Although these putties have had a long history and are particularly suitable for small lights in wood sashes, many other glazing compounds and sealants have been devised, especially for metal windows and large lights. Some of these are semi-hardening and remain fairly soft. They are compounded for applications where differential movement of glass and sash, caused by temperature changes, may be expected. For large lights, sealants derived from synthetic polymeric materials are employed. Gaskets based on rubber and other polymers are also used.

7.7 Casement Windows

Casement windows are side-hung and swing in or out; outswinging ones are more common. The wood casement windows described below are used to illustrate general principles, but there are many variants.

7.8 Frame

a. Window frames have three chief parts: the top or *head*, the sides or *jambs*, and the bottom or *sill*. Although *jamb* is derived from the word for "leg," the term *jamb* is also used to denote the head; thus "side jamb" and "headjamb." Wood casement frames are almost always "plank" frames, i.e., they are made of nominal 2″ stock cut and shaped to receive the sash. Shaping the head and the jambs consists of cutting rebates or "rabbets" $\frac{1}{2}''$ deep and $1\frac{1}{2}''$ or more wide to accommodate $1\frac{3}{8}''$ or thicker sash. A second rabbet is commonly added to accommodate screens and storm windows.

b. Figures 7.3 and 7.4 show details of outswinging and inswinging casement windows in frame walls. Heads and jambs are practically identical. They are wide enough to extend through the wall from the outside of the sheathing to the inside of the wall surface, and they clear the trimmer and header studs by only a small amount. Sheathing and building paper are carried in as close to the frame as is practicable.

c. The sill generally extends through the wall to the interior surface line. The outer edge, unlike head and jambs, projects beyond the sheathing line far enough to provide a base upon which the outside casing rests and forms a projecting shelf which protects the joint between the window frame and the siding or other exterior finish. The lower side of the sill should be plowed (grooved) to allow the siding to fit in snugly and prevent rain from being swept under the sill. A separate projecting subsill may be employed, thus allowing the main sill to be the same width as the jambs and the head. This is a manufacturing convenience.

d. The sill slopes down and outward at the rate of about 1″ in 5″ so as to shed water readily. Its upper surface (the *wash*) is usually rabbetted (figure 7.4) to form a snug watertight fit for the window sash or for screens and storm sashes. Although wood screens are shown in figure 7.3, metal screens are common. They may be placed in separate fixtures for interchangeability with storm sashes.

7.9 Inswinging Sash

The lower rails of inswinging sashes require special treatment to prevent rain from penetrating between the rail and the sill. Generally, the upper interior edge of the sill is provided with an upstanding lip, and the lower edge of the lower rail with a corresponding rabbet as shown. For further protection, a drip molding is fastened to the lower rail to prevent rain from being driven against the lower edge of the rail.

7.10 Mullions and Meeting Stiles

If several casement windows are in a row in one frame, they may be separated by a vertical member called the *mullion* (which is simply a

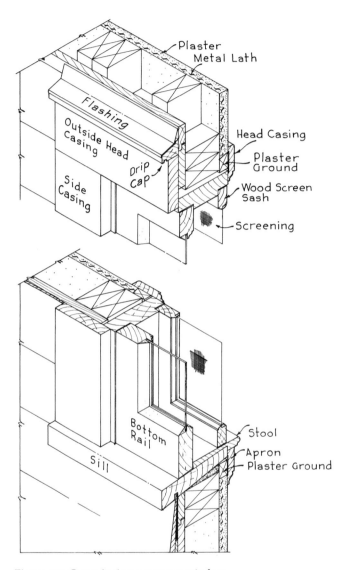

Figure 7.3 Outswinging casement window.

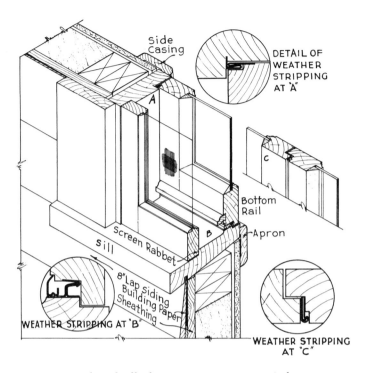

Figure 7.4 Jamb and sill of inswinging casement window.

two-sided jamb), or they may close against one another in pairs. A typical mullion detail is shown in figure 7.5a. Sections at the meeting of two casements are shown in figures 7.4 and 7.5b.

7.11 Casing

a. The casing, both exterior and interior, finishes and closes the joint between the frame and the wall. Since it seals that joint and keeps wind and rain from penetrating there, it is a building detail of considerable importance.

b. The exterior casing runs up the two sides (side casing) and across the top (head casing). It is attached firmly to the frame while being preassembled in the shop, and it should be "back-primed" (i.e., the back and cut ends should be painted at the time of assembly). It is also nailed against the sheathing or provided with anchoring devices for field attachment to the sheathing or frame. Sheathing paper must be brought in under the casing so as to form a seal where siding or other

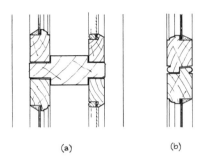

(a)   (b)

Figure 7.5 (a) Solid mullion. (b) Meeting stiles (rabbetted).

exterior finish abuts the casing. Across the top of the head casing is usually placed a sloping molding, provided with a small vertical fillet at the back, which is called the *drip cap*. Flashing covers this and is carried up under the exterior finish. This detail can be simplified by merely sloping and flashing the top of the head casing, but the projecting cap provides a positive drip.

c. The interior casing forms a part of the interior "trim" or finish of the house.

d. At the bottom (figure 7.3), starting at or on top of the wood sill and projecting into the room, is a horizontal flat piece called the *stool*. Under it and covering the space between the stool and the wall finish is the *apron*. Starting from the top of the stool and running up the side to the top is the side casing, and across the top is the head casing.

e. The stool may be omitted with inswinging casements (figure 7.4). If this is done, the side casing is carried down to meet the apron in the same way it meets the head casing. The apron, in effect, becomes the bottom casing.

7.12 Plaster Grounds

If the interior is plastered, the plasterer needs a guide of some kind or he may leave slight waves in the surface of the plaster. In order for the casing and the apron to fit snugly against the plaster, strips of wood or metal called *grounds* (the thickness of the plaster) are applied around the opening, and the plaster is finished flush with these strips. Moreover, the casings are slightly hollowed in back so that they can pass over slight irregularities. (See chapter 12.) With gypsum boards, plaster grounds are unnecessary.

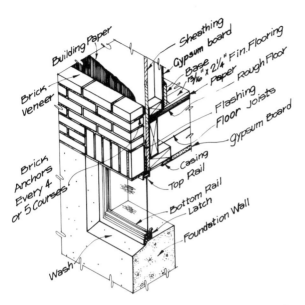

Figure 7.6 Steel basement window and cast-concrete foundation walls.

7.13 Metal Windows

a. Metal window frames and sashes are often employed in dwelling construction. The most common metals are aluminum and steel.

b. Residential aluminum sashes and frames are generally constructed of extruded tempered aluminum alloy of various strengths and hardnesses, depending upon the application. The extruded aluminum members are often tubular (closed hollow box) in cross-section, occasionally semi-tubular (semi-hollow or open), seldom actually flat. Corner joints are generally mortise-and-tenon or mitered and internally reinforced, and are held by aluminum rivets, stainless steel screws, or welds (helium-arc or electronic flash), which should be milled to a smooth finish. The typical factory finish is "as extruded" or "standard mill," protected by two dip coats of clear methacrylate lacquer, or satin finish, caused by a slight caustic etch, protected by clear acrylic lacquer. A more corrosion-resistant finish is available at extra cost by factory anodizing of the aluminum members after extrusion, to provide either a "natural" aluminum or a uniformly colored surface, a wide range of colors being available. For installation in wood-frame construction, aluminum windows are provided with integral aluminum nailing flanges or fins, pre-punched for nailing to the wood frame. The glazing of aluminum windows may be accomplished with butyl glazing compound and spring clips, with extruded aluminum glazing channels attached with screws, with "snap-in" glazing moldings of formed aluminum or rigid plastic (extruded polyvinyl chloride), or with synthetic rubber gaskets. Direct contact of unprotected aluminum with concrete or mortar masonry is generally to be avoided. In such construction, the aluminum should be anodized or protected with zinc chromate primer and bitumastic or a lacquer such as acrylic.

c. Residential steel sashes and frames are typically constructed of solid hot-rolled low-carbon billet steel. The combined weight of the sash and the frame in pounds per linear foot is generally specified, rather than the thickness of the metal of the various parts of the window. Steel casements and projected sashes are generally required to have continuous two-point weathering contacts around the entire perimeter of each ventilator sash to minimize air infiltration. The steel may be protected by pickling and galvanizing with a hot-dip "spelter" coat of molten zinc, or it may be electro-galvanized, phosphatized, and primed with baked-on enamel at the factory. Since the joints of steel sashes and frames are generally welded, the protective coatings should be applied after fabrication, and the joints should be ground smooth at the weathering contacts between the sash and the frame to provide a continuous seal. Steel frames are generally provided with anchors or flanges (pre-punched) to engage the masonry or wood frame for installation purposes. Glazing is usually accomplished with non-hardening glazing compound and spring clips or steel glazing beads attached with screws.

d. Metal windows must be handled with great care prior to installation, to avoid bending or warping. A vent sash in a frame which is out of square or out of "wind" (twisted) is difficult to operate and to close tightly.

e. Basement windows are commonly metal (figure 7.6). If the foundation wall is to be of cast concrete, the window frames may be built into the forms (chapter 4) so that when the concrete is placed the projecting legs of the frame are anchored directly and tightly into the concrete. Frames may also be inserted later, as shown in figure 7.6. Similarly, when the foundation is to be of masonry, such as concrete block or brick, the frame may be built directly into the wall or may be

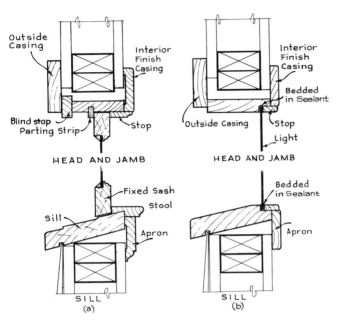

Figure 7.7 Fixed lights. (a) Separate sash. (b) Glass set directly in frame.

inserted later. In any event, the wash provided at the sill should be steep — a slope of approximately 1 to 3 is sufficient — in order to shed water quickly. Water should not be permitted to stand in contact with frames; otherwise rapid corrosion may occur.

7.14 Fixed Windows

a. Often it is desired to have windows stationary. Glass in such windows may be set in sashes, in much the usual way, or may be set directly into the frames without any sashes. A fixed light, especially when large, is more easily installed and removed when set in a separate sash, but a larger clear area is obtained if the sashes are omitted.
b. Fixed lights in separate sashes can be casement windows minus the hinges, or they may be single sashes in double-hung frames (section 7.15ff.) as shown in figure 7.7a. Evidently, no provision need be made for screens, but storm sashes may be desired.
c. Figure 7.7b shows one method of installing lights directly in frames. The critical point is at the sill, because the joint must be tight against rain outside and condensate inside. Back-putting is essential.

7.15 Wood Double-Hung Windows

In double-hung windows, two counterbalanced sashes slide up and down in the frame. In the past, cast-iron counterbalances were commonly attached to one end of a cord fastened at the opposite end to the sash and carried over pulleys set in the upper ends of the sides of the frame. These weights slid up and down in "weight pockets" between the window frame and the studs. Figure 7.9b shows this arrangement. Today, a variety of springs and otherwise-activated balances are used to offset the weight of the sash (figures 7.8, 7.9).

7.16 Sashes

a. Double-hung window sashes are in pairs, with the upper and lower sashes slightly different. The lower rail of the upper sash and the upper rail of the lower sash are shaped with a double bevel to fit snugly against each other when closed but to move apart without friction when opened. These two rails are called the *meeting rails.* Each projects beyond the parting strip (section 7.17b), whereas the rest of the rails and stiles do not.

b. With sash weights and certain types of spring balances, the stiles are grooved at the edges adjacent to the jambs so that the sash cords or balances can be carried down past the edge of the sash.

7.17 Frames and Casing

a. A double-hung frame contains more parts than a casement frame, although like the casement frame it consists essentially of a head, two jambs, and a sill. In this type of window, the entire side of the frame is called the *jamb,* but this particular part of it is called a *stile.* It is nominal 1″ material. The corresponding piece of the frame overhead is called the *yoke.* Terminology is not uniform; the terms *side jamb* and *headjamb* are common.

b. The stile (and generally the yoke) has a longitudinal groove in the center. In this is placed a rectangular *parting strip,* which separates the sashes from one another and which forms tracks in which the sashes move up and down. The parting strip may be of wood or of a metal such as aluminum.

c. Figure 7.8 illustrates a standard double-hung frame and sash. There are many variants. A blind stop is attached to the outer edges of the frame to form a recess or rabbet into which the screen and the storm

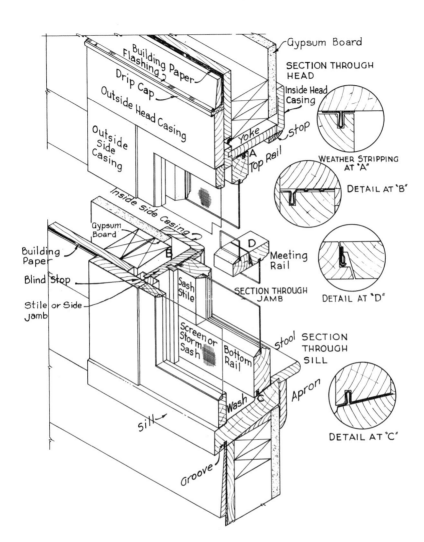

Figure 7.8 Double-hung window, weatherstripped.

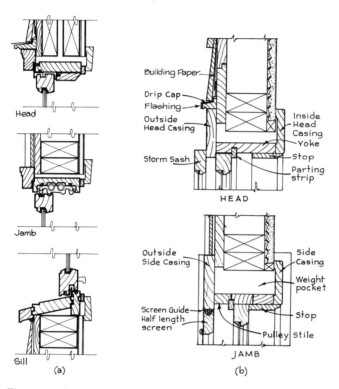

Figure 7.9 (a) Variant of double-hung window with flexible jamb liner and sill extension. (b) Simple "cottage" frame with weight pocket.

sash can be fitted. Outside of that is the outside casing, which extends far enough to overlap the sheathing and be nailed through it (with casing nails) to the studs. Sheathing paper is carried past the casing to protect the joint between the casing and the outside wall finish (such as bevel siding or shingles). At the top, the head casing is provided with the same cap or drip molding that is found on casement windows.

d. The sill of a double-hung frame has a sloping face to facilitate the shedding of water. Generally this face has one or two breaks in it: one immediately under the lower sash, and another between the sash and the outer edge of the sill to form a seat for the screen and the storm sash. These breaks obstruct the rain water that falls on the sill and keep it from being driven under the sash.

e. Interior trim around the window — casing, stool, apron — is much the same as on casement windows except that the stool is always present. There is an additional piece called the *stop*, which is a thin, narrow molding covering the joint between the interior finish casing and the frame. It forms the inside edge of the track in which the lower sash travels.

f. One variant of the standard wood double-hung window is shown in figure 7.9a. A spring-loaded flexible vinyl jamb liner is pressed against the sash stiles but is flexible enough to permit the sash to rotate about a pivot for cleaning the outer surface of the double insulating glass. Spring balances are concealed behind the jamb liner. The regular sill does not project, but a secondary sill is attached to provide a lip. Sealing this joint is important, as is the use of preservative-treated wood. In this particular detail, the stool is omitted at the sill and the inside casing is carried around the sides, the top, and the bottom. The interior wall surface is drywall (chapter 12).

g. Figure 7.9b illustrates a simpler frame known as a *cottage frame*. The blind stop is omitted. This frame makes it difficult to hang full-length screens or storm sashes. Screens are usually half-length, sliding in channels. Storm sashes must be placed against the outside casing instead of being fitted into a rabbet. Figure 7.9b shows an old-style frame with a weight pocket. The stile is called a *pulley stile* because it contains a pulley at the top, over which the sash cord runs.

7.18 Masonry Veneer

A metal double-hung window in brick veneer is shown in figure 7.10. At the head, the brickwork is carried across the opening by a steel lintel. The hollow window frame is shaped to provide a channel for the sash at the head and the jamb. The sill is shaped to provide a step for the lower sash and a rabbet to accept the screen, which fits into corresponding rabbets at the jamb and the head. Projecting legs at the head and the jambs provide for nailing to the wood framing. On the inside, the metal casing and stool meet the interior wall finish, and nailing is provided below the stool to the wood framing. The metal sill rests on a brick rowlock subsill (sections 5.52, 10.8ff.).

7.19 Mullions

When several double-hung windows are in one frame, they are separated by mullions (figure 7.11). The two stiles can be brought close together, or can be merged into a single, narrow, solid mullion.

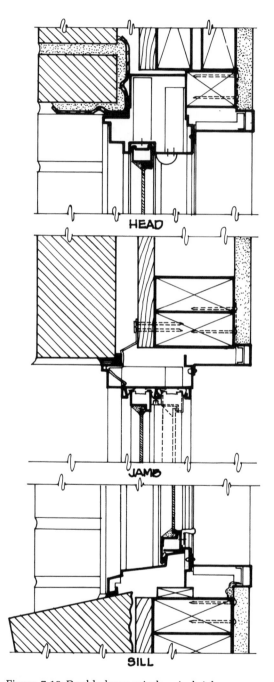

Figure 7.10 Double-hung window in brick veneer.

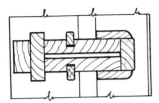

Figure 7.11 Mullion of double-hung window.

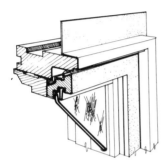

Figure 7.12 Plastic-covered wood window. PVC covers sash and exposed parts of frame and provides a lip for attachment to wood frame and sheathing, and flashing at head. Double insulating glass is held by plastic glazing gasket.

7.20 Plastic-Covered Windows

The wood parts of wood windows are good insulators against heat loss because wood has low heat conductivity. But wood shrinks and swells with changes in moisture content, and it must normally be kept painted. Metal windows, unless thermal breaks are introduced, transmit heat readily, are likely to be cold on the inside, and may condense moisture on the metal surfaces. Steel usually requires repainting from time to time, and aluminum is subject to attack in some atmospheres. To get around these limitations, windows may be made with a plastic overlay. A wood window with a vinyl (PVC) overlay is shown in figure 7.12. With such coverage, changes in moisture content — and, therefore, swelling and shrinkage — are minimized. Repainting is unnecessary. The plastic cover must be carefully formulated and fabricated to remain snugly attached to the wood with changes in temperature, because the plastic has a higher coefficient of thermal expansion than the wood. (See section 7.24.)

7.21 Metal Double-Hung Windows

a. A metal-plus-plastic (aluminum and PVC) double-hung window is shown in figure 7.13. The essential features are the same as in the wood window: head, jamb, meeting rails, and sill. Because extruded metal and plastic are used, the details are in general smaller and finer than in wood, but the functions are similar.
b. To avoid rapid conduction of heat outward through the metal, with consequent chilling and condensation, thermal breaks are introduced by making parts of the sash and frame of rigid vinyl, interlocking with the aluminum. At the head, upstanding lips provide a means of fastening the window to the house. A similar detail exists at the jambs and at the sill.
c. Double insulating glass (section 7.26) is used.

7.22 Horizontally Sliding Windows

a. A horizontally sliding window is shown in figure 7.14. Many of the details are similar to those of figure 7.13, with a combination of aluminum and vinyl extrusions to provide a thermal break. The major difference is that the sash slides or moves on rollers horizontally instead of moving vertically, and sash balances are not needed. Evidently, combinations of moving and fixed sashes can be employed.
b. Extending a window down to the floor creates a horizontally sliding door which functions in much the same manner as the windows shown. Because doors are customarily larger than windows, and traffic damage is more likely, the frames, the sash, and the tracks are generally heavier than those for windows.

7.23 Projected Windows

A projected metal window is shown in figure 7.15. In this instance, the sash and frame parts are solid sections rather than tubular extrusions. Single glazing set in glazing compound is shown, but double glazing evidently could be employed. Extended lips of the metal frames can be set in wood or masonry.

7.24 Plastic Windows

All-plastic window frames and sashes are made of extruded plastic (polyvinyl chloride) with integral color. The low thermal conductivity of the plastic is, like that of wood, an advantage. Although not subject

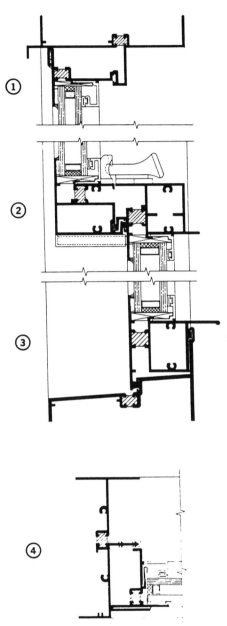

Figure 7.14 Horizontally sliding (rolling) aluminum window pair with PVC thermal breaks and sealed double glazing. (1) Head. (2) Sill, showing roller and weep holes. (3) Jamb. Courtesy of American Architectural Manufacturers Association.

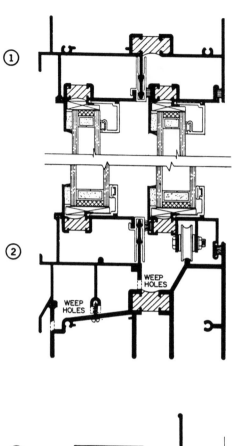

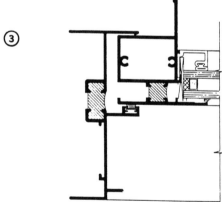

Figure 7.14 Horizontally sliding (rolling) aluminum window pair with PVC thermal breaks and sealed double glazing. (1) Head. (2) Sill, showing roller and weep holes. (3) Jamb. Courtesy of American Architectural Manufacturers Association.

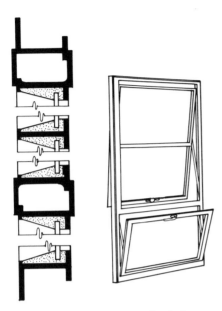

Figure 7.15 Metal projected window.

to moisture-induced dimensional changes, as woods are, plastics have higher coefficients of thermal expansion than the metals used in windows (chapter 15).

7.25 Weatherstripping

a. All windows allow some air to filter past them when there is a breeze blowing, but the amount of infiltration depends upon how tightly the windows have been installed. If the sashes fit well, the leakage is very much less than if they are loose. To reduce infiltration, a number of systems of weatherstripping have been devised to provide a tortuous path and various blocks for the air to traverse, and thereby to reduce the leakage.

b. Practically all systems rely upon shaped, thin metal strips which fit tightly against the sash and the frame or against other metal strips. The simplest of these are thin brass or zinc strips tacked to the frame and bent out to bear against the sash. Because of their inherent springiness they shut off the crack between the sash and the frame. Double-hung windows have a piece of this strip tacked against one meeting rail so that it bears against the other.

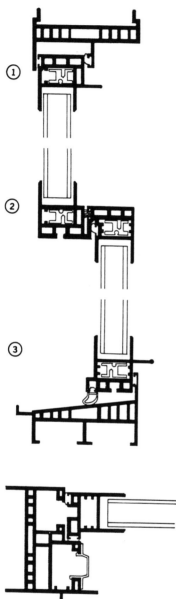

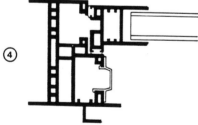

Figure 7.16 Plastic (PVC) double-hung window with sealed double glazing. (1) Head. (2) Meeting rail. (3) Sill. (4) Jamb at lower sash. Courtesy of American Architectural Manufacturers Association.

c. Somewhat more complex types call for grooves to be cut in the rails and stiles. The stripping consists of U-shaped strips of metal fitted snugly into the grooves and tacked to the frame. Meeting rails are provided with two-member strips, half tacked to each rail, so formed that the two halves engage each other when the window is closed (figure 7.8).

d. Weatherstripping of metal windows is accomplished with strips of stainless steel, soft extruded vinyl plastic, or woven mohair wool pile (generally silicone-treated) attached to one or both of the meeting members. Extruded vinyl plastics and treated woven pile are also used with wood windows.

e. For comfort and to reduce heat losses, it is advisable to reduce air infiltration, particularly on the exposed sides of the house and in rooms which are used most for living purposes. On the other hand, some infiltration is desirable to provide the fresh air necessary for health and comfort. Furthermore, fireplaces and other heating units require sufficient air for combustion and draft, and it must come from the inside of the house. If doors and windows are too tight, other means of ventilation must be provided or combustion is unsatisfactory.

f. Tables 7.2 and 7.3 afford a comparison of infiltration through unweatherstripped and weatherstripped windows.

Table 7.2 Infiltration through Double-hung Windows, Unlocked on Windward Side

Type of Double-Hung Window	Infiltration (cu ft/min), per Linear Foot of Crack											
	5[a]		**10**		**15**		**20**		**25**		**30**	
	No W-Strip	W-Strip	No W-Strip	W-Strip	No W-Strip	W-Strip	No W-Strip	W-Strip	No W-Strip	W-Strip	No W-Strip	W-Strip
Wood Sash												
Average Window	0.12	0.07	0.35	0.22	0.65	0.40	0.98	0.60	1.33	0.82	1.73	1.05
Poorly Fitted Window	0.45	0.10	1.15	0.32	1.85	0.57	2.60	0.85	3.30	1.18	4.20	1.53
Poorly Fitted but with Storm Sash	0.23	0.05	0.57	0.16	0.93	0.29	1.30	0.43	1.60	0.59	2.10	0.76
Metal Sash	0.33	0.10	0.78	0.32	1.23	0.53	1.73	0.77	2.3	1.00	2.8	1.27

[a] Boldface numbers are wind velocities (mph).
Source: ASHRAE Tests

Table 7.3 Infiltration through Casement-Type Windows on Windward Side

Type of Casement Window and Typical Crack Size		Infiltration (cu ft/min), per Linear Foot of Crack					
		5[a]	10	15	20	25	30
Rolled Section—Steel Sash							
Architectural Projected	$\frac{1}{32}$″ crack	0.25	0.60	1.03	1.43	1.86	2.3
Architectural Projected	$\frac{3}{64}$″ crack	0.33	0.87	1.47	1.93	2.5	3.0
Residential Casement	$\frac{1}{64}$″ crack	0.10	0.30	0.55	0.78	1.00	1.23
Residential Casement	$\frac{1}{32}$″ crack	0.23	0.53	0.87	1.27	1.67	2.10
Hollow Metal—Vertically Pivoted		0.50	1.46	2.40	3.10	3.70	4.00

[a] Boldface numbers are wind velocities (mph).
Source: ASHRAE Tests

7.26 Multiple Glazing

a. Heat loss through and condensation on glass are serious items, especially condensation in humidified houses (chapter 11).

b. The only practicable way to insulate glass areas against heat loss by conduction is by using several panes with air spaces between. Whereas a single thickness has a coefficient of heat transmission (chapter 11) equal to approximately 1.13, two sheets lower this to approximately 0.60 and three sheets to approximately 0.45.

c. There are various ways of installing the extra sheet or sheets of glass. The oldest is the winter window or storm sash, fitting into the screen space, put up in winter and taken down in summer (figure 7.17a). This installation has the advantage that it not only insulates the glass but also breaks the force of the wind, and when snugly fitted it largely eliminates the need for weatherstripping. The disadvantages are the necessity for putting on and taking off the sash and the frequent inconvenience of the installation. Various combination screen-and-sash installations are available in which sashes and screens, small and interchangeable, fit into permanent frames installed in the window frame.

d. A second method consists of small secondary sashes which fit into rabbeted spaces in the regular window sashes and are screwed, clipped, or otherwise fastened in place. These can be removed as desired but may be left in place the year around (figure 7.17b).

e. A third method calls for special double glass made up as a unit. Two sheets are sealed together with strips of sealing material at their edges and an air space approximately $\frac{1}{4}$″ to 1″ thick is left between the

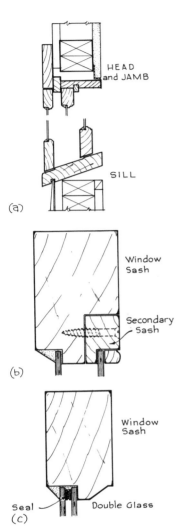

(a)

HEAD and JAMB

SILL

(b)

Window Sash

Secondary Sash

(c)

Window Sash

Seal   Double Glass

Figure 7.17 Multiple glazing. (a) Storm sash. (b) Secondary sash. (c) Double glass.

sheets. This space is filled with clean, dry air just before the edges are sealed. Double-glass panes are set in the sash in the same way as single lights and have the same appearance. They have almost as high an insulating value as double sashes, and condensation and dust are excluded from the inter-glass space as long as the seal around the edge remains unbroken (figure 7.17c). (See also figures 7.9, 7.12–7.14, and 7.16.)

f. Neither a double sash nor double glass has any effect on infiltration around a window. Weatherstripping is required to reduce heat loss. On the other hand, secondary sashes are easily removed and cleaned if necessary, and double glass simply remains fixed in place.

g. Radiant heat from the sun is not effectively stopped by several sheets of glass. Large glass areas must be so oriented and protected by overhangs as to avoid the sun's direct rays in hot weather. The best orientation in the northern hemisphere is south, because in summer the sun is nearly overhead during the hottest part of the day, but in winter it is low in the sky and can shine directly through the glass, thereby contributing to the heating of the interior.

h. With double glazing, whether by storm sash, double sash, or double glass, the temperature of the inner glass surface is markedly increased when outdoor temperatures are low. This greatly promotes comfort, inasmuch as the body radiation from occupants to cold glass surfaces is considerably reduced. Moreover, higher relative humidities are possible in the building because condensation does not occur readily on the warmer glass surface. Increased relative humidities in otherwise dry interiors promote comfort and probably health in addition to being better for woodwork and furnishings.

i. Special types of glass are made to absorb part of the sun's rays and thereby to reduce the amount of radiant energy. These high-iron heat-absorbing glasses absorb most strongly in the invisible infrared region, which constitutes about half of the total radiated solar energy, but they also absorb some of the visible red spectrum, and therefore have a slightly bluish cast. The absorbed solar energy causes the glass to rise in temperature and to re-radiate both inward and outward. The outward portion, constituting about 20 to 25 percent of the incident energy, is excluded from the building. Other glasses are tinted so as to absorb and exclude some of the solar energy in much the same way. Still other glass has an extremely thin mirrored surface which reflects part of the solar energy but still allows a considerable percentage of visible light to pass through. The reflected energy is not absorbed by the glass.

j. Low-emissity glasses, or "e-glasses," have surface coatings that significantly lower heat transmission, thus increasing the insulating value or "R value" (section 11.2) of the glass. A thin metal oxide or silver film may be deposited by sputtering in a vacuum or applied while the glass is being fired at high temperature. Alternatively, the low-emissivity film may be free-standing. Treated glass characteristically has a faint tinge. It reduces the amount of solar energy that passes, although the reduction of visible sunlight is usually not readily perceived.

k. Treated glass is used in sealed double glazing. The best position of the treated surface depends on whether the principal internal energy load is heating (winter) or cooling (summer), as shown in figure 7.18. Free-standing films ("heat mirrors") are placed in the space between the sheets of glass.

l. In addition to surface treatments and films, the inner space in sealed-glass units may be filled with an inert gas such as argon, further increasing the overall insulating or R value.

7.27 Skylights

Dome-shaped acrylic (chapter 15) skylights provide lighting from above in place of or supplemental to windows. A typical installation is shown in figure 7.19. The acrylic dome is vacuum-thermoformed to the shape shown. A curb is built up from the roof high enough to keep

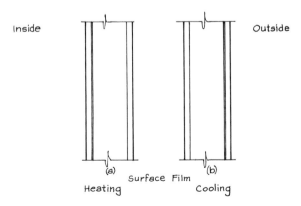

Figure 7.18

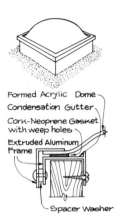

Formed Acrylic Dome
Condensation Gutter
Cork-Neoprene Gasket
with weep holes
Extruded Aluminum
Frame

Spacer Washer

Figure 7.19 Bubble-shaped skylight.

rain, snow, or slush from washing into the skylight. The dome is
clamped down by means of the interior and exterior metal sections
shown, with a gasket to act as a cushion and to permit the dome to
expand and contract differentially with respect to the metal. If the
dome is shaped properly, condensation forming on the inner surface
runs down to the gutter and out through the weep holes. In cold
climates, double domes reduce heat losses, much as double-glazed
windows do.

8 Roofing and Flashing

8.1 General

a. Roofs are more subject to weather exposure than any other house component. Among these exposures are precipitation (rain, snow, hail), mechanical exposure (wind, sliding snow and ice, maintenance traffic, thermal movement), and chemical exposure (sunlight and ultraviolet, aging, inherent chemical changes, pollution).

b. Building codes and insurance underwriters usually require various degrees of resistance to fire. Besides local codes, the most important insurance organization for standards and information are the Factory Mutual Engineering Corp. (1151 Providence Highway, Norwood, MA 02063) and Underwriters Laboratories Inc. (333 Pfingsten Rd., Northbrook, IL 60062).

c. Material standards and technical information on most roofing materials are published by insurance companies and industry sources, and are very useful for the design and construction of roofs. Specific information can be obtained from the organizations listed at the end of this chapter.

d. Roofing-system components can be classified as follows:

roof decking and structural substrate (plywood, planks, boards, steel, concrete)

shingle roofing (asphalt, wood, and metal shingles; stone slates; clay and concrete tile)

field-applied membrane roofing and insulation (liquid-applied foam and coating)

prefabricated membrane roofing (built-up, polymeric sheet, modified asphalt)

self-supporting metal roofing (articulated carbon steel, aluminum)

metal pan roofing (aluminum, steel, stainless steel, copper)

flashing (metal, polymeric, modified asphalt, built-up)

accessories and penetrations (hatchways, pipe penetrations, skylights, dormers, ventilators)

8.2 Principles Applicable to All Roofing Systems

a. All roofs should be sloped to drains (or should allow water to spill over the eaves), to avoid water accumulation on any part of the sur-

Revised by Werner H. Gumpertz, P.E., Senior Principal, Simpson Gumpertz & Heger Inc.

face. To prevent water entry, the edges (such as ridges, hips, valleys, eaves, rakes, and penetrations) must be protected and/or connected to adjoining house components by flashings. Roofs and roof decks are required, by public building codes, to support not only their own weight but also structural loads such as snow, ice, and wind (all as defined and quantified in such codes). In earthquake areas, roof structures require lateral resistance (as listed in the applicable code).

b. Insulation (chapter 11) is needed not only in the interest of fuel economy (enforced by building codes) but also to prevent excessive temperature gradients, which could cause discomfort and condensation problems as well as loss of energy. Insulations can be classified as follows.

Rigid boards: wood fiber, rigid glass fiber, foamed glass (now rarely used), extruded polystyrene foam, expanded polystyrene (EPS, bead board), polyurethane and polyisocyanurate foams, phenolic foam

Blanket insulation: glass fiber, mineral fiber

Sprayed insulation: polyurethane, polyisocyanurate foam

Poured insulation: mineral fill, fire-treated shredded newsprint, glass fiber.

In addition to serving as thermal protection, insulation can be used to improve the substrate (by providing a good base for roofing systems) and to attenuate substrate movement to prevent damage to membrane roofing. Insulation also serves to stop circulation of air where needed to stop heat losses and discomfort from convection. In some cases, insulation can be used as a partial fire retarder.

c. Slope. All roofs, including built-up systems, must be sloped sufficiently to dispose promptly of any water, even after the roof structure has deflected from elastic and creep movement. Ponding of water is unacceptable to the industry, because experience has shown that standing water damages membranes. In addition, in case of membrane failure in a ponded area, large and sometimes uncontrollable quantities of water can enter the building.

d. All roofs must be sufficiently anchored to prevent wind uplift. The most critical roof areas are perimeters, and especially roof corners, where uplift forces can be a multiple of the stalling pressure of the wind. In hurricane areas, uplift forces can reach 90 lb/sq ft. Insurance institutions, such as Factory Mutual Laboratories, now require roof insulation to be mechanically fastened to steel and wood decks to ensure adequate anchorage. Perimeter flashing must be well nailed with annular-ring nails (chapter 14) to prevent the wind from entering at the edge and peeling back the whole roofing system. Perimeter gravel stops should be anchored with a continuous heavy-gauge hook strip to develop the necessary anchoring force.

e. Vapor retarder. In cold climates, a vapor retarder is needed on the warm side of a roof structure to prevent moisture from accumulating in the roof from movement of water vapor under high pressure (in the interior of the house) to the ambient low pressure (on the exterior) and condensing when it reaches the dew point (chapter 11). Aluminum or kraft paper facing on blanket insulation is often used; recent practice favors continuous coverage of the warm side of the wall or roof with polyethylene sheeting. Either way, it is important to seal all edges and laps of the membrane to prevent significant vapor penetration.

f. Venting. It is important to keep the attic or the roof framing vented (chapter 9) to prevent condensation. In attics, this is accomplished by the use of appropriate ridge and eave vents to allow circulation of air. In flat roofs, the space directly under plywood decking must be vented to prevent condensation, which can cause swelling of, and damage to, plywood roof decking.

g. Structure. For successful application of a built-up roofing membrane, the structural roof deck must be stable enough to prevent locally significant movement that could tear the membrane. Roof "control" joints must be installed along the lines of deck discontinuity, where differential movement can occur.

If local discontinuities over beams are accompanied by excessive deflections of joists or decks (exceeding $\frac{1}{180}$ of the length of the span), tears in the membrane are possible. The presence of insulation increases the gap over the beams because of geometry. Creep deflections (in concrete and wood) can be a multiple of the computed elastic deflection. Control joints in the membrane can absorb movement and prevent damage.

Different deflection and movement patterns cause differential movements in lines between deck direction, frequently reflecting in differential vertical shear movement and cracking of the membrane. Again, control joints in these critical areas can prevent damage. The same applies to a line where beams or joists change in span length, because this can produce differential deflection in reentrant (interior) corners of the roof and where no work adjoins existing roofing.

h. Roof decking must not only be capable of supporting live and dead loads imposed on the roof, but must also be dimensionally stable and capable of serving as a base for attachment of all types of roofing, as discussed below.

Plywood: The roofs of most houses are wood-framed. By far the predominant roof decking material is plywood, generally identified as APA 1-83 "C-C exterior" grade, $\frac{5}{8}''$ to $\frac{3}{4}''$ thick and in 4' × 8' sheets. Like all other materials, plywood moves with seasonal moisture changes and must be installed with $\frac{1}{8}''$ joints to prevent buckling. Grade CDX should not be used for roof sheathing.

Particleboard has been used as a cheaper replacement for plywood. This board is made up of wood in various forms (flakes, chips, strands, or a combination thereof). This material should be used with caution, because of its high movement coefficient under varying temperature and moisture conditions, its susceptibility to damage from moisture and water exposure, and its limited nail-holding ability.

Tongue-and-groove boarding, sometimes applied diagonally, is now rarely used because of its high labor and material costs.

The *thickness* of roof decking is being reduced by some standards as an economy move. Use of thin sheathing may be approved by industry associations and even building codes, but it should be recognized that there is a reduction in the margin of safety with respect to deflection, structural adequacy, and depth of nail anchorage.

i. Some fire-retardant chemicals tend to deteriorate wood to the point of slow but certain disintegration. They may also corrode some fasteners.

j. Sheathing should be attached with coated annular-ring nails (chapter 14), spaced as recommended, to prevent corrosion, loose connections, and reduction in the diaphragm resistance needed to keep the roof structurally stable. All plywood edges must be supported adequately by rafters or solid bridging.

k. The problem of vapor migration from the interior to the outside calls for an appropriate vapor barrier, depending on the details of construction, the location of thermal insulation, and the ventilation (chapter 11).

8.3 Asphalt Shingles

a. Because of their fire resistance and economy, and the choice of colors, asphalt shingles are the first choice of cover for steep roofs. Many municipalities have legislated against wood shingles, because of the fire hazard, but permit asphalt shingles.

b. Composition. Asphalt shingles are made with a base of asphalt-impregnated organic or glass-fiber felt covered with a layer of colored ceramic granules. Good felt-based asphalt shingles have a practical life expectancy of 15 to 30 years, depending primarily on their solar exposure (north vs. south) and on the quality of the mineral surface granules and their embedment. Glass-fiber felts, now widely used, are sensitive to bending (especially during cold weather) and are easily broken. Durability depends on the quality and quantity of the base felt and the impregnating asphalt, and on the weight of the shingle. Weights range from approximately 280 to approximately 350 pounds per 100 square feet. Whereas the standard asphalt "shingle" originally was a 9″ × 12″ rectangle, asphalt shingles are now applied in strips, usually 36″ long and 12″ wide from butt to top. These may be embossed to give the appearance of random-width individual shingles, or they may be slotted every 12″, with a half-slot at each end. In either case, when the successive courses of shingles are laid to cover the ends of the embossed depressions or the slots, the final appearance is that of individual shingles. Other patterns are also common.

c. Appearance. Because ordinary asphalt shingles, unlike wood shingles, do not taper to a heavy butt and are fairly thin, they do not give a pronounced shadow line and the roof may consequently be rather uninteresting in appearance. To overcome this drawback, heavy-grade asphalt shingles are sometimes double-coated at the butt to provide horizontal and vertical shadows.

d. Wind uplift. To keep shingles from being raised and blown off in high winds, they are provided with spots of a thermoplastic mastic-based adhesive along the line which will be just under the butt of the next course above. When the hot sun shines on the roof, these spots soften and adhere to the butts of the succeeding course, bonding them and preventing them from being raised by wind. In areas of low winter temperatures combined with snow and alternating freezing and thawing, shingles must be sealed by hand; in warmer climates, the sun will cause the adhesive to bond properly without any other action.

e. Underlayment. Many of the principles governing the laying of asphalt and wood shingles are similar (section 8.4). There are some important differences, however. Before application of asphalt shingles, an underlayment of roofing felts is first needed to protect the decking against water leakage and to prevent excessive air circulation (figure 8.1). No. 15 or 30 felt (ASTM D226 or D2626) is employed.

f. Ice dams. Ice-dam flashing along the eaves is vital in snow regions, especially on non-monolithic roofs, such as those covered with asphalt, wood, or slate shingles or tiles. Accumulated snow and ice above a heated space, such as an attic, may melt and run down to a colder area, such as the eaves, and freeze, forming an ice dam (sections 9.4g, 11.4d) that blocks water, causing it to back up the roof under the roofing and into the interior. Where ice dams are likely, a waterproof membrane such as a strip of 50-lb or heavier smooth-surfaced roll roofing (section 8.6) is laid along the eaves over the underlayment (figure 8.1) to prevent water backed up by the ice dam from penetrating under the roofing to the interior. The upper edge of the membrane should extend up the roof far enough to be at least 12″ inside the line of the house wall, farther for shallower pitches. Edges and overlapping seams of the membrane must be thoroughly cemented. Other suitable membranes include simple built-up felts applied with hot or cold asphalt cements, or by application of a self-adhering polyethylene and modified asphalt prefabricated membrane (sections 8.8, 8.9). In northern regions of the United States, ice-dam aprons are made from metal sheets, properly sealed along their joints, to facilitate snow sliding off. The problem can be alleviated by omitting gutters that trap ice and snow.

g. Support. Asphalt shingles are relatively soft and will droop if allowed to project unsupported at the eaves. For this reason, a wood-shingle supporting course or metal drip support is often laid first (figure 8.1). In any event, a strip-shingle starting course with slots or

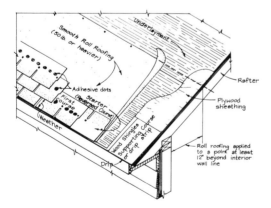

Figure 8.1 Starting courses and weather, asphalt-strip shingles.

embossed edge pointed upward is laid so that the continuous edge of the strip lies along the edge of the eave. The first regular course then is laid with the slotted or embossed edge down. Figure 8.1 shows both a wood-shingle supporting course and a doubled strip-shingle starting course. Succeeding courses are shifted horizontally one-half or one-third the width of shingle, or according to whatever pattern is wanted.

h. Weather exposure. The amount exposed to the weather can be varied slightly to make the courses come out even at the ridge.

i. Application. Shingles should be laid to chalk lines, although with a little care strip shingles can be made self-aligning. One nail or staple is driven at the end of each strip and two equally spaced between. In addition to the method of laying just described, there are numerous others, such as interlocking, which are variations of the standard method.

j. Ridge and hip details (figure 8.2) are almost identical to those employed for wood shingles (section 8.4), except that the Boston hip and ridge are made by using single shingles instead of pairs, the one shingle simply being bent over the ridge or hip and nailed down on both sides. No flashing is necessary.

k. Open valleys (figure 8.3) are the same as for wood shingles (section 8.4, figure 8.9), except that a strip of coated roofing felt (section 8.7) may replace the metal flashing.

l. Closed valleys on roofs covered with individual asphalt shingles are handled in much the same manner as wood shingles, but strip asphalt shingles frequently are run, "woven," into the valley from one side and a short distance, 12" minimum, up the roof on the other, the procedure alternating from course to course as shown in figure 8.3. The shingles are thus self-flashing. Strip shingles may also be run up a short distance, 12" minimum, on one side and the shingles on the

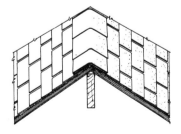

Figure 8.2 Ridge, asphalt shingles.

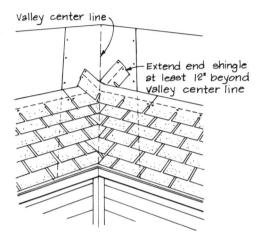

Figure 8.3 "Woven" closed valley, asphalt shingles.

other side cut parallel to but 2″ short of the center line of the valley (figure 8.4).

8.4 Wood Shingles

a. Wood shingles are sawn and are usually red cedar, or sometimes white cedar or redwood. Wood shingles come in four standard grades (Nos. 1, 2, 3, and 4) and three standard lengths (16″, 18″, and 24″). Number 1 shingles are all heartwood vertical or edge grain, and are entirely "clear" (that is, free of defects). They should be used for all first-quality work. Number 2 shingles are blemish-free three-fourths of their length above the butt, allow a 1″ strip of sapwood, and are mixed flat and vertical grain; they can be used for good-quality roofs. Number 3 shingles are clear for 6″ above the butt, allow more sapwood, and are mixed flat and vertical grain. They are useful for economy and secondary buildings. Number 4 shingles are used mainly for temporary purposes.

b. Wood shakes are red cedar split to produce an irregular, rustic appearance. Standard lengths of shakes are 18″, 24″, and 32″. Hand-split and resawn shakes are first split and then resawn along a diagonal center line to provide two shakes, each with one split and one sawn face. Butt thicknesses vary from $\frac{1}{2}″$ to $\frac{3}{4}″$ for the smaller, thinner varieties and from $\frac{3}{4}″$ to $1\frac{1}{4}″$ or more for the larger ones. Other shakes are split to a taper, or are straight split. When the pitch of the

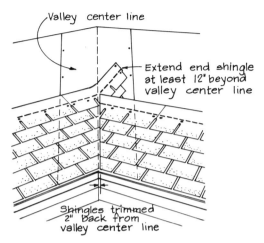

Figure 8.4 "Cut" closed valley, asphalt shingles.

roof is 4:12 or steeper, the recommended exposures are $7\frac{1}{2}''$, 10", and 13" for 18", 24", and 32" shakes, respectively. Because shakes do not lie as snugly against one another as sawn shingles, a layer of 30-lb roofing felt is recommended with each course of shakes; the lower edge of the roofing paper is held above the butt line at slightly more than double the exposure so that it will not show through the joints between shakes. Other details are similar to those for sawn shingles, including ridges, hips, valleys, and doubled or tripled starter courses. The first (under) course for the latter can be special 15" shakes made for the purpose.

c. Wood shingle-support strips, in place of solid decking, are sometimes employed with wood shingles and shakes for ventilation from below, to combat decay that can be caused by water penetrating between shingles, especially in humid conditions. Where high winds may drive water under shingles, especially on fairly shallow slopes, causing leaks, continuous sheathing is needed, together with roofing felt (section 8.3). Figure 8.5 shows an open cornice with tight tongue-and-groove sheathing visible from below to the wall line, followed by shingle strips. These are spaced apart the same distance as the "weather" or coursing of the shingles.

d. Starting course. The starting course is doubled and projects beyond the lowest roof board approximately $1\frac{1}{2}''$ to form a drip which forces rain water to fall clear of the roof. Along the rake (sloping edge)

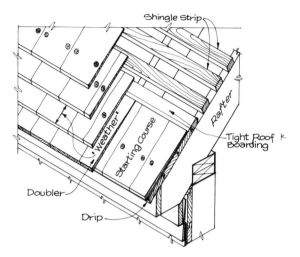

Figure 8.5 Detail at eaves, wood shingles.

of a gable roof, the end shingles project at least $\frac{1}{2}''$ for the same purpose. Joints in the second layer of the starting course and in each successive course must miss ("break") those in the preceding layer or course by at least $1\frac{1}{2}''$; otherwise rain water may find its way down through successive courses and eventually through the roof.

e. Succeeding courses are set back from the preceding ones a distance which depends upon the length of the shingle and upon the effect desired. Standard 16" and 18" shingles are usually exposed 4" to $5\frac{1}{2}''$ to the weather, the exact "weather" depending upon the pitch of the roof and upon the distance from eaves to ridge, which is divided into a full number of courses.

f. Installation. Courses may be kept straight by laying shingles to a line. This may be done by laying the butts along a chalk line struck for every course, or by tacking a straight edge (straight board) to the roof, laying the shingle butts against the board. Sometimes every sixth or seventh course is doubled to give a heavier shadow line and break the plane of the roof; sometimes shingles are laid at random in no set courses at all; sometimes they are staggered so that alternate shingles project beyond their neighbors; sometimes the courses are made wavy to simulate thatch. These are all merely variations; the basic principles remain the same.

g. Nailing. Each shingle should be held with two nails or staples (chapter 14) driven not more than $\frac{3}{4}''$ from the edge. Heads should be driven just flush with the shingle; driving too far tends to cause splitting, and projecting heads keep the shingles above from lying snugly against those below. The most commonly used nails are heavily galvanized or aluminum flat-headed nails. Nails must be long enough to penetrate the several thicknesses of shingle and the stripping or deck. Three-penny nails are customary for 16" and 18" shingles, 4d for 24". Longer nails may be needed at ridges and hips (see below). Nails should have annular-ring grooves (chapter 14) for permanent anchorage into the deck, and to avoid gradual backout.

h. Spacing. Shingles should be laid with approximately $\frac{1}{4}''$ space between adjacent shingles, depending upon their width. Shingles shrink and swell as they dry or become wet, and they must have room to move.

i. Ridges and hips require closure details, and similar details are used at both. The simplest type of ridge is the saddle, flashed or unflashed. The top shingles are cut off at the ridge, and a pair of saddle boards are nailed along the two slopes of the ridge. If these are not flashed, the nails should be driven through an elastic cement and the nail heads completely covered with mastic. The better way is to cover the saddle boards with rust-resistant metal flashing (figure 8.6) and fasten the edges of the metal indirectly through concealed cleats or hook strips.

j. The Boston ridge (figure 8.7) (not suitable for shakes) uses shingles

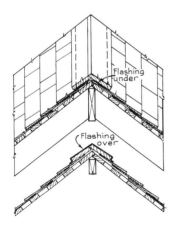

Figure 8.6 Saddle ridge, wood shingles.

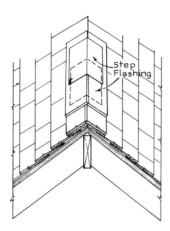

Figure 8.7 Boston ridge, wood shingles.

of all the same width, laid with their long edges parallel to the ridge instead of perpendicular to it. They are lapped the same amount as on the rest of the roof. Alternate shingles lap over the ridge. A piece of flashing is laid under each pair of shingles to make this detail watertight.

k. Finishing of ridges and hips. Because of their similarity, hips and ridges can be finished in much the same manner. Saddle boards can be carried down the two slopes of the hip and made tight in much the same manner as the saddle ridge. There is this difference, however: Saddle boards along the hip merely rest on the butts of the shingles and leave wedge-shaped openings, which must be filled in with wooden wedges; otherwise rain can drive in under the saddles. The same holds true of the Boston hip; otherwise it is the same as the Boston ridge (figure 8.8). To avoid the use of wedges, the Boston hip may be laid in the same manner as a slate hip (section 8.5 and figure 8.14). This requires close fitting of the shingles and adequate flashing at the juncture of regular shingles and hip shingles.

l. Valleys are either "open" or "closed." That is, either shingles are carried right across the valley without a break or they are stopped a few inches short of the valley line, the intervening space being left open and protected by flashing.

m. Open valleys (figure 8.9) are much easier to build and to flash than closed valleys. A strip of flashing metal (at least 16″ wide for pitches 6:12 or greater, and 20″ wide for lesser slopes) is placed in the valley

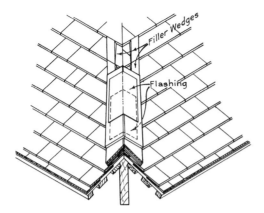

Figure 8.8 Boston hip, wood shingles.

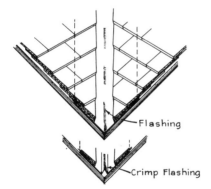

Figure 8.9 Open valley, wood shingles.

and turned up on both sides. If the valley lies between two roofs of approximately equal area, the flashing is turned up the same amount on both sides; if one roof is considerably smaller than the other, the flashing is turned up farther on the smaller roof because the greater volume and force of water coming down the larger roof is likely to force some of the water up the smaller roof. To prevent this, the valley metal is best crimped into an inverted V at the valley center to form a dam, as shown in the lower diagram in figure 8.9. With the flashing in place, the shingles are laid so that the exposed portion of the valley is 4″ to 6″ wide at the top. This distance can be increased by 1″ in 8′ toward the foot of the valley to provide a taper to facilitate drainage

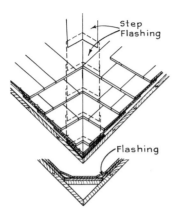

Figure 8.10 Closed valley, wood shingles.

and minimize troubles from ice and snow. To prevent leakage, metal flashing should be set into cement if there is an underlayment.

n. Closed valleys (figure 8.10) use courses of shingles carried across the valley from one side to the other. The upper sketch shows courses meeting at the valley bottom. The lower sketch shows a board or boards straddling the valley and shingle courses carried across it. Each course of shingles must be flashed separately, with a sheet of flashing laid with its lower edge just above the butt line of the succeeding course and carried at least 6″ up onto each valley slope. This dimension is increased on shallow roofs.

8.5 Slate

a. Slate is one of the best and most durable of all roofing materials, outlasting both wood and asphalt shingles many times. Because of its laminar structure, slate can readily be split into thin sheets. For roofing purposes it ought to be at least $\frac{3}{16}$″ thick, and often is much thicker.

b. Slate used for roofing and other purposes comes mainly from Pennsylvania and nearby areas, and from Vermont and neighboring portions of New York. Pennsylvania slates are dark gray and blue gray, often with streaks of darker color, called ribbons, apparently of the same composition as the rest of the slate. Vermont slates are green, purple, red, and mottled. Ribbons are not found in Vermont slates.

c. Framing. The framing for a slate roof must be more substantial than for wood or asphalt, or for any other kind of roofing except tile,

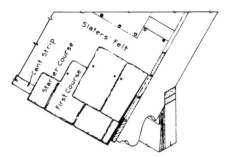

Figure 8.11 Eave detail, slate roofing.

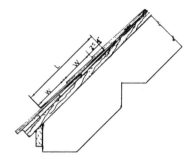

Figure 8.12 Determining "weather," slate roofing.

because of the weight of the slate. Decking is continuous, instead of in strips as may be employed for wood shingles (section 8.4). A slate roof should pitch not less than 4″ per foot.

d. Underlayment. Before slates are laid, the roof is covered with 30-lb asphalt-impregnated slater's felt, lapped at the edges and ends 2″ to 3″ and nailed with large-headed shingle nails (chapter 14) or metal disks. When ice dams may occur, the precautions set forth in section 8.3f should be observed.

e. Application. Slates are laid in much the same manner as wood shingles, with some important differences. At the eaves (figure 8.11) there is a cant strip thick enough to give the starter course the same slant as subsequent courses with respect to the roof surface. The starter course is laid with the long dimension of the slates parallel to the eaves.

f. Weather exposure. The second course above any particular course should lap over that course by at least 2″, and the first course above should lap half the remaining length (figure 8.12). From this rule, the following formula determines the "weather":

$$W = (L - X)/2,$$

where W = exposure to weather, L = length of slate, and X = length of head lap. The value of X should be 4″ for slopes of 4″ to 5″ in 12″, 3″ for slopes 8″ to 20″ in 12″, and 2″ for steeper slopes, all varied slightly to provide even coursing from eaves to ridges.

g. Attachment. To match the permanence of the slate, nails should be of a corrosion-resistant material, such as copper or copper alloy. Heavily zinc-coated nails are also common. Care must be exercised to drive the nail heads just flush with the surface of the slate. Too-heavy driving cracks the slate, and projecting heads prevent the next course from lying snugly against the preceding one. On large roofs, various sizes of slate are often employed, starting with large thick slates at the eaves and gradually reducing size and thickness toward the ridge. The starting slates are, in this case, often as much as 2′ long and as much as 2″ thick, whereas ridge slates may be only 10″ long and $\frac{3}{16}$″ thick. Standard sizes vary from 24″ × 14″ to 10″ × 6″. This not only gives a variation in texture; it also causes the roof to look much larger than it actually is.

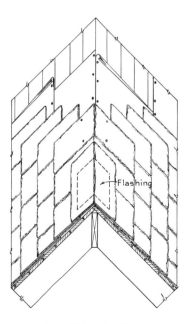

Figure 8.13 Ridge detail, slate roofing.

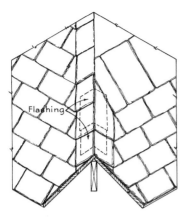

Figure 8.14 Boston hip, slate roofing.

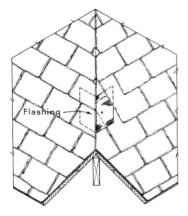

Figure 8.15 "Tight" hip, slate roofing.

h. Ridges and hips (figures 8.13–8.15) are only slightly different from wood shingles (section 8.4 and figures 8.6–8.8). The Boston ridge (figure 8.13) and the saddle ridge are quite common. In the saddle roof, slates laid end to end generally take the place of saddle boards, although saddle boards can be used. Tight and Boston hips are both found. The Boston hip is made by cutting the course slates to fit the hip slates; it results in a tight joint, provided that plenty of cement is used under the slates at the point and that the flashing is good (figure 8.14). A hip detail sometimes found on steep roofs is the "close" or "tight" hip (figure 8.15). Slate courses are laid to the hip, and the end slates are merely mitered to the slope of the hip. Flashing and liberal quantities of elastic cement are necessary to make this detail water-tight.

i. Open and closed valleys are handled in the same manner as wood shingles (section 8.4, figures 8.9 and 8.10). The transition from one side of a closed valley to the other is sometimes made more gradual by laying a secondary roof board in the valley as shown in the lower detail of figure 8.10. Slate are cut to fit into the trough of the valley and make the change from one side to the other without a sharp break.

8.6 Clay and Concrete Tile

a. Tiles are the aristocrats of roofing materials. The traditional details represent centuries of European experience. Tiles are heavier, need stronger roof framing, and must be laid with more care than other roof coverings. Traditional standards require the installation of horizontal wood roofing nailers to facilitate drying of the tiles on the underside. Nails of copper or some other durable metal are used to match the longevity of the tile, with annular-ring shanks to prevent loosening with time or wind uplift.

b. Although historically most tiles have been made of burnt clay, with its familiar red color, some are of concrete, with their colors depending on the pigments added. Clay tiles can also be colored. When glazed, clay tiles may be almost any color, with vivid and brilliant reflection. Glazed tile prevent water absorption by the clay; but poorly made glazing can spall off within a short time.

c. Shingle tile. The simplest kind of tile is a flat or slab (bottom corrugated) rectangular block which is applied to the roof in a manner similar to slate. These tiles are nailed near their top edges, and nail holes must be formed during manufacture. Copper or other corrosion-resistant nails are used, their length depending upon the thickness of the tile, which varies from $\frac{3}{8}''$ to $1''$ or more (figure 8.16a,b).

d. Interlocking. Tiles are made in various interlocking shapes (figure 8.16c) designed to cover the roof with a small amount of head and side lap. The interlocking designs are usually made with a small gutter at the side to carry off water, and with an upward-projecting lip at the head of the tile to provide both a bulkhead against water driven upward by high winds and a key to hold two adjacent courses together. A special wood cant strip supporter is needed at the eaves. A closure tile is needed at the rake. Additional stripping is needed at the ridge to support the special ridge roll which covers that point. An-

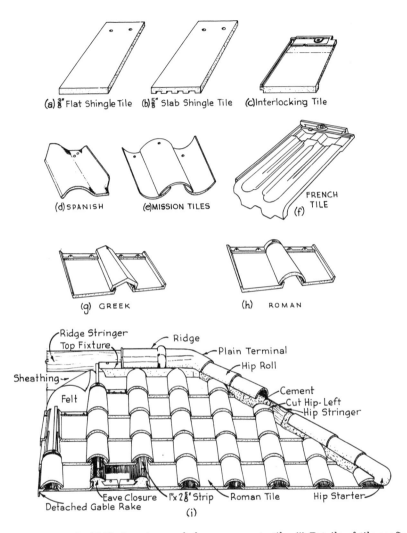

Figure 8.16 (a–h) Various types of clay or concrete tile. (i) Details of tile roofing.

other special piece is needed to cover the hip. At hips and valleys, special triangular pieces, made to fit the pitch of the roof, are required to make the joint (figure 8.16c).

e. *Mission* and *Spanish* tiles (figure 8.16d,e) are the familiar curved tiles. Of the two, the mission tile is the simpler, inasmuch as it is merely a curved piece. The roof is covered by turning adjacent tiles alternately concave (*pans*) and convex (*covers*), the covers fitting down over the upturned edges of the pans. Both are nailed with a single nail at the upper end. The convex tiles rest on 1″ × 4″ wood strips set on edge, running from eave to ridge. At the eaves, special closure pieces cover the opening which would otherwise occur under the convex tile. The rake of the roof is usually covered with a tile turned down over the edge, but special rake pieces are also employed. Ridges and hips require special rolls, and special tiles are needed at hips and valleys. Spanish tiles differ from mission tiles in that the convex and concave parts are formed in one S-shaped tile. The details of laying are otherwise much the same.

f. A variation of the flat shingle tile is the *French* tile (figure 8.16f), which is heavily grooved on top and has corresponding projecting lugs on the lower side which fit into the grooves of the next lower course. These tiles interlock and thus provide maximum coverage with minimum material. Special return pieces are required at the rakes. Special hip and ridge rolls are needed. Hip and valley tiles must be made to a triangle depending upon the pitch of the roof. Special wood strips or stringers are called for under hip and ridge rolls. Cement and lime mortar spacers are often used at these points as means of attachment in addition to, or in place of, metal fasteners.

g. *Greek* and *Roman* tiles (figure 8.6g,h) are both combinations of flat tiles with upstanding outer edges and curved or angular covers. Covers are tapered so that succeeding courses fit snugly, and edges of flat tiles are tapered to fit. Special eave closures, top or ridge fixtures, ridge and hip rolls, gable rake closures, and triangular hip and valley tiles are required in addition to the various wood stringers which support the covers and rolls.

h. Underlayment. Since tiles are not fully waterproof at their side joints and at nail holes (except possibly at slopes exceeding 9:12), a waterproof underlayment is important. Unless tiles are set exclusively into masonry mortar (a method much favored in southern Florida), the membrane underlayment must have some water resistance around nail penetrations. Pullout of fasteners can be avoided by the use of annular-ring nails, and by employing stable wood underlayment to anchor those nails. All tiles require a tightly sheathed roof covered by the best 30–40-lb roofing felt or special modified asphalt plastomer waterproofing. At hips, valleys, ridges, eaves, and other discontinuities, and on low-pitched roofs, the felt must be reinforced with metal flashing, or be doubled. Another material is prefabricated polyethylene-modified asphalt. This material is self-adhering and has some ability to self-seal around penetrating fasteners.

i. General assembly. This is shown in figure 8.16i. Critical areas requiring attention are valleys and eaves, especially at low slopes. All underlayment should be examined for integrity immediately before the tiles are applied; twisted or damaged tiles must be found and discarded to prevent excessive water penetration and point bearing, which could lead to breakage under foot traffic.

j. Slopes. Slopes should be fairly steep to prevent leakage through nail holes. Although most manufacturers recommend a minimum slope of 3:12, a 4:12 slope or better is advisable.

8.7 Built-Up Roofing

a. Built-up roofing is commonly found on "flat-roofed" commercial buildings but may also be employed on shallow-pitched or flat roofs of dwellings. The commonly accepted limit of shallow slope is 2:12.

b. Built-up roofing consists of layers of a cold- or hot-applied bituminous mopping in which sheets of roofing felt are embedded as shown in figure 8.17. Depending on the number of plies wanted, successive layers of felt are offset from the one below by $\frac{1}{2}$, $\frac{1}{3}$, or $\frac{1}{4}$ the width of the roll (2-ply, 3-ply, 4-ply, etc.). If the substrate is wood, a first layer of sheathing paper is commonly nailed to the deck, to prevent a continuous bond between the roofing and the substrate. The concept of built-up roofing is that of a multi-layered sandwich, in which the bituminous mopping is the interply adhesive and waterproofing, and the felts serve as the reinforcing layer.

c. The conventional and higher-quality system uses heated asphalt cement (ASTM D312) interlaced with prefabricated glass-fiber felts (ASTM D2178). Occasionally, organic (paper) felt is still employed. Generally where top quality is not required the industry has systematically degraded the quality of these felts (ASTM D226 or D2626) so that their quality is no longer adequate. The asphalt is heated not only

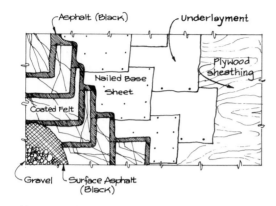

Figure 8.17 Built-up roofing, showing roof sheathing, underlayment, base sheet, mopped-in felt plies, and roofing gravel.

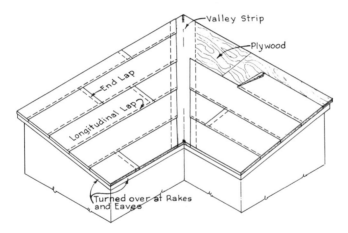

Figure 8.18 Mineral-surfaced cold-applied roofing; low slopes, with valley.

to make application possible but also to produce tight bonding. In some limited cases, when the slope does not exceed $\frac{1}{2}''$ in $12''$, the mopping is coal-tar pitch.

d. *Cold-applied* roofing (figure 8.18) uses emulsions (asphalt suspended in water) or asphalt cutbacks (asphalt softened by hydrocarbon solvents) to serve as adhesive and waterproofer. The top felts are usually coated with mineral granules. Cold-applied systems have a lower life expectancy than hot-applied systems, because their adhesive and waterproofing qualities depend too much on workmanship and on the ability of the carrier (water or solvent) to escape from the roofing membrane without leaving weaknesses or uncoated spots between the felts. Their life expectancy, at best, is 5 to 12 years, unless they are used on very steep roofs, where they function more as large shingles.

e. For protection from the sun's rays, a layer of light-colored granules of gravel or slag is embedded in the top or flood coat of hot-applied asphalt while it is still liquid. If a "cold" process is used, cap sheets with factory-applied granules provide protection against solar exposure.

f. Flashing is used to terminate membranes at perimeters, rising walls, and penetrations, to keep water from getting into the roofing and the building. In snow areas, perimeter flashing must be high enough to prevent overtopping by melting snow. Where roofs intersect with rising walls, the perimeter flashing must also be protected by through-wall flashing to prevent water from penetrating the wall, bypassing the roof flashing, and entering the building's interior.

8.8 Polymeric Sheet Roofing

a. Polymeric roofing is used in half of all low-slope and "flat" roofs. In time its use may be reduced by developments in the field of modified asphalt roofing, but it is likely to retain a significant share of the total market. Various types of material are used; they fall into the following two basic categories:

Elastomers (artificial rubbers) are thermosetting; that is, their shapes are set during the manufacturing process. The most prominent material is EPDM (ethylene-propylene-diene), which comes in factory made-up widths up to 20'; CR (Neoprene), usually in 5' or 6' wide rolls, and IIR (butyl). These materials are usually bonded with two-sided tapes or contact adhesives.

Plastomers (plastic sheets) are thermoplastic; that is, they can be softened and reshaped by heating or by appropriate solvents. The specific materials in this class are PVC (polyvinyl chloride), CSPE (Hypalon), and CPE (chlorinated polyethylene). These materials are usually bonded by heat welding or solvent welding, without any external bonding material.

b. Some polymeric sheets — especially plastomers — are reinforced, which gives them much-needed strength and dimensional stability. Elastomers are less likely to be reinforced because, by nature, they are more stable. EPDM has considerable resistance against deterioration by exposure to weather, as does butyl. Neoprene must be protected by paint. The main weakness of plastomers is their dependence on plasticizers, without which they would be too rigid for roofing. Plasticizer migration is a significant problem, caused by exudation with time and accelerated by contact with certain other materials (especially bituminous elements). Loss of plasticizer causes sheets to shrink and to become brittle, resulting in widespread cracking and separation of roofing sheets.

c. Lap bonding of polymeric sheets is relatively simple; however, it requires significant skill, because of lack of redundancy (the system relies on a single sheet and a perfect bond in the laps). Elastomeric roofing cannot be welded, because it is thermosetting and its consistency cannot be modified. Laps are usually bonded by cleaning both contact surfaces, applying a butyl-based contact cement, and pressing the surfaces together with a roller. The resulting joints cannot be better than the skill of the mechanic allows them to be. Since most sheets are coated with anti-stick surfacing, the preparatory cleaning of the contact surfaces, which is crucial to success, is difficult to achieve. Joints are usually caulked along the lap edges (this procedure is mostly symbolic) and to protect the seam adhesive during curing time. Sealants are not a real protection against failure of lap bonding. Plastomers are usually welded by heat or solvents, which gives joints a more secure and easier-achieved bond. However, the "window" of bonding can be narrow — a "low" temperature can fail to produce an intimate bond, and a "high" temperature can cause degradation (and failure) of the surfaces to be bonded. In addition, some plastomers (including CPEs) lose some of their thermoplastic capabilities with age, making heat or solvent bonding excessively difficult or impossible. This can become a problem as early as 6 months after construction.

d. Single-ply polymeric sheet roofing can be applied to a roof deck by one of the following three methods:

Full bonding calls for properly constructed insulation boards as a base, and is achieved with an appropriate contact adhesive applied to the insulation. The sheet is then applied to the contact adhesive; but the joints between sheets must be bonded securely, with a separate splicing adhesive or appropriate welding, as described above.

Loose-laid sheeting is spliced in the manner described above, but it is adhered to the building only at the perimeters and around penetrations. Wind-uplift resistance is provided by an appropriate quantity of large ($1\frac{1}{2}''$ to 2″) pieces of rounded river gravel (to avoid puncture), or by application of precast concrete pavers (which also provide considerable protection against physical damage). The structure of the roof must be designed to resist the extra weight of the ballast.

Mechanically attached membranes are held down by continuous metal strips or plate systems, screwed securely into the roof deck and spaced as needed for adequate hold-down power (usually at spacings of 5′ to 10′ on center). The metal strips or plates must be covered by membrane sealed to the original sheets for waterproofing. Some systems use fasteners with large washers lined up along the splices. The permanence of the mechanical attachment is uncertain, especially where wind pulsation may damage the fasteners, the washers, or the membrane itself, or where the fasteners may back out from the deck.

e. Flashing (section 8.12) for polymeric sheet is relatively simple, as these materials are "self-flashing." The flashings are of the same composition as the base material, and are bonded to the horizontal sheets by the same splicing methods as the base material. Their continuity and shape are as important as with any other type of flashing. Counterflashings are designed in the same manner as for other types of roofing. Flashing is easily formed of uncured rubber.

f. The same venting precautions recommended for built-up roofing (section 8.7) apply to work with single-ply roofing, to prevent damage from condensation.

8.9 Modified-Asphalt Roofing

a. Reinforced modified felt roofing, impregnated and coated with asphalt modified with plastic resins such as SBS (styrene-butadine-styrene copolymer) and APP (atactic polypropylene), is gaining widespread acceptance after extensive and successful use in Europe. The addition of plastics reduces the membrane's modulus of elasticity, making it less brittle (especially during cold periods) and therefore more able to survive differential deck movements. The reinforcing contributes to the membrane's strength, which also makes it more resistant to movement forces imposed on it by changes in the deck geometry, temperature, and moisture-induced deformations.

b. The handling and application of modified-asphalt membranes is similar to that of standard built-up roofing and usually involves two plies. Hot asphalt or cold adhesive (with the same limitations as cold-process roofing) can be used for inter-ply mopping, or the membranes can be bonded to the substrate and to one another by torching. In this technique, flame torching is used to melt the coating on the felts so that it serves as the continuous inter-ply adhesive. This process is neat and effective in the hands of a skilled mechanic, but incomplete bonding during this process can lead to a seriously defective membrane. Complete bonding is facilitated on large areas by use of a "dragon wagon" (a wheeled rack with multiple torches); on small areas, hand-held torches are used. Either method must soften all asphalt surfaces effectively to produce 100% bonding. Care is needed to prevent fire, especially in the presence of combustible insulation. Experience has shown that a fire guard is needed on the roof for at least one hour after the completion of any torching work.

c. The application of flashing (section 8.12) is similar in concept to that for standard built-up roofing. Special flashing felts can be torched on or mopped. Metal flashing is applied exactly as with built-up roofing and deserves the same attention to solid and permanent nailing for stability and uplift protection.

d. On venting and condensation, see section 8.7.

8.10 Liquid-Applied Roofing

a. Liquid-applied roofing systems are based on synthetic elastomeric rubbers such as polyurethane or silicone. They are applied by roller or spray, usually in several coats, and cure to a rubbery membrane. They can be used over flat and curved surfaces. They are especially useful on compound curves, such as domes and hyperbolic paraboloids, which are difficult to form with sheet materials. As is true of all thin surfacing materials, the substrate must be carefully smoothed or cracks and imperfections will show. Joints should be filled and smoothed, and high spots leveled. Surfaces must be clean, dust-free, and dry.

b. Because liquid-applied roofing does not depend on any specific substrate shape, it has at times been applied over existing roofs, sometimes with inadequate preparation. This has led to early disintegration because of substrate instability and blistering from enclosed moisture. For the same reason, discrete substrate elements, such as wood boards, plywood, and insulation boards, are likely to cause movement in the joints, breaking the membrane. Concrete is a better surface because of its continuity, but shrinkage and structural cracks are likely to destroy the integrity of the membrane. In general, liquid-applied coatings are very sensitive to even small movements in joints and cracks, making this type of roofing unreliable. Its best chances for success lie with concrete slabs of compact shapes, pre-stressed in at least two directions, since such structures are unlikely to develop cracks.

c. Another method of using liquid-applied membrane is to spray the roof deck with urethane foam insulation as a base. As long as this is done skillfully and with a total absence of moisture, the coating can be applied to such insulation, which acts as an attenuation layer to avoid reflected cracking from discrete deck movement. For this combination, success depends on sloping the insulation base to drain any standing water, and on applying the coating on the same day the foam insulation is applied. In any event, this type of roofing is vulnerable to physical damage, including damage from hail.

d. The flashing of liquid-applied roofing is simple and integral. The spray application is continued over all surfaces to be flashed at the same time the roofing is applied. The surfaces to be flashed must be stable, dry, clean, and not subject to movement after application of the coating.

8.11 Sheet-Metal Roofing

a. Sheet metal, such as copper, lead, and zinc, has been used for centuries for roofing. These traditional materials have been joined by aluminum, stainless steel, galvanized (zinc-coated) steel, and terne (plain steel or stainless steel coated with a lead-tin alloy). These corrosion-resistant metals must be used with care. All constituents of the roof must be the same metal or metals close to one another in the galvanic series (table 8.1). Any metal in the series will be corroded by those below it under certain conditions, such as the presence of rain water. The greater the separation, the more rapid the corrosion. Contact between copper and aluminum, for example, will lead to rapid corrosion of the aluminum. Acidic conditions usually favor corrosion, as in the cases of iron and steel. Aluminum is attacked by alkaline conditions, such as are created by concrete and mortar.

b. Weathering may change the color of sheet-metal roofing. Copper, for example, may turn blue-green in urban areas, brown in suburban or rural conditions, and black in industrial atmospheres.

c. Metals expand and contract with changes in temperature, which are likely to be extreme in roofs. This must be allowed for by attaching

Table 8.1 Galvanic Series of Metals (Electrochemical Order of Sensitivity to Corrosion)

Material	Single electrode potential	Nobility
Magnesium	+ 2.34	less noble
Aluminum	+ 1.67	
Zinc	+ 0.76	
Chromium	+ 0.71	
Steel	+ 0.44	
Stainless Steel	+ 0.42	
Cadmium	+ 0.40	
Nickel	+ 0.25	
Tin	+ 0.14	
Lead	+ 0.13	
Copper	− 0.35	more noble

the metal in such a way that it can expand and contract freely. Customary thicknesses and coefficients of expansion of some building materials are given in table 8.2.

d. A metal roof requires a solid deck to prevent wind uplift and air infiltration. Attachment cleats are crimped and folded into seams in such a way that the metal sheets (*pans*) can expand and contract. Figure 8.19 shows cleats employed with flat and standing seams and battens. Battens are slightly tapered inward toward the bottom to allow clearance for expansion of the sheets. Standing seams and battens are employed only along the slope of the roof; horizontally they would be barriers to rainwater runoff. As a general principle, metal should be solidly fastened to the deck in only one place, to allow thermal movement without restraint. All other fastenings should be movable, to prevent crimping and buckling.

8.12 Flashing

a. When dissimilar materials come together in joints, or when the possibility of leakage arises because of the type of construction, it is usually necessary to insert *flashing* (sheets or membranes of waterproof materials) to turn back the water. The details of flashing are generally the same regardless of the material; only materials with very high thermal coefficients (such as lead) require special attention. Because of its brittleness, its sensitivity to damage from condensation, and its high thermal coefficient, zinc is no longer in general use.
b. Cap flashing is usually metal, but base flashings are commonly

Table 8.2 Thickness and Thermal Coefficients of Expansion (Approximate)

Material	Recommended thickness (10^{-3} in.)	(mm)	Recommended gauge or weight	Coefficient of expansion (10^{-6}/°F)
Wood (fir), parallel to grain				2.1
Wood (fir), across grain				20[a]
Plywood[b]				
Brick masonry				3.3
Sheet glass				4.7
Concrete, standard structural				5.5
Galvanized steel (Type 1008)	19	0.48	26 ga	6.5
Copper (Type 100)	21	0.54	16 oz	9.3
Stainless steel (Type 304)	19	0.48	26 ga	9.6
Aluminum (Type 3003)	32	0.81	20 ga	12.8
Hard lead	34	0.86	2 ga	15.1
Acrylic	—	—	—	28–50
Polycarbonate	—	—	—	37
PVC	45 to 60	1.0 to 1.5	—	28–56
Elastomeric sheets	45–60	1.0 to 1.5	—	—

[a]Swelling across grain due to moisture changes greatly exceeds temperature expansion (chapter 5).
[b]Moisture-induced expansion exceeds temperature expansion, but is in the range of 0.5% going from oven-dry to saturated.

heavy impregnated fabric or felt, or sheet plastic. The metals most commonly used are copper, aluminum, stainless steel, monel, terne, zinc, lead, leaded copper, and galvanized steel.

c. Dissimilar metals must be kept out of contact, because water acts as an electrolyte to promote corrosion similar to the action occurring in a battery. A small electrical current is set up and the more active metal is corroded. If copper and aluminum, for example, are in contact, the aluminum is corroded. Galvanic or sacrificial protection operates in zinc-coated iron and steel. If the zinc coating is broken, it continues to protect the iron underneath until the zinc is eaten away so far that it can no longer protect the iron. Tin coatings, on the other hand, may accelerate the corrosion of the iron if the coating is broken, because the iron now acts sacrificially. Generally, "noble" metals corrode less than "less noble" metals with which they are in contact (table 8.1).

d. Thermal expansion of metal flashings requires that metals be free to move with changes in temperature. If flashings are confined, the stresses set up in trying to change dimensions eventually cause buckling, crimping, or fatigue cracks. Plastics have still higher coefficients.

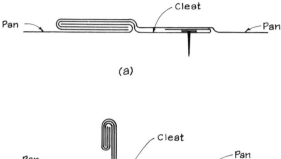

(a)

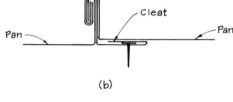

(b)

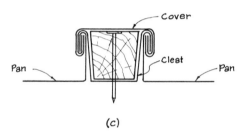

(c)

Figure 8.19 (a) Flat roofing joint. (b) Standing-seam roofing joint. (c) Batten-seam roofing.

Short strips less than 12″ wide can be fastened along both edges without much danger; wider sheets must not be confined at all but must be free to move. The coefficients of expansion of some common materials are given in table 8.2.

e. All flashings should shed water, especially to protect unsealed joints. Joints must be so made that water could work through them only against the force of gravity. A further qualification is that it must be impossible for driving winds to force water through. This usually requires either that the joint provides a tortuous path in which the driving force of the wind is dissipated or that the laps in the joint be so long that water cannot possibly be driven through.

f. Copper flashing is generally 16-oz "cold-rolled." Heavier copper is

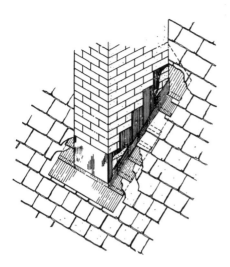

Figure 8.20 Cap and base flashing.

required for heavy-duty flashing, such as around certain kinds of tile roofs; lighter copper (not less than 12 oz) can be used in relatively protected points. Table 8.2 gives the thickness of several flashing materials.

g. Where a chimney penetrates a roof (figures 8.20, 8.21), the juncture must be flashed with cap and base flashing, a detail common where roofs and vertical masonry surfaces intersect. The lower (base) flashing is fitted into the shingles, and the upper (cap) flashing is built into the brickwork. The downstanding portion of the cap flashing folds down to lap 4″ or more over the upstanding portion of the base flashing. One piece of base flashing is required for each course of shingles, and is laid with its lower edge just above the butt line of the succeeding course of shingles. It should extend onto the roof at least 4″; 5″ or 6″ is better. Cap flashing is usually one brick (8″) or more wide, and its lower edge is cut on a diagonal to fit the pitch of the roof. Cap flashing must be built into the chimney as the brickwork is laid, and it should extend into the mortar joint at least 3″. In fact, many specifications require it to be built in 4″ and to be turned up against the flue lining 1″ or 2″. At the lower edge of the chimney the base flashing becomes a single sheet or apron which rests on top of the shingles, and the cap flashing is a continuous piece which laps down over the base flashing.

h. At the rear of the chimney, unless it straddles the ridge, a small gable called a *cricket* should be built to keep snow and dirt from

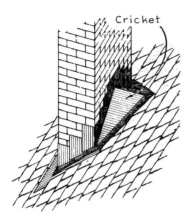

Figure 8.21 Cricket flashing.

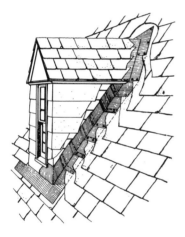

Figure 8.22 Dormer flashing.

collecting. This is covered with a single piece of flashing metal carried well up under the roofing and turned up the back of the chimney under the cap flashing (figures 8.20, 8.21).

i. The intersections of dormers and roofs are flashed similarly to chimneys (figure 8.22). The apron in front is also turned up under the wall covering. If the window sill rests on the roof, the apron is carried back under the sill, where it is turned up behind it an inch to stop rain from being driven under the sill and into the interior.

j. Where a roof changes slope (as in a gambrel, or where a porch or ell roof adjoins a steeper roof), it is necessary to flash the break if the

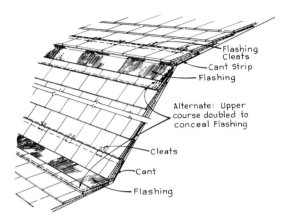

Figure 8.23 Changes in pitch in gambrel roof.

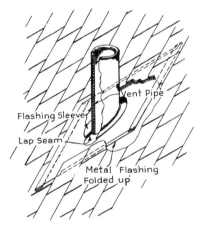

Figure 8.24 Vent-pipe flashing.

roofing cannot be shaped to conform (figure 8.23). In the case of shingles, the flashing is carried under the upper course of shingles and out on top of the lower course, but it may be completely concealed by doubling the lower course. In this instance, nails driven through the lower portion of the flashing should be embedded in washers made of lead or some other durable material to prevent leakage. Modern modified asphalts and polymer can often be used to avoid the damage from metal movement under the influence of thermal changes. In any event, the roof must be shaped to avoid snow traps in cold regions.

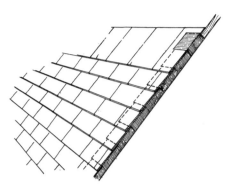

Figure 8.25 Flashing on rake.

k. Special flashing (figure 8.24) is required where the upper end of a plumbing stack extends through the roof, or where any other pipe protrudes. This flashing consists of a sheet of metal approximately 16″ square in which a circular opening is cut. To the opening is soldered a collar the proper size to fit snugly around the pipe. This is slipped over the pipe, and the collar is brought over the top and down the inside. The sheet forms an apron resting on top of the shingles below the pipe and fitted under the shingles above. Prefabricated elastomeric boots are available for many penetrations.

l. Thick inflexible roofing units, such as heavy slates and tiles, leave large wedge-shaped openings between courses at the rake or a gable roof (figure 8.25). These must be filled with individual pieces of flashing turned down over the edge of the rake at each course. Flashing should extend in under the shingles at least 4″ and be bedded in plastic roofing cement. In all sloped roof edges and terminations, step flashing (as recommended for chimneys) is a wise precaution against water leakage.

8.13 Sources of Technical Information on Roofing

Material standards are published by the ASTM (1916 Race Street, Philadelphia, PA 19103), by the ANSI (1430 Broadway, New York, NY 10018), and by all manufacturers.

Specialty-industry groups publish valuable and detailed information on their types of roofing materials and assemblies:

Sheet Metal and Air Conditioning Contractors National Association, POB 70, Merrifield, VA 22116

National Slate Association, c/o Vermont Structural Slate Co., Inc., Fairhaven, VT 05743

Asphalt Roofing Manufacturer's Association, 6288 Montrose Road, Rockville, MD 20852

Aluminum Association, 900 19th Street, NW Washington, DC 20006

Copper Development Association, Inc., Greenwich Office Park 2, Box 1840, Greenwich, CT 06836

Lead Industries Association Inc., 292 Madison Ave., New York, NY 10017

Metal Building Manufacturer's Assocation, Inc., 1230 Keith Building, Cleveland, OH 44115

National Tile Roofing Manufacturer's Association Inc., 3127 Los Feliz Boulevard, Los Angeles, CA 90039

The Society of the Plastics Industry, 355 Lexington Ave., New York, NY 10017

Red Cedar Shingle and Handsplit Shake Bureau, 515 116th Ave., NE, Bellevue, WA 98004

Single Ply Roofing Institute, 104 Wilmot Road, Deerfield, IL 60015

Thermal Insulation Manufacturer's Association, Inc., 7 Kirby Plaza, P.O.B. 686, Mount Kisco, NY 10549

Zinc Institute, Inc., 292 Madison Ave., New York, NY 10017

9 Cornices, Gutters, and Leaders

9.1 General

a. Although cornices and gutters are considered together here, cornices in actuality are almost always built before roofing is applied, and gutters are usually not hung until painting is finished unless the gutter is an integral part of the cornice detail. As a matter of fact, the exact sequence in which windows, roofing, and cornices are installed depends very much on their details. Roofing may not be applied until the house is practically finished, with windows, exterior finish, cornices, and gutters all in and the interior well along. In such an event, heavy roofing felt must be applied to keep the roof tight until the final roofing is in place, and be securely fastened and sealed against leakage at all joints and seams (chapter 8).

b. The usual sequence is cornice, roofing, windows, exterior doors, and exterior finish. An exception occurs when exterior finish is masonry veneer, which may have to be applied before the cornice is built because the lower part of the cornice laps over the top of the veneer (section 10.8).

CORNICES

9.2 General

Cornices may be classified as open or closed, depending on whether or not the ends of rafters are exposed to view. Open cornices are usually, but not necessarily, simpler in their details than closed ones. There are many variations of both kinds.

9.3 Open Cornices

a. Rafter ends are exposed at the eaves. Since the rafter ends are open to view, they should look well, be straight, and show no defects. Because the material used for rafters is apt to have knots and other imperfections, false rafter ends, terminating a short distance back of the wall line, may be used. In this case the actual rafters terminate at the plate and are concealed by the closure boards. In addition to looking well, false rafters can be uniformly spaced along the length of the building, allowing the spacing of the actual rafters to be whatever is required by the framing (figure 9.1).

b. The outer ends of rafters usually are faced with a board known as a *facia* or *fascia*. To prevent wind and rain from sweeping into the attic, the spaces between rafters are sealed at the building line by a vertical

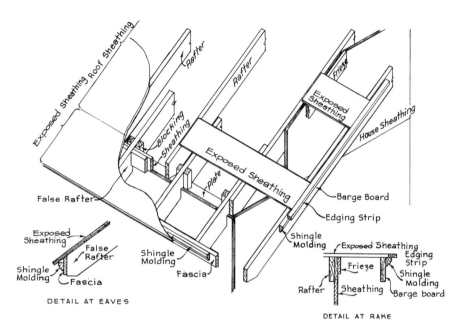

Figure 9.1 Construction details of open cornice.

or inclined closure board (*frieze*), or by a combination of a closure board and a molding forming an ornamental detail. To obtain tight and substantial construction, short blocks are nailed to the sides of the rafters to provide nailing and firm support for the closure boards.

c. Since the roof sheathing is exposed underneath, it must be of good-quality clear material. Better-grade stock is therefore substituted for the ordinary sheathing. It may be patterned boards. It is run up beyond the line of the house wall, and the ordinary sheathing begins there.

d. With a gable, gambrel, or shed roof, substantially the same detail as at the eaves is repeated along the rake, except that no rafter ends protrude from the wall. An outer rafter, variously known as a *flying rafter*, a *verge board*, and a *barge board*, is employed along the edge of the roof (figure 9.1).

e. The projecting end of the roof sheathing is exposed to view. It is therefore of better stock than ordinary sheathing. The latter is mostly cut off at the edge of the building but at frequent intervals is cut back to the first rafter behind the edge so as to support the barge board in cantilever fashion. Wide overhanging rakes may be carried on brackets fastened to the wall or framed as shown in chapter 5.

f. For better appearance, the end of roof sheathing is cut back an inch and a narrow edging strip is nailed the full length of the rake. The joint between edging strip and sheathing occurs directly above the barge board (or the shingle molding, if a shingle mold is used). Roof shingles project beyond the edging strip approximately $\frac{1}{2}''$, and the edging strip in turn projects beyond the barge board or shingle molding the same amount.

g. Along the building wall, just under the roof, is a board called the *frieze*. It corresponds to the closure board or frieze between rafter ends along the eaves and usually has the same details.

9.4 Closed Cornices

a. The *simple cornice* (figure 9.2) consists merely of a plain fascia board or a molding (such as "crown") nailed to the ends of the rafters and carried down against the wall. The rafters are cut off at the outer edge of the plate or project beyond it only $1''$ or $2''$. The fascia or molding is wide enough to cover the ends of the rafters and may run past the lowest roof board to the underside of the shingles, or it may butt against the lower side of the lowermost roof board, which projects beyond it to form a drip. Where the molding bears against the wall there may or may not be a frieze board.

b. Another kind of cornice is the *box cornice* or *boxed rafter* (figure 9.3). Although there may be additional ornament, it consists essentially of three members: the *fascia*, a vertical piece fastened to the outer ends of the rafters; the *soffit* or *plancia*, a piece which fastens either directly to the lower edges of the rafters or to secondary horizontal pieces called *lookouts*; and the *frieze*, a vertical piece which fastens to the building wall directly under the plancia. The fascia projects down beyond the outer end of the plancia, thus forming a drip. The soffit runs from fascia to building wall. The frieze is brought up against the soffit to make a tight joint against the wall.

c. When the gutter is fastened to the eaves, it covers a large part of the fascia and the fascia is just a simple board carried up to the underside of the lowest roofing board. When the gutter is free-standing, a shingle molding may be run along the upper edge of the fascia and may either bear against the lower side of the lowest roofing board or run up beyond it to bear against the underside of the shingles.

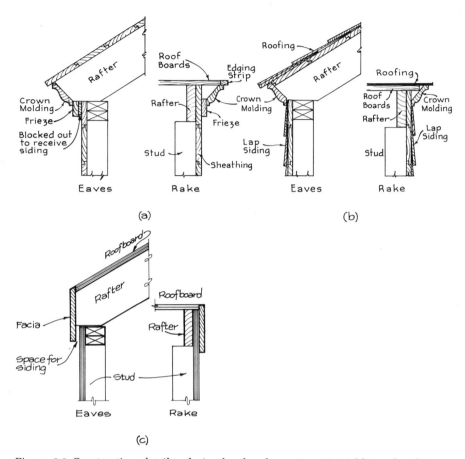

Figure 9.2 Construction details of simple closed cornice. (a) Molding plus frieze. (b) Molding alone. (c) Flat.

d. The soffit may be a single board if the cornice is not very wide, or it may be several boards wide, or it may be plywood or other exterior wallboard.

e. Friezes may be simple, consisting of a piece of molding or narrow board, or they may be wide and ornate, made up of several boards of varying thickness with moldings of several kinds added to provide the proper details and shadow lines.

f. Eaves and rakes are usually the same in detail but somewhat different in construction. Along the eaves, short horizontal lookouts run from rafter ends to the house wall to support the soffit, unless the soffit follows the slope of the rafters. Along the rake, lookouts are

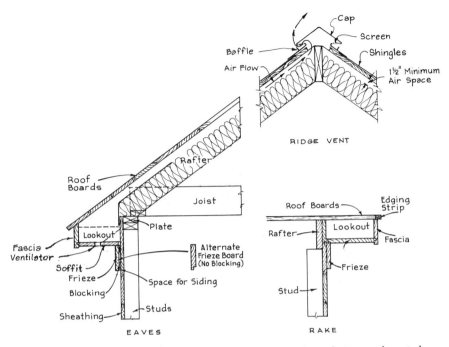

Figure 9.3 Construction details of simple box cornice, roof insulation, and vented ridge.

necessary to support the fascia, which is nailed directly to their outer ends. Since the lookouts act as small cantilevers, they must be fastened especially well to the wall. See chapter 5 for additional framing for projecting eaves.

g. In cold climates, snow and ice melting above the attic space may run down to the colder overhanging portion of the roof at the eaves and freeze, forming an ice dam (section 8.3f) that backs up the water coming down from above, forcing it under shingles and into the attic space. To prevent this, continuous ventilating slots or ventilating spots, protected by fly screening, are built into the soffit to allow cold outside air to penetrate into and ventilate the space above the thermal insulation usually found between ceiling joists or rafters (chapter 11 and figure 9.3). Eave ventilation is made more effective by ventilators installed along the ridge to provide an outlet for air from the attic space (figure 9.3). Air flows from the eaves ventilator upward and outward at the ridge through ventilating openings screened against insects. Insulation, if placed between rafters, must allow at least $1\frac{1}{2}''$ of

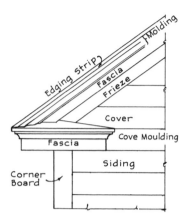

Figure 9.4 Return of box cornice.

space for air flow. Baffles prevent snow and rain from blowing into the openings. The ridge ventilator must be strong and rigid enough, or be supported, to withstand wind, snow, and rain.

h. In gable roofs, louvers at the gable ends provide an opportunity for ventilating air to flow from attic spaces.

i. At the corners of the building, the eaves cornice may be carried a short distance (approximately equal to the width of the cornice) along the end walls. The rake cornice is brought down on top of the eaves cornice at this point. This detail is known as a *return* (figure 9.4).

GUTTERS AND LEADERS

9.5 Gutters

a. Gutters or eavetroughs catch rain water from a roof and carry it to leaders or downspouts extending to the ground, where the water is delivered to cast-iron or terra-cotta drain pipes discharging into dry wells or storm sewers. Without this system of drains the rain water would fall off the roof at the eaves. On small buildings, such as sheds, gutters are seldom used; on small houses, they are sometimes omitted in favor of a concrete, masonry, or gravel splash strip set in the ground under the eaves to break the fall of the water.

b. Gutters are of many kinds and shapes. They are commonly made of wood, metal, or plastic, all of which give satisfactory service if properly installed. Certain basic requirements must be met by all gutters: They must be large enough to handle the discharge.

They must have sufficient pitch to carry the water off quickly and not leave any pockets of standing water.

They must not leak.

There must be no obstructions to free flow.

They must be so installed as to avoid danger of backing up snow and ice under the roofing material with consequent leakage into the building.

9.6 Wood Gutters

a. The simplest wood gutter is a vee formed by fastening two boards together. To be satisfactory it must be lined with metal or some other waterproof material, such as heavy asphalt-impregnated roofing felt, because the bottom of the vee otherwise soon opens and lets the water through. This is probably the oldest type of wood gutter, and is still found on old farmhouses and their replicas. Otherwise it is seldom used (figure 9.5).

b. The commonest wood gutter is molded from a solid piece of Douglas fir, cypress, redwood, cedar, or some other durable species. It has an ornamental molding (ogee) on the outside and a semicircular channel on the inside. This type of gutter usually forms a part of the cornice detail, and thus performs a double function (figure 9.5).

c. Figures 9.5a and 9.5b show cross-sections and splicing details of such gutters. Wherever a splice is necessary, the two ends are carefully and snugly butted, after which the channel is cut away deep enough to take a small sheet of lead or soft copper, which is fitted over the joint, bedded in elastic cement, and tacked down securely. All joints are finally filled with elastic cement. The same procedure is followed whenever a corner occurs; the ends are carefully mitered and the joint is lined with metal bedded in cement. A similar lining, cut to fit around the head of the leader, forms the joint between it and the gutter.

d. Although such a gutter can be completely lined with metal, this is neither necessary nor desirable. The danger of rotting is small, provided the joints are sealed against the penetration of water and provided the gutter pitches sufficiently and uniformly enough to prevent water pockets from forming after a rain. The periodic wetting from rains is soon dried, and the sun beating down on the gutter during the rest of the time keeps the wood too dry to rot. Standing water and water seeping into joints, however, may quickly cause decay.

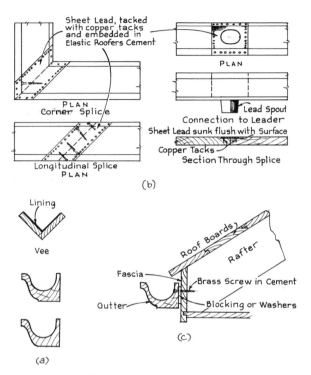

Figure 9.5 Wood gutter. (a) Ogee. (b) Splicing sections of ogee gutter. (c) Installation details.

e. Wood gutters are usually fastened to the fascia. Certain precautions must be taken:

1. Fastenings should be brass or other noncorroding metal, bedded in elastic cement to prevent leakage around the fastenings (preferably screws).

2. The gutter should not be fastened directly to the fascia, but should be held away from it $\frac{1}{4}''$ by small wood strips or by metal washers (figure 9.5c). This allows ventilation of the joint between the fascia and the back of the gutter and reduces the decay hazard. Moreover, if the gutter becomes stopped up by ice and snow in the winter, and melting water overflows or is backed against the back of the gutter, the water can seep over the back and drip to the ground. Otherwise it is likely to work into the house. This precaution is necessary with any kind of gutter, wood or metal.

3. The gutter should be far enough below the ends of the projecting

shingles at the eaves to prevent any water from backing up under the shingles when the gutter is full. In addition, if the gutter fills with ice and snow, it should spill over on the outside and not build up to the point where it can back up under the shingles. This is true of all kinds of gutters, wood or metal.

4. Distances between leaders for wood gutters, or any other gutters which form part of the cornice detail, should be kept short for the sake of appearance. Gutters must have some pitch or they will not shed water properly, but cornice lines should be kept as nearly horizontal as possible. A long gutter is noticeably higher at one end than at the other and destroys the appearance of the cornice. Moreover, long gutters are much more likely to form pockets of standing water than are short ones.

9.7 Metal and Plastic Gutters

Gutters are commonly made of aluminum, copper, leaded copper, zinc, galvanized iron, or plastic. Aluminum, copper, and galvanized iron are most common. Copper and aluminum are more durable, but first cost often dictates the use of galvanized iron. Plastic gutters do not rust or rot, but may degrade otherwise unless made of proven weather-resistant materials, typically PVC (figure 9.6).

9.8 Attached Gutters

a. The simplest and commonest type of attached metal or plastic gutter is the simple half-round eavetrough (figure 9.6a) with a single or double bead. The single-bead type is the most common. This is the cheapest and most efficient gutter from the standpoint of maximum use of metal, since it is easiest to form, and the semi-circular cross-section carries the most water for a given perimeter.

b. The other common type of metal or plastic gutter is the box gutter, usually with an ogee-molded face and a straight bottom and back. This, like the ogee wood gutter, generally forms part of the cornice detail.

c. Attached or "hung" gutters are usually hung from the roof by strap hangers, which are nailed to the roof boards before the shingles are applied (figure 9.6b). They should be close enough together to avoid sagging between them. Spacing depends upon the material, but is in the vicinity of 30″ to 36″. They should be installed to form a straight line with uniform pitch not less than $\frac{1}{16}$″ per foot so that when the

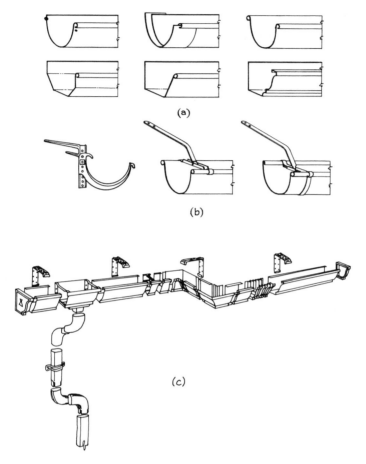

Figure 9.6 (a) Typical sections of hung gutters. (b) Hangers. (c) Plastic gutters and leaders.

gutters are subsequently hung to them proper runoff is provided. Wire hangers, cheaper and lighter than strap hangers, are common with smal gutters, but these must be spaced closer together. Metal brackets may be used to support large gutters, which carry fairly heavy quantities of water.

d. Hung gutters should ordinarily be held away from the fascia, for the reasons already given in the discussion of wood gutters. If the gutter must be set directly against the fascia, the back of the gutter should be carried up in one piece well under the lowest courses of shingles so that any water, ice, or snow which is backed up cannot

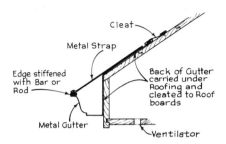

Figure 9.7 Molded metal gutter.

work through the roof (figure 9.7). This becomes essentially a molded gutter.

e. Attached gutters must be free to expand and contract with changes in temperatures. This is accomplished most simply by allowing one length of gutter to lap the next in the direction in which water is to flow. A somewhat more watertight joint is secured with a separate short section in which both lengths of gutter fit and slide (figure 9.6). Slip joints should be provided every 25' to 50'; intermediate joints can be soldered together.

f. Materials that have high coefficients of thermal expansion — such as aluminum and, especially, plastics — must be permitted to move or buckling and splitting may occur. A variety of motion-permitting joints have been devised for these materials.

9.9 Leaders

a. Leaders are simply vertical pipes which carry water from gutters to ground drains. They may be round or rectangular, corrugated or plain. They must be large enough to carry water away as fast as it comes (figure 9.8a).

b. The joint between a gutter and a leader is ordinarily an S-shaped piece, called a *gooseneck* or *elbow* (figure 9.8b), which curves in from the gutter to the wall and meets the top of the leader. It may join directly to the top of the leader in a slip joint, or it may first empty into an ornamental box (called a *leader head*) attached to the top of the leader. The box performs no particular function and is primarily an ornament.

c. Where the leader pierces the gutter, a strainer of some kind, usually a small inverted basket made of wire, is inserted. This prevents leaves,

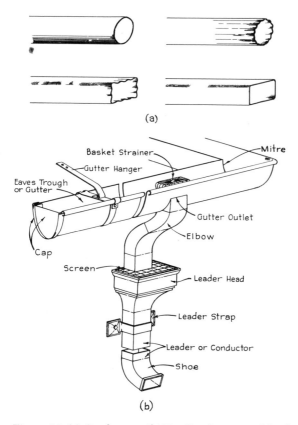

Figure 9.8 (a) Conductors. (b) Details of gutter and leader.

twigs, and other rubbish from clogging the leader and the underground drainage system. The strainer must be of such a design that it
will not readily stop up but will hold back rubbish; at the same time,
it must not slip down and jam in the leader.

d. Figure 9.8b shows the parts of a gutter-and-leader assembly. In
addition to the parts already described, it shows leader straps and a
shoe. If water is to be allowed to splash upon the ground or to run into
some surface drain, a shoe should be provided. If the bottom of the
leader is to connect into a vertical pipe leading into the underground
drainage system (chapter 3), the shoe is not necessary.

10 Exterior Finishes and Water Tables

10.1 General

a. The usual exterior finishes for frame construction are the following:
Siding
   drop (novelty)
   lap, bevel, clapboard
   vertical boarding
   horizontal flush boarding
Shingles
   wood
   asphalt
Sheet materials (see sections 5.2, 5.3, 12.15–12.17)
Masonry veneer
   brick
   stone
    rubble
    ashlar
Stucco (see sections 12.30–12.33)
Each of these calls for its own materials and techniques.

b. At the base of the frame, where the foundation and the superstructure meet, a special detail called the *water table* may be found. It may be simple or ornate, depending upon the detailing.

SIDING

10.2 Drop (Novelty) Siding

a. This is probably the simplest of exterior finishes because it combines sheathing and siding in one piece. Since it must afford a weathertight wall in one thickness of wood, the individual pieces are best tongued and grooved and must be driven up tightly against one another when they are nailed in place.

b. After studs are up, drop siding is nailed into place to form the finished wall (figure 10.1). Extra weathertightness may be afforded by stretching building paper across the studs before siding is nailed on, but the paper is usually omitted altogether. Siding is run from the sill to the plate, and is cut at window and door openings, the same as sheathing. Window and door frames are installed after the siding is on, which makes it difficult to flash the heads of these frames (figure 10.1b). At the corners, the ends are roughly cut off and the corner is

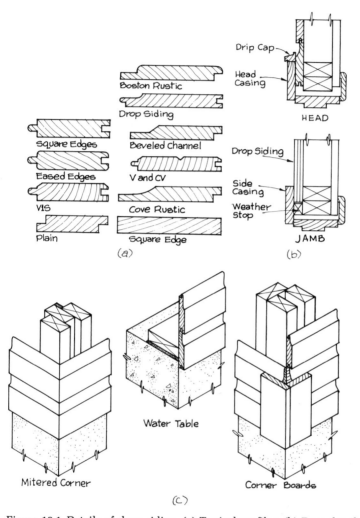

Figure 10.1 Details of drop siding. (a) Typical profiles. (b) Door details. (c) Details of corners and water table.

finished by nailing on a pair of vertical boards called *corner boards*, or ends are mitered at the corners (figure 10.1c).

c. Drop siding is usually beaded and otherwise shaped to various patterns (figure 10.1a). Where window and door casings are nailed over the siding, the beads and cutaway portions leave openings through which wind and rain can find their way unless they are sealed. Sealing is accomplished by nailing wood strips or weather stops over the cut-off ends of the siding before window and door frames are set (figure 10.1b).

d. Drop siding alone is not considered a good finish for permanent structures or those which are to be weathertight. It is mostly found on temporary structures, or on structures which must merely provide the minimum of shelter, such as storage sheds for non-perishable goods and inexpensive garages.

e. Used over sheathing, drop siding is a satisfactory wall covering and falls into the class of horizontal boarding (sections 10.5a, 10.5b).

10.3 Lap Siding

a. This is also known as *bevel siding* and, when narrow, is commonly called *clapboards*. Lap siding is made by rip-sawing a square-edged board along its length and diagonally across the cross-section (figure 10.2a). The result is two boards, narrow at one edge and wide at the other. The thick edge may be rabbeted to form shiplap.

b. Siding is applied after the sheathing and the building paper are on. Ordinarily it is put on in bands as high as men can conveniently reach, starting at the top of the building and working down to the sill, to avoid marring the finished surface with scaffolding. Application starts at the bottom of each band, since each succeeding board laps over the lower one much like shingles. The amount of overlap depends on the width of the boards and on the amount which is to be exposed to the weather — i.e., on the spacing. Narrow boards lap each other approximately $\frac{1}{2}''$ to $1''$. Wide ones lap $1''$ to more than $2''$, although the lap is sometimes less than $1''$.

c. Spacing is varied to suit conditions. On the side of a house, for example, there may be one spacing from the foundation line to the first-story window sills, another between the first-story window sills and the window heads, another one for the band between the first-story window heads and the second-story window sills, another from those sills to the window heads, and still another from the window

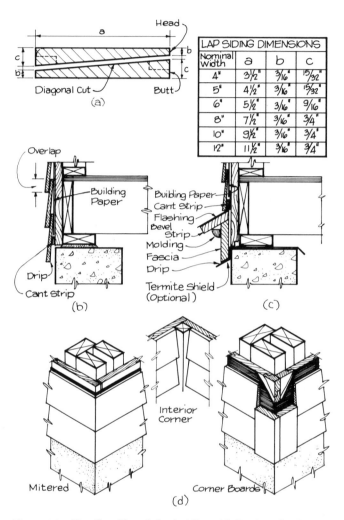

LAP SIDING DIMENSIONS			
Nominal width	a	b	c
4"	3½"	3/16"	15/32"
5"	4½"	3/16"	15/32"
6"	5½"	3/16"	9/16"
8"	7½"	3/16"	3/4"
10"	9½"	3/16"	3/4"
12"	11½"	3/16"	3/4"

Figure 10.2 Details of bevel (lap) siding. (a) Cutting. (b) Starting and lapping. (c) Water table. (d) Corners.

heads to the eaves. On a gable end there may be still further changes in spacing to the peak of the gable. Usually the variation in spacing is quite small and is not noticeable, particularly with narrow siding. This is one of the advantages of lap siding over drop siding, since the latter cannot be varied in its spacing.

d. Individual lap siding boards are nailed along the lower edge. Some carpenters prefer to drive nails through the butt of the upper board and through the top of the lower one; others prefer to nail above the top of the lower siding board. An exception is narrow clapboards, which frequently are nailed along the top instead of at the butt. Nails are usually 6d, 7d, or 8d box or siding nails, either plain or coated (chapter 14).

e. At the eaves, the top siding board slips under the lower edge of the frieze board to make a weathertight joint (chapter 9). The frieze is made to allow space for the top edge of the siding, either by rabbeting the lower back edge of the frieze board or by furring out the frieze from the wall. Along the rake the siding boards are carefully cut to fit against the lower edge of the frieze, which is not furred.

f. Corner boards may or may not be employed with lap siding. If they are, they are nailed on first and the siding is carefully cut to fit snugly against them (figure 10.2d). It must similarly be fitted snugly against door and window casings. At all these points building paper (section 5.12) must be carried continuously across the joint so that any water which may drive between siding and casing or corner boards is prevented from working through the wall. When corner boards are omitted, the siding boards from the two adjoining walls are brought together in a miter joint (figure 10.2d). Interior corners may employ corner strips (figure 10.2), or siding boards may be butted alternately left and right.

g. Figure 10.2c illustrates a typical water table for lap siding. The sheathing is brought down flush with the edge of the foundation wall. To it is nailed the water-table fascia. The lower edge of the fascia extends down beyond the top of the foundation wall and should be grooved or beveled to form a drip. If a termite shield is employed, the bottom of the fascia is beveled to fit the top of the termite shield, which projects beyond it approximately 1″.

h. The top of the fascia is beveled and is topped with another member, which projects beyond it and in turn forms a drip. If this member projects very far, or if the water table is to be accentuated, a piece of molding can be nailed under it. The top strip is covered with flashing carried up the wall 2″ or 3″ under the lower edge of the building paper. If thick-butt siding is used, the butt of the lowest siding board should be beveled to fit snugly to the top of the water table.

i. Usually, there is no water table. The lower edge of the lowest siding board is brought down approximately 1″ below the top of the foundation wall. Before it is nailed on, narrow wooden "cant" strips are tacked to the lower edge of the sheathing to give the lowest siding board the same flare as the upper ones (figure 10.2b).

j. Aluminum, plastic (PVC), plywood, and hardboard are also employed for siding.

k. Aluminum siding is formed to have the appearance of lap siding (figure 10.3) and is finished with anodized or baked-on finish in plain or embossed patterns, white or colored. The upper and lower edges are crimped to interlock as the successive courses are applied, and slots are provided at the upper edges for nailing. Because metal expands and contracts with changes in temperature, the slots allow for such motion. Nails, therefore, should be driven snugly but not so tightly as to prevent motion.

l. Because metal is impervious to the passage of water vapor, and because a wall should be allowed to "breathe," provision should be made — usually by openings along the bottom of the lower or butt edge — to permit ventilation.

m. The insulating value of thin metal is negligible. Consequently, the aluminum siding may be backed with plastic foam or fiber board. The denser fiber boards also provide backing for the metal to help to prevent denting.

n. Accessories include corner boards for exterior and interior corners, and window and door trim which permit the ends of siding strips to slip into a slot and to move with changes in temperature. Starter strips are employed to anchor the first course.

o. Extruded PVC is shaped to have the appearance of lap siding. Colors are integral rather than applied. Surfaces may be plain or embossed. Upper and lower edges are formed to interlock as successive courses are applied (figure 10.4), and slots are provided at the upper edge for nailing. Plastics generally, including PVC, have higher coefficients of expansion than metals, so it is essential to allow movement to occur with changes in temperature. Nails should, therefore, be

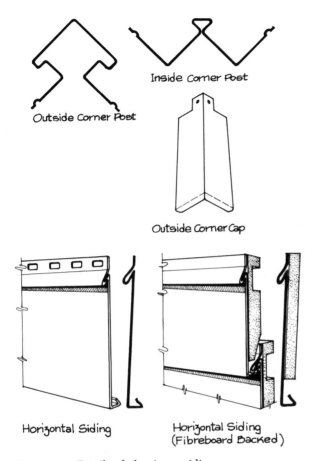

Inside Corner Post

Outside Corner Post

Outside Corner Cap

Horizontal Siding

Horizontal Siding
(Fibreboard Backed)

Figure 10.3 Details of aluminum siding.

driven snugly but not so tightly as to prevent motion, or buckling in hot weather and possible cracking in cold weather may occur.

p. Plastic siding, like metal, is essentially impervious to the passage of water vapor. It is, therefore, essential to permit the siding to breathe, usually by incorporating ventilation openings in the lower edge of the siding strip. Unlike metal, it is not easily dented and does not need the backer for that purpose, but an insulating backer enhances the overall thermal insulation of the wall.

q. Accessories include corner boards and closures, window and door trim, and similar details needed for a complete installation.

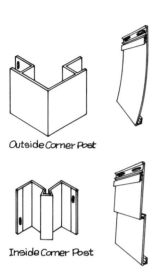

Outside Corner Post

Inside Corner Post

Figure 10.4 Details of plastic siding.

r. Plywood may be cut into strips and applied in a manner similar to standard lap siding. The strips are usually considerably wider than the usual lap siding, and may have a variety of surface textures (brushed, striated, rough sawn, and slotted or kerfed). It is sometimes prefinished with factory-applied paint, baked-on finishes, and other surface coatings.

s. Where adjacent siding strips butt together in a vertical joint, wood shingle wedges are recommended to support the joint and allow it to be firmly nailed; otherwise the two strips might tend to bow in and out away from each other.

t. Tempered lignocellulose hardboard, approximately $\frac{1}{2}''$ thick, may likewise be cut into strips and applied as lap siding. Widths vary. Edges are beveled to form a drip. Surfaces may be smooth or textured. These strips are available primed on the face and sealed on the back.

10.4 Vertical Boarding

a. The vertical boarding often found on walls of barns and sheds is also used quite commonly as exterior covering for houses. In this instance extra precautions are taken to make the joints weathertight.

b. As usual, the sheathing is covered with building paper; then tongued-and-grooved or square-edged boards are nailed vertically, with each board running the entire height of the wall if possible.

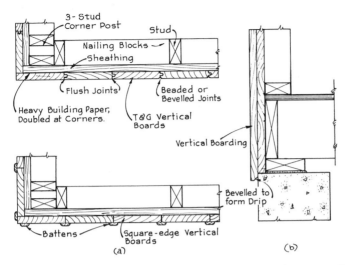

Figure 10.5 Details of vertical boarding. (a) Horizontal sections. (b) Simple water table.

Figure 10.1 shows a few patterns. Joints are best coated with paint just before the boards are nailed on, and succeeding boards are driven up tightly against the preceding ones. If nothing further is done, a plane unbroken surface results, unless the edges of the boards are beveled to accentuate the joint (figure 10.5).

c. In order to break the surface and further to protect the joints, battens are often nailed over the joints. Before they are applied, their backs are best coated with paint. The boards themselves are coated similarly unless they are not to be painted later, so that when the battens are applied, the joint is filled and sealed (figure 10.5a). If the joints are not to be covered with battens, the vertical boarding should be tongued and grooved; if battens are employed, square-edged material is satisfactory.

d. Generally no special water table is employed with vertical boarding. The bottom ends of the boards are merely carried down 1″ or so past the top of the foundation wall and are cut off on a bevel to form a drip (figure 10.5b). If a water table is desired, the bottom ends of the boards are brought down and fitted to the sloping top of the top member of the water table (figure 10.2c). Flashing of the usual type is required at a water table and at door and window heads (chapter 7).

e. Aluminum strips, similar to those used for lap siding, may be em-

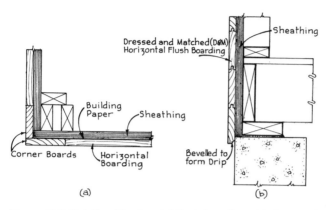

Figure 10.6 Details of horizontal flush boarding. (a) Corner. (b) Simple water table.

ployed as vertical siding. Instead of the beveled appearance of horizontal siding, profiles resembling board and batten or V-groove or both may be employed. Round or trapezoidal corrugations provide other profiles. The same precautions respecting thermal motion and ventilation must be observed as for horizontal siding. Usually, these strips are open at the bottom and can be vented at the top with appropriate closure strips or eaves details.

f. Plywood, hardboard, and reconstituted board sheets are often grooved, striated, formed to simulate board and batten or other surface textures, painted, provided with baked-on surfaces, or faced with film and/or foil. These are applied vertically to provide appearances similar to vertical wood boarding. Wallboards are discussed at greater length in sections 5.3 and 12.15–12.17.

10.5 Horizontal Boarding

a. Boards may be horizontal instead of vertical, in which case they are in practically the same category as drop siding applied over sheathing. Various patterns may be employed (figure 10.1). If the boards are not patterned but have square corners, a plane unbroken wall results. This material may be tongue and groove or shiplap. Like vertical boarding, the joints between boards should be coated with paint, and boards must be driven up tightly when nailed (figure 10.6).

b. A water table may or may not be employed. If it is called for, its construction is much the same as for lap siding; it is flashed on top, and the lowest board is beveled to fit snugly against the top member

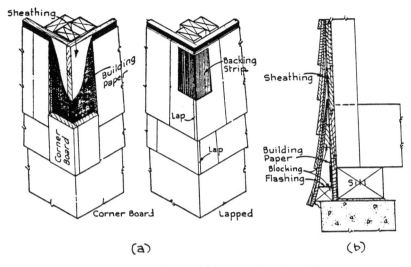

Figure 10.7 Details of shingled wall. (a) Corner. (b) Water table.

(figure 10.2c). Flashing at door and window heads is the same as for lap siding (chapter 7).

SHINGLES

10.6 General

a. There is little difference between the application of shingles to roofs and to side walls, whether the shingles are wood, asphalt, or any other kind.

b. Unlike lap siding, shingles are started at the house sill and are carried up the wall instead of being applied in bands starting at the top and working down.

c. Because water is less likely to work through shingles on side walls than on roofs, the exposure to weather can be increased. Moreover, instead of laying all courses with the same weather, successive courses may be made wide and narrow, or some other pattern may be worked out to break the regular coursing. Asphalt shingles are made in a variety of forms and shapes and are applied in different ways to correspond to these shapes. Wood shingles for side walls are often uniform in width, so regular patterns can be worked out readily.

d. See chapter 8.

10.7 Wood Shingles

a. The same precautions respecting snug joints at corner boards and casings must be observed as with siding. When wood shingles are returned at the corners, unlike the miter corner return in bevel siding, the shingles are butted and the butt joint is carried into the corner alternately from each side in succeeding courses. Each pair of corner shingles should be flashed or backed with a strip of heavy building paper to ensure a tight corner (figure 10.7a). To emphasize the butt lines, shingle courses are sometimes doubled, with Number 3 or 4 shingles for undercourses (chapter 8).

b. Under window sills, the tops of shingles are fitted into the groove in the lower face of the sill in much the same manner as with siding. Drip caps above the head casing are flashed in the usual manner (chapter 7). At the eaves the tops of shingles are fitted under the frieze board, and along the rakes they are cut to fit snugly against the frieze. The spacing is varied up the height of the wall in the same manner as with lap siding (section 10.3) so that butt lines come out even at window sills and heads.

c. Water-table details are ordinarily simpler than those for lap siding. The lowest shingle course simply extends down beyond the sill line and is doubled, like any starting shingle course. To form a better drip, it is furred out at the butt $\frac{1}{4}''$ to $\frac{1}{2}''$. If greater emphasis is to be placed on the water table, it may be flared as shown in figure 10.7b.

MASONRY VENEER

10.8 General

Masonry veneer may be brick (section 5.47ff.), rubble, or ashlar (section 4.25), with brick the most common. Construction is essentially the same for all three, differing only in minor details. Masonry veneer is simply another outside covering for a frame building, and does not alter its essential character. However, masonry veneer is brittle, especially at the mortar joints, and likely to crack if the supporting frame (e.g., lightweight studs) yields under lateral loads such as wind. The frame must be stiff enough to resist such deformation.

10.9 Details

a. Foundations. Because standard brick are $3\frac{3}{4}''$ wide and because space must be left between brick and sheathing to take up any irregu-

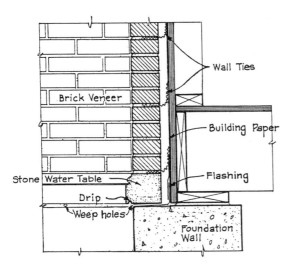

Figure 10.8 Brick veneer.

larities in construction, the sheathing line is held back $4\frac{1}{4}''$ to $4\frac{1}{2}''$ from the outer face of the foundation wall. Brick veneer therefore requires a foundation wall thick enough to carry the wood sill in addition to the veneer. The thickness must be made greater for stone veneer because ashlar is at least 5″.

b. Paper. Although masons often fill the space between veneer and sheathing with mortar, it is best left as an open cavity against water penetration, and to allow the ties to move as the frame shrinks. However, this space really is never quite open at the bottom, inasmuch as mortar falls in during the course of construction; hence it should be built as if it were solidly filled. This requires that heaviest-grade waterproof building paper be applied over the sheathing before bricks are laid. The paper is needed not only to keep the frame dry as the wall is built but also (even more) to keep rain water from penetrating, because thin masonry veneer cannot be expected to be entirely weathertight.

c. Brick and mortar. Sections 5.47 and 5.50–5.53 discuss brick and mortar. For masonry veneer, brick should be at least MW (moderate weathering). Mortar containing lime tends to be more workable under the trowel than the higher-cement types. No matter what kind of mortar is used, a wall cannot be expected to be reasonably weathertight or structurally sound unless all mortar joints, both horizontal and vertical, are completely filled.

d. Ties. Since a 4" to 8" wall cannot stand unsupported for wall heights, the veneer must be tied to the sheathing at frequent intervals by wall ties or brick anchors, which are small strips of corrugated metal about 1" wide and 6" long. The best metal is copper, but zinc-coated iron is most common. One end of the tie is laid in a mortar joint; the other is turned up against the wall and nailed to the sheathing. Nails should be of the same metal as the anchor to avoid electrolytic action. Ties are needed every four or five courses in height and every 2' along the mortar joint (figure 10.8).

e. Construction. If there is no special water table, the first course of brick or stone is laid directly on the foundation wall and, unless it is random rubble, is carefully leveled to form a straight, horizontal base for succeeding courses. Before the first course is laid, flashing is placed on top of the foundation wall, with its outer edge turned down a short distance over the edge of the wall and its inner edge turned up against the sheathing several inches. Building paper is brought down over, not under, the flashing so as to shed any water which may drive through the veneer and trickle down the building paper to the sill. It is good practice, moreover, to expedite drainage of this water by providing "weep holes" (small metal tubes) several feet apart on top of the flashing, their outer ends flush with the face of the wall and their inner ends in the space between the brick and the sheathing.

f. Brick courses, like siding and shingles, are laid out to come out even at window sills and heads or at any other horizontal details in the exterior finish. This is done by slightly varying the thicknesses of mortar joints. Brick or stone sills are set under the wood sills of window frames (chapter 7). The best practice is to lay up the veneer to the window line, set the windows in the usual way, with window sills on top of the masonry sills, and continue with the veneer.

g. Veneer is carried over the heads of windows and doors on steel angles, usually 3" × 4" or 4" × 4", which rest in the veneer at each end (chapter 7). Heads of this kind must be flashed in the same way as the first course at the foundation. Here the flashing is laid on top of the outstanding leg of the angle and is carried up the upstanding leg to the sheathing. Building paper laps over the back edge of the flashing.

10.10 Water Table

Figure 10.8 shows an ornamental stone water table, sometimes found not only in brick veneer but also in solid masonry. It may or may not project beyond the face of the foundation. Often the water table is a rowlock or soldier course (section 5.52). The water table may be a course of molded brick or other specially formed burnt-clay unit. An ogee (cyma reversa, chapter 13) is a favorite detail. Like the rowlock or soldier course, it does not project beyond the foundation wall but curves back and up from the face of the foundation wall. The face of the veneer is, consequently, set back several inches from the face of the foundation, which must be made even thicker than is ordinarily necessary for veneer.

10.11 Wallboards

These are discussed briefly in section 10.4 and at greater length in sections 5.3 and 12.15–12.17.

11 Insulation

11.1 General

The practice of insulating houses against excessive heat loss or gain, once rare, is now standard. It therefore becomes necessary to consider what insulation may be expected to accomplish, where it does the most good, the various materials used for insulation, how they accomplish their task, and the ways in which they are installed.

11.2 Heat Losses

a. Heat losses from a building bear a direct relationship to the fuel bill. However, the total heat inherent in every pound of fuel is by no means lost through the structure of the building. Imperfect combustion in the burner usually accounts for a very large part of the fuel consumption. Unless the draft is regulated to supply the correct amount of air to the fire, and unless the burner is kept in good condition, large quantities of soot and partially burned gases are liberated. These constitute a distinct loss. Unless the heat-exchanging surfaces in the heater are properly designed for the particular type of fuel burned, only partial transfer of heat from the burning zone to the heating medium (air, hot water) takes place and a large part of the heat evolved escapes up the chimney. Proper care of the heater can often reduce heat losses more, at smaller cost, than can additional insulation.

b. Heat losses through the structure occur chiefly at foundation walls, at basement floors and floors on grade, at outside walls (above grade), at windows and doors, through infiltration of cold air, by loss through glass, and at the roof.

c. Some approximate typical rates of heat transmission through selected materials and constructions are given in table 11.1. The thermal conductivity (k) is the thermal transmission in British thermal units (Btu) of a material in unit time by conduction through 1″ thickness per sq. ft. per degree F difference, or watts per meter per degree Kelvin (Btu · in/h · ft^2 · F or W/m · K). The thermal conductance (C) is the thermal transmission for the thickness indicated (Btu/h · ft^2 · F or W/m^2 · K). The thermal resistivity (R) is the reciprocal of k or C. The thermal transmittance (U), or overall coefficient of heat transfer, is the thermal transmission of an assembly, including boundary air films (Btu/h · ft^2 · F or W/m^2 · K). R is the reciprocal of U (h · ft^2 · F/Btu or m^2 · K/W). R values are commonly employed.

Table 11.1 Thermal Transmission

Materials	Conductivity k^a	Conductance c^b	Resistance R	
			1/k	1/c
Boards				
Plywood, Douglas fir	0.80		1.25 (8.66)	
Particle board, medium density	0.94		1.06 (7.25)	
Hardboard, medium density	0.73		1.37 (9.49)	
Glass fiber board	0.25		4.00 (27.72)	
Expanded polystyrene, smooth skin	0.20		5.00 (34.65)	
Cellular polyurethane	0.16		6.25 (43.82)	
Fill				
Milled paper or pulp	0.27–0.32		3.70–3.13 (25.64–21.69)	
Perlite, expanded	0.27–0.42		3.70–2.40 (25.64–16.60)	
Vermiculite, exfoliated	0.44–0.47		2.27–2.13 (15.73–14.76)	
Concrete				
Sand, gravel or stone				
Not dried	12.0		0.08 (0.55)	
Oven dried	9.0		0.11 (0.76)	
Lightweight aggregates, also cellular; 20–120 lb/ft³	0.70–5.2		1.43–0.19 (9.91–1.32)	
Brick				
Common	5.0		0.20 (1.39)	
Face	9.0		0.11 (0.76)	
Wood shingles, 16″, 7.5″ exposure		1.15		0.87 (0.15)
Siding				
Wood bevel, 0.5″ × 8″ lapped		1.23		0.81 (0.14)
Plywood, 0.375″ lapped		1.59		0.29 (0.10)

Table 11.1 (continued)

Materials	Conductivity k^a	Conductance c^b	Resistance R	
			$1/k$	$1/c$
Construction		U^c		R (1/U)
Frame wall, ½″ fiberboard sheathing, bevel siding, ½″ gypsum board		0.225		4.44
with 3½″ glass fiber		0.069		14.44
Wood shingles on wood strips, rafters bare below		0.48		2.08
		0.056		18.00
With 4″ glass fiber		0.056		18.00
Glass, single thickness		1.13		0.88
double thickness		0.60		1.67
triple thickness		0.45		2.22

[a] Btu/h·ft²·in·F (W/m·K)
[b] Btu/h·ft²·F (W/m²·K)
[c] Btu/h·ft²·F (W/m²·K)
Source: *Fundamentals Handbook*, ASHRAE, 1981

d. From the standpoint of insulation, the ordinary roof is poorer than the ordinary frame wall, but it is better than the usual single thickness of glass in the windows, or the ordinary concrete wall or concrete floor. On the other hand, the differential between basement temperature and outside soil temperature is much less than the temperature differential between the upper rooms or the attic and the outside air. Soil temperatures rarely go much below 40°F, whereas outside air temperatures may drop well below 0°F.

e. In house construction, basement losses were once commonly ignored but basement insulation is now much more general. Furthermore, in slab-on-grade construction, losses through the slab are appreciable — particularly at the periphery, where the high conductivity of concrete results in chilled zones in the floor and at the floor-wall intersection. This can cause not only discomfort but also condensation on the floor and the lower portions of walls (see section 11.11c).

f. Building codes commonly specify minimum U or R values for various parts of a building. Figures 11.1 and 11.2 show typical requirements. Degree-days are calculated by summing the daily differences between standard indoor temperatures (commonly 65°F) and average outdoor temperatures over the total number of days in the heating season.

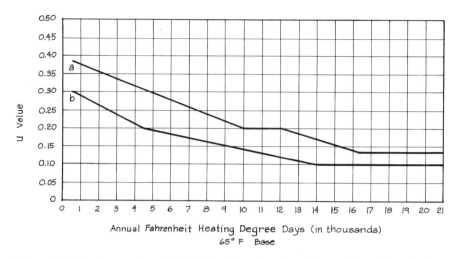

Figure 11.1 Maximum allowable U values for external wall assemblies. Line a is for one- and two-family dwellings; line b is for all other residential buildings not more than three stories high. Source: BOCA National Code, 1987.

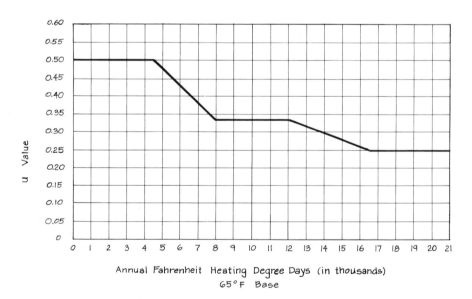

Figure 11.2 Maximum allowable U values for roof-ceiling assemblies. Source: BOCA National Code, 1987.

g. At first glance the figures given in table 11.1 seem to indicate that glass is the most important area to insulate, but the total area of glass is usually much smaller than the roof or the net wall area. Moreover, because warm air tends to rise, the warm zones likely to be found near the top of the house build up the temperature differentials at these zones and, consequently, increase the heat loss. Furthermore, insulation works both in summer and in winter, and in summer the hot sun heats the attic unless insulation is provided. For these reasons, one of the most important areas to insulate is almost always the roof, or the ceiling under the attic space.

h. Total heat losses through outside walls and through windows are usually about the same in most houses. From the comfort standpoint, however, the cold glass areas need more attention than the relatively warm interior surfaces of walls. Therefore, the glass areas, by and large, are at least as important from the insulation standpoint as the walls. In houses having very large window areas, the insulation of the glass may easily overshadow that of the walls in importance. Orientation of windows with respect to the sun becomes extremely important.

11.3 Mechanics of Heat Transfer and Reduction of Heat Loss

a. Heat is transferred by convection, conduction, and radiation. All three of these play a part in the loss of heat from buildings, and various methods of insulating combat one or more of these three sources of loss. Convection currents in the air transfer the heat from warm zones to cold. Solid parts of the structure transmit heat by conduction. Warm surfaces emit radiant heat energy, which passes through intervening space to colder surfaces.

b. The comfort of the occupants of a building depends chiefly on three factors: the temperature of the air, the differences between the surface temperatures of the bodies of the occupants and the surface temperatures of the exterior walls or windows, and the relative humidity of the air. The temperature of the air is less important than is often realized. It is possible to be comfortable even if the air is at a temperature much lower than usually considered comfortable, provided the surrounding walls are sufficiently warm to reduce the rate of radiation from body surface to walls. As a matter of fact, radiant heating systems keep the walls or floors warmer than usual, and comfortable conditions are obtained at air temperatures much lower than

are ordinarily considered necessary. Any method of raising the surface temperature of surrounding walls, floors, ceilings, and window areas by insulation reduces the air temperature required for comfort.
c. Dry air must be warmer than moist air to provide the same degree of comfort because the rapid evaporation of moisture from the surface of the body in dry air has a chilling effect. Hence, the relative humidity must be kept fairly high for comfort, but sufficiently high relative humidity in turn allows the air temperatures to be lowered for the same degree of comfort. Humidification is limited by the surface temperatures of walls and of glass areas. If these are cold, the moisture in the air becomes chilled and condenses even at low relative humidities. Since excessive condensation on walls and windows leads to deterioration of finishes, corrosion, and possible decay of woodwork, the amount of humidification permissible is limited by the temperatures of interior walls and glass surfaces. Proper insulation is therefore needed to keep these surface temperatures at higher levels.
d. Heat loss through a wall is a combination of radiation, convection, and conduction. Heat is transferred to the inner surface of the wall largely by convection currents and by radiation from warmer bodies, with conduction playing only a small part at this stage. The heat passes through the inner wall surface (wallboard or other covering) by conduction. Across the stud space from the inner wall covering to the sheathing, the transfer takes place chiefly by convection and radiation, with conduction usually playing only a small part (mainly at the studs) because wood is a poor conductor. (Metal studs are good conductors. Heavily pierced webs reduce heat-conducting paths.) Heat is transferred through the sheathing and the outside wall covering by conduction, and from exterior surfaces of the wall by radiation and convection.

11.4 Insulation against Convection

a. Without using any insulating material as such, convection losses can be reduced considerably in the stud spaces by proper construction of the house, particularly the frame.
b. Long vertical flues in the stud spaces should be blocked. Such construction considerably reduces the convection currents in the stud spaces, since the higher the flue the more rapidly the convection current travels. In figure 11.3a, not only is the inside wall warmer than the outside wall but the temperature T_2 near the ceiling is higher than

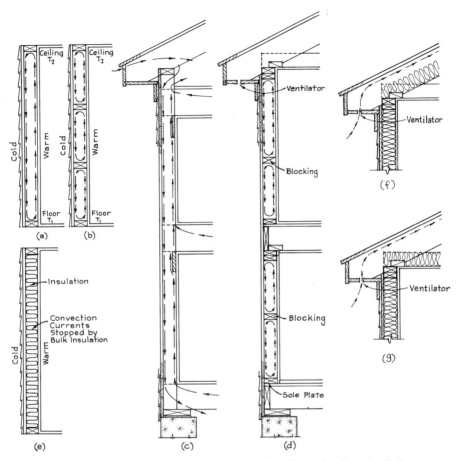

Figure 11.3 Air currents in walls. (a, b) Open stud height vs. headers. (c, d) Open sweep from basement to attic vs. blocking and platform frame. (e) Bulk insulation. (f, g) Details of prevention of ice dams in eaves.

T_1 at the floor. Cold air drops along the sheathing, and warmed air rises along the inner surface. The effect is noticeably stronger in the high stud space than in the blocked space (figure 11.3b).

c. There should be no continuity between inter-stud spaces and inter-joist spaces, but the joist spaces should be blocked at the exterior walls. Otherwise, particularly at the second-story ceilings, convection currents can sweep up from between studs and across under the attic floor, carrying heat to the cold attic and then out through the roof. Figure 11.3c illustrates an extreme case of continuity that promotes heat loss by convection and is also a bad fire hazard. In figure 11.3d the condition has been corrected by platform framing and blocking (see also chapter 5).

d. Cornices that are not tightly built may develop cracks through which air can penetrate in an irregular manner, adding to drafts (figure 11.3c). On the other hand, in hot weather it is desirable to allow air to sweep through screened ventilating slots or series of openings in the eave soffits into the attic space and out through gable or ridge vents (figure 11.3d and section 9.4). In cold weather the ventilators allow cold air to penetrate to the underside of the roof above the soffit and prevent ice dams (sections 8.3f, 9.4). Air should circulate above insulation (see below) in the attic floor or between the rafters (figure 11.3f,g).

e. These rather simple precautions, necessary for fire safety in any case, can substantially reduce heat losses without any extra insulating material.

f. Convection currents can be completely broken up in the inter-stud space by packing it with bulk insulating material. Quiet air is one of the poorest conductors of heat, and bulk insulating materials (figure 11.3e) provide quiet "dead" air by substituting an enormous number of very small air cells, in which convection is reduced practically to zero, for the large spaces between studs, joists, or rafters, in which convection is appreciable.

11.5 Insulation against Conduction

a. Conduction losses occur through the interior finishes of walls and ceilings, through the exterior coverings of walls, and through roof boards and roofing on roofs, as well as through any covering which may be attached to the undersides of rafters. By using materials which are poor conductors for these coverings, heat losses caused by conduction can be reduced. Because the heat must be carried by conduction to those surfaces from which it is transferred by convection and radiation, retarding conduction becomes an important method of reducing heat losses (figures 11.3e,f,g, 11.4).

b. Wood is in itself an excellent insulator, but numerous wallboards exist which, for the same thickness, have lower transmission coefficients and hence are better insulators. Whereas the R values of commonly used species of wood range from approximately 1.00 to 1.25, the coefficients of most wallboards are about 1.5 to 3.3. Insulating boards, like wood, provide a large number of dead air cells. When applied in the same thickness as wood, they form more retardant paths than wood and many more retardant paths than masonry materials or metals. Not only must a good insulator provide dead air cells; the solid portion of the insulating material must itself be a poor conductor. Thus cellular metal would not be a good insulator even if it provided an enormous number of minute cells, because heat would be conducted readily through the metallic portion of the mass.

c. Practically all insulating wallboards are designed to take the place of wood sheathing, and many are made to be used as interior wall coverings (chapter 12). Their efficacy must, therefore, be judged upon their replacements, not as additional insulation. For instance, if $\frac{1}{2}''$ wallboard with a resistance of 1.10 is substituted for $\frac{3}{4}''$ wood with a resistance of 0.95, there is a small net gain in insulating value. Using $\frac{3}{4}''$ insulating board, of course, shows a greater net gain as far as conduction is concerned. The reverse holds true of, for instance, $\frac{1}{2}''$ dense wallboard used as interior finish and sheathing versus $\frac{3}{4}''$ wood sheathing and interior finish. Not only the coefficients per inch of thickness but also the actual thicknesses must be compared to find the net gain.

d. Insulation against convection and against radiation is provided by placing an intermediate layer of insulating material halfway through the stud space (figure 11.4a,b). This provides a pair of intermediate surfaces, the inner one at nearly the same temperature as the back of the interior wall surface and the outer at nearly the same temperature as the back of the sheathing. Since the surfaces facing each other

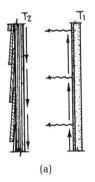 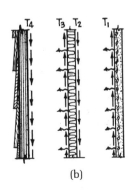

(a)   (b)

Figure 11.4 Radiation and convection in standard construction (a) vs. blanket construction (b). In diagram a, T_1 and T_2 differ markedly. In diagram b, T_1 and T_2 are nearly equal, as are T_3 and T_4; convection and radiation are reduced.

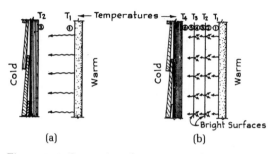

Figure 11.5 Comparison between standard construction (a) and use of bright metal foil insulation (b). In diagram a, T_1 is markedly higher than T_2; surface 1 is a good radiating surface and surface 2 is a good absorbing surface. In diagram b, there is only a slight difference between T_1 and T_2, between T_2 and T_3, and between T_3 and T_4; surfaces 2 and 4 are good reflectors, and surfaces 3 and 5 are poor radiators.

across each of the two air spaces are at nearly the same temperature, both convection in and radiation across the air spaces are reduced. Coupled with this is the low rate of conduction through the insulating layer. The effectiveness of this combination is much enhanced if the surface of the insulating layer is bright metal.

e. Heat transfer through the stud space is usually combated with full-thickness insulation, such as glass-fiber (section 11.10). To achieve additional insulation, the traditional 2 × 4 studs 16″ on center are commonly replaced by 2 × 6 studs 24″ on center (chapter 5).

11.6 Insulation against Radiation

a. The nature of a radiant surface has a great deal to do with the rate of heat loss. Very generally, a bright surface is a poorer radiator than a dull one; therefore, if surfaces of the materials composing wall coverings are made bright, they radiate less heat than do dull or dark ones. This is merely another way of saying that their emissive coefficients are low. Moreover (again very generally), bright surfaces are good reflectors and poor absorbers of radiant heat, so if the surfaces in a wall to which heat is being radiated are bright they absorb relatively little of the heat but reflect much of it (figure 11.5).

b. Since radiation plays an important part in losses through walls, it follows that bright surfaces interposed in the path of heat flow through a structure such as a wall or roof reduce the heat loss through that structure. The bright surfaces must, however, be free-standing to be effective, because wherever they are in contact with any part of the structure they may act as conductors. Bright metal surfaces, for instance, are apt to be good reflectors and poor emitters, but the metals are excellent conductors.

11.7 Insulating Materials

The insulating materials used in house construction fall into five chief categories:
wallboards (insulating)
blankets
sprayed-on insulation
fill
bright metal

11.8 Wallboards

a. Synthetic wallboards are made of a variety of materials, including pulped or mechanically separated wood or vegetable fibers and mineral or glass fibers. The fibers are recombined by matting and felting to form the many small air cells which give the boards their insulating properties.
b. The rigidity and strength of a fiberboard are functions of the pressure under which it was formed; the greater the pressure, the denser and stronger the board but the smaller its insulating value. Most insulating boards are therefore made under moderate pressure and are much softer than wood.
c. Although insulating wallboards are softer than wood, they can impart rigidity to a wall, when substituted for sheathing, because of their size (chapter 5). Commonly they are 4' wide and 8' or more long, and act as large webs when nailed to the wall. They can be used satisfactorily under siding, brick veneer, and the like, but if the walls are to be shingled it may be necessary to nail wood shingle straps to the walls first because shingle nails may not hold well in the soft matrix of insulating boards.
d. Foam boards are discussed in section 11.11.

11.9 Blankets

a. Often, blankets differ from insulating wallboards only in degree of stiffness and not in any inherent aspect of material or manufacture. For instance, blankets may be formed of pulped or mechanically shredded wood fibers, or they may consist of vegetable fibers — both materials also used for wallboards. In one case, the mass is compacted

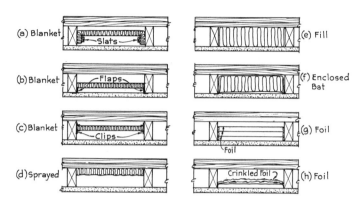

Figure 11.6 Methods of applying insulation.

enough to form a structural board; in the other it is loosely felted, will not stand unsupported, and must be attached to the frame. Blankets differ from wallboards, moreover, in that the loose material must be inserted between coverings such as paper to hold the mass in blanket form, and it may be quilted to hold it together better. Materials much used for blankets are mineral wools made of rock, slag, or glass; vegetable fibers; and wood flour (shredded wood) (figure 11.6a,b,c).

b. Blankets are usually inserted in the stud space and therefore may have an air space on each side. Each air space has practically the same insulating value in itself as the full air space originally in the inter-stud space; thus, in addition to the insulating value of the blanket, another air-space insulator has been added. This is a decided advantage. Between joists and rafters, insulating blankets are also placed so as to have an air space on each side (see also section 11.5).

c. Blankets are often attached by bending the edges against the studs and tacking them in place with wood or heavy paper strips. Many blankets are provided with special flaps at the edges which bend over the edges of studs and are tacked or stapled. Still others, which are stiff enough to stand with little support, are merely attached with small clips along the stud.

11.10 Fill-Type Insulating Materials

a. This class includes all insulating materials which completely fill the inter-stud space, and which fill a large part of the inter-joist or inter-rafter space. The materials may be loose and poured in place, or loosely matted blocks called *bats* may be placed as units (fig. 11.6e,f).

b. A great many materials fall into this category. It is the oldest kind of insulation. The oldtime icehouses with their double outer walls filled with sawdust are an example. Any loose, porous material which can be poured or packed into a space will do provided it does not gradually settle with time and vibration, leaving the upper portion of the wall open and producing a dense mass in the lower portion whose insulating value has decreased. Flake or cellular gypsum, crumbled cork, and vermiculite are examples of this kind of insulation. Loose mineral wool is often used as auxiliary packing in odd spaces. In existing uninsulated houses, mineral wool and other loose materials can be placed by removing some of the exterior wall covering, cutting holes in the sheathing, and blowing the insulation in through a large hose.

11.11 Foam Insulation

a. Plastics, glass, and concrete may be formed into efficient foams for thermal insulation. Glass and concrete foams are employed mainly for industrial and commercial buildings, but may also be used in houses. Glass foam is made into blocks, typically employed in the cavities of masonry and as roof insulation over concrete or steel decks. Foamed concrete is often foamed and poured into place on decks or into irregular spaces.

b. Foamed plastics are either prefoamed or foamed in place (chapter 15). The most common are polystyrene and polyurethane.

c. In house construction, one common use of prefoamed polystyrene planks and boards is as perimeter insulation in slab-on-ground construction (figure 11.7a,b), where otherwise heat loss through the concrete would cause chilled floors and lower walls. It is essential to make sure that concrete does not extend through to the outside, and that the outer one to several feet of floor are insulated, depending upon the severity of the cold outside. Polystyrene foams of this type have closed cells and are reportedly impervious to the passage of water or water vapor; consequently, they need no vapor barrier. Foundation walls are commonly insulated with such foam boards. If placed on the outside of the wall, the cells must be impervious to penetration by moisture (figure 11.7c).

d. Foam wallboards are extensively used as sheathing because of their insulating qualities. When applied in large sheets, they can impart considerable rigidity to a wall, but not as much as plywood and simi-

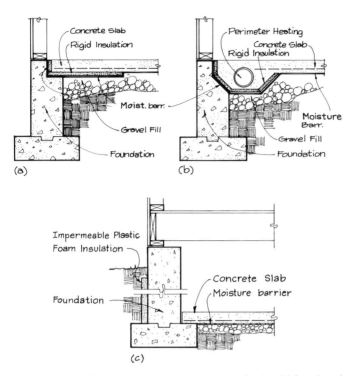

Figure 11.7 Slab-on-grade insulation. (a) Boards should be placed to provide a thermal barrier under the periphery of the slab and toward the outside. (b) Insulation carried under perimeter heating, with moisture barrier interposed. (c) Insulation board placed on outside of basement wall.

lar boards. It may be desirable, therefore, to use let-in braces of panels of plywood or other boards at corners to impart rigidity (section 5.12). **e.** Nail-holding power is low. Clapboards and other finish should be nailed through the foam boards into studs and other framing members, such as blocking, with nails long enough to provide the desired penetration (section 5.4) in addition to the thickness of the foam board. Shingles may require strapping.

f. Expanding-bead polystyrene insulation is used to fill irregular and hard-to-reach spaces. The beads are poured into the space, and heat is supplied by a live steam probe. The beads expand and fill the space.

g. Polyurethane is foamed in place by mixing the liquid ingredients and immediately pouring the mixture into the space to be insulated, where it can rise, fill the space, and solidify. This is particularly convenient for irregular and hard-to-reach spaces. Some pressure is exerted by the foaming mass, so the surrounding structure must be able to withstand it. Pressure can be lessened by allowing the liquid to froth almost to its final volume before pouring it.

h. Urea-formaldehyde is also foamed in place. It is generally legally banned because of formaldehyde fumes.

I. Polyurethane may also be mixed and sprayed in one operation. This makes it possible to spray to the back of sheathing in a stud space and allow the insulation to foam and harden in place (figure 11.6d). Cracks and joints are well sealed this way. Appropriate masks and inhalators should be worn, and good ventilation should be provided.

j. Other plastics, such as the phenolics, can be sprayed. The sprayable insulating materials can also be cast and cut into slabs and boards.

k. As is true of vegetable and wood-based fibrous insulation, the plastic foams can be destroyed by fire. Depending on the formulation, they may burn readily or slowly, or be self-extinguishing when flame is removed. Variable amounts of smoke and noxious or possibly toxic gases are given off. The smoke ranges from moderate to dense, depending on the composition of the foam and the availability of air. This is true of combustible materials generally.

11.12 Bright Metal

a. Radiation losses are combated by bright metallic surfaces, generally aluminum foil several thousandths of an inch thick. The bright surface of aluminum foil possesses high reflecting power and low emissivity. This combination is made effective by interposing several sheets of the foil in the inter-stud space, with air spaces between the sheets. Heat radiated from the back of the inner wall surface (e.g., wallboard) is largely reflected, and that portion which is absorbed is not readily emitted from the other side of the sheet. Each sheet thus forms a barrier against the transmission of heat across the stud space by radiation. At the same time, convection currents are reduced because of the constricted air spaces and because the temperature differential across any one space is fairly small. A free-standing sheet provides one reflecting surface and one low-emission surface, whether heat is traveling outward or inward. When foil is pasted to some backing, the value of one surface is lost.

b. Because of foil's fragility, free-standing sheets must be placed with care. Methods of applying several sheets are shown in figure 11.6g,h.

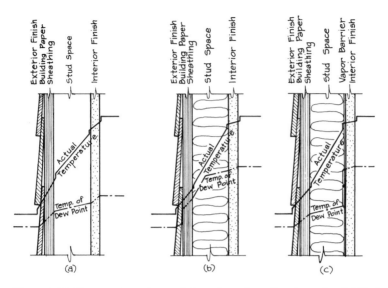

Figure 11.8 Temperature, dew point, and condensation in walls. (a) No insulation or humidification. (b) Insulation and humidification. (c) Insulation, humidification, and vapor barrier.

Foil is also applied to paper for support. Both faces must be covered to have the same two-sided efficiency as free-standing foil. The faces of batts or blankets may have foil on the free face of the cover sheet, and the backs of wallboards may be similarly faced. Such foils act as vapor barriers as well as low-emittance and high-reflectance surfaces.

11.13 Humidification and Condensation

a. Problem. The simultaneous use of insulation and humidification raises the potentially serious problem of condensation in exterior walls.

b. In any exterior wall a temperature difference exists from inside to outside in cold weather, beginning at the indoor temperature and descending in a broken line through the various parts of the wall until it reaches the exterior temperature at a point just outside the wall (figure 11.8a). The slope of actual temperature is steep in good insulating materials and shallow in good conductors. In uninsulated frame walls the gradient falls off most sharply through the sheathing and exterior finish. In insulated walls the steep portions of the gradient are found in the insulating material (figure 11.8b), which means that the temperature of the inside of the sheathing is lower in insulated walls than in uninsulated ones. Because a thin layer of quiet air is held at surfaces of materials, there is a temperature drop at those surfaces.

c. In addition to the temperature gradient there is an absolute humidity difference, which also starts at a high value in the interior and decreases through the wall until it reaches the absolute humidity of the exterior. The absolute humidity of the interior is higher because the warm air is capable of holding much more moisture than the cold outside air, and evaporation from objects and persons within the building (even if there is no humidification system) raises the humidity of the inside air. The higher vapor pressure inside the building generates a tendency for vapor to diffuse outward through the wall. Ordinary building materials, such as insulation, plaster, wood, and brick, offer relatively slight resistance to the diffusion of vapor, but there is enough resistance to cause the absolute humidity to decrease through the wall.

d. Cold air cannot hold as much vapor as warm air can. When air at any temperature is saturated with all the vapor it can hold, it has reached the *dew point* and any excess vapor must condense. In a building wall two tendencies are at work. As the temperature of the air in the wall decreases, its capacity for holding vapor drops in proportion to the temperature gradient (figure 11.8a,b). The actual amount of vapor in the air also decreases, and if it decreases so rapidly that at no point is the air in the wall saturated, condensation does not occur because the dew point is not reached (figure 11.8a). On the other hand, if the moisture content does not drop off rapidly enough, the dew point is reached somewhere and condensation can occur (figure 11.8b).

e. In ordinary uninsulated walls and in unhumidified buildings, the dew point is apt to be reached well out in the sheathing, and condensation is hardly likely to occur within the stud space (figure 11.8a). Experience shows that such walls have not caused trouble. In insulated walls, however, the dew point is reached much farther in, and if the building is humidified (so that the dew-point temperature starts at a much higher value) the likelihood of condensation is much greater (figure 11.8b). If condensation does occur, it generally results in blistered paint, discolored plaster, and warped interior trim. It can lead to decay in the frame.

f. **Remedy.** Any system of construction which depresses the humidity sufficiently to prevent the dew-point temperature from coinciding with the actual temperature automatically prevents condensation. It follows that when moisture is prevented from escaping from the interior of the building into the wall, the moisture gradient falls off very steeply, the dew point is at a much lower temperature, and condensation is much less likely to occur. The logical conclusion is that some sort of barrier must be erected within the wall, close to the interior, to stop the passage of vapor.

g. Metal is probably the only usable material that, to all intents and purposes, completely stops the flow of vapor. However, complete stoppage is not necessary; greatly retarded flow answers just as well. The most common barrier is 2–8-mil polyethylene film. Ordinary tar paper and light felt offer little resistance, but heavy, glossy-surfaced, asphalt-saturated paper, 50-lb or more, is satisfactory.

h. The best position for the barrier is immediately behind the interior wall finish (figure 11.8c). Vapor works its way through the interior surface and is stopped or retarded at the barrier, whose temperature is well above the dew point so that no condensation occurs. The small amount of vapor which does pass through is not sufficient to raise the relative humidity at any point in the wall to the dew point.

i. The barrier must be installed carefully. There must be no breaks in it, because vapor will flow toward and escape through any breaks which might occur. Any seams in the barrier sheets must therefore be sealed, or the seams must be made at studs, joists, or other framing members so that they can be securely fastened and closed tightly when the wall covering is applied. Aluminum foil insulation forms its own vapor barrier, but care must be taken to see that the foil is snugly attached to the framing members. The easiest way to install film or building paper as a seal is to fasten it to the studs in vertical strips long enough to run the full height of the room and turn out on the floor and the ceiling several inches. Seams are made at studs. If the walls are to be plaster on lath, the barrier must be bellied back into the inter-stud space so that the plaster will have room to push through and key itself to the lath.

j. Some insulating materials, especially the batts and blankets, are provided with vapor barriers. For example, vaporseal paper or foil is attached to one side and porous paper to the other, and when the insulation is installed the vaporseal side is turned toward the interior. The efficacy of these attached barriers must be judged, first, on the effectiveness of the barrier as a vapor retardant and, second, on whether the barrier is so arranged as to provide no breaks through which vapor can escape.

k. When film or paper is applied to the inside of the wall as a vapor barrier, it is not necessary to apply another barrier on the outside of the sheathing. In fact, it is better that the outer layer be omitted in insulated and humidified houses, because it is desirable that any vapor which gets into the inter-stud space be allowed to escape through the exterior of the wall as rapidly as possible. If outside paper or another air barrier is desired as an additional wind seal, it should be completely permeable to vapor.

l. Certain wallboards have the faculty of retarding vapor sufficiently to form their own barriers. Ordinary plywood, for instance, is not a good barrier, but plywoods made with synthetic-resin adhesives have been found to be good barriers because of the resin layers. Ordinary gypsum board is a poor barrier, but when backed with a sheet of foil it is a good barrier provided the joints between sheets are sealed.

11.14 Glazing

Standard window glass is inherently a good heat conductor, and such insulating value as it has is due almost entirely to the thin boundary layer of air (table 11.1). In high winds, the value of the boundary layer is diminished. Insulation therefore largely takes the form of multiple glazing (section 7.26), which may be augmented by low-emissivity glass (section 7.26j). Infiltration is another contributor to heat load; it is combated by weatherstripping (section 7.25).

12 Wallboard and Lath and Plaster

12.1 General

Interior surfaces of walls and surfaces of partitions and ceilings in dwelling houses are mainly finished with a variety of wallboards, in a style of construction sometimes called "drywall." Lath and plaster is the other most important method of interior finish.

WALLBOARD, OR "DRYWALL"

12.2 General

Wallboards used for interior finish include gypsum board, portland-cement board, fiber boards, plywood, and hardboard. Of these, gypsum board is the most widely employed.

12.3 Gypsum Board

a. Gypsum is a naturally occurring material, calcium sulfate, that contains two molecules of water per molecule of calcium sulfate. This is heated (calcined) to drive off most of the water, cooled, and ground to a fine powder. When water is added, the calcium sulfate recombines with the water to form a hard material that has good fire resistance, partly because the water bound up in it must be driven off.

b. The various forms of gypsum board are flat panels consisting of a gypsum core between surfaces of paper or other sheet materials. Because of the gypsum core they have good fire resistance, and because of their weight they can provide sound isolation, depending on thickness and method of installation. Depending on the surfacing material employed, they can provide various degrees of abrasion resistance. Their dimensional stability is good. They should, however, be employed in dry locations, because persistent moisture can cause disintegration of most gypsum boards.

c. Gypsum board is made in the following most important types:

Gypsum wallboard (figure 12.1) is used for the surface layer on interior walls and ceilings. It has a gray paper back and a special paper on the facing and edges. The paper is usually cream-colored and provides a smooth, even surface ready for finishing and decorating. When a layer of aluminum foil is applied to the back, gypsum wallboard becomes an insulating wallboard and a vapor barrier. Predecorated wallboard has a decorative paper or vinyl sheet bonded to the exposed face, and does not require further decorating. These wall-

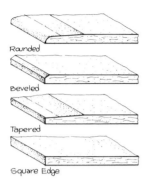

Rounded

Beveled

Tapered

Square Edge

Figure 12.1 Types of gypsum wallboard.

boards are $\frac{1}{4}''$, $\frac{3}{8}''$, $\frac{1}{2}''$, and $\frac{5}{8}''$ thick. The $\frac{1}{4}''$ thickness is used mainly for lining old surfaces or for direct application to substrates such as masonry. The $\frac{3}{8}''$ is used mainly as the outer layer of a two-ply system. The $\frac{1}{2}''$ is used as a single layer for walls and ceilings in new construction, and the $\frac{5}{8}''$ thickness is used for best quality and enhanced resistance to fire and the passage of sound.

Backing board is used as the base layer where two or more layers of gypsum board are applied. Backing board has gray paper on all sides and edges. When supplied with a layer of bright aluminum foil on one side, it becomes an insulating backing board and a vapor barrier.

Core board, which is 1'' thick, is employed for solid gypsum wallboard partitions. It forms the core, and additional layers of gypsum board are applied to it to build the required thickness of partition.

Type X is similar in every respect to the preceding boards except that the core has been made more fire resistant by the addition of glass-fiber reinforcements and other materials. It is used where the greatest degree of fire resistance is required.

Water-resistant backing board, which is more resistant to the absorption of water than ordinary, untreated gypsum board, has water-repellant face papers and a water-resistant gypsum core. It is used as a base for wall tile in baths, showers, and other wet areas.

d. Portland-cement-based backer board is similar to moisture-resistant gypsum board, but utilizes portland cement as the base in place of gypsum, taking advantage of portland cement's superior resistance to water.

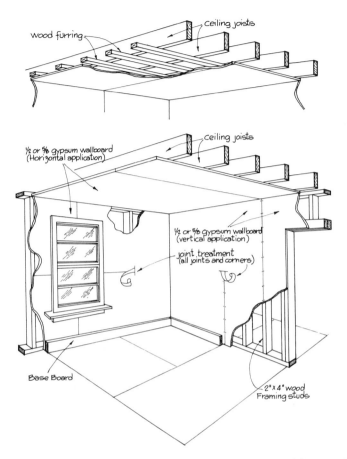

Figure 12.2 Application of gypsum wall board on wood framing. (left wall and ceiling) Horizontal application. (right wall) Vertical application. (top) Alternate application on furred ceiling. Joints are taped.

12.4 Application

Gypsum board may be applied in single or multiple layers (figure 12.2 and section 12.13), but in dwelling-house construction the single layer, employing regular gypsum wallboard, is most common. Gypsum board can be applied over any firm, flat base, such as wood or metal wall studs, ceiling joists or roof trusses, or furring (such as wood strips or metal channels) supported by underlying construction. Gypsum board can also be applied directly to masonry or concrete, but furring is generally preferred, especially on outside walls, to separate the wallboard from possible dampness in the masonry.

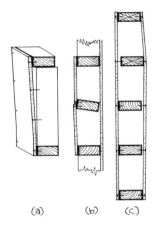

(a)   (b)   (c)

Figure 12.3 Faulty framing, to be avoided. (a) Uneven top plate. (b) Twisted stud. (c) Stud not aligned.

12.5 Supporting Structure

Gypsum board is applied to supporting structures. In dwelling houses this is mainly wood framing and furring, but metal supports are also found.

12.6 Wood Framing

a. Framing must be accurately placed so that the facings are all in the same plane to allow the gypsum board to fit flat against it. Irregularities leading to high spots and low spots, such as bowed or twisted studs, misaligned plates, and other imperfections, should be corrected before the gypsum board is applied, to avoid loose spots, bulges, cracks, and other blemishes (figure 12.3).

b. Spacing of framing members should not exceed the maximum recommendations given in table 12.1. Here the term *horizontal* means that the long edges of the wallboard are at right angles to the directions of the supporting members, whereas the term *vertical* means that the long edges are parallel to the supporting members.

c. Supports should be sufficiently rigid to prevent buckling or cracking of wallboard. Headers over openings, for example, should be strong and rigid enough to avoid excessive deflection under superimposed loads. Special construction should be provided to support wall-hung equipment and fixtures.

d. If spacing between framing members is greater than the maximum

Table 12.1 Maximum Framing Spacing for Application of Gypsum Board

| Gypsum Board Thickness | | | | Maximum Spacing | | |
| | | | | | Two Layers | |
Base Layer	Face Layer	Location	Application	One Layer Only	Fasteners Only	Adhesive Between Layers
3/8"	—	Ceilings	Horizontal	16" o.c.	16" o.c.	16" o.c.
3/8"	3/8"	Ceilings	Horizontal	NA	16"	16" o.c.
3/8"	3/8"	Ceilings	Vertical	NA	NR	16" o.c.
1/2"	—	Ceilings	Horizontal	24"	24" o.c.	24" o.c.
1/2"	—	Ceilings	Vertical	16" o.c.	16" o.c.	16" o.c.
1/2"	3/8"	Ceilings	Horizontal	NA	16" o.c.	24" o.c.
1/2"	3/8"	Ceilings	Vertical	NA	NR	24" o.c.
1/2"	1/2"	Ceilings	Horizontal	NA	24" o.c.	24" o.c.
1/2"	1/2"	Ceilings	Vertical	NA	16" o.c.	24" o.c.
5/8"	—	Ceilings	Horizontal	24" o.c.	24" o.c.	24" o.c.
5/8"	—	Ceilings	Vertical	16" o.c.	16" o.c.	24" o.c.
5/8"	3/8"	Ceilings	Horizontal	NA	16" o.c.	24" o.c.
5/8"	3/8"	Ceilings	Vertical	NA	NR	24" o.c.
5/8"	1/2" or 5/8"	Ceilings	Horizontal	NA	24" o.c.	24" o.c.
5/8"	1/2" or 5/8"	Ceilings	Vertical	NA	16" o.c.	24" o.c.
1/4"	—	Walls	Vertical	NR	16" o.c.	16" o.c.
1/4"	3/8"	Walls	NR	NA	NR	NR
1/4"	1/2" or 5/8"	Walls	Horizontal or vertical	NA	16" o.c.	16" o.c.
3/8"	—	Walls	Horizontal or vertical	16"[a] o.c.	16" o.c.	24"[a] o.c.
3/8"	3/8" or 1/2" or 5/8"	Walls	Horizontal or vertical	NA	16" o.c.	24" o.c.
1/2" or 5/8"	—	Walls	Horizontal or vertical	24" o.c.	24" o.c.	24" o.c.
1/2" or 5/8"	3/8" or 1/2" or 5/8"	Walls	Horizontal or vertical	NA	24" o.c.	24" o.c.

NA—Not Applicable
NR—Not Recommended

Spacing for Fasteners, Single Ply

Location	Nails	Screws
Ceiling	7" o.c.	12" o.c.
Walls and Partitions	8" o.c.	12" o.c.

[a] For single nailing. For double nailing, end nailing same; field nails in pairs 2" apart, spaced approximately 12" between centers of pairs.

Spacing For Fasteners Used With Stud Adhesives

| Location | Support Spacing | Fastener Spacing | |
		Nails	Screws
Ceiling	16 in. o.c.	16 in. o.c.	16 in. o.c.
	24 in. o.c.	12 in. o.c.	
Load-bearing Walls and partitions	16 in. o.c.	16 in. o.c.	24 in. o.c.
	24 in. o.c.	12 in. o.c.	16 in. o.c.
Non-load-bearing Walls and partitions	16 in. o.c.	24 in. o.c.	24 in. o.c.
	24 in. o.c.	16 in. o.c.	

Source: *Using Gypsum Board for Walls and Ceilings*, Gypsum Association, Chicago, Illinois.

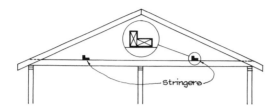

Figure 12.4 Method of aligning ceiling joists with horizontal and vertical stringers.

recommended for a particular board thickness, or if the surface provided by the framing members is not sufficiently flat, furring should be used (figure 12.2). The furring surface supporting the gypsum board should be at least $1\frac{1}{2}''$ wide if wood and $1\frac{1}{4}''$ wide if metal.

e. To provide sufficient stiffness, wood furring should be at least nominal $2'' \times 2''$ material, although nominal $1'' \times 3''$ is frequently used when wallboard is attached to the furring with screws rather than nails. If the furring is backed by solid construction, such as masonry, wood furring can be as little as $\frac{5}{8}''$ thick by $1\frac{1}{2}''$ wide.

f. Wood studs in load-bearing partitions are best nominal $2'' \times 4''$, and $2'' \times 3''$ in non-load-bearing partitions. In staggered partitions, $2'' \times 3''$ studs are employed at $16''$ on centers, staggered $8''$ apart in opposite rows, spaced $1''$ apart. If 2-hour fire resistance is required, studs must be $2'' \times 4''$.

g. Ceiling joists should be evenly spaced, with their bottom edges aligned in a level plane. Excessively bent and crooked joists should be avoided. Those that have a crown should be applied with the crown upward. Joists that are somewhat out of line can be brought into line by stringers or bracing members (figure 12.4). Where wide variations in joist spacing occur or where joists are not in a level plane, furring should be applied at right angles to joists at proper distances on centers.

h. Where roof trusses are employed — and particularly where some roof trusses extend their full length without intermediate partitions, whereas others have intermediate partitions under them — it is highly desirable to have the entire roof and other loads applied before the partitions are put into place. In this way, the roof trusses will have deflected their full amount; otherwise, the subsequent greater deflection of full-span trusses as compared with partially supported trusses causes unevenness and cracking in the wallboard ceiling. Intermittent snow loads still can cause difficulties.

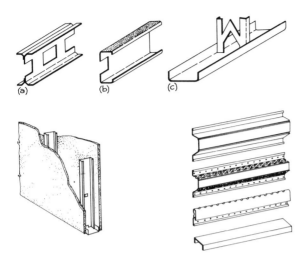

Figure 12.5 (top) Types of metal studs and runners. (lower left) Metal studs with applied board. (lower right) Types of furring — from top to bottom: plain, resilient, resilient, and cold-rolled.

12.7 Metal Framing

a. Although wood framing is most common in dwelling houses, metal framing is found, particularly in metal stud partitions (section 5.3w and figure 12.5).

b. Various configurations of metal studs are found. These are inserted between channel-shaped runners at top and the bottom, which take the place of the plates in wood partitions. The spacing for metal framing is given in table 12.1. Metal furring members are commonly rolled channels, special drywall channels, hat-section channels, or drywall steel studs (section 5.3w).

12.8 Fasteners and Attachments

a. Nails and screws are commonly used to attach gypsum board in either single- or multiple-layer installations. Clips and staples are used only to attach the base layer in multiple-layer applications.

b. Special drywall adhesives can be used to bond single-ply gypsum board onto framing, furring, masonry, and concrete. Such adhesives can also be used to laminate the face layer of multiple layers to backer board, sound-deadening board, or rigid foam insulation. Adhesives are generally supplemented with some mechanical fasteners.

c. When mechanical fasteners (particularly nails, staples, and screws) are employed, they should be the special varieties made especially for gypsum board. Ordinary wood screws, sheet-metal screws, and common nails are not designed to hold the board tightly and to countersink neatly.

d. Any fasteners should be placed at least $\frac{3}{8}''$ from the edges and ends of boards. It is best to begin fastening at the center of the board and to work outward toward the ends and edges. Nails should be driven with a crown-headed hammer to form a dimple not more than $\frac{1}{32}''$ deep around the nail head. It is important not to break the face paper or to crush the core with too heavy a blow.

e. Several types of nails used for gypsum board are shown in figure 12.6. Heads should be between $\frac{1}{4}''$ and $\frac{5}{16}''$ in diameter and tapered to avoid cutting the face paper when the nail is driven home. Nails should be long enough to go through the wallboard layer or layers and far enough into the supporting construction to provide adequate holding power. For smooth-shank nails, penetration should be at least $\frac{7}{8}''$; for annular-ring nails, $\frac{3}{4}''$ is adequate. The less the penetration, the less the chance that nail popping will occur (see section 12.14).

f. Several types of drywall screws are shown in figure 12.6. They are used to attach gypsum board to wood or steel framing or to other gypsum boards. Screws of this type pull the board tightly to the supports without damaging the board, and the specially contoured head makes a uniform depression without breaking the paper or providing ragged edges.

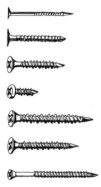

Figure 12.6 Fasteners. From top down: flat-head annular-ring nail, flat-head ratchet nail, Type S bugle screw, Type S pan screw, Type G bugle screw, Type W bugle screw, Type S trim screw.

g. Type W screws are designed for fastening gypsum board to wood framing or furring. The recommended penetration into these supports is $\frac{5}{8}''$.

h. Type S screws are designed for fastening gypsum board to metal studs or furring. They are self-drilling and self-tapping; the hardened drill point penetrates sheet metal with little pressure.

i. Type G screws are used for fastening gypsum board panels to gypsum backing boards. Regular drywall screws should not be used for this purpose, because they lack sufficient holding power. Nails or longer screws should be driven through both layers into the supporting wood or metal construction.

j. Staples are recommended only for attaching the base ply to wood members in multi-layered structures. These should be 16-gauge flattened galvanized wire with minimum $\frac{7}{16}''$ wide crown and spreading points. They should penetrate at least $\frac{5}{8}''$ into the wood.

k. Adhesives are employed to bond single layers of gypsum board directly to wood and metal framing, or to other substrates, or to laminate wallboard to such base layers as backing board. Adhesives are generally used in combination with nails or screws to provide supplemental support.

l. The principal types of adhesives are the following:

rubber-based wallboard and panel adhesives, for attaching panels to wood and steel framing members, existing walls and ceilings, rigid foam, and masonry surfaces

modified contact adhesives, for the same purposes and also for attaching gypsum board to gypsum board

laminating adhesives, for laminating gypsum wallboard panels.

12.9 Preparation

a. Job conditions are important — especially temperature and humidity, which can affect the performance of joint treatments, the quality of joints, and the adhesive bond (when adhesives are employed). During the winter season, buildings should have controlled temperatures of at least 55°F maintained for at least 24 hours before installation, and afterward until permanent heating is installed. During warm months, the building need not be completely glazed, but the material should be protected from the weather. Ventilation may have to be provided if humidity is excessive. Windows should be kept open to provide air circulation, and in enclosed areas fans should be used. In hot, dry weather, drafts should be avoided to prevent excessive and rapid drying of joint compounds.

b. Because lumber shrinks across the grain as it dries, the moisture content should be low enough to avoid excessive shrinkage and nail popping (section 12.14). Lumber should be no higher than 19 percent in moisture content and preferably should be at the final moisture content it will have when the building is in use (section 5.2).

c. Gypsum board should be delivered at the time of installation so that it need not be stored for excessive periods of time. When it is stored, it should be stored flat and in its original packing in reasonably dry conditions to avoid moisture pickup.

12.10 Cutting and Fitting

a. Careful attention and planning are necessary for successful installation of gypsum board. The boards, if at all possible, should span the entire length or width of ceilings and walls to avoid butt-end joints, which are difficult to finish. If butt-end joints must be employed, they should be well staggered, preferably away from conspicuous spots such as centers of walls and ceilings. Ends and edges of boards should fall on supporting members such as studs and joists and not between them. If they must fall between, additional blocking should be supplied. If possible, the long edges of wallboards should be installed at right angles to supporting members because greater stiffness results. On long walls, boards of maximum practical length should be used to minimize the number of end joints. Proper measuring, cutting, and fitting are important, and measurements should be made for each edge or end of a board. Inaccuracies in framing and furring should be corrected before boards are applied.

b. Straight-line cuts across the full length and width are made by scoring the face paper, snapping the core, and then cutting the back paper with a sharp knife. Gypsum board can also be sawn by cutting from the face side to preserve a smooth paper edge.

12.11 Single-Ply Application

a. Wall board may be single-nailed or double-nailed (figure 12.7). Nail spacing is determined more by requirements for fire resistance and rigidity than for sufficient strength to support the wallboard.

b. Ceiling panels should be installed first and then the walls. Joints should not be forced, but should only be loosely butted. Tapered

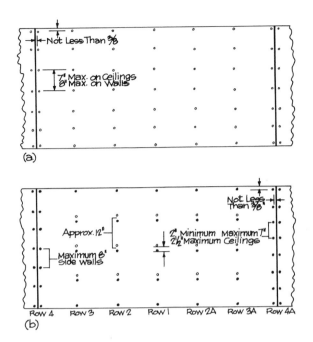

Figure 12.7 Nailing. (a) Single. (b) Double.

edges should adjoin, and square-cut ends should adjoin. Tapered and square-cut ends and edges should not adjoin, because the resulting ridge is difficult to conceal (figure 12.2).

c. On ceilings, nails should be spaced 7″ on centers; on walls, 8″ on centers along the supports (figure 12.7).

d. If double nailing is employed, the first set of nails is driven 12″ on centers in the middle of the panel. A second set is driven 2″ from each of the nails of the first set, which should be driven again to reset them firmly. Edges and ends falling over supports should be single-nailed 7″ on centers on ceilings and 8″ on centers on walls (figure 12.7).

e. Loose attachment (nailing in which the board is not driven firmly in contact with studs or other supports) should be avoided because it can lead to nail pops, or nail heads projecting beyond the surface of the wallboard. Loose attachment is avoided by having the supports in the same plane, avoiding too-tight joints, and making certain that the boards are driven tightly against the supporting surfaces.

f. When screws are employed, fewer fasteners are required (table 12.1). They should be spaced 12″ on centers on ceilings and 16″ on

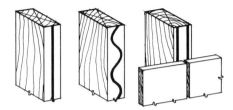

Figure 12.8 Adhesive beads.

centers on walls where framing members are 16″ on centers, or a maximum of 12″ on centers on walls and ceilings where framing members are 24″ on centers.

g. Adhesives and nails may both be employed to apply gypsum board, and result in a stronger, more rigid system than is true of nails or screws alone. Fewer nails are employed with less chance of defects and blemishes than with all-nail attachments (table 12.1).

h. Stud adhesives are applied with a caulking gun, either as a straight bead ¼″ in diameter or (especially where two adjacent panels join over a supporting member) as a serpentine or zigzag bead when a joint in ordinary wallboard will be subsequently treated and covered (figure 12.8). If pre-decorated wallboard is used, two parallel beads of adhesive should be applied, one near each edge of the supporting member, so that when adjoining pieces of wallboard are pressed against the surface the adhesive will not squeeze out into the joint.

i. Where wallboards are applied to studs with adhesives, only perimeter fasteners are required. These should be spaced 16″ on centers along edges and ends that fall along supporting members, and at each crossing of a supporting member. For ceiling applications, the same perimeter fastenings are employed but additional fasteners are spaced 24″ on centers in the middle of the field.

j. If pre-decorated wallboard is applied with adhesives, it is desirable not to use mechanical fastenings because they may show. In this case, it is desirable to pre-bow the wallboard so that as it is flattened against the supporting surfaces, it comes into close contact with them. Temporary bracing is required to hold the wallboard in place while the adhesive hardens. Bracing should remain in place at least 24 hours.

12.12 Double-Ply Application

a. Double-ply construction is seldom used in dwellings because of the high cost. It does, however, result in sturdier construction, greater fire

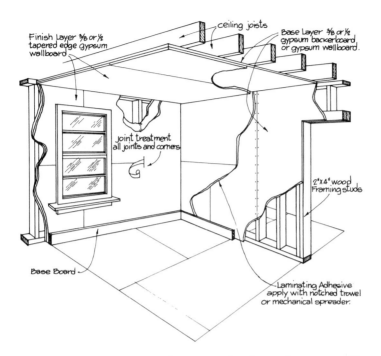

Finish Layer ⅜ or ½ tapered edge gypsum wallboard

ceiling joists

Base Layer ⅜ or ½ gypsum backerboard or gypsum wallboard.

Joint treatment all joints and corners

2"x4" wood framing studs

Base Board

Laminating Adhesive apply with notched trowel or mechanical spreader.

Figure 12.9 Double-layer application: surface layer of gypsum wallboard on base layer of backing board.

resistance, and enhanced acoustical isolation because of the greater mass, provided that other sources of acoustical leakage are stopped. Nail-popping (section 12.14) and other blemishes are reduced.

b. When double-ply construction is employed, the first ply is usually backer board; although wallboard may be used, it is more expensive. Special gypsum board and other sound-deadening boards may be used for enhanced sound isolation (figure 12.9).

c. The base ply is attached with nails and staples (for wood framing) or with screws (for metal). If the face ply is to be adhesively laminated to the base ply, nails and screws for the base ply are 7″ to 8″ on centers, and screws 16″ on centers. If the face ply is to be nailed or screwed, the nail or staple spacing for the base ply is 16″ on centers and screws are 24″ on centers. Floating corners are employed, as described below.

d. The face ply of wallboard is fastened to the base ply with nails, screws, or adhesives. If nails or screws are used, the spacing is the same as for single-ply attachment.

e. In double-ply construction, the face ply is often applied with adhesive, by sheet lamination, strip lamination, or spot lamination.

f. In sheet lamination, the entire back of the facing sheet is covered with laminating adhesive applied in a ridged configuration with a notched spreader, and the sheet is pressed firmly against the base. Any squeezeout at the edges and ends is promptly removed.

g. Strip and spot lamination are usually preferred in sound-rated construction because sound deadening is enhanced. In strip lamination, adhesive is applied in notched ribbons approximately 6″ wide, 16″ to 24″ on center. In spot lamination, spots of adhesive approximately 2″ to 3″ in diameter are applied 8″ to 10″ apart. The board is pressed firmly against the base.

h. Temporary supports are needed to hold the facing board in place until the adhesive has hardened. Such supports may be double-headed nails or temporary bracing. For fire-rated walls, permanent mechanical fasteners such as nails or screws are required around the perimeters of the boards and in the field.

12.13 Treatment of Joints and Fasteners

a. Joints between edges and ends of wallboard and joints at interior corners are usually reinforced with a paper tape embedded in a compound to provide a smooth, inconspicuous, monolithic appearance. Exterior corners and exposed edges are protected with corner and edge trim for appearance and protection.

b. The tape used for joint reinforcement is generally a strong fiber paper with feathered edges. It resists tensile stresses across and along the joints (figures 12.10, 12.2, 12.9). The paper is embedded in a compound or compounds. Taping or joint compound is used to embed and bond the taping at the joint. Finishing compound is employed for final smoothing and leveling over the joints to provide a smooth, inconspicuous appearance. All-purpose compounds combine the features of taping and finishing compounds.

c. Dry compounds are mixed with water to the proper consistency for handling with a heavy, broad knife. Some harden by evaporation of water and others by setting of the ingredients; the latter frequently have a gypsum base and must be used within specified time limits to avoid premature setting.

d. Taping compounds are used to bond tapes over joints, to fill depressions, and to conceal fasteners and edge and corner trim. They

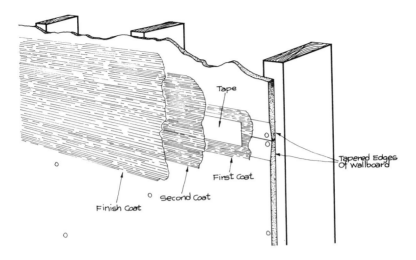

Figure 12.10 The taping of a joint. Tape is embedded in the first coat; then a smooth surface is built up with the second and finish coats.

are, therefore, sometimes called *embedding compounds*. Topping or finishing compounds are primarily used to conceal and smooth over embedded tapes, fasteners, and trim. All-purpose compounds are used for both taping and topping.

e. It is recommended that at least three coats of compound be employed with all taped joints. The first coat is an embedding coat to bond the tape, after which two finishing or topping coats are applied and smoothed off to a level surface with the surrounding board as shown in figure 12.10. To prevent excessive shrinkage, each coat should be allowed to dry thoroughly before the next coat is applied.

f. For flush joints, taping compound is spread into the depression formed by the tapered edges of adjacent boards, and over butted end joints. Tape is centered over the joint and smoothed, after which it is pressed into the compound with a broad knife under enough pressure to squeeze out excess compound. After the compound is dry, it may be sanded if the surface is too rough. Then a second coat of compound is applied and the edges are feathered 2″ to 4″ beyond the tape. This coat is also sanded after drying, if necessary, and a third coat of compound is spread with its edges feathered 2″ to 4″ beyond the second. It is blended smoothly with the wallboard surface. Taping and spreading of compound can be done by hand or by machine.

g. At interior corners, taping compound is applied to both sides of the

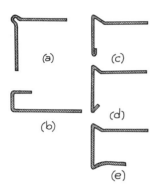

Figure 12.11 Corner beads and protective edging strips. (a) Corner. (b) U. (c) L. (d) LK. (e) LC.

joint, after which the tape is folded along a center crease and embedded snugly in the corner to form a right angle. The surfaces are then finished as described for flush joints.

h. Exposed corners of wallboard need to be protected against damage. This is often accomplished by wood trim, especially at window and door frames and in the form of baseboards at floors.

i. Metal trim, such as corner beads and casing beads, is commonly employed to protect exterior corners and exposed edges of wallboard. A number of standard shapes are shown in figure 12.11. Metal corner beads protect wallboard corners from damage, and other trim protects edges. Trim is generally nailed or screwed approximately 6″ on centers to the supporting construction. These various metal trim shapes require at least three coats of finishing with joint compound if a smooth surface is to be obtained and if the adjacent fasteners, such as nails or screws, are to be concealed.

j. The heads of fasteners, such as nails or screws, must be concealed, and this is generally done with joint compound at the same time that the joints are taped or otherwise protected. This is commonly done with a broad knife; the compound not only fills the depression at the fastener, but is feathered out to the surrounding board. The second and third coats are generally applied at the same time as the second and third coats to joints.

12.14 Damage and Blemishes

a. Nail popping may occur any time wallboards become loose. Looseness may be caused by shrinkage of the wood studs, joists, or other supporting members, if the moisture content of the wood is too high

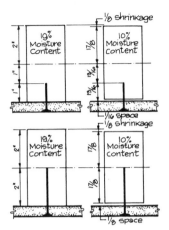

Figure 12.12 If wood shrinks after wallboard is nailed, long nails may cause separation, and their heads may push out (or "pop"). Short nails minimize separation.

to begin with and the wood dries in use (figure 12.12). For this reason, the shorter the nail used the better; the special nails for gypsum board described above are therefore recommended. Twisted, crooked boards out of line also lead to looseness and nail popping. The usual repair is to drive a new nail of the proper size about 1¼" from the popped nail by holding the board tightly against the framing. Then the popped nail can be re-seated or withdrawn. The damaged part and the new fastening should be filled smoothly with compound.

b. Cracks may be caused by a variety of circumstances, and they may be filled. If movement of the frame is a cause of the cracking, the cracks probably will open again and will need to be refilled from time to time.

c. It is not uncommon for cracks to occur in corners because of structural stresses where walls meet walls or where walls and ceilings meet. This may be minimized by floating-angle construction, which consists of omitting some fasteners at interior corners (figure 12.13).

d. As usual, wallboard should be applied to the ceiling first and should be fitted snugly at the ceiling-to-wall intersections. Framing members or blocking should provide solid backing, but fasteners, such as nails, are omitted at the corners. This means that the first nails are 8" from the intersection on the walls and 7" on the ceilings. When gypsum boards are applied to the walls, they butt against the ends of the ceiling panels; the wall panels are nailed along the edges.

e. When two walls intersect, the panels applied to the first wall are

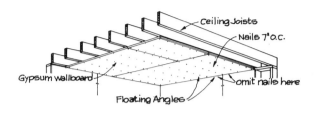

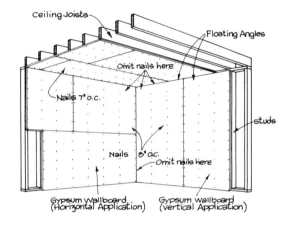

Figure 12.13 Floating-angle construction. The lower diagram shows vertical application of wallboard on the right wall and the ceiling. Horizontal application is shown on the left wall and in the upper diagram. Nails are omitted at the edge of the ceiling wallboard.

snugly fitted into the corner. Nails are omitted along the edge. When panels are subsequently applied to the other wall, these are butted against the panels of the first wall and are nailed along the edges.

f. By this procedure, at least one of the boards abutting the corner has some ability to move as the corner moves, and, therefore, to avoid building up stresses that can lead to cracking.

g. Ridges may occur, particularly where ends of boards meet. The reason may be expansion and contraction of the framing or other movement. It is just as well to allow enough time for the ridges to develop completely before attempting to correct them. Correction consists of sanding the ridges down to the reinforcing tape without actually sanding through the tape, and filling the sanded area with topping compound. After the compound has dried, it is blended into the repaired area with a light film of additional topping compound as necessary to bring it out to a smooth surface.

h. The most effective preventive measure is to use multi-layer gypsum-board systems, but this is not commonly done in dwelling-house construction. For single-ply construction, back blocking or strip reinforcing is employed to reinforce joints and to prevent the stresses that cause ridging.

i. Back blocking is employed when gypsum-board ends do not fall on framing members or furring. Gypsum-board back blocks extending the full distance between supports are laminated to the back of the wallboard to reinforce the joint and to prevent flexing or movement.

j. In strip reinforcing, strips of ⅜" backing board or scrap wallboard 8" wide are installed 24" on centers, perpendicular to the framing members as cross stripping, to support the edges and provide intermediate support in the field. Where butt ends occur, additional short strips are secured directly over the supporting members between the cross-stripping.

k. Laminating adhesive is applied to the strips in parallel beads, preferably with a split laminating head on the applicator. Wallboard is applied perpendicular to the framing members so that the long edges fall on the cross-stripping, and the ends are supported on the short intermediate strips.

l. Fasteners such as nails and screws are better thermal conductors than the surrounding wallboard and wood studs. Consequently, dust and moisture tend to collect on the surface of the compound over nail and screw heads. This causes a situation known as *shadowing*, which is simply a surface discoloration but often looks like popping. Shadowing is most likely to occur on exterior walls and under roofs or ceilings where marked indoor-outdoor temperature variations occur. Shadowing is best avoided by the installation of adequate insulation to prevent large temperature differences, by good ventilation, or by using multi-layer installation. It can be corrected by periodic washing or decorating.

12.15 Plywood and Reconstituted Boards

a. These materials are described in section 5.3.

b. For ordinary work no special pains are taken to select the wood for the face plies, except to see that no blemishes occur if the material is to be used for a finished face. The most common species used for ordinary plywood is Douglas fir (chapter 5). If surfaces are to be exposed, they are sanded; if not, sanding is unnecessary. For walls which are to be finished "natural" (i.e., to show the grain of the wood), specially selected face veneers may be used in place of the ordinary species because the latter may have an uninteresting figure. Numerous fine veneers exist which may be selected for this purpose, ranging from the most expensive exotic woods to the more common native species such as birch and white pine. These may be cut in any of a variety of ways to produce the best figures and may be arranged or "matched" in various patterns to produce the effects desired.

c. Plywood is applied directly to studs, joists, strapping, or furring. It should be nailed with small finish nails, such as 4d, and the heads should be "set" (driven below the surface) if the joints are not to be covered. If wood battens are to be nailed over the joints, ordinary flat-headed nails, such as 5d or 6d box, may be used. Nails should be fairly close together — not over 6" apart — and all edges must be nailed, even if intermediate blocking is required. In addition, the ply-wood sheets should be nailed to intermediate framing members and to the fire-stopping or similar blocks let in between the studs. For addi-tional rigidity, the edges of studs may be covered with water-resistant glue before the plywood sheets are applied.

d. As with all wallboards which do not cover the entire wall in one sheet, the treatment of joints between sheets is an important problem. Numerous methods have been tried, of which the following are the most common (figure 12.14).

Wood battens. This is the oldest and perhaps the commonest method. Molded or plain wood battens are nailed over the joint, and therefore form raised strips wherever joints occur. By proper arrange-ment of the sheets on walls and ceilings and by using additional battens even if no joints are to be covered, the effect of paneled areas can be secured. To obtain good paneled effects usually requires strap-ping, furring, or a solid base, so that the sheets can be applied without regard to the studs.

Accentuated joint. Instead of attempting to conceal the joint, it may be emphasized and made a part of the decorative treatment of the room by cutting it in a vee or a bead or otherwise making it promi-nent. When this is done, it is essential that edges be cut straight so that a good fit between sheets is obtained. By scoring or beading the sheets at other points than at the edges, and by arranging the sheets properly, decorative effects may be obtained.

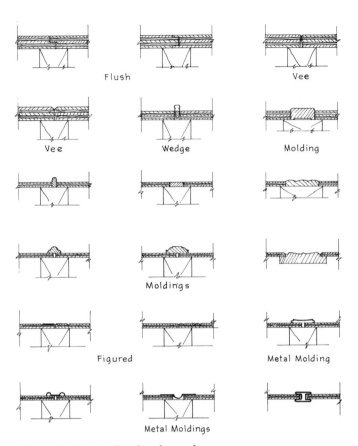

Figure 12.14 Joint details, plywood.

Moldings and beads. Instead of wood battens, small metal moldings may be applied over joints, or small metal or wood beads may be inserted between sheets of plywood and allowed to project from the wall, to provide the reverse of the sunken joint typical of the vee joint (figure 12.16).

e. Figure 12.15 illustrates a method of resisting small movements at the joints which may be caused by changes in moisture content of the studs or other framing members: fastening furring strips of plywood to the edges of the framing members before the plywood panels are applied. Dimensional changes in the cross-grain direction in the framing members are resisted by the face plies of the plywood furring strips, and joints in the plywood panels are therefore prevented from opening.

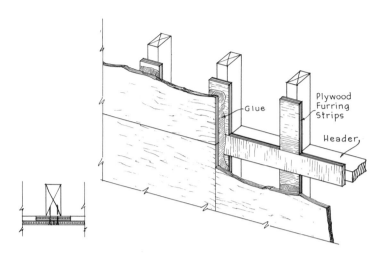

Figure 12.15 Reinforced plywood joints.

12.16 Fiber and Pulp Boards

a. Several different vegetable fibers are employed in the manufacture of fiber boards. A common one is bagasse, the pressed-out stalks of sugar cane. Wood pulp may be the product of mechanically shredded wood, or may be chemically separated wood fibers. In any event, the base fibers are usually mixed with other materials which help act as binders and to some extent as preservatives, and the resulting wet pulpy mass is rolled or flowed out into sheet form, pressed between rollers to dry and consolidate, and finally dried in large sheets, usually from $\frac{3}{8}''$ to $1''$ thick. The hardness and the weight of the board are functions of the pressures employed in the consolidating operation. Usually they are fairly soft and porous, which gives them better heat-insulating qualities than the denser and stiffer boards such as hardboard (below) and gypsum. On the other hand, soft boards do not withstand rough usage so well as the harder varieties.

b. These boards are applied in much the same way as plywood, with the same provisions for abundant nailing and blocking behind all edges. If nail heads must be concealed, finish nails are employed; if they are to be covered, flat-headed nails can be used. The latter are to be preferred, because these boards do not have the nail-holding power of plywood.

c. Treatment of joints is an important problem, and is met in largely

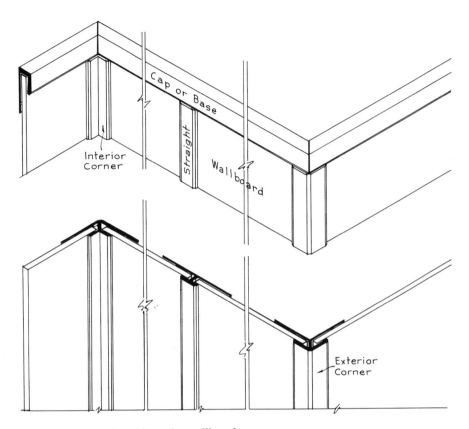

Figure 12.16 Metal moldings for wallboard.

the same way as for plywood joints, except that no attempt is ordinarily made to provide a concealed joint. Joints are commonly covered with wood battens, with battens of the same material as the board, or with fine metal moldings. The edges are often beveled, and the rest of the sheet may be scored with vees of the same shape as the beveled edges to form geometrical patterns on walls and ceilings. Paneled effects are obtained with moldings of the same shape as the battens.

12.17 Hardboard

a. Exploded-wood-fiber boards are somewhat different in composition from the wood-pulp boards (section 5.3n). Wood chips are subjected to steam under high pressure which is suddenly released and causes explosive separation of the fibers. These are recombined under heat

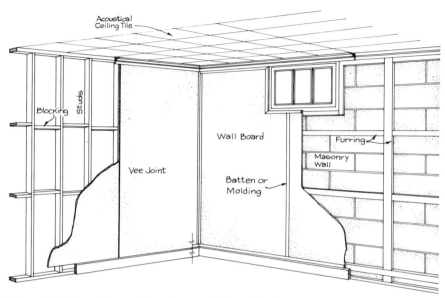

Figure 12.17 Applying wallboard over studs and furring.

and pressure into large sheets, the density and weight of which depend on the pressure employed. Soft insulating board is seldom used as a finished surface where there is any likelihood of contact with persons or objects, but the hard board provides a wear-resistant finished surface. Application and joint treatments are much the same as for plywood or other boards. Metal moldings are commonly employed for joints and corners (figure 12.16).

b. Typical installation details for wallboards are shown in figure 12.17. Vee-jointed boards are shown attached to blocked studs. Battens or moldings are shown covering the joints of wallboards applied over furring on a masonry wall. Lightweight fibrous sound-absorbing acoustical tiles are attached to furring strips on the ceiling. Baseboards at the floor and corner moldings at the ceiling cover the intersections with the walls.

LATH AND PLASTER

12.18 General

Lath and plaster has been the traditional method of finishing interior walls, partitions, and ceilings. The use of plaster goes back to ancient times.

12.19 Framing

The framing requirements for lath and plaster are similar to those for wallboard. In dwellings the framing is usually wood, but metal framing, especially studs and furring, is becoming more common (figures 12.2, 12.5, 12.9). Framing must be sturdy, rigid enough to avoid excessive deflection, and reasonably plane and level to avoid the requirement for excessive straightening by the lath and plaster, although lath and plaster can accommodate greater deviations from line and plane than wallboard.

12.20 Lath

At one time, most plaster was applied to 4' wood lath. Although this lath has now virtually disappeared, its influence still lingers on in the 4' dimensions of most wallboards and the 16" or 24" spacing of studs and other framing members. Today, when plaster is used in dwelling houses, it is usually applied to gypsum lath, and occasionally to metal lath.

12.21 Gypsum Lath

a. Gypsum lath is similar to the gypsum wallboards already described, except that the lath is made of gray porous paper on both sides and the edges are rounded. The most commonly used thickness is $\frac{3}{8}"$, and the common sizes are 16" by.48" (although 96" is also found). Veneer plaster (section 12.29), on the other hand, is commonly applied to boards 4' wide by 8' long. Gypsum lath may be plain, or may be perforated with holes to provide a mechanical key (figure 12.18).
b. Lath should be applied with its long dimension perpendicular to the framing members. The ends of lath must bear on a framing member unless special clip attachments are used.
c. Interior corners should be reinforced with "Cornerite" (figure 12.19), which consists of a strip of metal lath bent into the corner and secured to the lath with staples or wire.

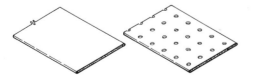

Figure 12.18 Gypsum lath. (left) Plain. (right) Perforated.

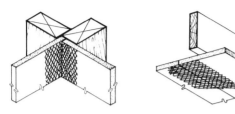

Figure 12.19 (left) Cornerite. (right) Strip reinforcement.

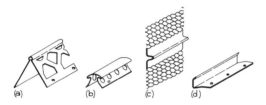

Figure 12.20 (a,b) Corner beads. (c) Base or parting screed. (d) Square casing bead.

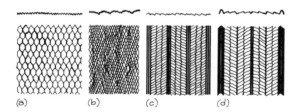

Figure 12.21 Metal lath. (a) Flat diamond mesh. (b) Self-furring. (c) Flat rib. (d) $\frac{3}{8}''$ rib.

d. Exterior angles are finished with corner beads (figure 12.20). Casing beads are used at windows and doors, and metal or wood grounds are used at openings, trim, and other places where it is essential that the finished plaster be brought to true thickness and a straight level surface. Picture molds are employed where pictures are to be hung.

12.22 Metal Lath

a. Metal lath consists of expanded metal or of wire fabric. The principal expanded types are flat and self-furring diamond mesh, flat rib lath with shallow stiffening ribs at intervals, and rib lath ($\frac{3}{8}''$ or $\frac{3}{4}''$).
b. Wire fabric lath is fabricated of copper-bearing cold-drawn steel wire. It is galvanized or coated with a rust-inhibitive paint after weaving or welding, or is fabricated from galvanized wire.

c. Lath must be securely attached to supports and should be placed with the lower sheet lapping over the upper. It should be lapped at the sides not less than ½" and at the ends not less than 1", and there should be a wire tie on side laps halfway between supports. End laps should occur only over supports.

12.23 Masonry Bases

a. A number of masonry materials provide adequate bases for plaster.
b. Brick forms a good base for plaster, provided it is sufficiently porous to allow for absorption and the development of a good bond.
c. Most concrete blocks provide a satisfactory base for plaster when the blocks are properly aged. Portland-cement plaster bonds well to concrete block. Plaster may be applied successfully to monolithic concrete, depending on the surface of that concrete. High-strength, dense, vibrated concrete with non-porous surfaces may not be satisfactory. Rough-surfaced concrete, devoid of oil or other parting materials, may provide a satisfactory base. However, if there is any chance of moisture getting into any kind of masonry wall, or of condensation occurring, it is far preferable to fur such walls and provide an air space or insulation behind the lath and plaster.

12.24 Plaster

a. Gypsum is the most commonly used plaster. It is manufactured by calcining naturally found gypsum to drive off most of the water of crystallization. When calcined gypsum is mixed with water, the water of crystallization is replaced and the material sets or hardens. Because this reaction can occur quickly, retarders are added to the gypsum to reduce the rate of set and to permit mixing and application before it stiffens too much to be worked. As normally employed, gypsum plaster hardens in a matter of several hours.
b. For finish coats, lime is commonly employed in combination with gypsum or Keene's cement. Lime is made by burning limestone, or calcium carbonate, into the form known as *quicklime*, or calcium oxide. This, in turn, is mixed with water to form *slaked lime*, or calcium hydroxide, the form in which lime is used as plaster. When it is mixed with water and applied to a wall, the calcium hydroxide slowly reacts with carbon dioxide in the air to convert the material back to the original calcium carbonate. This is a slow reaction; in thick layers, it may not go to completion.

c. Keene's cement is similar to gypsum, except that it is calcined at a higher temperature and the water of crystallization is virtually all driven off. The resulting material, when mixed with water, crystallizes as does ordinary gypsum plaster, but the final product is considerably harder and denser.

12.25 Plaster Aggregates

A number of materials, or *aggregates,* can be added to gypsum to provide bulk, reduce shrinkage, increase strength, and cut the cost.

Sand is the most commonly used plaster aggregate, because of its economy and general availability. For best results, the particle size should be distributed from fine to coarse. Proper gradation adds workability to the mix. The sand must be clean and usually has to be washed.

Perlite is frequently used as a plaster aggregate. Raw perlite is a volcanic glass which, when roasted at 1,400–2,000°F, expands into a frothy mass of glass bubbles 4 to 20 times the original volume. Thus it weighs only $7\frac{1}{2}$ to 15 lb per cu ft and effectively reduces the dead weight of plaster. Perlite plasters are effective fire barriers and are superior to sanded plasters.

Vermiculite is another lightweight aggregate. It is based on a form of mica which expands 6 to 20 times when heated at 1,600–2,000°F. Perlite and vermiculite, like sand, must be properly graded to form a satisfactory aggregate for plaster. Vermiculite weighs 6 to 10 lb per cu ft and, like perlite, therefore reduces the dead weight of plaster.

For smooth trowel finishes, fine silica sand or perlite fines are added. For float finishes where a textured surface is wanted, clean graded sand is added. Other aggregates, such as vermiculite, may also be employed.

12.26 Application

a. *Three-coat plaster* consists of (1) a scratch coat, applied to the plaster base and cross-raked after it has begun to stiffen, (2) a brown coat, which is brought out to the grounds, smoothed, and allowed to set and dry partially, and (3) the finish coat. Three-coat plaster is normally employed over metal lath and over gypsum lath on ceilings.
b. *Two-coat work* is similar to three-coat work, except that the scratch coat is not raked and the brown coat is applied or "doubled back" within a few minutes to the unset scratch coat. This method is nor-

mally employed in applying plaster to masonry and gypsum lath. It is faster than three-coat work.

c. *Plaster grounds* (chapters 7 and 12) are employed around openings, at baseboards, and at trim, generally to control the thickness and give the plasterer a straight line with which to work. On large surfaces, intermediate screeds may also be employed so that the plasterer has a guide.

12.27 Standard Base-Coat Plasters

a. Base-coat plasters are applied directly to the lath or masonry substrates and support the finished coats. They are also truing coats; they are brought to an essentially level surface and take up any irregularities that may occur in the substrates. They must be compatible with and capable of supporting the finish coat without cracking, spalling, or otherwise deteriorating.

b. Base-coat plasters come in several varieties:

Neat plaster, fibered or unfibered, is mixed with an aggregate such as sand, perlite, or vermiculite, plus water.

Ready-mix plasters contain all of the necessary aggregates.

Wood-fibered plasters are neat plasters containing wood fibers, and may be used without other aggregate.

Bond plasters are especially formulated for use on interior monolithic concrete surfaces, to provide a strong bond.

c. Mechanical mixing is preferred to hand mixing, but both are feasible.

d. Once mixing is completed, the plaster should be used immediately. A batch of plaster that has started to set should not be used.

e. Plaster may be applied by machine or by hand. Machine application is preferred; there is a shorter time between mixing and actual application to the wall, and greater uniformity and density can easily be obtained. One man handles the nozzle and applies the plaster. He is followed by other plasterers who darby the plaster. In hand work, the plasterer applies the plaster by hand, pressing it firmly to the surface and making certain that, in the case of metal lath, the plaster penetrates the metal lath and completely encloses it from the far side. He follows it with a brown coat.

f. Drying is extremely important to the quality of the base plaster. It should not occur before the plaster is set and thus leave insufficient water for the chemical reaction, nor should it occur after the plaster has set and thus impair the strength. Rapid changes of temperature should be avoided while plaster is setting and drying.

12.28 Finish-Coat Plasters

a. The finish coat provides the visible surface of the plaster. It must meet the user's requirements and be compatible with the base coats and substrates.

b. There are six principal types of finish coats:

smooth finishes
    gypsum-lime putty, trowel finish
    Keene's cement-lime putty, trowel finish
    prepared gypsum, trowel finish
float finishes
    Keene's cement-lime sand float finish
    gypsum-sand float finish
acoustical plaster

c. The gypsum used in finish plaster is known as gauging plaster. It is ground to a coarse texture with low consistency. It absorbs water readily and blends easily with lime and other constituents.

d. Trowel finishes are applied over the nearly dry base coat. Very thin applications are made, and suction by the base coat draws the finish into the pores of the base coat. After this has "drawn up," the second or leveling coat is applied and left smooth under the trowel.

e. For sand-float finishes, the base coat should be uniformly damp to avoid drying the finish before it can be floated; otherwise the application is quite similar to that for the trowel finish. A wood float is often employed first to give a rough surface which may be worked into final form with a rubber float.

f. Many special finishes can be applied, such as swirl and spatter.

12.29 Veneer Plaster

a. The term *veneer plaster* covers a multitude of gypsum plasters, almost all of them proprietary, which vary widely in strength, hardness, and composition. With such wide variations in physical characteristics, no meaningful generic description is possible.

b. Whereas a veneer plaster generally can be used over a veneer base (lath) other than that for which it was designed, each veneer plaster–veneer base combination is designed as a system, to provide optimum cost and performance for each market's requirements.

c. The surface finish desired dictates whether the veneer plaster will be mill-aggregated, job-aggregated, or unaggregated, and whether it will be a two-material (base coat and finish coat) or a single-material (finish coat) system.

d. To provide the optimum application and finishing characteristics, the thickness of veneer plaster must be held to not more than $\frac{1}{8}''$. At this thickness, in combination with the specified veneer base, it must yield adequate strength, hardness, impact resistance, and crack resistance to meet the design requirements of the assembly in which it is used.

e. With proper design, veneer plaster–veneer base systems can offer fire retardancy, sound control, crack resistance, and appearance at least comparable to those of most conventional wallboard and plaster systems.

f. Instead of standard gypsum lath, the base for veneer plaster is generally gypsum board 48″ wide and 6′ to 16′ long, the latter on special order. Thicknesses are $\frac{3}{8}''$, $\frac{1}{2}''$, and $\frac{5}{8}''$. Regular, Type X (fire-retardant), and foil-backed insulating bases are available.

g. The requirements for wood or metal framing and support members such as studs, joists, and furring are the same as for gypsum wallboard and lath and plaster. Spacing is not greater than 16″ on centers, except for $\frac{5}{8}''$ thick veneer base (for which a 24″ spacing is permissible for sidewalls) and for ceilings if the base is applied horizontally, i.e., with edges perpendicular to supporting members (joists or furring).

h. Veneer base is applied in much the same manner as wallboard and backing board, with nails, screws, and staples. Nail penetration into wood should be $\frac{3}{4}''$ to $\frac{7}{8}''$. Spacing of fastenings is essentially the same as for wallboard and backing board. Floating interior corners are recommended, as for regular gypsum board (section 12.14).

i. Backing board is employed for double-ply construction, with veneer base applied over it.

j. Joints and corners are reinforced with a mesh tape, commonly glass fiber. This is stapled to the veneer base. Special corner beads, casing beads, grounds, and other trim are applied.

k. The temperature and ventilation requirements are similar to those for gypsum wallboards. It is recommended that the temperature be maintained between 55° and 70°F for at least a week before application of plaster, during the plastering operation, and for at least a week afterward. Hot spots and drafts should be avoided. In hot, dry weather, windows should be opened only partially (3″ top and bottom), to avoid excessive drying; unglazed openings can be protected with open-weave fabric such as muslin or cheesecloth. On the other hand, once the plaster has hardened, excess water must be allowed to evaporate, and sufficient ventilation, free of local drafts, is needed.

l. Mixing must be in accordance with manufacturer's directions. These materials come ready-mixed and need only to have water added.

m. Plaster is applied by hand or machine.

n. In most cases, two coats are applied. Flat mesh-reinforced joints are first troweled over with sufficient pressure to embed the mesh and press the plaster against the base. The first or base coat is then immediately applied directly to the veneer base and straightened to a level surface between $\frac{1}{16}$″ and $\frac{1}{8}$″ thick.

o. The finish coat can be applied immediately as a "double-back" coat to green base coats, or it can be applied to partially dry or dry base coats. A smooth trowel finish is obtained by using a steel trowel to "scratch in" a thin layer of plaster securely to the base and doubling back to provide a true, hard surface. Textured finishes are obtained by troweling and building up to a true surface and finishing by floating with the appropriate tool. Finish-coat thickness is approximately $\frac{1}{16}$″.

p. Veneer plaster may be applied as a single coat by applying a properly formulated single-coat mix directly to the veneer base and building up to the required thickness.

q. Veneer plaster may be applied over masonry surfaces and cast concrete. Such surfaces must be free of dirt, oil, grease, and other contaminants. Mortar joints should be struck flush, but, if recessed, are first filled with base coat material firmly pressed in. Cast concrete surfaces should be treated with a bonding agent.

r. Any marked irregularities should be smoothed. Depressions should be filled in with base coat, scratched in, leveled off, and allowed to set.

s. A tight scratch coat is troweled over the entire area and doubled back to a thickness of $\frac{1}{16}$″ or more as needed to obtain a level surface. Finish coats are applied as described above.

t. The foregoing procedures and thicknesses are approximately correct, but individual manufacturers have their own formulations, and their recommendations should be carefully followed.

u. Under favorable conditions, if the recommended procedures are followed, veneer plaster may be hard and dry enough to permit finishing operations to go forward in as little as 24 hours, but it is probably safer to permit a longer time in many situations.

STUCCO

12.30 General

a. Stucco, or portland-cement plaster, makes an excellent exterior and interior wall covering, as is attested by its long and honorable history. Care, patience, and meticulous attention to detail are required to obtain satisfactory stucco, particularly in rigorous climates.

b. Lime has been used for centuries in stucco, but its slow hardening has led to the general adoption, in the United States, of more rapidly hardening cements. Portland cement is the most widely used. With white portland cement and lime, a wide range of colors is obtainable, particularly when colored sands and stone chips are employed with colored pigments.

c. If the surface to be stuccoed is masonry, two coats are applied; if the surface is metal lath, three coats are required. These are similar to the coats of plaster employed on interior wall surfaces.

12.31 Preparation of the Surface

a. Because stucco, like plaster, is a thin, hard, unyielding, and brittle material, its support must be strong and rigid. If walls must be of frame construction, they should be well braced and so framed as to avoid shrinkage and expansion in the frame and sheathing which would cause cracks in the stucco. With any kind of surface — masonry, concrete, or frame — foundations must be firm and unyielding, with ample and carefully proportioned footings, to avoid differential settlement, which would crack the stucco.

b. Masonry surfaces must be cleaned of all loose particles, dirt, and grease, and smooth surfaces must be hacked, sand-blasted, or otherwise roughened to improve the mechanical bond. Walls should be thoroughly hosed and then allowed to dry only enough to leave the surfaces well dampened before applying the base coat.

c. On sheathed walls, sheathing is covered with heavy waterproof building paper. Metal lath is applied over the building paper, and furred at least $\frac{1}{4}''$.

d. For furring on wood walls, self-furring lath (section 12.22), furring nails, or furring strips are employed. On masonry walls, furring is not generally necessary but may be employed over unsuitable surfaces. Furring must allow at least $\frac{1}{4}''$ between the surface of the wall and the undersurface of the lath.

e. Expanded metal lath, expanded stucco mesh, stucco netting, and wire fabric are most commonly employed types of metal reinforcement. Paper-backed metal fabric is available. Expanded lath and mesh should be copper-bearing metal. Reinforcements of all types should be galvanized or protected with rust-inhibiting paint.

f. Flat and self-furring expanded metal mesh are recommended.

g. Metal reinforcement is applied over wood or steel framing, flashing, masonry, and concrete if these do not provide satisfactory surfaces; over chimneys; and over unsound old stucco if it does not provide a satisfactory bond.

h. Bonding to masonry and concrete can be improved by using one of the bonding agents, usually a water-based emulsion. This provides a strong bond between the surface and the stucco.

12.32 Mixes

a. The first (scratch) and second (brown) coats are essentially the same mix. One part by volume of portland cement and 25 percent by volume of hydrated lime (to act as a plasticizer) are mixed with three to five parts by volume of damp, loose sand. The sand proportions vary because of the wide variations in sand. Trial mixes are made until the proper workability is achieved. Diatomaceous earth is also used as a plasticizer.

b. The portland cement employed should conform to ASTM C150 Types I, II, or III (section 4.15a). Masonry cement, ASTM C91 Type II, is also employed.

c. Finish coats are usually premixed by the manufacturers, and if true colors are wanted it is best to use such ready-mixed materials. For job mixing, if white or a color is wanted, white portland or waterproof white portland cement is employed. The usual mix is one part cement, up to $\frac{1}{4}$ part hydrated lime, and 2 to 3 parts fine-grade light-colored sand, plus mineral oxide pigments, the latter carefully weighed if uniformity from batch to batch is to be obtained.

12.33 Application

a. Stucco is often sprayed on. The first (scratch) coat should be applied with enough pressure (hand or machine) to make sure that it is pressed through the lath against the backing and completely embeds

Figure 12.22 Stucco. (upper left) Wire mesh attached over building paper with self-furring nails (above) and nailed to furring strips (below). (upper right) Wire mesh, scratch coat, brown coat, and finish coat. (lower left) Close-up of scratch, brown, and finish coats showing treatments and thicknesses. (lower right) Close-up of finish coat showing one type of texture.

the lath. It should be approximately $\frac{1}{2}''$ thick. After application, it is horizontally scored with a scoring tool to provide a good mechanical bond to the second coat.

b. The second (brown) coat is applied as soon as the first coat has set or hardened enough to carry the weight of both coats. This may take only 4 or 5 hours — perhaps less in hot, dry weather, more in cool weather. The first coat on open wood framing should be allowed to stand at least 48 hours to achieve enough strength to withstand the pressure of subsequent applications. The first coat should be kept damp, by fine spraying if necessary, until the second coat is applied. Just before the second coat is applied, the first coat should be evenly dampened.

c. The second coat is applied evenly, to approximately $\frac{3}{8}''$ thickness, over an entire area such as a wall, without stopping, if possible. Stopping points, if needed, should be at natural breaks in the wall such as corners, pilasters, and windows. Otherwise, the starting and stopping joints may show through the finish coat.

d. The brown coat is moist-cured for at least 48 hours and allowed to dry at least 5 days, or longer if possible, before the finish coat is applied. More uniform suction for the finish coat is attained by the brown coat under these conditions, and the result is more uniformity in texture and color.

e. The brown coat is uniformly dampened just before the application of the finish coat.

f. Many textures — from smooth and hard troweled, through float, to pebbled — may be attained in finish coats. They may be applied by hand or machine. Deep textures include "Spanish," "brocade," dashing, scoring, and combing. A pebbled or "rock dash" or "marblecrete" finish is attained by throwing or machine-blowing small pebbles or chips of marble or other stone against the freshly applied finish.

g. Moist-curing should begin the day after the finish coat is applied. Fog spraying should be used first, and moist-curing should be continued for at least a day.

TILE

12.34 General

a. Tile floors and walls are widely employed in bathrooms and similar spaces where water is apt to be splashed about and where an impervious, waterproof, easily cleaned surface is required. Tile may be baked clay, terra cotta, glass, concrete, or plastic. The baked varieties are usually employed for interiors.

b. Glazed, ceramic, and vitreous tiles are commonly used for walls, ceramic and vitreous tiles for floors. Colors may be on the surface or integral. The more glossy finishes usually contain surface colors; the duller-finished tiles usually have integral colors imparted by minerals added to the basic mixture and brought out by baking.

12.35 Wall Tiles

a. Wall tiles are set against a properly prepared scratch coat of cement mortar applied to metal lath, to special waterproof gypsum or port-

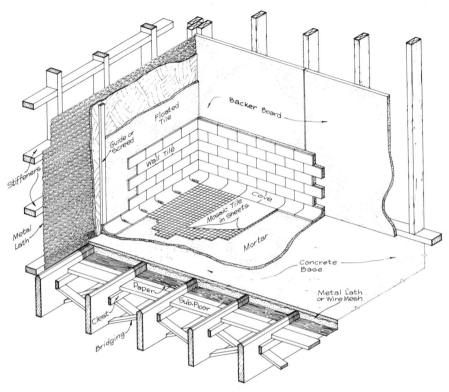

Figure 12.23 Tile walls and floor, with wall tile floated (left) and buttered (right), mosaic floor tile, and special cove.

land-cement backer board, or to a masonry surface. Because of the weight of the tile finish and the need for a completely rigid backing, it is best to set studs not more than 16″ on centers. When metal lath is employed, lines of horizontal blocking 16″ apart should be solidly nailed between the studs.

b. Metal lath must be carefully and firmly nailed to studs, with horizontal and vertical laps occurring at horizontal blocking or at studs.

c. Walls of brick or terra cotta tile (heavily scored surfaces) should have rough-struck mortar joints. Cork, gypsum block, and similar walls should be covered with wire mesh, expanded metal lath, or backer board.

d. Cutouts for pipes and fixtures should have the cut edges protected by a waterproof compound or adhesive tape.

e. Over boards, ceramic tile is applied with organic adhesives. These must be water-resistant.

f. Each manufacturer has his own set of instructions for applying tile, and these should be carefully followed.

g. On metal lath, two coats are applied to the wall: a scratch coat, to form a base, and a cement mortar, in which the tiles are embedded.

h. The scratch coat is composed of 1 part portland cement, about $\frac{1}{4}$ part hydrated lime, and 2 parts clean sand. It is mixed with sufficient water to form a thick mortar, and is applied in a coat at least $\frac{1}{2}''$ thick, or thick enough to form a true, even surface $\frac{3}{4}''$ back of the finished surface of the tile, if tiles $\frac{3}{8}''$ thick are employed, or to allow for a cement mortar bed $\frac{3}{8}''$ thick behind the tiles. The scratch coat is thoroughly scratched and allowed to harden at least a day before tiles are set.

i. The cement mortar is commonly 1 part portland cement to 2 parts clean sand plus 25 percent lime putty.

j. After tiles (except vitreous types) have been well soaked in clean water, and after the scratch coat has thoroughly hardened and has been thoroughly dampened with clean water, the actual setting of tiles may proceed either by "floating" or by "buttering" (figure 12.23).

k. When tiles are "floated" the procedure is as follows:

1. Wood guide strips are placed vertically against the wall in a thin bed of mortar, and are carefully plumbed.

2. Mortar is spread between the guide strips and brought out flush with them by hawk, trowel, and float rod.

3. Guide strips are removed, and the resulting grooves are filled with mortar.

4. A thin grout of pure cement and water is spread on the back of each tile as it is set.

5. Tiles are placed against the wall and carefully beaten into place with a block and a hammer.

l. Tiles are "buttered" in the following manner:

1. Small pieces of tile, set in mortar, are spotted about 30" apart on the surface of the wall, and their faces are carefully brought into a true even plane. These act as guides for the rest of the tiles.

2. As each tile is set, a wash of neat cement and water is spread on the back, followed by the proper thickness of mortar. Each tile is then set against the scratch coat and tapped into place until firmly set and plumb with the spotter tile.

m. Whether tiles are floated or buttered, the final steps are to fill the joints between tiles with a thin grout of white or gray portland cement and water, and finally to wipe off all traces of cement on the surfaces.

12.36 Floor Tiles

a. Preparation of floor framing and subflooring has already been discussed in chapter 5. After the subflooring and the framing have been covered with waterproof building paper, the base for the tiles is prepared as follows (figure 12.23):

1. A concrete bed of 1 part portland cement, 2 parts clean sand, and 4 parts small aggregate is placed to a depth of $2\frac{1}{2}''$ and leveled. This brings the concrete $\frac{3}{4}''$ to $1''$ above the tops of the joists, where the chamfered joist is employed (chapter 5).

2. Well-painted or galvanized wire mesh or metal lath is embedded in the top of the concrete to form reinforcement for the setting bed of mortar spread over it.

3. A setting bed of mortar, consisting of 1 part portland cement and 3 parts clean sand, is spread and leveled at an elevation $\frac{1}{16}''$ lower than the eventual elevation of the bottoms of the floor tiles. Screeds are employed for this purpose. Often a thin layer of dry portland cement is spread over the well-soaked surface of the concrete slab before the cement mortar is spread.

4. A $\frac{1}{16}''$ layer of dry cement is spread over the cement mortar just ahead of the setting tiles.

5. Tiles are soaked in water (except vitreous tiles), placed upon the cement mortar, and hammered and tamped into place.

6. Joints are grouted with a creamy mixture of cement and water. Dry cement is sprinkled on the floor, and the floor is finally cleaned with sawdust, excelsior, or similar material.

b. Mosaic tiles, usually ceramic, are commonly cemented to a sheet of paper, with the mosaic pattern worked into the arrangement at the factory. If separate borders are required, some cutting of the central field, where it abuts the border, is required. The tiles are bedded as noted above, but cannot be grouted until the paper has been removed. Tile sheets may be pre-grouted.

c. Where floors and walls join, special cove tiles are placed before either wall or floor tiles are set. Cove tiles provide a smooth transition from floor to wall.

d. If wall tiles do not run to the ceiling (that is, if only a tile wainscot is wanted), special dado tiles are used to form a finished edge for the top of the tile wainscot. If walls are "returned" into window and door openings, special bull-nosed tiles are used to make the return. Similarly, at re-entrant angles, special cove tiles may be employed, although this is not always done.

e. Towel bars, recessed soap and water-tumbler fixtures, and other special fixtures to match the tile are set at the same time as the rest of the tile.

13 Interior Finish

13.1 General

a. The interior finish includes all exposed woodwork in the interior of the building. This consists mainly of stairs, doors, built-in features such as cupboards and bookshelves, trim of all kinds, and finish floors. All require careful installation to ensure neat appearance, tight joints, and smooth surfaces, whether the protective coatings (paint, enamel, varnish, etc.) are to be transparent or opaque.

b. For painted (opaque) finishes the wood must be fine (close) grained and free of knots, pitch streaks, resin pockets, or other imperfections which cannot be concealed by paint. It must have a surface which will not "raise" (that is, parts of which will not pull away from the rest of the surface). It must be easy to work. Northern white pine is excellent, but less readily available than ponderosa pine and Idaho white pine.

c. Transparent or "natural" finishes call for decorative woods free of blemishes. Hardwoods such as oak, birch, maple, walnut, mahogany, and lauan are excellent. Redwood, white pine, Idaho white pine, ponderosa pine, gum, and others are also employed.

13.2 Care of Wood Finish

a. Wood finish is a valuable commodity and must be handled with care. The primary requisite is that it be kept dry and straight. It should be stored in dry warehouses at the supply house, should be covered when being transported in damp weather, should not be permitted in the building until the plaster and concrete are completely dried, and should be piled carefully and straight so that surfaces are not damaged and individual pieces do not become crooked. The best practice is to stand the individual pieces on end if they are not too long, rather than piling them on top of one another. The precaution of keeping wood trim dry cannot be overemphasized. Most troubles with faulty trim can be traced to material which was damp when installed and which dried subsequently. In damp cool weather, artificial heat must be installed in the building before the trim is brought in.

b. If trim is to be painted or enameled, it is excellent practice to have it primed (i.e., given the first coat of paint) at the mill, before it is shipped. This initial coat has some retardant effect on the penetration of moisture and slows swelling and shrinkage with varying humidity conditions. In any event, it is good practice to back-prime all trim (i.e., to paint the back faces) before it is installed. Such treatment helps to retard the penetration of moisture from the back and therefore aids in slowing swelling and shrinkage. Even if the front faces are to be finished "natural," it is wise to back-prime the material.

13.3 Joints

a. In ordinary framing no particular care is exercised to obtain neat, tightly fitting joints, and most members are simply butted or lapped. Strength and rigidity are important, but appearance is secondary because the frame, sheathing, rough flooring, and roof boards are subsequently covered. In trim and finish of all kinds, especially interior finish, appearance is of foremost importance, and the joints between members must receive close attention. Generally speaking, joints are either so made as to be permanently tight and completely inconspicuous, or they are worked into the design in such a way as to be inconspicuous if they do open.

b. Speaking very broadly, four principal types of joints — butt, miter, shiplap, and tongue and groove — are employed, each with numerous variations. Several of the typical applications of each are shown in figure 13.1. These are merely representative and by no means exhaustive.

c. Butt joints (figure 13.1a), either longitudinal or corner, are easily made but are weak, open easily, and may show end wood, which is usually objectionable because it is difficult to finish well and is considered unsightly. Butt joints may be strengthened and reinforced by dowels, splines, dovetails, and tenons. When snugly fitted and glued, these devices aid materially in keeping joints tight. Generally speaking, butt joints, especially in the end-to-end directions of the boards, are avoided in finish of highest quality. The principal exception to this general rule is in re-entrant, or interior, corners where plain or molded members meet. One member is, in this instance, butted and cut to fit (coped) against the other.

d. Miters (figure 13.1b), particularly at exterior corners, are almost always preferable to butt joints in finish work of all kinds. Plain miters are often reinforced with miter brads, splines, and numerous types of patented devices designed to prevent the joints from opening. To provide a snug firm joint, the miter is sometimes shouldered, especially when the parts are made in a shop instead of on the job. The corner is occasionally emphasized by a small re-entrant angle, called a quirk. Longitudinal miters are employed in baseboards, moldings, and

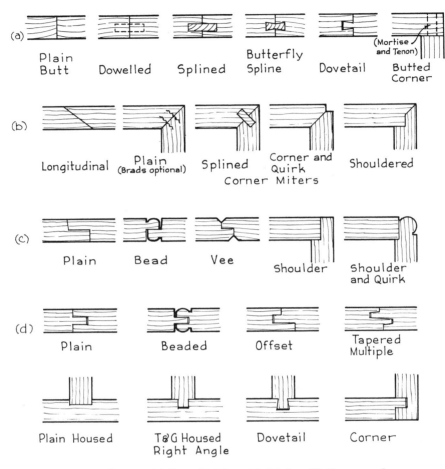

Figure 13.1 Typical joints. (a) Butt. (b) Miter. (c) Shiplap. (d) Tongue and groove.

other linear members too long to be made in one piece. If these miters open slightly they do not show as unsightly cracks, as do butt joints. **e.** Shiplap joints (figure 13.1c) are quite common in both rough lumber and millwork. Although more common along the edges of adjoining members, they are also found at the ends and at corners. To avoid a corner joint involving both side grain and unadorned end grain, a bead and quirk or similar molding is sometimes formed at the corner. Various methods of emphasizing shiplap joints, such as beads or vees, are commonly employed. **f.** Tongue-and-groove joints are widely employed for "rough" boards

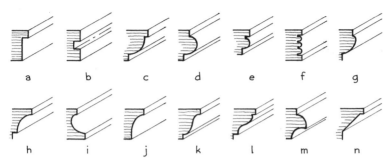

Figure 13.2 Basic profiles employed in moldings. (a) Raised fillet. (b) Sunk fillet. (c) Quarter round or ovolo. (d) Torus. (e) Bead or astragal. (f) Reeding. (g) Thumb or ovolo. (h) Cavetto. (i) Scotia. (j) Conge. (k) Cyma recta. (l) Cyma reversa. (m) Beak. (n) Splay.

and for finish (figure 13.1d), either in longitudinal joints involving ends and edges of boards or in joints involving angles such as reentrant corners. Tongue-and-groove joints may be plain, beaded, or otherwise emphasized; they may be provided with offsets to increase the overlap, or formed in multiples to obtain large gluing areas; they may be made by "housing" the end of one member into the side of another; or they may be provided with dovetails, rabbets (rebates), or other means of tying the two parts together.

13.4 Moldings

a. Much of the woodwork employed for trim and finish of all kinds is shaped, or "molded," to various profiles, depending on the ultimate use. Moldings are of two kinds: stock and special. Stock moldings are made in large quantities by millwork manufacturers and stocked by lumber dealers; hence the name. Special moldings are made to the special profiles specified for a particular application by the architect, and require special knives to be made up for the job. Special moldings are considerably more costly than stock.

b. Although the possible shapes and sizes of moldings are practically numberless, most are combinations of the basic shapes shown in figure 13.2. Differences in terminology exist, but the ones here employed are those of Webster's Dictionary.

c. Associations of millwork manufacturers have come to substantial agreement as to sizes and shapes of stock moldings. Many of these have also been standardized (see also chapter 5 for standard sizes of framing lumber). In addition to these generally accepted stock moldings, many millwork manufacturers make certain stock items of their own design.

d. It is beyond the scope of this book to discuss and illustrate the many stock moldings available, much less the specials which might be designed for a particular application.

STAIRS

13.5 General

a. The following discussion is based mainly on conventional stair construction, and the details shown are typical. The general principles are valid for conventional or for less traditional details. Figure 13.3 shows a typical conventional closed-riser stair of all-wood construction. Figure 13.4 shows a heavy-tread open-riser stair of wood and metal construction. Stairs are often installed by a separate craft. They may be plain and simple, and run in one flight between partition walls from floor to floor, or they may be ornate, open circular, or elliptical, with complex construction and ornamentation. Stairs have their own set of terms and parts, of which the principal ones follow.

b. A *flight* is a single set of stairs running as a unit from floor to floor, or from a floor to an intermediate *landing* or *platform*. Landings are used to break up what would otherwise be long and fatiguing flights, or to provide for turns in stairs.

c. A *tread* is the horizontal member forming the top of a single step. It is associated with a *riser* or vertical member of a step. The front edge of a tread is the *nosing*.

d. The terms *rise* and *run* each have two meanings. The *rise* is either the total height of a flight of stairs (the height from finish floor to finish floor or from finish floor to top of landing) or the height of a single step, from the top of one tread to the top of the next tread. The latter definition is the more useful, and is more commonly employed. To distinguish the rise in this sense from the total height, the latter is sometimes called the *total rise;* that term will be used below. The run, similarly, may mean the horizontal projection of the flight of stairs, or it may mean the horizontal distance from the face of one riser to the face of the next. In this discussion the run has the latter meaning, and the term *total run* will be used for the horizontal projection of the entire flight.

e. *Strings* are the sloping side boards of a flight, against which the

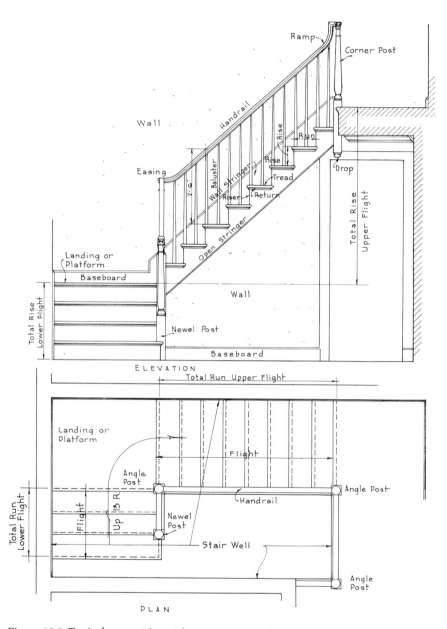

Figure 13.3 Typical open-string stairway arrangement.

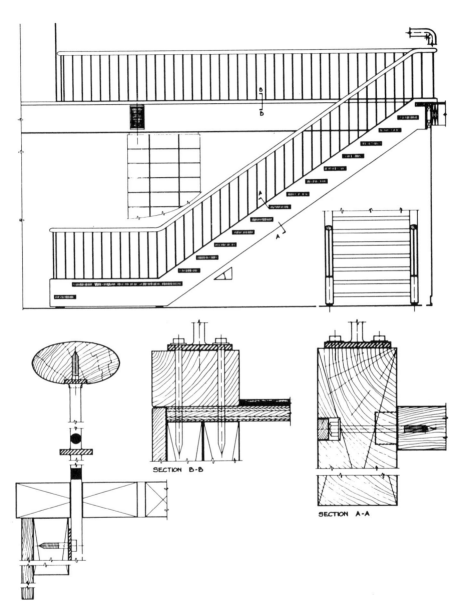

Figure 13.4 Open-rise stair. (top) Elevation and view from left toward stair. (lower left) Detail of rail, spindle, and attachment. (section B-B) Detail of upper rail and base. (section A-A) Detail of tread-stringer connection.

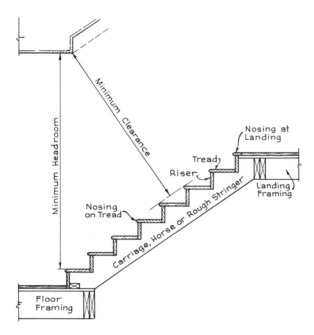

Figure 13.5 Minimum headroom and clearance.

ends of risers and treads are terminated. Three types of strings exist: *wall strings,* which rest against partitions or walls adjacent to the stairs, *open strings* (free-standing, not adjacent to a wall), the tops of which are cut to the profiles of the stairs, and which allow the treads to project beyond the outer faces of the strings, and *closed or curb strings* which, like open strings, are not adjacent to walls, but do not have their upper edges cut to the profiles of the stairs. Treads and risers, consequently, are terminated against their inner sides. Partitions may be brought up under open and curb strings, but the upper edges are free.

f. An *open* stair is one which is open to a room or hallway on one side (occasionally both sides are open). It calls, consequently, for open or curb strings on the open side. *Closed* stairs are enclosed by partitions or walls on both sides, and consequently employ only wall strings.

g. An ornamental or plain bar of wood or metal attached to an adjacent wall or attached directly to the stairs at a convenient distance above the level of the stairs, to be grasped by the hand, is called the *rail* or *handrail.* When the rail is attached directly to the stair treads, as in open stairs, the attachment is accomplished by means of *balusters,* which are vertical plain or ornamental sticks or bars fastened to the treads or strings and to the underside of the rail.

h. At the foot of an open stair the rail usually terminates against a post of some kind, and against a similar post at its head. This is called a *newel post.* Intermediate posts at landings or other breaks in the stairs are called *angle posts.* When an angle post projects down beyond the bottom of the strings, the ornamental detail at the bottom of the post is called the *drop.* Newel posts at heads of stairs are often halved because they are built directly against a wall. Sometimes the half newel is omitted and the rail is terminated by a small metal or wood plate fastened to the wall.

i. The clear height from a tread to the overhead construction above (such as the upper floor) is called the *head room.* It is essential that ample head room be provided, not only to prevent actual collision but also to give a feeling of spaciousness. Even when the head room provides clearance, if an individual using the stair has the impression that he is about to collide with the structure overhead the head room is not sufficient. For a feeling of roominess, an average person should be able to extend his arm fully forward and upward without touching the ceiling of the stair. In any event, the absolute minimum allowable when measured from the nosing of a tread vertically to the overhead construction is 6'6". This is not a comfortable height.

j. The finished stair must be supported on rough structural members underneath. These members go by the names *horse stringers, carriage stringers,* and (most commonly) *rough stringers.*

13.6 Rules for Laying Out Stairs

a. Stairs must be neither too steep nor too shallow, since either extreme is fatiguing. Risers over 8" high are too steep for comfort, and those less than 6" are too slow in their ascent. Best practice calls for risers slightly over 7" high, the exact height depending on the total rise. Since the risers must all be the same height, the total rise must be divided among some whole number of risers which gives a rise in the neighborhood of 7". For example, if the total rise is 114", 17 risers provide a rise of 6.71" and 16 risers a rise of 7.13".

b. For comfort, certain proportions between the magnitudes of rises and runs must be maintained. In general, the greater the rise the less the run and vice versa. For this reason, grand staircases often have shallow rises and wide runs, whereas secondary stairs for which a minimum of space is to be sacrificed may have high rises and narrow runs. A number of rules have been worked out for maintaining the proper proportions, of which the following are the most common:

rise times run equals 70 to 75

rise plus run equals 17 to $17\frac{1}{2}$

twice the rise plus the run equals 24 to 25. (This is found in some building codes.)

Any of these rules provides narrow runs for steep stairs and wide runs for gradually rising ones. In addition to these rules of thumb, a number of formulas have been devised to give comfortable proportions of treads and risers for various pitches.

c. In any one flight of stairs, there is always one less tread than the number of risers. Hence, if a single flight runs from floor to floor and has 16 risers, 15 treads are required; an intermediate landing reduces the number to 14; and so forth. Knowing the total rise and the number of risers, one can easily compute the total run per flight and determine the size of the stair well by adding to the space required by the stairs the amount of space needed for landings or for winders.

13.7 Stair Plans

a. Various arrangements of stairs within the stair well (opening in two adjacent floors within which the stair is located) are possible, some simple and others complex (figure 13.6).

b. The simplest is a single flight running from floor to floor. Because this type is fatiguing if the total rise is high, an intermediate landing may be built approximately halfway between floors. In buildings used by the public, laws often restrict the number of risers permissible per flight.

c. A single flight or several flights with landings may require a longer stair well than can be obtained. The stair may therefore be turned 90° or 180° at a landing and be continued to the next floor. This construction can be varied still further by using several landings with short flights running from landing to landing. The short flights may consist of only one or two risers or may be quite long.

d. Where space is at a premium, the landings are often omitted and the treads are carried around the angle by running their interior ends to a point at the turn of the stair (figure 13.6c). At this point, then, the

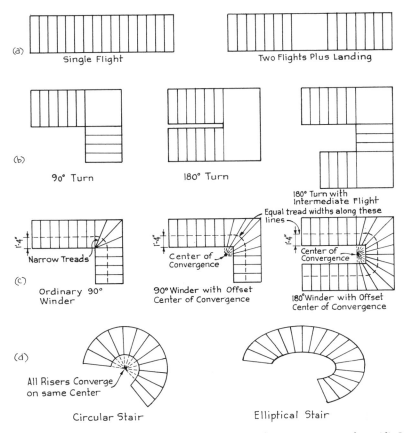

Figure 13.6 Typical stair plans. (a) Straight run. (b) Turns. (c) Winders. (d) Ornamental stairs.

ends of risers are directly above one another. This kind of construction, called a *winder*, should be avoided if at all possible. No adequate foothold is afforded at the angle, and there is an almost vertical drop of several feet if a number of risers converge on the same point. The construction is dangerous and may easily lead to bad accidents. It is poor planning so to restrict the stair well that winders must be employed. Winders are often illegal.

e. The sharp drop which ordinary winders afford may be lessened in a stair with a 90° turn if the center of convergence for the various risers of the winder is brought out from the corner 1' or more (figure 13.6c). The risers then do not converge directly at the corner but afford some foothold. The same holds true of a 180° turn if the corner is made broad, as would be the case in a stair with a short intermediate flight. The center of convergence in this instance is also brought out from the corner. The center of convergence should be so located as to provide treads of equal width along a line 16″ from the inner edge of the stair. This is the line of usual travel. The ordinary winder does not provide equal treads along this line.

f. A helical stair, usually called a spiral stair, is a continuous winder from top to bottom. Such a stair, of course, contains all the bad features of the winder multiplied several times.

g. Ornamental stairs are often built in the shape of a portion of a circle or an ellipse (figure 13.6d). This type of stair is almost always open on the underside, requiring the inner string to be open or curbed. Often the strings have to be fairly massive, because the stair may be open underneath (so that no carriages can be employed), and the curved section imposes torsion as well as bending in the inner string. Such strings may consist of a number of smaller pieces shaped to form and fitted, and then pegged, pinned, doweled, and glued together to form a single unit; or they may consist of thin boards bent to shape and glued together. For additional stiffness, flat steel bands may be fastened to the inner side of such a string, or be concealed in its interior. Strings may be entirely of steel.

h. Many special types of construction may be employed, e.g., cantilevered heavy open treads supported only at one end of the string. These must be designed around the special conditions of the installation. Prefabricated helical metal winders supported on central posts may have wood treads. There are many variants.

13.8 Stair Construction

a. Stairs may be built in place or they may be built as units in the shop and set in place. Both methods have their advantages and disadvantages, and custom varies with locality.

b. Built in place. Although exact details may differ, the procedure for building stairs in place is as follows (see figure 13.7):

1. Carriages are carefully cut to exact size and set in place, lower ends resting on the lower floor and upper ends framed against the header of the upper-floor construction (sections 5.24–5.28).

2. The wall string is "housed" at least $\frac{1}{2}$″ deep to the exact profile of the risers and treads. The bottom of the string is cut to the profile of the stairs at the backs of risers and treads, and the string is set in place

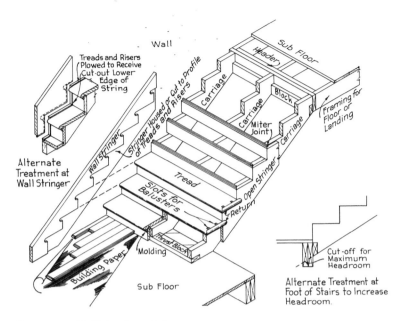

Figure 13.7 Built-in-place stairs.

against the wall, so that the back of the housed-out profile coincides with the profile of the carriages. Treads and risers are firmly nailed to carriages. Rear edges of treads are best grooved to fit tongues in the lower portions of risers, and tops of risers are tongued to fit grooves in the bottoms of treads. The projecting portions of treads, or nosings, are usually finished underneath with cove or other moldings.

3. The wall string is fitted over the treads and risers, or else the ends of treads and risers are inserted into the housed-out portion of the string at the time they are placed and nailed.

4. The open string is carefully cut to the same profile as the treads and rises and mitered to fit corresponding miters cut in the ends of risers. The ends of treads project out over the string, and the nosing is returned along this projecting end.

5. If the outer string is curbed, it is housed in the same manner as the wall string and is fitted over the ends of risers and treads. Setting the outer string, whether open or curbed, finishes the stair.

c. The built-in-place method of stair building is not particularly satisfactory for enclosed stairs, because the second string is not as easily fitted into place as in the case of the open stair. When so built, how-

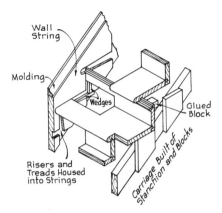

Wall String

Molding

Wedges

Glued Block

Risers and Treads Housed into Strings

Carriage Built of Stanchion and Blocks

Figure 13.8 Detail of shop-built stair.

ever, both wall strings are ordinarily fitted over the ends of treads and risers after the latter have been nailed into position on the carriages.

d. As figure 13.4 shows, many other means of fastening treads, risers, or both to strings can be devised. In this instance, only treads are employed.

e. Built in shop. This kind of stair is essentially a self-contained unit which is set in place after being fabricated elsewhere. It may be set either before or after the application of plaster or other wall finishes. If set before, carriages may be installed separately and the stairs fitted to them by an arrangement illustrated in figure 13.8. The carriage here consists simply of a stanchion to which blocks are nailed after having been fitted snugly under the treads. If, as is preferable, the bottom of the stair opening as well as the rest of the stair well is finished before the stairs are set, it is impossible to make this kind of stair rest snugly on pre-set carriages, and the carriages therefore must be incorporated into the stairs themselves at the shop after risers, treads, and strings have been assembled as described below. Except for being incorporated into a pre-built stair, such a carriage is essentially the same as the carriage for the stairway built in place. Ordinarily its lower edge is in the same plane as the lower edges of the strings, unlike the carriage shown in figure 13.8. Construction details are as follows:

1. Strings, instead of being cut or completely housed underneath to the profile of the stair, as are wall strings in the built-in-place type, are left solid their full depth to attain strength, and are only housed to receive the ends of risers and treads. The housing is made wider than

the actual thickness of treads and risers, and is flared on the under-side. Inner strings in open stairs are either cut to the profile of the stair (if the string is an open one) or housed in the same manner as the wall strings (if curbed). The curbed type is stronger and stiffer.

2. Risers and treads are best provided with tongue-and-groove joints in the same manner as the built-in-place type, and are firmly nailed together. Joints can, moreover, be glued together and blocks glued into the angles on the underside for additional reinforcement. The ends of risers and treads are inserted into the housed profiles in strings, and are tightened into place by wedges driven into the flared under-portion of the housing. Wedges are nailed and glued into place.

f. When finished, these stairs are set as units in the stair well. Need-less to say, they must be carefully made to fit the opening exactly, both in length and in width, and with proper rises and runs so that treads are level and risers plumb. A molding similar to a base mold (section 13.14a) is usually necessary on top of the string to produce a tight joint with the wall surface.

13.9 Rails and Balusters

a. Rails are required on all open stairs for protection as well as to afford hand holds, and must be carried around the edges of open stair wells. Along the slope of a stair, rails are approximately 30″ above the treads, depending on the pitch, when measured from the face of a riser. On landings and around open wells the height is the same as when measured from the center of a tread, namely 32″ to 34″.

b. Rails are often ended against newel and angle posts at an oblique angle. If it is desired to have all rails meet the posts at the same elevation, the upper ends of the rails may be flared upward in a curve called a *ramp* and then turned at right angles to meet the posts per-pendicularly to their vertical faces. The lower ends of rails may be curved in an *easing* to meet the vertical faces of the newels at right angles. Angle posts may be omitted and the rail carried up in continu-ous curves from bottom to top. In such instances the newel post is often omitted and the lower end of the rail is finished in a spiral resting on a cluster of balusters or on a large single baluster. Rails may be carried around bends and corners in continuous curves as shown in figure 13.4.

c. Balusters may be plain square or turned rods, or may be ornately turned and twisted, depending on the effect desired. In any event,

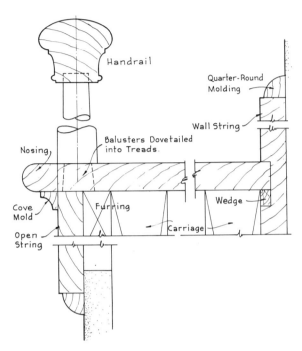

Figure 13.9 Details of stairway construction, showing baluster and handrail.

they must be firmly fastened to the rail and the treads so that the rail will provide firm support. The easiest and poorest way to fasten balusters is merely to nail them to the rail and the treads. Next easiest is to drill holes in the rail and the treads, round off the ends of balusters, and insert the rounded ends in the holes. Although this is better than nailing, it is not entirely satisfactory because balusters work loose and turn in the holes. The best way is to dovetail the lower ends of the balusters into the treads and fit upper ends into holes bored in the lower side of the rail. Dovetailing is accomplished by removing the return nosing of the tread and cutting rectangular holes in the treads just back of the nosing. These holes, or mortises, are flared out at the bottoms, and the balusters are slipped into the mortises from the side and tightly glued into place. After the balusters are firmly set, the return nosing is replaced, thereby concealing the joint. This dovetail joint is tight and rigid and cannot work loose.

d. The balusters of figure 13.4 are welded to a continuous metal plate, which is firmly fastened.

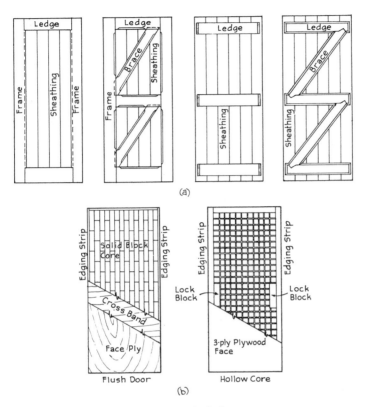

Figure 13.10 (a) Batten doors. (b) Flush doors.

e. Rails along enclosed stairs are commonly fastened to the walls with metal wall brackets. Such brackets must be substantial and should be not over 10' apart unless the rail is exceptionally rigid. Brackets must be securely screwed or lag-bolted to the frame of the wall or to blocking firmly nailed to the frame and set at the proper elevation to receive the brackets, since it is imperative that the brackets be sturdy.

DOORS

13.10 Types

a. There are several different types of doors, of which the commonest are *batten, flush,* and *paneled.* Each of these has several subdivisions.
b. A *batten* door (figure 13.10a) consists of boards nailed together in various ways. The simplest is two layers nailed to each other at right

angles, usually with each layer at 45° to the vertical. This construction is sometimes used for the cores of metal-clad fire doors. The second type of batten door consists of vertical boards nailed at right angles to several (two to four) cross-strips called *ledges* or *ledgers*, with diagonal bracing members nailed between ledgers. When vertical members corresponding to the ledgers are added at the sides, the verticals are called *frames*.

c. *Batten* doors are often found in places where appearance is not a factor and economy is important. Such doors may be dimensionally unstable because of so much wood running in the same direction, leading to shrinking and swelling in the cross-direction. Without braces they may sag. They are, therefore, loosely fitted in the door frames.

d. *Solid flush doors* (figure 13.10b) are perfectly flat, usually on both sides, although occasionally they are made flush on one side and paneled on the other. Flush doors sometimes are solid planking, particularly if authentic old details are required, but much more commonly they are veneered over a core of small pieces of white pine or some other wood that takes glue well and holds its shape. These pieces are glued together with staggered end joints, and the entire slab is dressed to the proper thickness. Other solid cores include particle board and various mineral boards; the latter offer maximum fire resistance. Along the two side edges and along the top and the bottom are glued $\frac{3}{4}''$ edge strips of the same wood (usually hardwood) that is to be used to face the sides of the door. The sides are then faced with one or two layers of veneer. If only one layer or ply is used, it is usually $\frac{1}{8}''$ to $\frac{1}{4}''$ thick; if two plies, the inner one is customarily $\frac{1}{16}''$ to $\frac{1}{8}''$ and the surface veneer is much thinner. The inner ply or cross band is laid at right angles to the core (i.e., horizontally), and the outer ply or face is laid parallel to the core (vertically, or the long way of the door). Two-ply faces are much more common than one-ply.

e. For interior doors, good but not maximum water resistance is needed; for exterior doors, the glue must have maximum water resistance. Thermosetting synthetic resin adhesives are rapidly replacing all others for all veneered doors, both interior and exterior.

f. *Hollow-core doors* (figure 13.10b), like solid flush doors, are perfectly flat, but unlike the solid doors, the core consists mainly of a grid of crossed wooden slats or some other type of grid construction, such as an impregnated paper honeycomb. The faces are three-ply plywood

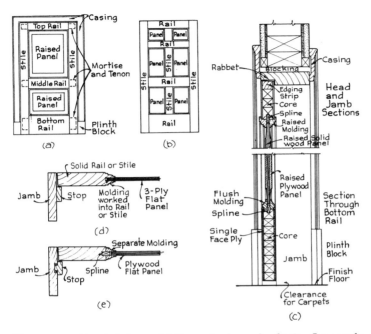

Figure 13.11 Paneled doors. (a) Two raised panels. (b) Six flat panels. (c) Section through interior door. (d) Simple jamb and stop. (e) Simple jamb and adjustable housed stop.

instead of one or two plies of veneer, and the surface veneer may be any species of wood (usually hardwood) possessing any figure or pattern desired. The faces may be hardboard (section 5.3n) laminate (section 13.17) or a similar material. The edges of the core are solid wood and are made wide enough at the appropriate places to accommodate mortise locks and butts. Doors of this kind are considerably lighter than solid flush doors.

g. Many doors are *paneled* (figure 13.11), with most panels consisting of solid wood or plywood, either "raised" or "flat," although many exterior doors have one or more panels of glass, or "lights." One or more panels may be employed; the number seldom exceeds eight. They may be horizontal, vertical, or combinations of horizontal, vertical, and square, and different sizes may be employed in the same door. Panel construction overcomes the problem of dimensional instability in batten doors, thus allowing much tighter fitting in the door frame.

h. Horizontal members are called *rails* (figure 13.11a,b). Every door

has a top and a bottom rail, and there may be one or more intermediate rails. The top and intermediate rails are usually the same
width, but bottom rails are wider than the other rails and stiles.

i. Vertical members are called *stiles* (figure 13.11a,b). There are at
least two stiles, one on each side, the full height of the door, and there
may be one or more intermediate stiles, which may or may not run
full height (i.e., from bottom rail to top rail). When intermediate rails
occur, the rails are continuous and the stiles are butted against them.
The rails must be the stronger members in order to keep a door from
sagging.

j. The set-in thinner sheets are called *panels* (figure 13.11). These are
held in place by the rails and stiles, either directly or through the
medium of moldings.

k. Paneled doors may be either "solid" or veneered. Ordinarily, exterior doors which are to be painted on the outside are made of
"solid" softwood, particularly white pine. Inexpensive interior doors
are also made of "solid" wood with Douglas fir a favorite material
(figure 13.11d,e). The term *solid* refers primarily to the rails and stiles,
which are run out of single pieces of wood.

l. Where the panels are fitted into rails and stiles, the edges of the
latter are worked down to an ornamental molding and are plowed
(grooved) to receive the edges of the panels. Running the molding is
called *sticking* or *stickering*. Lights must be removable, so the molding
on one side (the exterior side of an outside door) is made removable
and is held in place by brads.

m. Veneered doors (figure 13.11c) are used where better quality is
desired and where faces are to be hardwoods. This makes for both
economy and a better door, because thick hardwood stock is costly
and often has a bad tendency to twist. Veneering is usually considered
advisable even for woods such as mahogany, in which there is little
tendency to twist. Rails and stiles of veneered doors are made in
much the same way as solid flush doors (section 13.11d). Cores of
small pieces of softwood are first assembled, often by dovetailing, and
glued. The edges of cores are provided with edging strips of hardwood, and the faces are covered with veneer.

n. Panels are either flat (plane surface) or raised (beveled edges), and
may be solid wood or plywood. If plywood panels are to be raised, the
surface plies must be thick enough to allow for the beveling without
showing the cross-bands. By selecting and carefully matching sheets
of figured veneer, various patterns can be created in the panels.

o. Panels may be inserted directly into grooves plowed in the edge strips of the stiles and rails, or may be held in place by moldings. In the latter instance, splines are inserted into the plowed groove to fill in the space behind the edge of the panel. The splines are needed to prevent light from showing through the door between the molding and the edge of the rail or stile.

p. Three types of molding details are used. The simplest is the so-called *solid* sticking, in which the molding is run directly in the edges of the rails and stiles (figure 13.11d). When heavier ornamentation is desired, separate pieces of molding are bradded and glued into the corner between the panel and the rail or stile (figure 13.11c,e). Flush molding does not project beyond the surface of the door. Raised molding protrudes beyond the faces of rails and stiles.

q. Lights in exterior doors call for special details, because water running down the surface of the glass is likely to work its way behind the veneer and cause it to loosen. This may be prevented by inserting a piece of molding under the glass, extending it through the door, and turning it down over the face of the door on the outside to form a drip. The same result can be achieved by inserting a piece of sheet metal under the removable outer molding that holds the glass in place, and turning the metal up behind the glass and down slightly over the face of the door so that a narrow edge of metal shows (figure 13.12c).

13.11 Construction

a. Many doors are made to manufacturers' specifications and stocked by dealers in their warehouses; others are made especially to architects' specifications. Stock doors commonly are $1\frac{1}{8}''$, $1\frac{3}{8}''$, and $1\frac{3}{4}''$ thick. For interior work, $1\frac{3}{8}''$ is the thickness often used for ordinary medium-size doors up to 34″ wide and 6′10″ high. Exterior doors, doors larger than those just mentioned, and doors which are to receive a great deal of use should be at least $1\frac{3}{4}''$ thick. Very large exterior doors should be 2″ or $2\frac{1}{4}''$. The $1\frac{1}{8}''$ doors are used in closets and minor rooms, particularly if the openings are quite small. Stock doors are made in 2″ increments of width and height; odd sizes must be obtained by cutting down standard-size doors, or must be made to order.

b. The frame of a doorway is that portion of the ensemble to which the door is hung and against which it closes. It consists of two sides or jambs and a head, with an integral or attached stop against which the door closes.

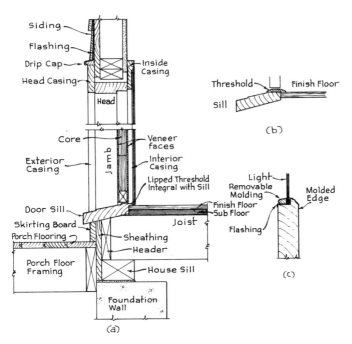

Figure 13.12 Details of exterior door. (a) Section through door in wall frame. (b) Door sill with separate threshold. (c) Light in exterior door.

c. Exterior door frames (figure 13.12a) are ordinarily of softwood plank, with jambs and head rabbeted to receive the door in exactly the same way as casement windows (chapter 7). At the foot is a sill, almost always made of hardwood to withstand the wear of traffic and sloped down and out to shed water. A threshold is provided to keep water from driving under the door. This often is integral with the sill and consists of a raised lip at the back whose width is the thickness of the door but which is slightly beveled at the front to allow the front face of the door to project and form a drip. The back of the lip laps over the finish floor and conceals the joint.

d. Thresholds may be separate pieces of hardwood (figure 13.12b) placed over the joint between the sill and the floor and hollowed on the bottom to fit snugly against the sill and the flooring. Such thresholds must be tightly fitted and securely nailed or screwed after the underside has been liberally coated with a sealant to seal the joint. Thresholds may also be of metal, such as brass. The same precautions must be followed when setting metal thresholds as when setting

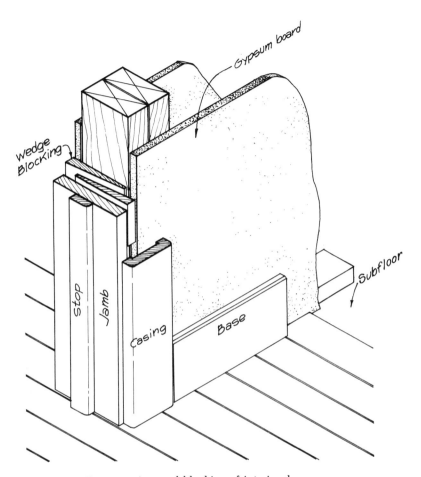

Figure 13.13 Frame, casing, and blocking of interior door.

wood. Metal thresholds are often employed with stone sills, particularly if the adjacent floor is of tile or some other masonry material.

e. One may set interior frames on the rough floor and then fit the finish floor around the bases of their jambs, or the finish floor may be laid first and the frames set on top. It is easier to obtain a tight joint by the latter method, but the former anchors the frame more firmly in place. Rough-framed openings must be wide enough to allow for the thickness of the jambs, and to provide an extra inch for blocking (figures 13.11c, 13.13) between the backs of the jambs and the rough framing (chapter 5). The blocking is firmly wedged to bring the jambs and the head to plumb and level straight lines, after which the frames are nailed solidly to the rough framing through the blocking. Finish nails are used, and the nail heads are set (chapter 14).

f. If rabbeted interior frames (figure 13.11c) are employed, the stock must be thick enough to allow the depth of the rabbet; if the stops are attached (figures 13.11d,e, 13.13), the frame is commonly $\frac{3}{4}''$ thick. Attached stops are small molded pieces firmly nailed to the faces of the frame so as to leave a space on the door side equal to the thickness of the door. The door is hung with its hinge or butt edge (chapter 14) in line with the edge of the frame. Attached stops may simply be nailed to the frame or they may be tongued in back and set into a groove plowed in the frame. The simple nailed stop makes it easier to re-hang a door to swing the other way, because the stop need merely be reversed and nailed in its new position. Rabbeted and tongued stops provide lightproof joints which, moreover, make it impossible to open a door by inserting a thin strip between the stop and the frame and pushing back the latch.

g. Door casings (figures 13.11a,c, 13.12a, 13.13) have the same functions as window casings (chapter 7): to set off the doorway and to cover and seal the space between the frame and the rough opening.

h. Casings may be simple or ornate, depending on the architectural design. The simplest treatment consists of two side pieces and one head piece. They are installed most simply by carrying the head casing across the full width of the opening plus the side casings and butting the side casings against the head casing. More commonly the joint is made by mitering the three pieces. The mitered joint is satisfactory as long as the wood does not shrink or swell, but with changes in width the joint opens at either the inner or the outer end. To guard against this, fine miter joints are reinforced in a variety of ways; by doweling and gluing the joint, by mitering only the face and half-lapping and gluing the back, or by mitering the front and mortising, tenoning, and gluing the back. Sometimes special metal ties are employed.

i. Next in order of increasing complexity is the casing plus backband. The backband is a narrow molding nailed to the outer or "back" edges of the casing. The joints in the backband are mitered. The casings may be butted or mitered. Backbands are used particularly to accentuate the outside edge of the casing without using heavy stock for the casing.

j. Wide and ornate casings are built up of several pieces, with moldings either run in the casing or attached to the casings as a part of the architectural profile. Ornamental pilasters often are made a part of the casing in ornate entrances, and the head is then made in the form of a pediment. No matter what the detail may be, an essential part of the construction is plenty of blocking to which the parts may be attached.

k. In thick walls, the door frames are augmented by additional casings called *jamb casings*. These may be paneled to match the paneling of the door or molded and ornamented to match the regular side casing. A refinement of this type of jamb casing in very thick walls is to have the sides splayed to give additional width and perspective to the opening. Again, no matter what the detail, it is essential to provide plenty of blocking, carefully set and true to line, to which the paneling and other ornament are attached. Setting the blocking is often the most important part of the work from a construction standpoint, because it must be accurately and sturdily built so that the finish will fit perfectly and be given adequate support.

l. Short blocks called *plinth blocks* are sometimes provided at the bottoms of side casings. They are thicker than the casing itself and are usually fairly plain. They form a stop for the baseboard as well as a base for the side casing (figure 13.11c). At the juncture of the side and head casings, ornamental corner blocks are occasionally found.

m. Prefinished and prehung doors, complete with frame, casing, and hardware, are commonly employed, thus considerably reducing the field work. To make it possible to install a prehung door, frame, and casing, the entire jamb is split longitudinally into two pieces, with the door and the casing for one side attached to one half of the jamb and the casing for the other side attached to the other half. The door half is carefully fitted and placed with the casing snug against the wall, and the other half-jamb and casing is then slid in from the other side, meeting the first half-jamb at the split joint (which is usually covered by the door stop) (figure 13.14).

MILLWORK

13.12 General

Millwork comprises all trim and finish woodwork and therefore includes a number of items which, for convenience and completeness or because of their individual importance, are taken up elsewhere. Window trim is discussed in chapter 7, stairs in sections 13.5–13.9 of

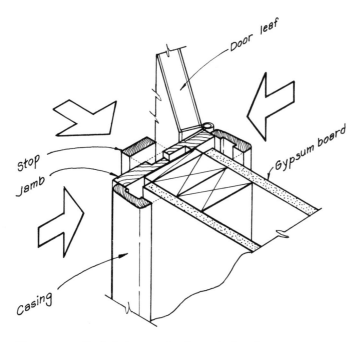

Figure 13.14 Exploded view of split-jamb door frame.

this chapter, and doors and door trim in sections 13.10–13.11. Other customary items of interior trim will be discussed here.

13.13 Baseboards

a. Baseboards, also variously called *mopboards*, *skirting*, or *skirting boards*, are found at the junctures of floors and walls. Ornate baseboards may consist of two or three parts, including a sub-base put down before the finish flooring, a center board or base proper, and an upper molded piece called the *base molding*, which might either be flush or raised, similar to the moldings employed in paneled doors. More commonly, baseboards are fairly plain and quite narrow, with simply molded top edges, or with narrow simple molding nailed along the top. The backs of baseboards should be hollowed as are window and door casings so that they will hug the wall finish closely along the edges. Baseboards are nailed to the studs through plaster or wallboard with 8d or 10d finish nails. At internal corners one piece is butted and coped to the profile of the other, but at external corners the pieces are mitered and firmly nailed together. Where baseboards ad-

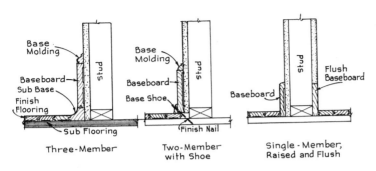

Figure 13.15 Types of baseboards.

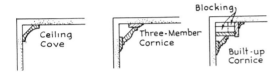

Figure 13.16 Cornices.

join door openings, the ends of the baseboards are carefully fitted to the edges of the casing or to the plinth blocks (figure 13.11a,c).

b. Baseboards may be put in place either before or after the finish floor is laid. If before, the finish floor usually ends against the baseboard; if afterward, the finish floor is carried under it.

c. Often the joint between baseboard and flooring is covered with a small molding, either quarter-round or similar, called a *base shoe* or *carpet strip*. The base shoe is best not nailed to the finish floor or to a baseboard, because shrinkage in either causes it to move away from the other and open a crack. Nails should be driven through to the subfloor, which has little tendency to move.

13.14 Chair Rails and Cornices

a. Chair rails are horizontal strips of wood applied to the walls at the height of chair tops to prevent the latter from marring the walls. When window sills are at the proper height, the chair rail is continuous under the stool and takes the place of the apron.

b. Cornices (figure 13.16) consist of single-piece or multiple-piece ornamental details at the junctures of walls and ceilings. Generally no cornice is used at all. When employed, the cornice is often a wide crown mold set into the corner and nailed to studs and joists. It may be made a trifle heavier by attaching a narrow frieze board to the wall first, or a frieze may be employed on the wall and a similar piece on the ceiling, with the molding nailed to both. The frieze may be further ornamented with any detail the architect may desire. As far as construction is concerned, the cornice consists of a number of horizontal strips of plain or molded wood nailed to one another or to the studs and joists. Dentils and similar details have to be nailed on separately. In order to obtain a snug fit between plaster or wallboard and wood, the wall finish must be applied straight and without any waves. This can be accomplished with grounds. Heavy cornices require blocking.

13.15 Mantels

a. Most mantels are stock items in standard sizes, but some are custom-made. Little can be said in general about the construction of mantels, since those built to architects' details almost all are different. A mantel may consist merely of a shelf, called the *mantelpiece*, at the top of the fireplace masonry, or the entire front of the fireplace may be faced with wood, marble, limestone, or some other ornamental material, leaving only a narrow edge of masonry showing around the fireplace opening. The mantelpiece is often omitted entirely.

b. No matter what the facing of the fireplace may be, the opening should be edged with masonry material such as brick, tile, or stone, because the heat of the fire causes materials such as wood to char if they are brought to the very edge of the opening. If bricks or tiles are used, the fireplace opening must be designed to fit the sizes of these units, in order that a full number may be carried up the sides and across the top without requiring any to be cut. Stone slabs and rubble can be fitted to desired dimensions.

c. The principles underlying the construction of paneled fireplace fronts are the same as for any paneled work. Rails and stiles hold the panels in place. If the chimney juts into the room, the paneling is returned at the sides and may be continued as part of the wainscot. A jutting chimney may be paneled up to the ceiling to emphasize the importance of the fireplace in the room. In any event, as far as construction is concerned, it is essential to provide plenty of solid blocking, carefully set to line, plumb and level, to which the finished woodwork is applied. Since this woodwork is likely to be warmed a great deal of the time and consequently to become very dry, it is advisable to use only very dry wood in its original construction because otherwise joints are apt to open.

d. Figure 13.17 illustrates a typical mantel installation, in which simple molded trim surrounding a brick-faced opening is surmounted by a one-piece mantelpiece with supporting molding, face, and small pilasters. The wall is finished with random-width vertical boarding tongued and grooved into molded separating strips. All woodwork is simply nailed to blocking inserted among the studs of the partition and to furring strips built around the brickwork.

13.16 Cabinets

a. Probably no part of the house has received more intensive study recently than the kitchen. Equipment makers have employed engineers to study the activities carried on in the kitchen, to arrange the equipment in the most efficient manner, and to work out floor plans to give the maximum of convenience in the minimum of space. Various plans have been evolved, and refrigerators, sinks, stoves, and cabinets have been worked into them for greater efficiency.

b. Kitchen cabinets (figure 13.18) ordinarily are in two parts: a rather wide lower portion surmounted by a counter, and a shallower upper portion, starting approximately 16″ above the counter and extending to the ceiling. The cabinets contain drawers and shelves, often have special compartments, and usually possess bread boards and chopping boards which slide into slots under the counter. Most are now factory-made.

c. To prevent toes from being stubbed at the bottoms of the cabinets and to allow closer approach to the counters, the bottoms of cabinets are recessed approximately 3″ and the bottom shelf is raised off the floor approximately 4″. This provides a toe space and greatly increases the comfort of a person working at the counter.

d. Shelves in the best-constructed cabinets are housed into the side of the cupboard with dovetail joints and do not, consequently, have to be nailed (figure 13.1d). Shelves and cupboard sides are firmly joined and cannot separate. In less expensive work, shelves are supported on cleats fastened to the sides and backs of cupboards. In kitchens, shelves are usually fixed in place, but they may be made adjustable by movable brackets which fit into slotted standards fastened to the sides and backs of cupboards. Ordinarily $\frac{3}{4}″$ stock is used for shelves, and

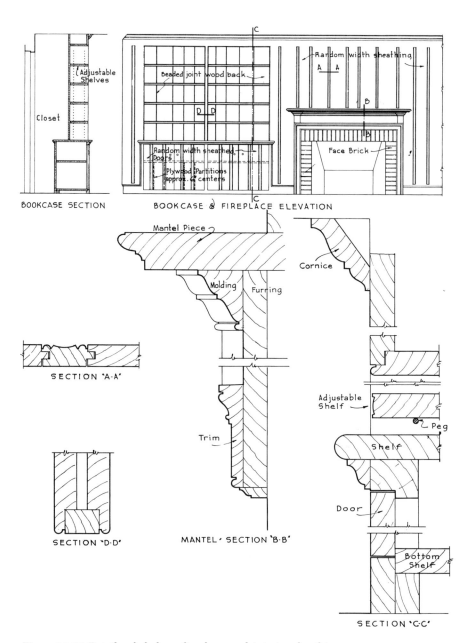

Figure 13.17 Details of shelves, fireplace, and interior sheathing.

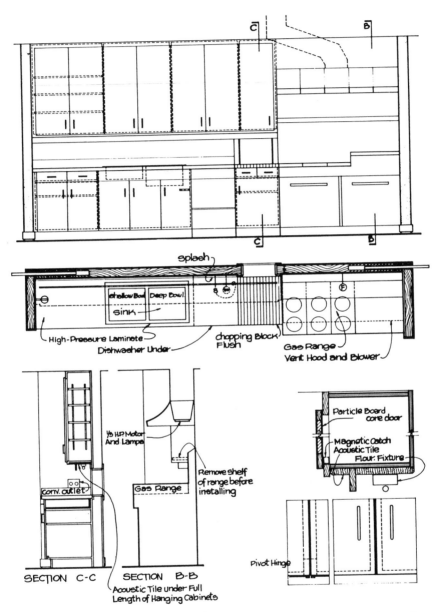

Figure 13.18 Kitchen cabinets. (top) Elevation and plan. Sections B-B and C-C show shelves, drawers, counters, toe space, and exhaust. Details of hanging cabinets are shown at lower right.

sound knots are considered no detriment inasmuch as the shelves are concealed behind cupboard doors.

e. To prevent sagging, sticking, and loss of shape, drawers must be carefully and sturdily built. The sides should be dovetailed to the front, and the back should be housed into the sides. The bottoms should be of rigid material (plywood is excellent) and should be inserted into slots plowed in the front and the sides, and not merely nailed to the bottom. For best results, the parts should be glued as well as nailed together, and the drawers must, of course, be squared and true. Drawer fronts may be flush or lipped. Drawers must rest on sturdy slides firmly fastened to the frame of the cupboard and set perfectly level. The bottoms of large drawers should have intermediate reinforcing strips, which should run in auxiliary slides to keep the drawers moving straight. Wide drawers are otherwise apt to become skewed and to bind against the sides. Between drawers, intermediate panels of plywood or other sheet material, called *dust panels*, should be placed to keep dust from dropping into the contents of one drawer from the bottom of the drawer above it. Dust panels are usually omitted in kitchen cabinets, but should be present in furniture.

f. For greater ease of operation, especially of large drawers, metal slides with roller bearings or small wheels which run on metal tracks are employed.

g. Doors may be paneled, provided with lights, or flush. Flush doors are easier to clean than paneled doors.

h. Paneled doors are made in the same way as the "solid" paneled doors already described, but the rails and stiles are thinner (commonly $\frac{3}{4}''$ to 1"), and the molding is run or "struck" directly to the rails and stiles. Panels may be plywood, hardboard, glass, or other materials, sometimes solid lumber and sometimes raised. Flush doors have plywood, lumber, or particle-board cores with veneer or other hard facing and solid edging strips, hardboard, or combinations. Plywood doors are more easily made and can be cut to size from large sheets, whereas the other type must be made to order or purchased from stock. On the other hand, screws for the hinges and butts (chapter 14) do not hold so well in the edges of plywood as they do in solid lumber, and plywood doors may twist more readily than lumber-core doors.

i. Where doors close against the frame of a cabinet, a rabbeted joint much like shiplap should be used unless the doors have lipped edges. The adjoining edges of pairs of doors should also be rabbeted, since a square edge does not provide as tight a joint as does the rabbeted type.

j. Counter tops are usually the same elevation as tops of stoves and kitchen sink drain boards and are in effect continuous with them. Although the tops may be exposed wood, which is enameled, painted, or oiled, the majority are covered with some sheet material, most commonly decorative high-pressure laminate. This is often carried at least partway up the wall over a coved corner and molded down over the front edge. Other water-resistant sheet materials, such as PVC-faced sheets (chapter 15), are suitable for covering counters. Commonly the edges are finished with stainless-steel strips.

k. Factory-made metal cabinets for kitchens have come into general use. The doors, drawers, shelves, backs, sides, and fronts are enameled pressed-steel sheets. The doors are almost always hollow flush doors with concealed hinges. The shelves are often adjustable. The drawers in the better cabinets move on roller slides; others move on friction slides similar to those in wood cupboards.

l. Metal cabinets are generally made in unit sizes, often two doors wide, which are put together in multiples for any particular plan. It is generally necessary, therefore, to plan the cabinet arrangement to fit standard units. The same holds true of standardized wood cabinets, or cabinets made of a combination of materials.

m. Figure 13.19 shows details of built-in lavatories and cabinet work. Shelves, doors, toe space, and counters are typical.

13.17 Bookshelves

a. Bookshelves are much the same as cabinets in their construction, except that doors are usually omitted and the fronts left open. Glass doors, either swinging or sliding on rollers resting on metal tracks, are occasionally found.

b. Bookshelves are commonly adjustable rather than housed into the ends. A simple adjustable shelf may be obtained by providing the ends of cases with vertical wood strips pierced with a series of holes bored at short intervals (figure 13.17). Wood pegs or small metal brackets inserted in these holes support the shelves. Various metal standards with adjustable brackets are common (figure 13.19).

13.18 Closets

a. Hook strips and shelves are found in clothes closets. The hook strips are high enough to be within convenient reach and yet provide sufficient height to permit garments to hang free of the floor. Clothes

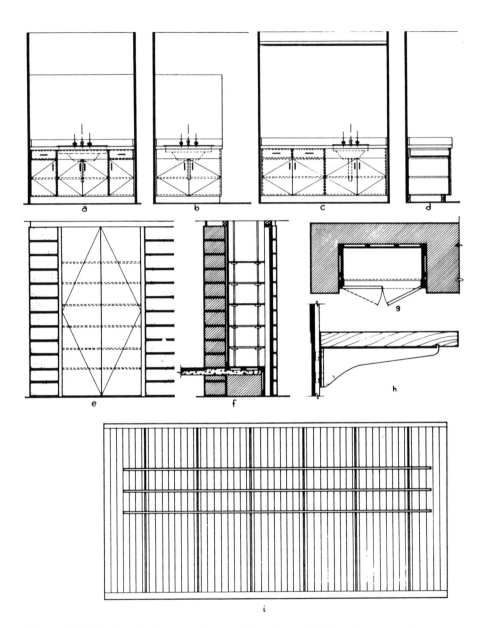

Figure 13.19 Details of cabinet work. (a–c) Elevations of built-in lavatory and
cabinets. (d) Cross-section of a–c showing shelves, counter, and toe space. (e–g) Elevation, section, and plan of cabinet built into masonry wall, with recessed carpet in
concrete floor. (h, i) Open shelves on vertically boarded wall with shelves and adjustable shelf support.

rods fastened to opposite hook strips permit clothing to be hung free of the wall and allow many garments to be hung in a small space. Hook strips must be firmly nailed to the framing of the walls; if the studs are not properly spaced to provide nailing, blocking must be provided. Shelves rest on top of the hook strips or, if hook strips are omitted, on narrow cleats nailed to the wall framing or to blocking.

b. Clothes closets may be provided with sets of shelves and drawers to accommodate various articles of apparel. For instance, at the bottom may be special inclined racks with heel strips upon which shoes are placed. Above this may be a set of drawers with ventilated fronts to receive garments which can be laid away flat. Above this and at full length, to one side, may be a space provided with a clothes rod to accommodate other garments which must be hung on clothes hangers. Shelves may be provided with compartments instead of being open, and may be covered to exclude dust.

c. Linen closets are commonly supplied with both shelves and drawers. The shelves may be slatted so that linens, woolens, and other folded materials may be ventilated from below and kept dry and fresh. Drawer fronts are often ventilated for the same reason.

d. Increasing attention is being given to the design of closets for maximum efficiency and convenience. Closets are made wide and shallow rather than narrow and deep, doors often run the full width, and whole walls are sometimes built as compartment closets with separate doors for the individual compartments. In small houses, where space is at a premium, closet design is especially important.

FLOORS

13.19 Materials

a. Both hardwoods and softwoods are regularly used for finish floors, but the hardwoods are generally considered to be better and more attractive. Hardwoods (e.g., red or white oak, maple, beech, birch, pecan) and softwoods (e.g., southern yellow pine, Douglas fir, western larch, western hemlock, redwood) are commonly used for finish flooring. The last possesses superior durability when the heartwood is used, and is mainly intended for exposed places such as porches.

b. All species are available in various grades, but not all species are graded the same. Oak is classified as *quarter-sawed* (with two subgrades: clear and select) or *plain-sawed* (clear, select, No. 1 and No. 2

Table 13.1   Hardwood Flooring

Nominal Size (in.)	Actual Size (in.)	Nails
$^{25}/_{32}$ x 3¼	Same	7d or 8d screw nail or cut nail
$^{25}/_{32}$ x 2¼	"	"
$^{25}/_{32}$ x 2	"	"
$^{25}/_{32}$ x 1½	"	"
⅜ x 2	$^{11}/_{32}$ x 2	Always on subfloor. 4d bright wire casing nail
⅜ x 1½	$^{11}/_{32}$ x 1½	
½ x 2	$^{15}/_{32}$ x 2	5d screw, cut, or casing nail
½ x 1½	$^{15}/_{32}$ × 1½	"

common, 1¼′ shorts). Beech, birch, and maple have first, second, and third grades plus special combinations. Pecan has first-grade red and white, second-grade and second grade red, and third grade. All these species are available in "nested" flooring bundles consisting of mixtures of grades and lengths.

c. Finish flooring (figure 13.20a) is made in strips, tongued and grooved and end-matched so that they can be driven tightly sidewise and lengthwise to provide tight joints, with each strip held in place by its neighbors. Thicknesses of hardwood flooring and recommended nailing are given in table 13.1. The lower faces of flooring strips are hollowed so that they will bear firmly along both edges and so that difficulties in laying caused by irregularities in subflooring are minimized.

d. Resilient flooring, including plastic (PVC), rubber, and cork, can be applied over a variety of substrates. The principles of installation are discussed below (section 13.25ff.).

13.20 Preparing the Subfloor

a. Subflooring is commonly plywood or reconstituted wood, with or without an underlayment surface (sections 5.3m–q, 5.22). Building paper is rarely employed.

b. It has already been pointed out (chapter 5) that subflooring of wood boards should preferably be laid diagonally (figure 13.20c). Before the finish flooring is laid the subfloor should be carefully inspected for tightness and levelness. The floor should be cleaned and covered with a good grade of building paper, lapped at ends and edges. The paper helps to make the floor draft-tight so that dust does not work up from

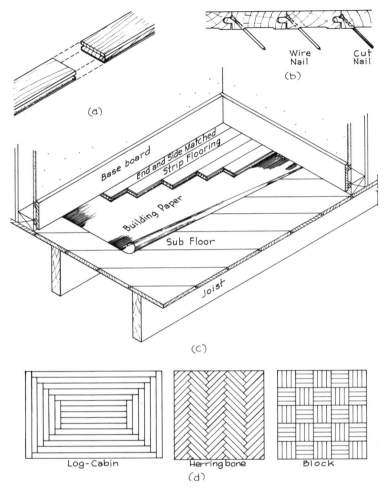

Figure 13.20 Wood flooring. (a) End- and side-matched flooring strips. (b) Blind (toe) nailing. (c) Laying strip flooring. (d) Flooring patterns.

below, particularly from basements and crawl spaces. A vapor-seal paper helps to exclude moisture from below.

13.21 Laying

a. Flooring strips are blind-nailed or toe-nailed (figure 13.20b) — that is, the nails are driven into the angle between the tongue and the front edge of the strip. The nails used are 8d wire flooring nails or cut steel flooring nails (chapter 14). Nails are driven at an angle of 45° to 50° to the horizontal, and can be driven flush but are usually driven by nailing machines struck with a mallet. Very hard woods or those that split easily may have to be drilled for nail holes — particularly if wire nails are employed, because these have a splitting action whereas the blunt-ended cut nails punch through the wood. Nails should be from 10″ to 16″ apart in thick flooring, and not over 8″ apart in the thinner varieties.

b. The first strip of flooring (figure 13.20c) is selected for straightness and is nailed down firmly parallel to and close to the side of the room, held just far enough away from the baseboard to be covered by the base shoe which is nailed down later. If no base shoe is employed, the flooring is carried under the baseboard just far enough to be covered or is butted against the baseboard. This first strip is face-nailed along the back edge and is often also blind-nailed. Subsequent strips are driven up tightly against the first strips, and all are blind-nailed. Flooring strips are made in random lengths ranging from about 2′ to 12′ or more, with the longer lengths predominating in the higher grades and the shorter length in the lower grades. The bundles should be sorted over and the longer pieces reserved for the larger and more important rooms, leaving the shorter pieces for smaller rooms, closets, or small halls. Strips are laid end to end. When the end of the room is reached, the last piece is cut to length and the cut-off piece is used to start the next stretch.

c. Various patterns (figure 13.20c,d) can be worked out in the flooring. The simplest method is to run all the strips in the same direction, which should be the long dimension of the principal rooms. The direction can be varied if the long dimensions of rooms do not run in the same direction. In such cases the change is usually made under doors to conceal the joint when doors are closed.

d. A second method is to lay the flooring parallel to all four sides of the room, which makes changes in direction from room to room unnecessary. The ends of strips parallel to one side butt against the sides of strips parallel to the adjacent sides, which makes them appear to lap one another. This kind of pattern is often called *log cabin*.

e. *Parquetry* is a term applied to a floor in which the strips are cut and laid to a geometrical pattern. The most common are the so-called *herringbone* and *block* flooring. In herringbone, short pieces, perhaps 1′ to 2′ long, are laid zig-zag so that they are all at 45° to the side walls and at right angles to one another. Block floors consist of squares of short lengths of flooring (usually 6″ to 12″ square), which are usually

assembled into units in the factory and then laid as blocks on the
subfloor. When laid on wood subfloors they are blind-nailed along the
tongued edges; when laid on concrete they are usually cemented
down with stiff mastic. Many $\frac{1}{4}''$-thick prefinished parquet tiles are
available.

f. Parquetry may be ornate. When made up to some pattern laid out
by a designer, and with various colors and figures provided by different species and cuts of wood, gives the intricate patterns sometimes
found in pretentious buildings. In such instances the individual
pieces of flooring must be cut to pattern and then be completely laid
out on the floor, and each piece must be individually fitted into its
proper place.

g. End-matched wood-strip flooring $\frac{25}{32}''$ thick may be laid directly
across joists without subflooring. Joists should not be more than 16"
on centers, and both ends of a single piece of flooring should not be in
the same joist space.

13.22 Precautions in Handling Flooring Material

Finish flooring is a carefully manufactured product, cut and shaped to
precise sizes and cross-section and dried to a low moisture content. It
is a valuable commodity, and should be treated as such. The principal
precaution, and one which cannot be stressed too much, is that *it
must at all times be kept dry.* Flooring is commonly kiln-dried to a
moisture content of 6 to 8 percent, which content it will maintain if
kept in dry storage and not permitted to become damp. If it is exposed
to dampness it quickly absorbs moisture, swells, twists, and otherwise
gets out of shape, so that strips no longer fit well together. Furthermore, dwellings are commonly dry in winter because of artificial heat
and lack of sufficient humidity, and flooring laid down in a moist
condition shrinks, leaving unsightly open joints between adjacent
strips. Flooring should be stored in dry sheds at the supply yard,
should be covered during transportation from yard to house during
damp weather, should be stored in dry conditions in the house,
should not be brought onto the premises until everything in the house
(e.g., concrete floors) has completely dried, should be laid as soon as
possible after delivery, and (unless prefinished) should be finished
immediately after it is laid. Flooring should preferably be one of the
last items in the construction.

13.23 Sanding

Formerly all floors were scraped by hand with special floor scrapers. Today, sanded finishes are achieved with motor-driven floor-sanding machines which consist of a revolving drum on which is mounted sandpaper of varying degrees of fineness depending upon the stage of the sanding operation. Sanding is begun with coarse paper to break down any irregularities in the floor and to provide a plane surface that looks coarse. Subsequent sanding with finer papers brings out the figure of the wood and provides a smoother surface. The degree to which the polishing is carried depends on the fineness of the paper in the final sanding operation.

13.24 Specialties

a. To simulate plank floors, flooring is obtainable in *random widths and lengths*. Widths usually vary from 4″ to 10″ or 12″ in multiples of 1″ or 2″, so that two or three narrow boards can be made to match the width of a wide one. Often this flooring is cut from specially selected knotty material such as oak. Such floors may be blind-nailed or may be nailed and pegged to simulate the appearance of old plank floors.
b. When it is desired to lay a new floor over an old one in an occupied house or to avoid the delay caused by applying finish coatings, *ready-finished flooring* may be used. This is commonly provided with a vee joint instead of tongue and groove. It is often already stained, sealed, or otherwise finished, and ready for use as soon as it is laid. Because great care must be exercised in laying such flooring to avoid marring, the edges are often factory-drilled for nails, and the strips are carefully wrapped in packages for delivery.

13.25 Resilient Flooring

a. The principal types of resilient flooring used in house construction are vinyl (PVC, chapter 15) and, rarely, cork. Vinyl flooring is made as both sheet and tile, and cork as tile. Vinyl, may be all-vinyl (homogeneous) or may have mineral fibers, as well as other ingredients and pigments, added to produce a harder but somewhat more brittle formulation.
b. In all of these materials the wearing layer may go through the entire thickness, or it may be only partial. Common overall thicknesses range from $\frac{1}{16}″$ to 0.090″.

c. Some vinyl sheet materials have a felt back for adhesion to a substrate. Others have a thin foamed-plastic base to add a soft, resilient cushion, especially useful where hard substrates might otherwise lead to fatigue.

d. Although resilient flooring may have its surface improved by periodic waxing, the denser, harder formulations dispense with waxing.

e. A wide variety of colors, textures, and figures is possible. Mottled, plain, chips in a matrix, embossed to simulate brick and tile, smooth, and other surface characteristics are available.

f. The term *resilient flooring* is applied to these materials to distinguish them from hard materials such as concrete and ceramic tile (chapter 12). They are softer underfoot, but they should not be so soft as to show permanent indentation under long-continued or impact loads. Such indentation is more likely to occur at elevated temperatures because the vinyls are thermoplastic. At lower temperatures they become harder.

13.26 Installation

a. Resilient flooring may be installed over a variety of substrates, but concrete and wood are the most common in house construction.

b. Concrete may be suspended, that is, have an air space below it; it may be at grade, or it may be below grade. The latter two cases are most common in dwelling houses, as exemplified by slab-on-grade and basement construction.

c. Suspended concrete floors do not pose any particular problem. Fresh concrete must be dry enough so that a good bond can be achieved, and there must be enough ventilation under it to allow the water in the concrete to escape from the lower surface.

d. Concrete on soil may present a problem. A bed of gravel or other porous material should be placed under the concrete, and it should be well drained. A moisture barrier should be placed under the slab, but even then it is entirely likely that dampness will exist in the concrete which will tend to migrate to the upper surface. Such slabs should be allowed to dry, after curing, for the longest possible time before resilient flooring is applied.

e. Alkaline water below the slab, or even the alkalies in the concrete itself, may cause difficulties with some cements or adhesives. Only adhesives and cements formulated for such conditions should be employed, but when they are, satisfactory results can readily be obtained with vinyl floors.

f. Rough surfaces, such as are likely to be found on rough-cast concrete, are almost certain to show or "telegraph" through a resilient floor. Consequently, such floors must be smoothed, usually with a topping layer. This may be a concrete mortar, which must be thick enough not to crack later under traffic. Such material cannot be feathered successfully. If the topping must be thin, it should be based on a latex rather than straight portland cement, and the formulation must be alkaline-moisture resistant if on a slab on soil.

g. Wood makes a satisfactory substrate for resilient flooring, but the problem of telegraphing defects exists here as it does with concrete. This is particularly true of the joints between rough subflooring, especially if the boards are wide (more than 3" or 4") and not tongue and groove. In such instances, it is best to apply an underlayment of underlayment-grade plywood, hardboard, or reconstituted board (chapter 5). The most common substrates are plywood and reconstituted board with underlayment surface (section 5.22).

h. Once the substrate is prepared, resilient flooring may be installed. Because of differences among proprietary materials and cements or adhesives, and different substrates, it is essential that manufacturers' directions be closely followed. For tile, the cement is applied over the entire surface of the substrate, in small enough areas at a time to permit the tiles to be placed and pressed down firmly before the adhesive becomes too dry for a good bond. For sheet materials, adhesive may be spread over the entire surface, or in strips, e.g., 6" along perimeters and 8" (4" each side) along intermediate joints. Any such adhesive must be resistant to water that may seep down into the joint.

i. Special cove strips are made for use with resilient flooring. These provide a smooth curved transition between the floor and the wall, and perform the same function as a baseboard. In some instances, sheet materials are warmed and bent into a gradual curved cove at the floor-wall interface, but the specially formed cove provides a surer detail less prone to difficulty.

14 Hardware

14.1 General

Builders' hardware is divided into two general categories: *rough* and *finish*. Under rough hardware are lumped such items as anchor bolts and other bolts, rough screws, nails, hangers, strapping, and similar miscellaneous iron and steel which is not of a heavy structural nature. Finish hardware includes butts and hinges, locks, door knobs, window fasts, drawer pulls, and similar items.

14.2 Nails

Nails are the almost universal means of fastening the wood members of a house together. Wood and metal pins are occasionally found, screws and bolts have some use, and the use of adhesives is growing, but nails are easily the most important of all fastening means. Two principal types are employed, *cut* and *wire*, with wire nails far overshadowing cut nails in importance. In the following discussions, only those nails are included which are at all likely to be found in building operations. In other chapters, reference is made to the types of nails employed for the particular operation under consideration.

14.3 Cut Nails

Cut nails are the older variety. They are cut or sheared from flat iron nail plate of the proper thickness, and heads of various types are formed at the wide end. The shank tapers along the two edges, but the two sides are flat. The point is blunt (figure 14.1).

14.4 Wire Nails

a. Wire nails, first introduced during the second half of the nineteenth century, have nearly superseded all others. Most are manufactured from mild steel wire of the proper gauge, but galvanized steel, aluminum, copper or copper alloy, and stainless steel are employed for corrosion resistance. They may have any one of a number of different kinds of heads or no head at all, and may be pointed in a variety of different ways. The shank is cylindrical and of uniform diameter. The holding power of the nail depends to a considerable extent upon friction caused by the pressure of wood fibers pried apart by the point of the nail as it penetrates the wood. Because of the point, wire nails have a greater tendency to split wood than cut nails.
b. Lengths of nails are in general designated by the "penny," an ex-

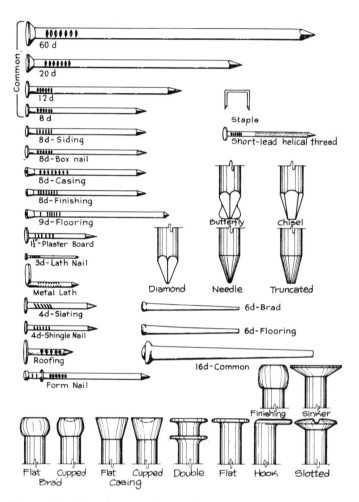

Figure 14.1 Typical wire and cut nails.

pression whose origin, although known to be English, is difficult to trace. One theory is that the word originally referred to the cost; for example, a 6-penny nail cost 6 pence per hundred. Another theory is based upon the fact that the symbol "d" was originally used for both pound and penny, and a 6d nail therefore was one which weighed 6 pounds per thousand. Whatever the origin, the symbol "d" is still used to designate length. In general, the range is from 2d to 60d, or 1 inch to 6 inches, as shown in table 14.1.

c. Diameters of shanks vary with the use to which the nail is to be put. For heavy work they are large (low wire-gauge number); for fine work the shank is thin (high wire-gauge number) (see table 14.1).

d. Depending on the use, nails may have flat, tapered (sinkers), or countersunk heads. Flat heads provide the greatest surface area and the greatest gripping power. They are used when the head may be permitted to show, and are driven flush with the surface. Common nails, spikes, box nails, siding nails, roofing nails, lath nails, and shingle nails are examples. With the exception of brad heads, countersunk heads are conical and are only slightly larger than the shank. Brad heads are partially spherical and are even smaller than the conical. Both are designed to be driven below the surface (countersunk) with a nail set, and almost always are concealed by putty. Common brads, nails and brads for flooring, casing nails, and finishing nails have countersunk heads. Special types of heads are round or oval; hooked as in metal lath nails; and double-headed, as found in concrete form nails, which must be driven home firmly for holding power but which must subsequently be easy to withdraw. A few types of heads are shown in figure 14.1.

e. Practically all nails used in building have the ordinary diamond point shown in figure 14.1. Blunt-pointed nails may be employed with refractory woods which split easily (an ordinary diamond point when blunted by striking with a hammer is a satisfactory substitute). A few other types of points are shown in figure 14.1.

f. Shanks for most building applications are cylindrical, but many other types are found. These include barbed, fluted, grooved, knurled, threaded, and twisted types. Twisted shanks are square in cross-section. Threaded nails, in particular, are used for superior gripping power. Threads may be annular or helical, and result in alternate ridges and depressions in the shank. Annular-threaded nails are often

Table 14.1 Wire Nails

Size	Length (in.)	Common[a] Gauge No.	Common Shank Diam. (in.)	Common Head Diam. (in.)	Box,[b] Casing Gauge No.	Shank Diam. (in.)	Head Diam. In. Box	Head Diam. In. Casing	Finish Gauge No.	Finish Shank Diam. (in.)	Finish Head Diam. (in.)	Flooring[c] Gauge No.	Flooring Shank Diam. (in.)	Flooring Head Diam. (in.)
2d	1	15	0.072	$11/64$	$15\frac{1}{2}$	0.067	$3/16$	0.098	$16\frac{1}{2}$	0.058	0.086	15	0.072	$9/64$
3d	$1\frac{1}{4}$	14	0.080	$13/64$	$14\frac{1}{2}$	0.076	$7/32$	0.113	$15\frac{1}{2}$	0.067	0.098	15	0.072	$9/64$
4d	$1\frac{1}{2}$	$12\frac{1}{2}$	0.098	$\frac{1}{4}$	14	0.080	$7/32$	0.120	15	0.072	0.105	13	0.091	$5/32$
5d	$1\frac{3}{4}$	$12\frac{1}{2}$	0.098	$\frac{1}{4}$	14	0.080	$7/32$	0.120	15	0.072	0.105	13	0.091	$5/32$
6d	2	$11\frac{1}{2}$	0.113	$17/64$	$12\frac{1}{2}$	0.098	$17/64$	0.142	13	0.092	0.135	$11\frac{1}{2}$	0.115	$13/64$
7d	$2\frac{1}{4}$	$11\frac{1}{2}$	0.113	$17/64$	$12\frac{1}{2}$	0.098	$17/64$	0.142	13	0.092	0.135	$11\frac{1}{2}$	0.115	$13/64$
8d	$2\frac{1}{2}$	$10\frac{1}{4}$	0.131	$9/32$	$11\frac{1}{2}$	0.113	$19/64$	0.155	$12\frac{1}{2}$	0.098	0.142	$11\frac{1}{2}$	0.115	$13/64$
9d	$2\frac{3}{4}$	$10\frac{1}{4}$	0.131	$9/32$	$11\frac{1}{2}$	0.113	$19/64$	0.155	$12\frac{1}{2}$	0.098	0.142			
10d	3	9	0.148	$5/16$	$10\frac{1}{2}$	0.127	$5/16$	0.169	$11\frac{1}{2}$	0.113	0.155	10	0.135	$\frac{1}{4}$
12d	$3\frac{1}{4}$	9	0.148	$5/16$	$10\frac{1}{2}$	0.127	$5/16$	0.169	$11\frac{1}{2}$	0.113	0.155	10	0.135	$\frac{1}{4}$
16d	$3\frac{1}{2}$	8	0.162	$11/32$	10	0.135	$11/32$	0.177	11	0.120	0.162	9	0.148	$9/32$
20d	4	6	0.192	$13/32$					10	0.135	0.177			
30d	$4\frac{1}{2}$	5	0.207	$7/16$										
40d	5	4	0.225	$15/32$										
50d	$5\frac{1}{2}$	3	0.244	$\frac{1}{2}$										
60d	6	2	0.263	$17/32$										

[a] Aluminum and copper shank diameters are slightly different.
[b] Commonly cement-coated. Shanks are generally 1 ga. smaller. Also supplied galv.
[c] Also flooring brads, brad head, slightly different shank diameters.

Brad. Common: $3/8''$ to 60d, brad head $0.050''$ to $0.331''$.
Clinch. 2d to 20d, duckbill or clinch point. Oval head.
Concrete. Hardened steel, $\frac{1}{2}'' \times 0.135''$ to $3\frac{1}{2}'' \times 0.207''$, countersunk head.
Dating. Galv. copper, brass. $3/8''$ to $\frac{1}{2}''$ flat numeral head.

Double-headed. Concrete forms. 1¾" x 0.113 to 4" x 0.207", ³⁄₁₆" to ⁷⁄₁₆" double heads.

Fiberboard. Low-carbon or hardened. 1" x 0.054" to 2" x 0.062", needle point.

Gypsum-lath. Bright or blued. 1" to 1¾" x 0.092", ¹⁹⁄₆₄" to ⅜" head. 1" x 0.120" to 1½" x 0.148", ½" head. Alum. alloy 1⅛" x 0.099" to 1½" x 0.105", ¹⁹⁄₆₄" or ⁵⁄₁₆" head.

Gypsum-wallboard. Smooth or annular thread. 1⅜" x 0.062" to 2" x 0.105", ¼" to ¹⁹⁄₆₄" head.

Hardboard. Bright, colored lacquer, or galvanized. Medium carbon or hardened. Annular or helical thread. 1" x 0.058" to 3" x 0.115". Small flat to countersunk head.

Hinge. 1¼" x ³⁄₁₆" to 4" x ⅜", flat or oval countersunk, long diamond or chisel pt.

Insulation board. Zinc, nickel, or cadmium plate. 1¼" and 1¾" x 0.054", ³⁄₃₂" head, needle pt.

Masonry. Hardened, knurled, vertically threaded, fluted, plain or zinc coated. ½" to 4" x 0.148" to 0.250", flat or checkered ⁵⁄₁₆" to ⁹⁄₁₆" head.

Roofing. Plain, galvanized, copper-coated steel; aluminum. Flat, checkered, small to large, reinforced, lead and cast-lead heads plus lead, neoprene, plastic washers. ¾" x 0.092" to 2" x 0.150", heads ¼" to ⅝".

Shake. Galv. steel and alum. 1¼" x 0.086" to 2½" x 0.092", heads ⅛" to ⁵⁄₃₂".

Shingle, wood. Bright or galv. steel, alum., plain or threaded shank, heads ⁷⁄₃₂" to ⅞₂", med. or blunt diamond pt.

Siding, aluminum. Plain or helical thread. 1" x 0.099" to 2½" x 0.135", ¼" to ⁵⁄₁₆" hd.

Siding, wood. Bright, colored lacquer, steel alum., or stainless steel. Plain or threaded. 1¾" x 0.080" to 3" x 0.148". Flat, casing, or sinker head. ⁵⁄₃₂" to ¹³⁄₃₂".

Slating. Galv. steel, alum., copper. 1" x 0.106" to 2" x 0.148". ⁵⁄₁₆" to ⁷⁄₁₆" head.

Underlayment. Low, medium-carbon or hardened steel. Annular thread. 1" x 0.080" to 3" x 0.148", flat or countersunk head.

Wallboard. Low, medium-carbon or hardened steel. Colored lacquer. Plain or annular thread. 1⅛" x 0.062" to 2" x 0.083", countersunk head.

called *ring nails*. Withdrawal resistance from side grain in particular is much enhanced over plain-shank nails, especially after wood has shrunk and swollen several times with changes in moisture content. Drive screws have helically threaded shanks and are likely to have slotted heads. They are made to turn when driven with a hammer and can be retracted with a screwdriver.

g. Most nails are made of wire cold-drawn in the final stages and therefore are bright, smooth, and covered with a thin film of lubricating oil. Lath nails turn blue when they are cleaned of oil and sterilized. A coating derived from resins or shellac provides a temporary bond between nail and wood and protects against corrosion in storage. Etching increases holding power. Shingle and roofing nails, and others destined for exposure to severe atmospheric conditions, are usually zinc-coated.

h. Nails may be of metal other than mild steel. Aluminum is used for its corrosion resistance. Copper is especially desirable for roofing. Zinc, brass, Muntz (yellow) metal, and copper-bearing steel have increased corrosion resistance. Stainless steel and monel metal have special uses. Coatings, in addition to the widely used zinc, may be tin, copper, cadmium, or brass. Nickel- and chromium-plated nails are used in conjunction with trim of the same metal. "Parkerizing" increases the paint-holding power.

i. Where greater hardness is needed, as in nails to be driven into masonry or concrete, the steel may be medium- to high-carbon, heat-treated to produce greater hardness and resistance to bending than usual.

j. Many special types of nails are made for special purposes. Some of these are described in other chapters of this book in connection with those topics (e.g., gypsum board). A few others are listed in table 14.1.

k. Much framing is now done with threaded nails driven by pneumatic nail guns.

14.5 Screws and Bolts

a. Wood screws. Screws are made with various shapes of heads and threads for various uses. The following are the types usually employed in building:

flat head
round head
oval head

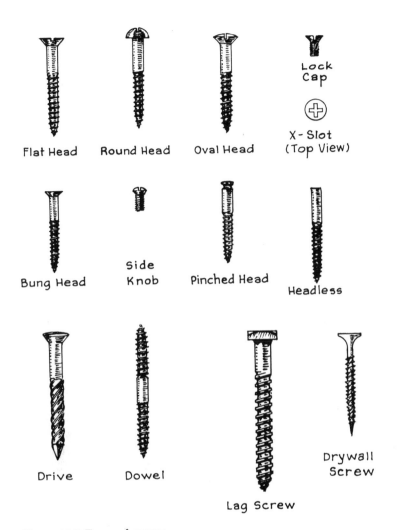

Figure 14.2 Types of screws.

clove head
bung head
winged head
pinched head
headless
drive
dowel

Of these, flat-head screws are used much more than all the others combined, round-head screws rank second, and the first three listed above fulfill almost all building requirements. The others are used for limited specialized applications. Heads may be slotted across for flat-ended screw drivers, or have x-shape slots for x-shaped screwdrivers.

b. Most items of hardware (see section 14.6ff.) are applied with flat-head screws. Round-head screws are used for surface hinges and for other applications where appearance is a factor. Oval-head screws find some use for applying interior trim which must be removed periodically.

c. Standard metals for wood screws are steel and brass, although bronze, monel metal, and other special metals may be employed, and the screws may be plated for special purposes. Steel screws are ordinarily made in lengths from $\frac{1}{4}''$ to $5''$, and brass screws from $\frac{1}{4}''$ to $3\frac{1}{2}''$. Sizes are given in table 14.2.

d. Lag screws. These are large, gimlet-pointed steel screws provided with square or hexagonal heads to be turned by a wrench instead of by a screwdriver. Lag screws are used for fastening heavy framing members and for attaching structural iron such as angles, channels, and strap iron to wood members.

e. Holes for all types of screws should be pre-bored. In soft woods,

Table 14.2   Wood Screws

No.	Diam. (in.)	No.	Diam. (in.)	No.	Diam. (in.)
0	0.060	6	0.138	12	0.216
1	0.073	7	0.151	14	0.242
2	0.086	8	0.164	16	0.268
3	0.099	9	0.177	18	0.294
4	0.112	10	0.190	20	0.320
5	0.125	11	0.203	24	0.372

 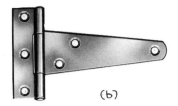

(a)   (b)

Figure 14.3 (a) Strap hinge. (b) Half-strap hinge.

holes for the smaller sizes of screws may be approximately equal to the diameter at the base of the thread, but in hard refractory woods it is often necessary to bore two holes: one for the threaded portion and a larger one (slightly smaller than the shank diameter) for the un-threaded portion of the screw. Lubricating with wax, soft soap, or paraffin often helps to drive the screw home in hard refractory woods.

f. Bolts. Bolts are used to fasten the sills to foundation walls, to join heavy wood framing members, and to attach metal framing members to one another or to wood.

g. Holes for bolts are bored $\frac{1}{16}''$ larger than the diameter of the bolt unless an absolutely snug or "driving" fit is required, in which instance the bolt hole is the same diameter as the bolt.

FINISH HARDWARE*

14.6 Butts and Hinges

a. A *hinge* is, strictly speaking, a pair of straps joined together by a pin which allows the two straps to rotate about the pin (figure 14.3). A *butt*, often mistakenly called a hinge, is the butt end of a hinge, that is, the portion near the pin but with the long portion of the straps omitted (figure 14.4).

b. Today the term *hinge* is usually applied to a member screwed to the surface of a door and the term *butt* to a member mortised into the edge. Most doors are hung on butts rather than on hinges. For the most part, hinges are employed on batten doors and similar doors not easily mortised.

c. The round central part of the butt or hinge is the *knuckle* and the flat portions are the *flaps* or *leaves*. The pin, which is contained in the knuckle, when made removable is called a *loose* pin, otherwise it is a

*This section was prepared by W. R. Haverkampt of Sargent and Company.

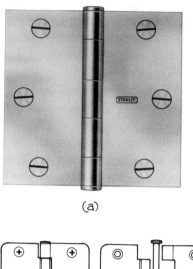

(a)

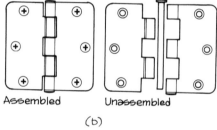

Assembled   Unassembled

(b)

Figure 14.4 (a) Butt. (b) Assembled and unassembled butt.

fast pin. Loose pins sometimes have a tendency to rise when leaves are worked back and forth because the pin binds and rotates only one way. Consequently, specially designed *nonrising* pins, forced to rotate both ways, may be substituted. If the pin is so made that it cannot be withdrawn when the door is closed, it is a *self-locking* pin. This prevents doors from being tampered with and removed from their hinges when closed.

d. The proper location of a hinge on a door is determined by using the formula illustrated in figure 14.5a,b.

e. In addition to ordinary butts and hinges, several types of butts, hinges, and pivots are made for special purposes. Open or enclosed springs may be incorporated at the pin to provide a self-closing feature. Such hinges are especially common on screen doors, which must be kept closed as much as possible (figure 14.6).

f. Invisible hinges consist of a number of small flat plates rotating

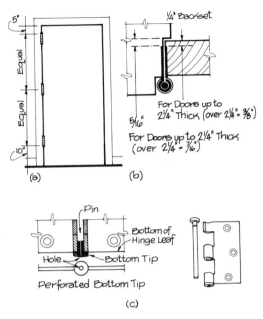

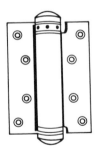

Figure 14.5 (a) Arrangement of door and butt. (b) Clearances. (c) Non-rising pin with perforated bottom tip.

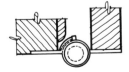

Figure 14.6 Spring hinge.

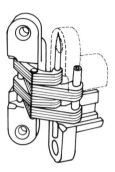

Figure 14.7 Invisible hinge.

Figure 14.8 Floor hinge for double-acting door.

about a central pin and provided with shoulders which are mortised into the edges of doors and frames. When closed, the hinges are completely out of sight (figure 14.7).

g. Doors that are required to swing both ways (in and out) are called *double-acting* doors. These doors are usually hung on double-acting floor hinges.

h. Floor hinges (figure 14.8) for double-acting doors are provided with springs which either permit the door to stand open at 90° or cause it to close to its central point if the door is released when open less than 90°. A mortise pivot is provided at the top. "Checking" floor hinges are provided with hydraulic chambers as well as with springs. The liquid causes the door to close slowly and quietly. (See also section 14.11.)

i. Butts must be wide enough to allow a door to swing clear of the surrounding trim when the door is opened. The manner in which this is determined is shown in figure 14.9a,b. Wide-throw hinges are used to swing the door clear of exceptionally wide trim.

j. Another door that is required to swing both ways is a cafe or dwarf

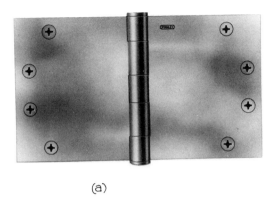

(a)

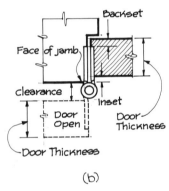

(b)

Figure 14.9 (a) Wide butt. (d) Determination of inset and clearance for wide-throw butt.

door. This type of door is generally of louver-type construction and very light. This particular door is hung on gravity-type pivot hinges (figure 14.10).

k. Cabinet doors today generally come pre-hung from the cabinet manufacturer. Hanging of these doors generally falls into three categories: *flush, overlay,* and *lipped* (figure 14.11).

14.7 Locks and Latches

a. Both locks and latches are devices for holding doors in the closed position. Generally speaking, the latch consists of a beveled or otherwise shaped bar, called a *latch bolt*, which slides into position when the door is closed. Generally, also, the device for opening the latch is

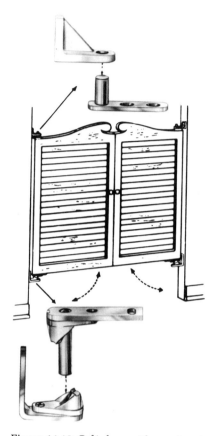

Figure 14.10 Café door with gravity pivot hinge.

a knob or lever, connected with the latch. These are called *operating trim.* In some instances the latch is so arranged or fitted that it can be opened by such a device from one side only and must be opened from the other side with a key.

b. A *dead bolt* is a rectangular bolt that does not slide into place automatically but must be thrown into place by a key or a turn knob. It is common practice in builders' hardware to combine latch bolts and dead bolts into the same unit. Such combinations are simply called *locks.* When a lock has a dead bolt only, it is called a *deadlock.*

c. Various types of locks and latches are used in today's construction. They are generally named after the type of construction and installation they require. Basically there are mortise, unit and integral, cylindrical and tubular, and special-application locks and latches.

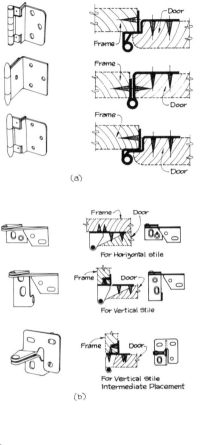

(a)

(b)

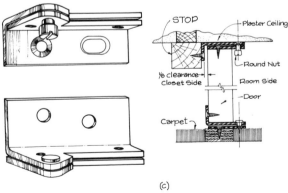

(c)

Figure 14.11 (a) Hinges for lipped or flush doors. (b) Pivot hinges for vertical and horizontal stiles. (c) Pivot hinges for full-height wardrobe door.

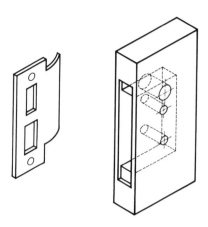

Figure 14.12 Mortise and strike.

d. Mortise locks and latches are designed to fill a cavity or hole placed in the edge of a door (figure 14.12). They are concealed except for the face or portion showing at the edge, the knob or lever, the cylinder, and the operating trim.

e. A *mortise lock* is made up of a lock body that contains the following features (figure 14.13):

latch bolt (described earlier).

guard bolt — Prevents the latch bolt from being retracted by surreptitious means when it is depressed.

dead bolt (described earlier).

cylinder (See section 14.18.)

stop works — Slide stops operating on split hubs which engage the outside knob hub so it cannot be turned and the latch bolt cannot be retracted from that side without a key. Stop works are operated by a pair of buttons on the face of the lock. When one is depressed, the other is raised and the knob is stationary on one side.

operating trim — Can be either a knob or lever that comes in various design and finishes.

functions — Mortise lock functions are made by combining the above-mentioned features in various ways. A manufacturer's catalog should be consulted when selecting the proper function.

f. The *unit lock* is a factory-preassembled lock that fits into a door cutout (figure 14.14). The *integral lock* is also a factory-preassembled lock that fits into a door mortise (figures 14.15, 14.16). These similar

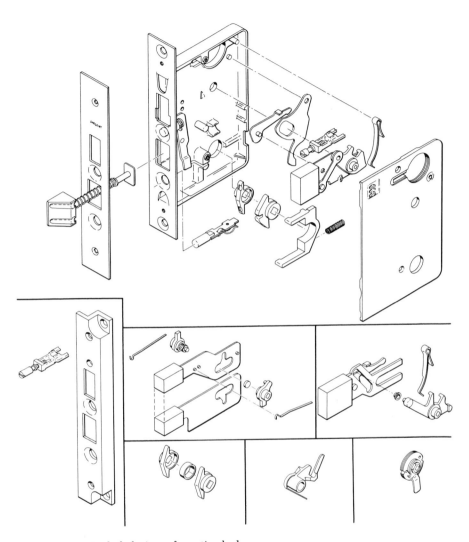

Figure 14.13 Exploded view of mortise lock.

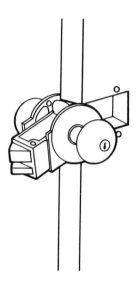

Figure 14.14 Unit lock.

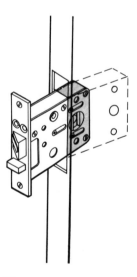

Figure 14.15 Mortise lock inserted in mortise.

Figure 14.16 Integral lock.

Figure 14.17 Bored-in lock.

locks offer the same basic features as a mortise lock (latch bolt, guard bolt, dead bolt, stop works, and operating trim) except that the cylinder is placed in the knob, and they have limited functions when compared to mortise locks.

g. *Cylindrical* and *bored* locks feature a key-in-knob principle with rapid installation. They are designed to fit into a hole that is bored in the edge and lock stile of the door (figures 14.17, 14.18). The following components make up a cylindrical lock (figure 14.19):

latch tube — Contains both the latch bolt and the guard bolt.

aligning tube — A cylindrical housing which receives the latch tube and the knobs, and provides threads for the roses to fasten to.

knob assemblies — An outside and inside knob assembly that snaps into the aligning tube or cylindrical housing.

cylinder — Placed in the knob, generally the outside knob.

button stops — Also placed in the knob. Generally the inside knob contains the buttons that lock the outside knob.

Cylindrical and bored locks are used today mostly in dwelling-

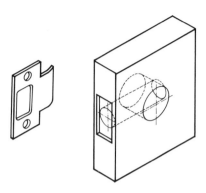

Figure 14.18 Cutting and boring for bored-in lock.

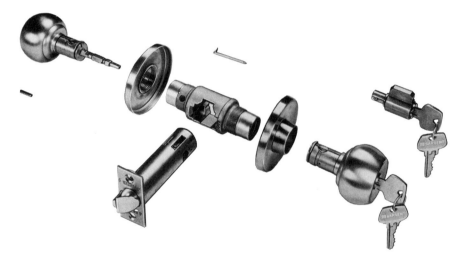

Figure 14.19 Exploded view of cylindrical lock.

Figure 14.20 Rim deadlock.

Figure 14.21 Rim night latch.

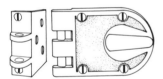

Figure 14.22 Rim lock.

house construction because they are easy to install and inexpensive. **h.** The more common special-application locks and latches found in dwelling-house construction are rim night latches, rim deadlocks, jimmy-proof rim locks, and sliding-door locks. Rim locks are used to provide additional security when required. Sliding-door locks generally come with the sliding-door assembly, directly from the manufacturer.

14.8 Cylinders

The locks mentioned above have cylinders with keyways, cylinder pins, and drivers. Normally five or six pins are used for locks keyed alike or differently (figure 14.23). The mechanism of a cylinder for a mortise cylinder lock consists of a cylinder or shell containing a cylin-

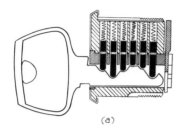

(a)

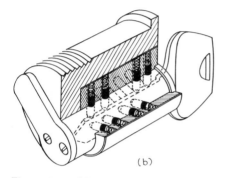

(b)

Figure 14.23 Maximum-security cylinder. (a) Cylinder showing pins lined up in barrel by notched key. (b) Key turning barrel and cam.

drical barrel. The barrel is slotted lengthwise and requires corresponding slots or keyways in the side of the flat key. At right angles to the barrel and cylinder shell are holes containing the cylinder pins, the drivers, and the cylinder springs. The key is notched along one edge in such a way that when it is inserted it raises the pins. If the notches are correctly cut, the breaks between the cylinder pins and the drivers line up where the barrel and the shell meet, allowing the barrel to be rotated. Otherwise, the cylinder pins obstruct the rotation of the barrel. Rotation of the barrel turns a cam which engages the deadbolt lever, the latch-bolt lever, or both, and withdraws the bolt or bolts, allowing entry. Key-in-the-knob cylinders are substantially the same as the above except that the doorknob acts as the cylinder shell.

14.9 Operating Trim

a. In conventional mortise and bored-in locks, the operating trim or the combination of knob, spindle, and hub makes it possible to retract

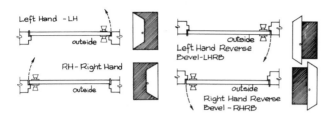

Figure 14.24 Hands of doors.

the latch bolt when the door is closed. The operating trim comes in various designs and finishes to complement the various types of dwelling-house construction seen today.

b. Operating trim varies so widely that the manufacturer's catalog should be consulted when selecting design.

14.10 Handing the Door

a. In order for the various locks and latches and hinges previously described to function properly on the door, they must be *handed*. The manner in which a door swings determines its "hand" and the hand of the lock required (figure 14.24).

b. The hand of a door is determined from the "outside" — i.e., the street side of an entrance door, the corridor side of a room door, the space between twin doors, and the side of the door against which it is to be locked if the door communicates from one room to another. In general, the outside of a door is the side which must be opened by key, if the door requires locking. The "outsides" of closet doors and cabinet doors of all kinds are the room sides.

A *right-hand* (R.H.) door swings away from you to the right. You cannot see the hinges from the outside when the door is closed.

A *left-hand* (L.H.) door swings away from you to the left. You cannot see the hinges from the outside when the door is closed.

A *right-hand reverse-bevel* (R.H.R.B.) door swings toward you to the right. You see the hinges when the door is closed.

A *left-hand reverse-bevel* (L.H.R.B.) door swings toward you to the left. You see the hinges when the door is closed.

c. The four hands apply to descriptions of hands for door locks. This is necessary because the swing of the door must be known (and also the outside hand for the key when keyed locks are required, and the bevel of the front of the lock where beveled doors occur). In the case

Figure 14.25 Pneumatic door closer.

of hinges only, two hands occur: right or left. With cabinet doors, again only two hands occur: right or left.

14.11 Door Closers

a. Door closers or "checks" are designed to close a door quickly without the slamming that occurs with ordinary springs and spring hinges. In dwelling-house construction, two general types are employed: liquid and pneumatic. The liquid or hydraulic type is used to control larger doors; the pneumatic type is almost exclusively used on screen doors, or gates (figure 14.25).

b. The hydraulic closer is generally used on garage doors that enter directly into a house and on front and rear entrance doors. Fire regulations today call for a self-closing "C" label fire door between a garage and a house. These doors are generally large enough to require hydraulic closers (figure 14.26).

14.12 Miscellaneous Hardware

In this category may be lumped many small items of commonly found hardware, the functions of which are more or less self-evident. Cabinet door catches and locks, tracks and sliding sheaves for sliding cabinet doors, overhead tracks and hangers for heavier sliding doors, drawer pulls, door stops, coat and hat hooks, supports for adjustable shelves, and many other items fall into this group.

14.13 Window Hardware

Window hardware is no longer the worrisome problem that it was years ago. The reason is that the manufacturers now supply windows complete with all hardware. Sash weights, ropes, and pulleys have been eliminated from today's pre-hung windows.

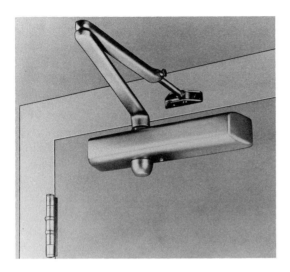

Figure 14.26 Hydraulic door closer.

14.14 Materials and Finishes

a. The metals commonly employed in finishing hardware are brass, bronze, aluminum, iron, steel, and stainless steel. These metals can be cast, forged, extruded, or wrought. The cast, forged, or extruded metals are a minimum of 0.080″ thick and are generally much too expensive for use in dwelling-house construction. The less-expensive wrought materials, 0.050″ thick, are more commonly employed in dwelling-house hardware. Of the wrought materials, brass and bronze finishes are used most often.

b. All hardware finishes are obtained by the careful processing of the above-mentioned metals. When required, a clear protective coating is electrostatically applied and cured in a high-temperature oven.

c. Many factors should be considered when selecting a finish, e.g., the design surface, whether sculptured, etched, or smooth, matching decor, interior or exterior exposure, and climate. In areas where the finish is to be subjected to strong corrosive vapors, humid climate, sea air, or salt spray, aluminum or stainless steel finishes are recommended for durability and minimal maintenance.

d. Finishes of one color tone are suggested for smooth surface designs. Ornamental designs with irregular surfaces are usually more

Table 14.3 Finishes

BHMA Code Symbol	Finish Description	Nearest US Equivalent
600	Primed for painting	USP
605	Bright brass, clear coated	US3
606	Satin brass, clear coated	US4
609	Satin brass, blackened, satin relieved, clear coated	US5
610	Satin brass, blackened, bright relieved, clear coated	US7
611	Bright bronze, clear coated	US9
612	Satin bronze, clear coated	US10
613	Oxidized satin bronze, oil rubbed	US10B
616	Satin bronze, blackened, satin relieved, clear coated	US11
617	Dark oxidized satin bronze, bright relieved, clear coated	US13
618	Bright nickel plated, clear coated	US14
619	Satin nickel plated, clear coated	US15
620	Satin nickel plated, blackened, satin relieved	US15A
621	Nickel plated, blackened, matte, relieved, clear coated	US17a
622	Flat black coated	US19
623	Light oxidized bright bronze, clear coated	US20
624	Dark oxidized statuary bronze, clear coated	US20D
625	Bright chromium plated	US26
626	Satin chromium plated	US26D
627	Satin aluminum, clear coated	US27
628	Satin aluminum, clear anodized	US28
629	Bright stainless steel	US32
630	Satin stainless steel	US32D

attractive when two-tone oxidized finishes are specified. The darker oxidation remains in the lower surface areas, to accent the highlighted upper portions where the oxidation has been removed.

e. Some ornamental finishes are actually the result of using "handmade" processes to achieve an effect such as aging. Finishes are many and varied; a few of the more common ones are given in table 14.3, following the listing of the Builders Hardware Manufacturers Association. In the table, the nearest US equivalents are also given.

15 Plastics and Coatings

PLASTICS AND RESINS

15.1 General

a. Plastics, also known as *synthetic resins*, have entered into house construction in numerous ways. Because they have become important constituents of many coatings employed in buildings, they are combined with a discussion of coatings in this chapter. These plastics are a family of some 20 to 30 giant molecules called "high polymers." All plastic materials, at some stage, are plastic; i.e., they can be formed into whatever shape is desired, usually by pressure, heat, or both. Some are simply cast. Some plastics are plastic only once; having hardened, they cannot be softened. These are called *thermosetting*, because the earliest ones needed heat to harden them. Other plastics can be softened by heating and hardened by cooling any number of times. These are *thermoplastic*. These two types cover a wide range of properties, from soft and flexible to hard and brittle, from fully transparent to fully opaque, from highly weather-resistant to rapidly deteriorating outdoors, and from infinitely colorable to only moderately colorable.

b. All plastics can be destroyed by fire, but some do not support their own combustion and, in the presence of a fire, are slow-enough burning to be considered noncombustible under code provisions. Others burn rapidly. Plastics may burn with a clear flame and give off nothing but carbon dioxide and water, or they may give off a good deal of smoke and noxious or toxic gases. Here they are similar to materials such as wood and fabric.

c. The outdoor durability or weathering resistance of plastics varies with the materials and their compositions. Some have been exposed outdoors 25 years or more and have stood up well. Others have deteriorated badly in less than a year, depending on the composition and exposure conditions. None of the plastics have been used in buildings as long as wood, stone, brick, concrete, and glass.

d. Plastics unmodified by fillers or reinforcements have variable strength properties, generally comparable to those of good-quality wood parallel to the grain and to the compressive strength of commonly used concrete. When a plastic is reinforced with high-strength filaments such as glass or carbon, its strength approaches that of the best high-strength steel at a fraction of the weight. These composites are widely employed in space vehicles.

e. The stiffness of unmodified plastic materials, by and large, is low. Some are soft and flexible; others are hard and rigid, but even these are less stiff than wood parallel to the grain. When a plastic is modified with high-strength fibers, such as glass, its stiffness is considerably increased (section 15.6ff.). The toughness of some plastics is outstanding, and their resistance to wear and abrasion may also be excellent. Flexibility may be extremely high.

f. Although plastics are used without alteration, their properties are commonly changed by modifiers. Among the most important are:

plasticizers; change hard rigid materials to soft and flexible,

fillers; change strength, hardness, durability, cost, and other properties,

colors; dyes for transparent colors, pigments for opaque colors.

15.2 Thermoplastic Materials

Among the most important of the thermoplastics used in house construction are the following.

a. Polyvinyl chloride (PVC), usually called simply "vinyl," is fairly hard and rigid, but when it is combined with plasticizers or copolymerized with other plastics it becomes soft and flexible. PVC may be transparent or may be colored with dyes and pigments.

b. Acrylics are widely used for tough, breakage-resistant skylights and glazing and for lighting fixtures. They have infinite colorability with either dyes or pigments, and may range from fully transparent to fully opaque.

c. Polystyrene has excellent electrical characteristics, is fully transparent to fully opaque, and is infinitely colorable with dyes or pigments. Normally brittle, when copolymerized with acrylonitrile and butadiene it becomes tough, impact-resistant ABS. In building, polystyrene's chief use is as foam for thermal insulation (section 11.11).

d. Nylon is tough and wear-resistant, and is easily molded into intricate shapes. It is not fully transparent and has moderate colorability.

e. Polyethylene, a soft, flexible plastic, is most often used in building as film. When unmodified, it is waxy, light gray, and easily molded into a large variety of shapes, e.g., drainage pipe. Carbon black greatly increases its weather resistance.

f. Cellulosics include primarily cellulose nitrate, cellulose acetate, and cellulose acetate butyrate. These materials are used for extruded architectural moldings and molded articles such as impact-resistant tool handles. Cellulose nitrate is highly flammable, especially as thin sheet or film; but cellulose acetate and cellulose acetate butyrate burn relatively slowly. Cellulose nitrate provides tough lacquer (section 15.10).

g. Polyvinyl butyral is mainly used as an exceptionally tough upholstering material, with or without fabric backing. It forms the interlayer in safety glass.

h. Polypropylene, similar to polyethylene in some of its properties, is somewhat harder and more temperature-resistant than ordinary polyethylene. It is used for piping and for intricate molded parts generally.

i. Polycarbonate, a tough transparent material, is used mainly for applications where the breakage hazard is high. It has many of the same uses in building as acrylic.

j. Fluorocarbons, exemplified by the commercial material Teflon, have outstanding resistance to high and low temperatures and to weathering generally. They also have extremely low coefficients of friction. Other fluorocarbons are used as protective surfacing films against weathering and attack by sunlight.

15.3 Thermosetting Plastics

a. Phenolics are the oldest of the thermosetting plastics. In houses they are used mainly for knobs, handles, switchplates, small electrical parts, and similar items. They are dark in color, ranging from green through purple, red, blue, and black. For ordinary molding, they are modified with wood flour; for electrical purposes, with mica.

b. Urea formaldehyde and melamine formaldehyde are used for light-colored molded cases. In building, the major use of melamine is as a constituent of the decorative high-pressure laminates widely employed for counter tops, table tops, and furniture (section 15.7).

c. Polyesters of the unsaturated variety are mainly constituents of reinforced plastics (section 15.6). The *epoxies* find widespread use in building applications as adhesives, because they bond strongly to many different kinds of materials. They also provide surface finishes (section 15.11).

d. Polyurethanes are mainly employed as foams for insulation, as soft, flexible upholstery materials, and for tough surface finishes. They are joined by polyisocyanurates and tripolymers for foams.

e. Silicones are mainly used in building as sealants for joints and for difficult glazing applications. They are also applied as liquid sprays to masonry walls for increased moisture repellency. Their weathering resistance is generally outstanding, as is their resistance to higher temperatures than are normally allowable with plastics.

PLASTIC-BASED COMPOSITE MATERIALS

15.4 General

Plastics are often combined with other materials to form composites that have properties unattainable by the individual constituents. The most common composites are particulate, fibrous, and laminar.

15.5 Particulates

In particulate composites, particles are embedded in a matrix. The most important particulate composite, of course, is portland-cement concrete (section 4.15). If unsaturated polyesters are substituted for portland cement and suitable aggregates are used, a "polyester concrete" results. It has higher tensile strength, substantially equal compressive strength, and great toughness in comparison with portland-cement concrete, but less fire resistance, although it can be made to achieve a non-flammable rating. Particle boards are made of wood particles bonded with urea or phenolic resins (section 5.3m ff.). Fine inorganic solids, such as marble dust combined with epoxide or other binders, are used for molded lavatories and similar fixtures.

15.6 Fibrous Composites

When fibers are incorporated into a plastic matrix, a fibrous composite results. The most commonly used fiber is glass. Glass drawn into extremely fine fibers is as strong as the strongest steel, at one-third the weight. Such fibers may be incorporated into plastic matrices, most commonly polyester. The resulting material is a *glass-fiber-reinforced plastic* often called *fiberglass*, although glass fiber is only one of the two constituents. The glass fiber may be incorporated as continuous filaments, or as chopped fibers varying from $\frac{1}{2}''$ to $2''$ in length in a random matted configuration, or as a woven fabric. For building purposes, the most common is chopped fiber. Carbon, graphite, and aramid fibers are employed in high-performance applications such as space vehicles, at higher cost than glass.

15.7 Laminates

Laminar composites consist of sheets or layers of material bonded together and frequently interpenetrated by a resin binder. In decorative high-pressure laminates, a decorative facing sheet, usually printed paper but possibly fabric or wood veneer, is saturated with melamine formaldehyde, and over that is laid a thin film of melamine formaldehyde in a cellulosic veil. This decorative sheet is backed with layers of high-strength kraft paper impregnated with a phenolic resin. The combination is pressed and fused together at 1,000 to 2,000 lb per sq in. at a temperature of 350°F. The resulting decorative sheet is applied to a variety of substrates such as plywood and particle board.

15.8 Sandwiches

a. Structural sandwiches consist of two relatively thin facings of hard, dense, strong material bonded to a relatively thick core of softer, weaker less stiff material. The geometry of the sandwich results in stiffness and strength combined with lightness. In addition, the facings provide the appearance and resistance to weathering and wear and tear; the core provides most of the thermal insulation and supports the facings against buckling under load, and the combination, in addition to strength and stiffness, provides whatever acoustical value and fire resistance there may be.
b. Common facing materials for dwelling-house sandwiches are plywood, hardboard, high-pressure laminates, and metals such as aluminum and plain or coated steel. Cores include foamed plastics, phenolic-impregnated kraft paper honeycomb, egg-crate construction, wood strips, plywood, particle board, fiber board, and inorganics such as silicates.

15.9 Applications in House Construction

A few building applications are briefly listed below and are referred to in other parts of this book:
counter tops (section 13.16)
floor coverings (sections 13.19, 13.25, 13.26)
foams (sections 5.12, 11.11)
gutters and leaders (sections 9.5, 9.7, 9.8)
piping (sections 3.5–3.7)
sealants (section 7.6)

sky lights (section 7.28)
vapor and moisture barriers (sections 4.27, 11.13ff.)
wall coverings (section 12.3)
windows (sections 7.20, 7.24)

COATINGS

15.10 General

Protective and decorative coatings employed in dwelling-house construction consist largely of transparent to opaque white or colored systems comprising a liquid vehicle or binder that hardens by chemical action or evaporation, with or without pigments and other ingredients. They are commonly classified as paints, varnishes, lacquers, and stains.

Paints are essentially mixtures of drying liquids acting as vehicles or binders for various kinds of pigments in suspension. Other ingredients may be added for special purposes. Binders may be natural oils, resins, resins and oils, latexes, or water (section 15.2). Pigments may be opaque or transparent (sections 15.12, 15.13). Other ingredients include driers and thinners or solvents (section 15.14). Fillers (section 15.14) may be employed, as well as with varnishes, lacquers, and stains.

Varnishes are resins essentially similar to the oil-resin binders in paints without the pigments. At one time commonly consisting of fossil or synthetic resins combined with linseed or tung oil, varnishes today are mostly based on alkyd, epoxy, phenolic, and urethane resins (section 15.3).

Lacquers used in building applications are completely unlike the sap-based oriental lacquers. Building lacquers are solutions of resins in volatile solvents. As the solvent evaporates, a hardened film of the resin is left on the surface. Water-white lacquer is transparent with no apparent color; clear is transparent but may have some color such as amber; flat is clear lacquer plus clear pigment to diffuse reflected light. *Shellac* can be considered a special kind of lacquer consisting of the exudation of the lac insect dissolved in alcohol. It may be the natural color (orange) or bleached (white). *Builders' enamels* are suspensions of pigments in lacquer.

Stains (oil-based or water-based), used mostly on wood, are intermediate between paint and varnish, with pigment contents ranging from light tints and high transparency to "solid" or highly opaque colors. They are employed chiefly to impart color or tint without hiding the surface, rather accentuating features such as texture. Oil stains are oil-soluble powders in oils such as alkyds (section 15.11). Water stains contain water-soluble pigments in water. These tend to raise the grain of wood and may need sanding. Non-grain-raising stains have water-soluble powders in non-aqueous solvents. Water stains may be based on acrylic emulsions (section 15.11).

15.11 Binders, Vehicles, and Film Formers

a. Among the principal coating systems in general use are those based upon the following:

Natural Drying Oils. Paints may employ drying oils alone, but they are mostly combined, e.g., alkyds (see below). These oils do not dry; they harden by oxidation. The outstanding natural drying oil has for years been linseed, "raw" as pressed from flax seed, and heat-treated with chemicals, or "boiled." Among the other important natural drying oils are tung oil, oiticica oil, safflower oil, soybean oil, dehydrated castor oil, and fish oil. Natural oils may be subject to mildew unless specially treated, and may bleach in sunlight while yellowing in the dark; soy and safflower oil are superior in this respect.

Alkyds. These are synthetic resins modified with various vegetable oils (soya, safflower, linseed, tung, etc.) to produce clear resins much harder than ordinary oils. Because of their versatility, they have displaced natural oils used alone, the properties of the resultant film depending on the relative volumes of resin and oil. Hardening is by both evaporation of solvent and oxidation. Other ingredients may be added for such features as increased color retention, resistance to blistering and dirt collection, and gloss retention. They should not be used directly on alkaline surfaces such as fresh concrete, masonry, plaster, and stucco.

Latex paints. These are based upon water emulsions. The most widely used emulsions are acrylic, vinyl-acrylic, styrene-butadiene, and vinyl acetate. The use of these paints has increased rapidly because of their ease of application, quick drying, freedom from solvent odor, minimum fire hazard, and ease of cleanup with soap and water only. They adhere well to many surfaces, have good color retention, and are of varying degrees of flexibility. They should be used above 50°F and must be kept from freezing. Traditional water paints use water as the vehicle. In calcimine, glue or casein is added; pigment is powdered calcium carbonate with or without added colored pigments. Whitewash is lime and water.

Epoxy and epoxy ester. Catalyzed two-part epoxy coatings are mixed just prior to application, since their pot life ranges only from a few minutes to a day. A chemical reaction produces a hard film, resistant to solvents, abrasion, traffic, and cleaning agents. Epoxy esters, produced by modifying epoxies with oils, harden upon oxidation without catalyst, and, therefore, have no pot-life restrictions. Less hard and chemically resistant than catalyzed epoxies, they are easy to apply, they dry quickly, and they produce hard, tough films commonly used as single-component paints. Epoxies, although durable, tend to yellow and chalk in exterior applications.

Polyurethanes. These can produce especially abrasion-resistant fast-hardening coatings. They may be made as two-component formulations that are mixed just prior to use and have variable pot life, depending on the formulation, or they may be one-component formulations that cure by evaporation and reaction with moisture in the air (30 to 90 percent relative humidity). Some formulations are modified with oils and alkyds.

Vinyl-solution coatings. These solutions of PVC and vinyl esters dry rapidly by evaporation of the solvent, so spraying is the best method of application. Individual coats are thin, but to build up thickness, multiple coats can be applied in rapid succession because of the quick drying. Vinyl coats characteristically have low gloss, high flexibility, and inertness to water, but are sensitive to some solvents. Weather resistance is excellent.

Oleoresinous coatings. These are primarily oil-based but contain resins that make them harder, with higher gloss and better durability than straight oil coatings. At the other end of the scale are resins, modified with oil in varying amounts, that harden by evaporation and oxidation.

b. An important consideration in paint formulation is the pigment volume concentration (PVC), the ratio of pigment to total volume of pigment and binder. The critical point (CPVC) is the formulation at which there is just enough binder to coat each pigment particle and fill the voids between them. Less binder tends toward "flat" finishes; more binder tends toward increased gloss and hardness. The abbreviation PVC as used here is not to be confused with polyvinyl chloride, commonly called vinyl.

15.12 Pigments

a. Pigments hide, color, or do both to a greater or lesser extent, and may perform some other functions such as corrosion resistance or ultraviolet absorption.

b. White pigments are by far the most important, and generally form the base of colored or tinted paints as well. Pigments are held in the vehicle and fill the many pores and interstices which otherwise would be present in the hardened film formed by the vehicle. Opaque white pigments impart color and hide the surface.

c. Basic lead carbonate — white lead — is the oldest and formerly one of the most widely employed white pigments. It mixes well with drying oils and is an excellent base for tints. With good-quality drying oils it forms an excellent paint film of high durability. As is true of lead pigments generally, its use is restricted because of possible toxic effects. Basic lead sulfate, considered interchangeable with white lead, is also banned.

d. Zinc oxide is used by itself or in combination with other pigments. Its color is unaffected by atmospheric gases, and it is therefore often used around seashores and in chemical plants or other areas where hydrogen sulfide would discolor some other pigments.

e. Titanium pigments have the highest hiding power per pound of any of the white pigments. Because of this, and their other generally good qualities, they have rapidly become some of the most widely used of all the white pigments, especially in mixtures. Of the two commonly used types, anatase promotes chalking, sometimes excessively; rutile causes much less (section 15.17).

f. The most commonly employed transparent pigments are barium sulfate, magnesium silicate, silica, clay, and calcium carbonate. Transparent pigments, often called fillers and extenders, have essentially the same functions as colored pigments at lower cost, but have no marked coloring or hiding power.

g. For maximum durability outdoors, inorganic pigments are needed. For indoors and where maximum durability is not required, organic pigments generally offer a greater range of colors, tints, and brilliance than inorganic ones. Among the inorganic pigments, some of the best for color and general usefulness are lead-bearing, including chrome yellows, chrome oranges, and chrome greens. Lead-free pigments include iron oxides (red) and iron blues, ultramarine blue, siennas (brown), nickel titanate, zinc yellow, cadmium compounds, and chrome oxides. Organic pigments encompass a large assortment of chemical types, yielding a wide range of colors and tints. Blacks are based on carbon, such as lampblack.

h. Metallic aluminum is used in two forms: finely ground metal in dry powder form, or very thin metal foil broken into very small flakes and dispersed in a thinner to provide a paste. When spread on a surface in a binder such as varnish, the flakes overlap or "leaf." Bronze leafing pigments provide a range of simulated gold colors. Zinc dust used over metal (ferrous) can afford a considerable degree of corrosion protection.

i. Corrosion protection of ferrous metals, in addition to the zinc dust mentioned above, is afforded by red lead and by zinc chromate, both used widely either as primers or complete paint systems.

15.13 Mixed Pigments

Mixed pigments are often favored over pigments of only one type. Various formulations of differing mixes are available with different white pigments such as zinc and titanium, colored pigments, and transparent pigments combined to meet the requirements of particular applications. By mixing pigments, an attempt is made to obtain some of the best characteristics of each while minimizing deficiencies, at minimum cost.

15.14 Additives and Fillers

a. *Driers* are catalysts that hasten the oxidation and hardening of oil and alkyd binders. Once mostly lead oxides, they are now mainly cobalt and manganese compounds or soaps. Manganese, otherwise suitable, tends to discolor white paints. Auxiliaries to the primary cobalt and manganese "driers" promote uniform drying.

b. *Thinners* or solvents are needed to "thin" or reduce the viscosity of coatings, to promote adhesion, and to assist in "leveling" the wet film to uniform thickness. For oils and alkyds, the most common thinner or solvent is mineral spirits, derived from petroleum. Turpentine, at one time almost the exclusive thinner for oils, has largely disappeared because of cost and odor. Epoxies require more complex combinations. Other thinners include naphtha, and solvents with slower evaporation rates for use in hot weather.

c. Other additives include ingredients for color and gloss retention, resistance to blistering and dirt collection, anti-skinning and coalescing agents, defoamers, emulsifiers, freeze-thaw stabilizers, wetting agents, and preservatives.

d. Fillers are needed with those hardwoods whose large pores must be filled if a smooth finish is to be attained. The more commonly found "open-grained" woods are ash, butternut, chestnut, elm, hickory, mahogany, African mahogany, Philippine hardwoods, oak, and walnut. The more commonly found hardwoods which do not have large pores (close-grained woods) and therefore do not need filling are alder, aspen, basswood, beech, birch, cherry, cottonwood, gum, maple, poplar, and sycamore. None of the softwoods requires filling. Birch does not have to be filled to obtain a smooth surface but has pores large enough to be accentuated by colored fillers.

e. Fillers ordinarily consist of ground silica paste which is thinned to a thick creamy consistency before application. They are spread on the surface and thoroughly rubbed in; then the excess is wiped off, leaving the large pores filled with the paste. Colors may be added.

15.15 Formulations

a. With so many coatings, bases, and combinations to choose from, a great multiplicity of combinations can be formulated to meet the needs of exterior and interior protective and decorative coatings for many different materials under diverse climatic and other environmental conditions. It is manifestly impossible to cover them all, and only a few indicative types can be examined briefly.

b. For wood siding and trim, depending on the degree of gloss and whether only white or tints or deep colors are wanted, systems may be based upon linseed or similar drying oil, alkyd, acrylic latex, PVC latex, and alkyd enamel. For staining, such as siding and trim, redwood and red cedar shingles and shakes, stains may be based on alkyds and acrylics. If clear, tough finishes are wanted, as on siding or hardwood exterior doors, varnishes and urethanes may be chosen.

c. Brick, stucco, and concrete walls free of chalky deposits, and concrete block and cinder block walls may be coated with PVA, PVC, acrylic emulsions, alkyd-epoxy, or alkyd-urethane combinations.

d. For ferrous metals that must be protected against corrosion, a rust-inhibitive primer (e.g., zinc dust, zinc oxide, or zinc chromate) is often used, followed by finish coat or coats. Depending on the color and degree of gloss wanted, systems may be based on alkyd, acrylic, and epoxy esters with zinc chromate, red lead, or aluminum flake. Galvanized metal is a special case. It must be free of the oil normally left as a result of processing. Cleaning may be by extended weathering or solvents.

e. Aluminum may be coated with systems based on alkyd, acrylic, epoxy esters, or oleoresinous binders.

f. Drywall construction may be coated, e.g., with alkyd, acrylic latex, vinyl-acrylic latex, and epoxies. Wallboards with unfinished paper surfaces, e.g., gypsum board, must be sealed first.

g. Plaster, depending on the color, texture, hardness, and wear-resistance wanted, may be coated with alkyd, acrylic latex, PVA latex, or styrene-butadiene.

h. Painted interior woodwork and trim may be coated with alkyd enamels, acrylic latex, drying-oil paints, or alkyd-drying oil paints, depending on the color, degree of gloss, and hardness wanted.

i. Natural and stained finishes on interior woodwork and trim may be achieved with shellac, lacquers, and varnishes based on alkyds, urethane, vinyls, and copolymers. Latex, oil, and water-based stains may be employed for colored transparent finishes.

j. Wood floors may be finished with shellac, standard varnishes, or coatings based on alkyds, epoxies, and polyurethanes, the latter for especially hard finishes.

k. Finishes on concrete and concrete block include cement, drying oils, acrylic, PVA, alkyd, epoxy, styrene-butadiene, and two-component urethane, the latter especially for floors. Where concrete is below grade and dampness is a problem, alkyd resin and chlorinated rubber is a useful combination.

l. For fire resistance, *intumescent paints* based on modified PVC latex may be applied. When heated, as by the approach of flames, these paints evolve an inert gas that causes the paint to bubble into a froth that insulates the surface below.

15.16 Application

a. For successful application, the surface to be coated must be properly prepared. Most coating systems require clean, dry surfaces, especially free of grease, oil, dust, and moisture, although some

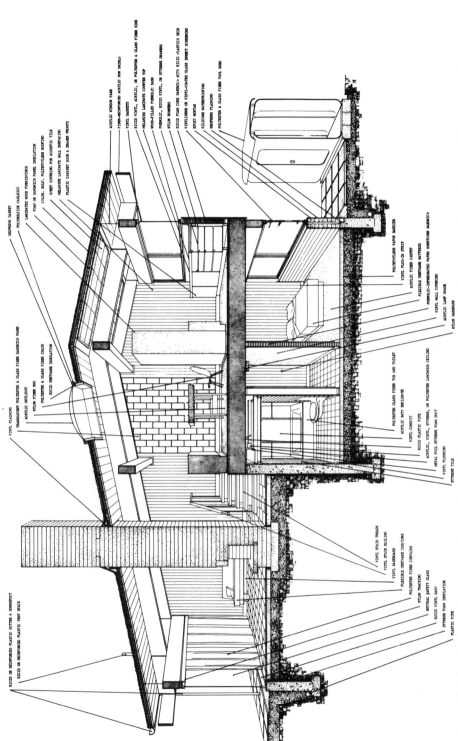

Figure 15.1 Illustration of hypothetical house showing where plastics may be applicable. Source: Hamilton, Goody, and Clancy, Architects.

formulations can be applied to damp or even wet surfaces. Strongly alkaline surfaces such as fresh concrete and plaster may have to be neutralized if oil-based paints are to be applied. Resinous wood, such as knots and pitch pockets, are likely to strike through ordinary paints, and should be coated (e.g., with shellac) over the prime coat before finish coats are applied. With the many formulations available, manufacturers' directions must be followed.

b. Most coating systems require a primer or prime coat, followed by one or two finish coats, although some systems can be applied in one coat, especially if sprayed. Application is usually by brush, roller, or spray.

c. The thicknesses of the various coats are critical. Recommended thicknesses for prime and subsequent coats are often given in terms of square feet per gallon to be covered, or, more accurately, in wet film thickness. This latter thickness is usually expressed in mils (thousandths of an inch). Wet film thickness can be converted to square feet per gallon by noting that one gallon is nearly 230 cu in. One square foot is 144 sq in., from which it follows that one gallon, or 230 cu in., will cover nearly 1,600 sq ft, one mil thick. If a thickness of 4 mils is called for, the spreading rate is 400 sq ft per gallon.

15.17 Paint Deterioration and Defects

a. Paint films are expected to deteriorate with time and to require renewal at intervals. All other things being equal, the most rapid deterioration takes place where exposure to sunlight is most intense and prolonged. Several stages are observed:

soiling, in which dirt collects on the surface

flatting, in which the gloss disappears

chalking, in which the surface becomes powdery and the accumulated dirt is at least partly thrown off, leaving the surface dull but fairly clean

fissuring, either checking (in which small superficial cracks eventually penetrate to the wood) or cracking (in which the fissures pass through to the wood almost immediately)

disintegration, either crumbling (which develops from checking and causes small fragments cut off by the checking to fall away) or flaking (in which the small scales caused by cracking curl up at the edges and finally fall away)

b. From the time that deterioration in the form of cracks reaches the wood surface, the nature of the wood controls the speed with which further deterioration occurs. The density of the surface, especially the proportion and width of summerwood bands, markedly influences the rate of deterioration after this stage.

c. Chalking pigments may tend to soil more rapidly than others in the first stages, especially in urban areas, but chalking usually sets in rather early and the dirt is thrown off readily, leaving a clean, if faded and chalky, surface. Rutile titanium and zinc oxide generally reduce excessive soiling and chalking.

d. If surfaces are repainted before deterioration reaches the wood, it is seldom necessary to remove the old paint. If disintegration reaches the wood, removal of old paint often cannot be avoided.

e. Defects may be divided into two types: defects caused by poor paint, and defects caused by improper preparation and maintenance of the surface of the wood or by poor workmanship.

Widespread checking and alligatoring. The surface is unusually heavily checked, or is broken up into a larger and more prominent alligator pattern than is normal. The cause may be too-soft undercoats, either because the formula was wrong or because not enough time elapsed between application of coats.

Heavy cracking and scaling. Pigments which promote hardness and brittleness in the film are generally responsible for this condition.

Blistering and peeling. Moisture in the wood behind the paint film almost always causes this condition, either because the wood was too wet when it was painted or because moisture has found its way behind the paint film. Incompatible successive coats may also cause this and alligatoring, cracking, and scaling.

Spotting, or loss of gloss. This is almost always caused by too-thin paint films, which cause excessive absorption of oil by the wood and permit early loss of gloss, fading, and chalking.

Washing. Soluble pigments in the paint film may be washed out by rains and run down over foundations or other surfaces, causing streaks and causing the film to lose its hiding power.

Wrinkling. Excessively thick coats of paint may skin over quickly without hardening underneath until wrinkles develop.

Running and sagging. These are associated with wrinkling in that they are also caused by too thick coats of paint. A paint high in oil content and applied too freely is apt to run down the wall, or to form a surface skin and then to sag under its own weight.

Excessive soiling. If the surface film contains too much oil, it is apt to be soft and tacky and to collect dirt in excessive amounts.

Mildew. Mildew may be mistaken for soiling. It is apt to occur in warm, damp, shaded areas in which ventilation is poor.

16 Manufactured Housing and Mobile Homes

MANUFACTURED HOUSING

16.1 General

a. The preceding chapters have discussed the principles of house construction in the field, the customary procedure by which houses are built. Manufactured housing, the production of complete houses in the shop, has become a sizable segment of the housing market. Shop fabrication has introduced increased utilization of mechanized tools, assembly-line production, and sophisticated production equipment such as robotics, thereby lowering the labor segment appreciably. In spite of such changes, manufactured housing is essentially based on the platform frame or "2 × 4" or "stick-built" system described in this book, a highly flexible open system adaptable to either site or factory operations. Books can be and have been written about manufactured housing. This chapter briefly sets forth only a few principles and typical details.

b. Many elements of shop fabrication have already become common in site construction, including roof trusses (section 5.33o), prehung prefinished doors (section 13.11), prefinished cabinets (section 13.16), and other prefinished items such as flooring, wallboard, and primed or finished wood, metal, and plastic siding.

c. Manufactured housing, or prefabrication, is hardly new. Prefabricated house parts are reported to have been shipped from the east coast of the United States to California and Australia during their gold rushes. Prefabricated barracks and field hospitals were employed during the Civil War. There are numerous other examples.

d. Various degrees of factory fabrication of houses are practiced. "Precutting" is the oldest and simplest form. This method involves factory cutting of the shell elements, which are then marked, bundled, and shipped to the building site. Precut packages usually include components such as doors, windows, and all other elements, including nails and shingles, necessary to complete the shell. Precutting increasingly uses automated and computer-linked machines, linked in turn to com-

The section on manufactured housing was prepared with the major assistance of Frances Fleetwood, a graduate student in the Department of Architecture at MIT. The section on mobile homes was prepared by Arthur D. Bernhardt and Norman Y. Quinn, with assistance from Jeffrey Ng. Eric Dluhosch reviewed the chapter and offered many suggestions.

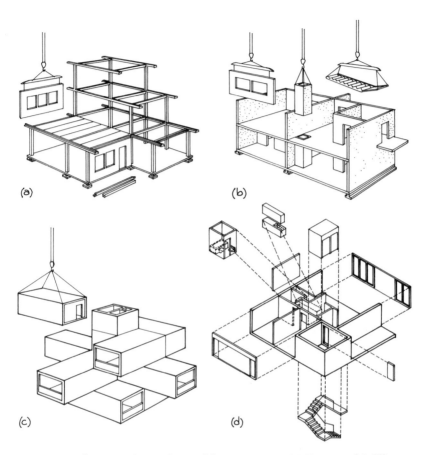

Figure 16.1 Elements of manufactured home systems. (a) Frame and infill: post-and-beam frame supporting infilling wall, floor, and roof panels. (b) Panel: load-bearing panels form a complete shell. (c) Volumetric elements (big boxes, modules), stacked to form a building. (d) Combination of various elements.

puter-aided design to allow considerable variations in design without increasing production costs.

e. The "frame and infill" (figure 16.1a) is the next step in the sequence of industrialization. It consists of a structural frame comprising the carrying elements of the floor, the walls, and the roof (e.g., girders, posts, trusses), to which are attached infill elements (e.g., small wall, floor, and roof panels) capable of transmitting imposed loads such as wind and live loads to the structural elements. Post and beam construction (section 5.40) lends itself to this approach.

f. "Panelized houses" (figure 16.1b) involve precutting all shell elements and assembling the wall panels and, sometimes, floor and roof panels. Windows and doors are usually inserted into the wall panels. The panelized package includes the many precut pieces and elements needed to complete the shell at the site.

g. "Volume elements" or big boxes (figure 16.1c), often referred to as *modules,* are completely factory-fabricated three-dimensional dwellings or segments of dwellings. They are finished as completely as possible at the factory. Bathrooms, kitchens, and interior finishes are all factory-installed. The foundation and the utility hookups comprise most of the work needed to complete the dwellings at the site. The materials and methods employed vary from system to system and from manufacturer to manufacturer.

h. Many systems combine aspects of frame and infill, panels, and volumetric elements (figure 16.1d).

i. In this chapter, it will be neither possible nor desirable to discuss factory prefabrication or fabrication in detail. The essential features differentiating manufactured homes from standard on-site construction will be presented briefly.

j. Manufactured houses have become international in scope. Scandinavian manufacturers, in particular, are shipping elements to the United States and other parts of the world. Japanese manufacturers, who have adopted the "2 × 4" system, are also shipping abroad, as are manufacturers in the United States.

16.2 Precut Construction

Precut houses differ little from standard construction in detail and theory. They may be assembled more quickly than conventional houses since most of the cutting is done at the factory. The principal advantages are simplified purchasing of materials and step-by-step directions for erecting a selected house. This type of manufactured home often appeals to the novice owner-builder.

16.3 Panel Construction

a. Much panel construction is adapted from standard platform construction in order to meet differing local codes. A typical simple panel consists of studs 16″ or 24″ on centers and an exterior grade of plywood or other board or factory-applied siding, with a down lap to cover the exposed floor construction at the edge (figure 16.2). Insulation and interior finishing material are generally applied in the field,

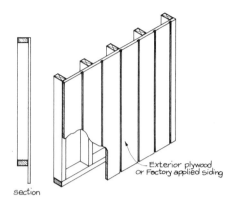

section

Figure 16.2 Typical wall panel element, based on platform framing: studs, sole plate, and plywood with downlap.

after wiring has been installed in the wall, thereby conforming to standard practices.

b. Other panelized homes are being produced from stressed-skin and sandwich panels (section 5.45), which are the most efficient structural wood systems for walls, floors, and roofs.

c. Wall panels are classified by their lengths. "Small" panels range from 2' to 8' in length. Any panels larger than 8' are called "large" and may range from 9' to 40' in length. Panels longer than 40' may require special road permits for their transport. Panels smaller than 16' usually do not require cranes or special mechanical equipment. Small panels may be lifted by a standard building crew of four men.

d. Panel height and length are typically controlled by the economies available by using standard material sizes such as 4' and 5' widths and 8' and 9' lengths. For example, panels tend to be close to 4', 5', 8', 10', etc. in length.

e. Panel systems may be either load-bearing or post-and-beam (section 5.40). Load-bearing panel systems are most common and economical, especially when large panels are used, but small load-bearing panel systems offer more design flexibility. Post-and-beam panel systems are gaining in popularity. They are often used with stressed-skin or sandwich (section 5.45) infill, in which the posts and beams support the structure. However, stressed-skin or structural sandwich panels may be used as the total load-bearing wall, floor, and roof construction.

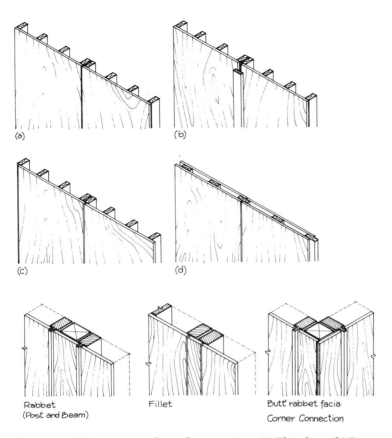

Figure 16.3 Various types of panel connections. (a) Plain butt. (b) Butt covered with batten. (c) Lapped joint. (d) Tongue and groove with covers bonded to ribs for stressed skin. (below) Variants with post, fillet, and corner.

16.4 Panel Construction Details

a. Panel construction differs from traditional construction in the details of panel connection. Panel joints are either edge or right-angle connections. They can be considered part of the traditional family of wood joints, except that panel joints involve two and sometimes three elements: the exterior skin, the frame, and occasionally the interior skin. Often one element in the panel may butt while another element may pass, forming a lap joint.

b. Several possible joint configurations are shown in figure 16.3. These are all adaptations of the types of joints discussed in chapter 13.

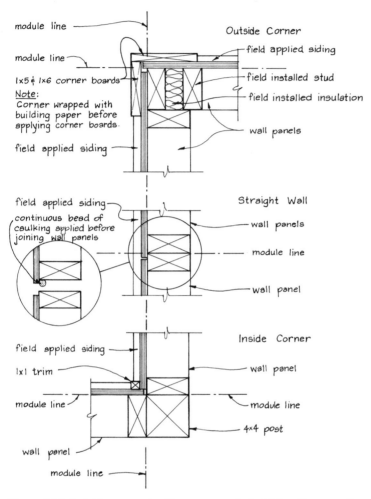

Figure 16.4 Outside corner, inside corner, and straight-wall connection details of panel construction. Source: Acorn Structures.

c. The most important step in the erection of a manufactured home is starting with a level and square foundation. Half-inch tolerances are usually acceptable and can be accounted for in the sill details. Time spent in starting right by aligning and leveling the sill is repaid many times in the simplicity with which the rest of the building goes up. Conversely, careless alignment of the sills causes recurring problems throughout erection.

d. Figure 16.4 shows details of outside and inside corners and straight-wall connections. Corner boards, trim strip, and siding are

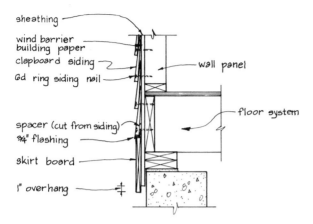

sheathing

wind barrier
building paper
clapboard siding
6d ring siding nail

wall panel

floor system

spacer (cut from siding)
¾" flashing

skirt board

1" overhang

Figure 16.5 Sill details of panel construction. Sheathing downlap projects down beyond top of foundation wall. Siding and skirt board are field-applied. Source: Acorn Structures.

applied in the field, after wind-barrier paper. The framing crew installs an additional stud plus insulation at the outside corner, and a 4 × 4 post at the inside corner. At the straight-wall connection, the sheathing of one panel overlaps the stud of the adjacent panel. A caulking bead makes the joint tight.

e. Figure 16.5 shows a sill detail. The sill is raised above the foundation wall and projects beyond it to allow leveling and straightening to compensate for slight unevenness in the foundation. The downlap of the sheathing projects down beyond the top of the foundation. Clapboards, skirt board, and flashing are field-applied.

f. Steps in the erection of a typical panel system are shown in figures 16.6–16.9. The floor consists of precut joists and headers and precut panelboard rapidly assembled on the foundation. Wall panels and roof trusses all come in one truckload. Wall panels are placed and roof trusses upended into position. Roof panelboard is nailed into place, and the house is closed in in one day. Interior partitions are all non-bearing and are assembled later from precut stock.

16.5 Volumetric Elements

a. Also called *modules,* these "big boxes" may consist of factory-assembled three-dimensional units employing standard framing, stressed skin, sandwiches, or combinations. The obvious advantage is that exteriors and (especially) interiors can be more nearly completely

Figure 16.6 Floor of precut joists.

Figure 16.7 Truckload of wall panels and roof trusses.

Figure 16.8 Erecting wall panels.

finished in the factory than is the case with other systems. Disadvantages are the bulk of the units, transportation restrictions on size, possible greater difficulty of making field connections, and lessened flexibility of design.

b. Figure 16.10 shows large volumetric elements being hoisted and stacked to form two-story multiple housing. To a large extent, such elements are constructed in a conventional manner, although in many instances greater use of glued construction is employed, because of good shop control, than is normally possible in the field. Shop production is accelerated by shop equipment and assembly lines not readily adaptable in the field.

16.6 Flexibility in Design

One of the goals of panelized housing is the development of highly prefinished panels of a minimum number of standard sizes which can be put together in practically unlimited arrangements to meet the requirements of an individual family building on a specific site at the lowest possible cost in a minimum amount of time. Although most producers of panelized houses have traditionally tended to move in the direction of a standardized plan or series of plans and variants, the advent of computer-aided design and control of increasingly sophis-

Figure 16.9 Placing roof trusses.

ticated production equipment have considerably advanced the goal of flexible arrangement, utilizing standardized panels but not standardized plans.

MOBILE HOMES

16.7 General

a. Mobile homes represent the ultimate in completely prefabricated and largely furnished dwellings, ready to be transported on wheels

Figure 16.10 Volumetric units being stacked.

and connected to utilities at a permanent or temporary site and ready for occupancy.

b. Since its inception in the early 1920s, the mobile-home industry has developed as a major producer of housing. One of the industry's principal characteristics is its cost performance. Completely finished and furnished units have typically been produced at average F.O.B. factory prices substantially less than the equivalent per square foot costs for on-site home building. Transportation costs are variable. Because of high volume, it has been possible to design for the maximum use of the minimum amount of material, preassembly of components, mass purchasing, and efficient use of labor, accompanied by a corresponding high degree of organization and management.

c. The industry has developed a production and delivery system that integrates production, transportation, and distribution with financing, materials, land supply, and the regulatory functions of highway and building code regulation, taxation, and land-use controls. This chapter is limited to the characteristics of mobile-home construction.

d. Road restrictions limit dimensions and weights. There is essentially no flexibility; the purchaser takes the product as it is, especially the spacial arrangement. The same is true of equipment and such attributes as thermal and acoustical adequacy.

16.8 Product Rationale

a. The mobile-home industry's objective is to provide an easily standardized, low-cost living unit by fully exploiting the techniques of mass production to produce a unit transportable from the factory to its eventual site.

b. Aside from the requirements for transportability, many of the design criteria of the mobile home are similar to those for the conventional home. It must be a suitable shelter of dimensions usable by human beings. It must accommodate various generally needed facilities: lighting and electricity, waste and water transport, and heating or full air conditioning. It must be adequately insulated. It must be structurally sound.

c. Although the design criteria are similar to those of conventional homes, the physical details are radically different. An attempt is made to utilize the properties of materials to the fullest practical extent, avoiding many structural redundancies. Standardization and interchangeability of components promote fast assembly-line construction.

d. Mobile homes are commonly based on platform construction (section 5.6ff.), with aluminum and steel framing when economical.

e. In meeting the requirements of transportation, the mobile home consists of four major assemblies: chassis frame, floor assembly, wall assembly and roof assembly, plus cabinetry and windows and doors.

f. The chassis frame is the structural base, receiving all the vertical loads and transferring them either to the wheels when in transit or to the foundation at the stationary site. By contrast, in traditional homes,

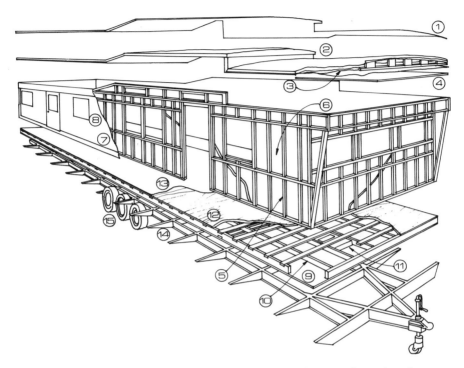

Figure 16.11 Details of mobile home. (1) Galvanized roof. (2) Insulation board over roof truss. (3) Fiberglass blanket insulation. (4) Polyethylene vapor barrier. (5) 2″ × 3″ studs 16″ o.c. (6) Natural wood interior panels. (7) Aluminum exterior sheet, baked-on enamel finish. (8) Awning-type windows. (9) Asphalt fiber board plus fiberglass blanket. (10) 6″ floor joists. (11) Aluminum heating ducts. (12) ⅝″ flooring panels. (13) Nylon carpet throughout except in bath, kitchen, dining area. (14) 10″ I beam. (15) Running gear.

the vertical loads are transferred directly to the foundation. Floor, wall, and roof components serve the same function as in traditional homes: enclosing and insulating the living space and producing a structure rigid against wind forces and other loads. Plumbing, electricity, and heating ducts are housed within these assemblies. Figure 16.11 shows an exploded view of a mobile home.

16.9 Chassis

a. The basic chassis frame differs from that of an automobile in load capacity and size. Common dimensions for the chassis are approximately 12′ to 14′ wide by approximately 60′ long, limited by highway requirements. The basic chassis consists of two steel I beams or tubular beams running the full length of the chassis. These are reinforced by steel cross-members. Outriggers are cantilevered from the sides of the two beams. In front of the chassis frame is an A-frame made up of two tongue members and the coupling mechanism, forming a hitch assembly.

b. The beams are typically 8″ or 10″ in depth, with built-in camber to ensure that the mobile home will be level when the weight of cabinet walls and other assemblies is added at points not supported by the axle assembly. The cross-bracing members are Z, I, or open-web joists spanning the distance between the beams. The tapered outriggers may be either open-web steel joists or steel beams. Additional longitudinal beams reinforce the axle assembly, giving added support at the area of load concentration.

c. The tongue members of the A-frame are usually 6″-deep steel beams or tubular steel. Each starts at the die-pressed steel hitch plate and extends through the front cross-member to the main longitudinal beams. The coupling mechanism is a socket through which the mobile home is coupled to the towing vehicle. The running gear includes springs, spring hangers, axles, bearings, wheels, brakes, rims, and tires.

16.10 Floor Systems

a. The standard floor system is attached directly to the chassis frame. It utilizes steel-spliced 2 × 4 to 2 × 8 floor joists spaced 16″ on centers, running parallel to the length of the chassis. Dadoed 1″ × 4″ cross-members spaced 48″ on centers act as cross-bracing for the floor joists and as nailers for the subfloor on top and under siding on the bottom. The standard decking material is 4′ × 8′ sheets of $\frac{5}{8}$″ plywood or particle board, screwed, nailed, and glued to the floor joists.

b. Ductwork and piping are laid principally in the longitudinal direction. For transverse distribution, openings in the floor joists must be made. Careful attention must be paid to the size and location of the opening to avoid structural weakness. The sizes of the horizontal distribution heating ducts are limited. Openings in the decking accommodate heating ducts, vents, furnace, and plumbing.

c. Typically, fiberglass blankets are placed between floor joists and heating ducts. Polyethylene vapor barrier is used beneath the fiberglass. Often, a vapor barrier is placed on the inside floor structure to protect the fiberglass from condensation. Next, a moisture-resistant, rigid insulation board is fastened in place. The floor system is thus sealed at the bottom against moisture and rodents.

d. The floor covering is typically nylon carpeting, vinyl, or both. Usually it is installed in one piece over a pad. The vinyl flooring may be tile or, generally, rolls the width of the floor section. A glued-on $\frac{1}{4}''$ overlay is often used over the subflooring, with the vinyl to give added wear and provide a cushion when walking.

e. Another floor system is the *cavity floor*. Rigid insulation board laid on top of the chassis cross-members serves as the bottom of both the chassis and the floor system, dropping the floor system area 4″ to 6″ and forming a "basement." This provides space for longitudinal plumbing pipes and heating ducts. Above the basement level is an upper level with floor joists placed transversely. Heating and plumbing occur at two levels, the main distribution longitudinal at the basement level and horizontal distribution connecting to this main spine at the upper level with heating ducts and plumbing parallel to the transverse floor joists. Other features, such as decking and joists, remain the same as in the standard floor system. The floor is rigidly secured to the chassis at each floor joist.

16.11 Walls

a. The wood framing of the sidewalls consists of a top and bottom plate with 2″ × 3″ studs spaced 16″ on centers reinforced by horizontal belt rails. At sidewall openings, the studs and headers are doubled. For reinforcement, $\frac{3}{4}''$ diagonal steel strapping ties the floor, walls, and roof into one complete unit, primarily to aid in resistance against sliding caused by loading, or overturning by wind.

b. To ensure further continuity between exterior walls and floors, the walls may be tied directly to the floor system or may have wall studs extend past the bottom plate and lap the longitudinal floor side members.

c. Horizontal bracing is provided by two to four, usually three, 1″ × 3″ dadoed belt rails extending over the full length of the wall. All wood framing members are both glued and nailed at the joints with metal splice plates at critical points. Bottom plates of walls are either glue-nailed or bolted to the floor. Floor-to-wall connections are reinforced with steel plates. Steel gusset plates may occur at the corners.

d. Standard fiberglass insulation varies from $1\frac{1}{8}''$ to 2″ blankets to $2\frac{5}{8}''$ batts.

e. The common but not the only exterior finish is crimped 0.024″ prefinished aluminum. The color is paint, baked acrylic, or both, preapplied to both sides of the aluminum made rigid by horizontal or vertical crimping. The number of colors used varies from one to three. Other exteriors include prefinished wallboards, plastics, and steel.

f. All joints are sealed against leakage. A drip rail is installed the entire length of the unit on each side. In addition, all sidewall openings (other than windows and doors) are protected from leakage by aluminum visor drip caps. Siding is attached to the studs or asphalt insulation broad by rustproof screws.

g. Interior walls are finished with prefinished $\frac{1}{4}″$ plywood, or other board, often grooved to simulate random-plank paneling, and nailed and glued to the studs.

h. The plywood or other board nailed and glued to studs utilizes the stressed-skin principle, thus allowing smaller studs and thinner sheathing than would otherwise be possible (section 5.45).

16.12 Roof

a. The roof design is one of the distinctive features of the mobile home. It is a lightweight component somewhat similar to the trussed rafters described in chapter 5.

b. The mobile home roof truss is a jig-fabricated bow-string generally varying from about 2″ high at the ends to 6″ to 8″ at the center. It consists of a 2″ × 2″ bottom chord and a 1″ × 2″ cambered top chord, with plywood plates $\frac{1}{4}″$ thick glued and nailed on each side. The result is a lightweight curved form to withstand snow loads and provide water drainage.

c. Trusses are arranged 16″ on center and are tied together by two longitudinal 1″ × 2″ side members extending the length of the roof and so placed as to allow $\frac{1}{2}″$ bearing for the roof trusses on the top plates of the side walls. Additional longitudinal members are sometimes used for reinforcement.

d. The exterior subroof is installed on the tops of the trusses. Many kinds of materials are used, but the standard is $\frac{3}{8}″$ rigid insulation board. The exterior roofing of 26- or 30-gauge rubberized and fibered galvanized steel or aluminum decking is attached to the subroof.

e. The ceiling, usually $\frac{1}{4}″$ plywood fastened to the bottoms of the trusses, completes roof system. It also provides a backup board to which acoustical tile, planks, or custom-textured ceiling panels are attached.

f. Fiberglass blanket is the most common form of insulation. The thickness ranges between $\frac{1}{2}''$ and $3\frac{7}{8}''$ and extends the full width of the roof. Single or double vapor barriers are placed below or above the trusses, or in both positions. Besides the insulation board used for the exterior subroof, an additional insulation board may be placed above the finished ceiling. This double insulation lessens sound transmission from outside and inside. It also lessens heat loss in winter and gain in summer.

It is important to ventilate the roof space with open cavities and ventilation holes to avoid trapping warm moist air under a cold roof and causing condensation.

g. The types of ceiling finishes show large variation, from textured acoustical ceiling or acoustical planks with $\frac{1}{4}''$ plywood backup to $\frac{1}{4}''$ thick wood pulp board or other insulation board applied directly to the bottoms of roof trusses.

16.13 Windows and Doors

a. The most frequently used window is an all-aluminum awning type, usually 12" high, placed, when possible, to provide cross-ventilation. A bay window often appears at the front. Windows are installed with non-hardening, rubberized sealant. Screen units are usually removable. The interior garnish is anodized.

b. Exterior doors, commonly 32" wide by 72" high, are prehung in extruded aluminum frames. Doors are usually all-aluminum, insulated in the core with fiberglass or foamed polystyrene (chapter 15) and commonly equipped with a jalousie-type ventilating sash.

c. Interior doors, commonly $1\frac{3}{8}''$ thick, are usually finished with a $\frac{1}{4}''$ plywood or other board to match the interior paneling, as is true of closet and cabinet doors.

16.14 Double-Wide Units

a. "Double-wides" (two separately transported coaches), once on the site, are bolted together through the floor and roof assemblies, creating a home twice the width of one coach. One coach unit is the heavier of the two, containing the bathroom and kitchen; the other unit generally contains either bedrooms or the living room. For double-wides, roofs tapered upward toward a common central ridge are most common (as opposed to the bow-string truss used in single-wides).

b. To ensure close tolerances, double-wides may be assembled on the assembly line with the two units attached together. When a double-wide is to be transported, the two units are separated and transported independently to the site. While in transit, dummy walls are erected to cover openings in the wall the two units share. These dummy walls are of stud-and-plywood construction or may consist simply of plastic sheets. When the two units are fastened together, the dummy walls are taken down. The joints between the units are made watertight at the site. Roof shingling and wall siding are completed as required. A metal strip covers the junction of the two floors and is carpeted or tiled. Appropriate baseboards and molding are installed at the joints.

Conversion of English to Metric Units

To convert	to	multiply by
inches (")	meters (m)	2.540×10^{-2}
feet (')	meters (m)	3.084×10^{-1}
square inches (sq. in.)	square meters (m²)	6.452×10^{-4}
square feet (sq. ft.)	square meters (m²)	9.290×10^{-2}
cubic inches (cu. in.)	cubic meters (m³)	1.639×10^{-5}
cubic feet (cu. ft.)	cubic meters (m³)	2.832×10^{-2}
pounds (lb)	newtons (N)	4.448
tons	kilograms (kg)	9.072×10^{2}
pounds per square inch (lb/sq. in.)	pascals (Pa)	6.895×10^{3}
board feet (bd. ft.)	cubic meters (m³)	2.360×10^{-3}
British thermal units (BTU)	joules (J)	1.055×10^{3}
conductance (BTU/h · ft² · F)	W/m² · K	5.678
resistance (h · ft² · F/BTU)	m² · K/W	1.761×10^{-1}

Source: American Society for Testing and Materials

Index